Praise for

CHECK THE TECHNIQUE

"Brian Coleman has produced the best kind of oral history, getti
est figures in hip-hop (and some of the most important obscur
the music, straight up. If you listen to it and love it, or if yo
where it comes from, *Check the Technique* is the source-point.

"All producers and hip-hop fans must read this book.It really shows how these albums were made and touches the music fiend in everyone."
—DJ Evil Dee of Black Moon

"A rarity in mainstream publishing: a truly essential rap history."
—Ronin Ro, author of *Have Gun Will Travel*

"Brian Coleman gets props for the exhaustive effort it took to interview the writers
and producers of three dozen seminal hip-hop albums for *Check the Technique*. He
doesn't merely compile fresh liner notes and anecdotes from stars like Q-Tip,
Chuck D and Too $hort. He captures hip-hop's spirit from the '80s to the mid-'90s,
when inner-city kids discovered music through samples crammed into SP-1200
drum machines, learned the biz from shady contracts, and built their personae
from their stage names up. Most admirably, Coleman sits back and lets these born
storytellers talk. Grade: B+."   —*Entertainment Weekly*

"The rap must-read of the year."   —*Boston Herald*

"For hip-hop heads, and even casual fans, *Check the Technique* is highly addictive
reading. Coleman's writing is snappy, but even better is his ability to draw out
hugely entertaining and revealing tales from a pantheon of hip-hop artists."
—Washington *Express*

"Impressive. [One of] the season's must-reads."   —*Vibe*

"You know and I know that the rap industry is not the most focused when it comes
to the administrative side of life. Fortunately our friend Brian Coleman put together *Check the Technique*, a reference book of '80s and '90s record factoids that
fills in all the blanks. . . . CliffsNotes for Hip-Hop 101!"   —*The Fader*

"Easy to read and informative . . . Coleman's volume, covering 400 tracks and 75
artists all told, is a valuable, entertaining inside look at the creative processes behind
some of the best-selling albums of their (or any) time."   —*Publishers Weekly*

"Indispensable for tried-and-true hip-hop heads."   —*SF Weekly*

"The expansion [of *Rakim Told Me*] gives the book an extra heft, not only in size,
but also as an overview of the hip-hop album's ascension as an ambitious form and
a major market force. Grade: A–."   —*The Onion*

"Where others might want to intellectualize the stories of an urban artist's rise from obscurity to legendary status, in Coleman's hands these tales are anything but academic. . . . More often than not, Coleman's introductions to the albums actually outshine the artist-led track commentary, and his enthusiasm and sense of humor are infectious." —*Alarm*

"We're duly impressed with the exhaustive research Brian Coleman put into *Check the Technique*. . . . Through in-depth conversations with major players like Chuck D, Wyclef and Q-Tip, the author takes us back to a time before hip-hop was dominated by bling and Snoop cameos, offering no less than 500 pages of track-by-track history on how a genre was built." —E! Online

"Artists and their work can get paved over and forgotten pretty quickly in these days of cultural amnesia. So a few uncorny hip-hop hoorays are due to Brian Coleman. . . . Deep, informative and hilarious liner notes via interviews with the artists and producers who were there." —*Time Out New York*

"Coleman's lengthy chapter introductions are meticulously thorough and informative, putting each album into its proper context. But the real strength of *Check the Technique* lies in the Boston-based writer's ability to extract the right information from his interview subjects. Coleman writes with the warmth and enthusiasm of a hip-hop addict eager to share his findings with like-minded individuals, rather than with the superior know-it-all smugness sometimes attributed to music experts. . . . *Check the Technique* is a must-read for both old fans who grew up on many of the albums included here, and younger heads eager to learn some history. Rating: 5/5." —*Blues & Soul*

"A must-have book that should sit alongside your CD [and] record collection." —AOL BlackVoices

"*Check the Technique* is the antidote to surface-level stagnation, a descent into behind-the-scenes territory to offer an in-depth oral history of hip-hop record-making in the '80s and '90s that's both rare and revealing. . . . [It gives] intimate access to the brains and schemes behind the curtain of a seminal, high-stakes genre." —New York *Metro*

"Super-bionic-genetically-enhanced liner notes . . . *Check the Technique* is a fine case of intimate journalism from a veteran writer who has managed to make storied albums that much more legendary, by providing a looking glass into the genius behind their conception. Coleman has paid a great debt to the music that has so greatly influenced him and codified for us many cherished opuses that we can now relive over and over again." —AllHipHop.com

"Using the artists' own words, Coleman's enthralling, mercifully non-academic approach pulls back the curtains on the creation of dozens of classics, from the Fugees' *The Score* to 2 Live Crew's *As Nasty As They Wanna Be*." —*Urb*

CHECK
THE
TECHNIQUE

CHECK
THE
TECHNIQUE

Liner Notes for
Hip-Hop Junkies

BRIAN COLEMAN

2007 Villard Books Trade Paperback Edition

Published in the United States by Villard Books, an imprint of
The Random House Publishing Group, a division
of Random House, Inc., New York.

VILLARD and "V" CIRCLED Design are registered trademarks of Random House, Inc.

Originally published in different form in the United States
by Wax Facts Press, Somerville, Mass., in 2005.

Library of Congress Cataloging-in-Publication Data

Coleman, Brian.
Check the technique: liner notes for the hip-hop junkie / Brian Coleman.
p.   cm.
ISBN 978-0-8129-7775-2
1. Rap (Music)—History and criticism.   2. Rap musicians—United States.   I. Title.
ML3531.C65 2007
782.42164909—dc22   2006100800

Printed in the United States of America

www.villard.com

2   4   6   8   9   7   5   3

Designed by Stephanie Huntwork

$12 $25 used good
Amazon

Published 2007
Check The Technique
Hip Hop Junkies

54

To every hip-hop pioneer in this book,
for never raising your hand and
asking for permission.

FOREWORD

Since I got a record deal in '93, my peers have always chided me with the "Ahmir, you need to get out more often" talk. But I stay inside too much. I can't help it. I'm a stickler for all the information I can get out of music.

Ever since I absorbed all twenty-four pages of the liner notes to Stevie Wonder's *Songs in the Key of Life,* I realized—even as a five-year-old—that the information about how a record got made was just as important as (and in some cases more important than) the product itself. Those details always got me closer to that fly-on-the-wall experience, watching the creation of music.

And that's why the packaging of most hip-hop records was frustrating to me. Aside from a wacky De La project or your amazement at the amount of text Chuck D was able to hold in his head for his thank-yous (by the way, Chuck—can the Roots get Extra Strength Posse status now?), there wasn't much in the way of information for the music that I was supporting. With no Internet and only the obligatory *Rap Pages/Right On!* feature, I was left to my own devices. So I asked my own questions whenever I could.

Some cats couldn't wait to spill the goods. (Yeah right, Pete . . . you wanna convince us that you fit *all* those loops in the thirteen-second, handicapped SP-1200 for "Number One Soul Brother" with *one pass*?!?!) Some engineers are *still* in therapy over their experiences. (Brian, make sure you and Dave Tompkins do an engineer tell-all book so Tom Coyne can give you his well-executed tale of mastering and sequencing (in four days at that!!!!!!!!!) Raekwon's *Only Built 4 Cuban Linx . . . .)* And some cats, I just plain scared them off (my bad, Tip . . . a "Hello, I'm Ahmir" woulda done fine).

When Brian Coleman's *Rakim Told Me* came out, I was elated and jealous at the same time, more the former than anything. Finally, someone had put in perspective the stuff I had been *dying* to know about: the method of Paul C's madness, or Ced Gee's undervalued work on many a classic recording, or even the rat-infested environment the Jungle Brothers had to endure to make their debut LP. (My jealousy arose only because I was having a lot of "Why didn't I think of that!?!?!" moments as I kept reading.)

In pop and rock music, you are often given a *thorough* view of the landscape, and you are the wiser for it. Rock critics are constantly dissecting and breaking down the champions (*Sgt. Pepper's* and *Rumours*) and the underdogs (*Pet Sounds* and *Shoot Out the Lights*). But it's not so easy for hip-hop fans with the music we love.

Back in the day, hip-hop *barely* got a recording budget, let alone decent packaging. On top of that, with the marketplace being what it is, if the monetary rewards on an album weren't reaped, it was forgotten.

Well, not in the hearts of those who still care.

Check the Technique is a book that's been a long time coming. Better late than never!

And Brian, hurry up with the next installment . . . we're waiting.

Ahmir "?uestlove" Thompson
October 2006
Illadelph

AHMIR "?UESTLOVE" THOMPSON is a Philadelphia-born-and-bred drummer, producer, DJ, and all-around music junkie. He cofounded the influential live hip-hop band the Roots and has produced and performed on eight Roots albums since 1993. In his spare time, he has also found time to collaborate with artists ranging from John Mayer and Fiona Apple to Al Green and Dave Chappelle. For more information on Ahmir and the Roots crew, visit www.okayplayer.com.

PREFACE

"One time, in probably 1983, I was in the park in Brooklyn. I was getting beat up by about eight kids, I don't even remember why. But as it was happening, this dude was walkin' by with one of those *big* boom boxes. And as he's walking by, we hear [imitates the unmistakable intro drum pattern from Run-DMC's 'Sucker MCs,' loudly]. They all stopped beating me, and we all just stood there, listening to this phenomenon. I could have run, but I didn't, I was just so entranced by what I heard. Then the dude with the box passed by and the kids continued to beat me up. But it didn't matter. I felt good. I knew right then that I *had* to get into this hip-hop shit."
—*Pras of the Fugees, 2003*

I love that Pras story, which he recounted to me a couple years back as we were discussing the Fugees' own phenomenon, *The Score.* I know that feeling he's talking about. Maybe not the feeling of getting beat up by eight kids in a park in Brooklyn . . . but I do know the sensation of being frozen with delight after hearing a hip-hop track. It's a feeling that everyone should experience in their lives, with any kind of music, and as often as possible. It's the kind of thing that reminds you that you're really *alive.*

There are so many frostbite-inducing moments in this book for me. And I know I'm not the only one who has been messed up by geniuses like Public Enemy, De La Soul, Pete Rock & CL Smooth, A Tribe Called Quest, Black Moon, and the Roots, to name just a few. The hip-hop that runs through my veins and does laps around my 1200s has two traits that never waver: originality and innovation.

When I put out *Rakim Told Me* in 2005, I had one goal: to let people eavesdrop on some amazing conversations I've had with hip-hop legends over the years. This book you hold in your hands continues my exhibitionism and vastly expands it, featuring more than seventy-five interviews with many of the most important innovators in hip-hop. If you have a copy of *Rakim Told Me,* a couple of the chapters will be familiar to you. Others, like Ice-T's *Power* and De La Soul's *3 Feet High and Rising,* have been greatly expanded since the last edition. But beyond that, there are a crateload of new chapters, many of them focusing on classic albums from the nineties.

The format is the same as the last time around, something I call Invisible Liner Notes. (I *still* haven't figured out why hip-hop albums never had them!) One chapter, one artist, one album. Each chapter starts with background on the creators of these masterworks to let readers know where they were in their careers when the classic album in question was made. Then we get their own thoughts and memories about as many album tracks as I could squeeze out of them. Whenever possible, I stay out of the way and let the legends speak.

I have done everything I could to verify the accuracy of claims made by interviewees, double-checking information and attempting to get corroboration for important incidents or anecdotes. You will also see my "Author's Notes" sprinkled throughout the text. Overall, my hope is that *Check the Technique* will serve as a fact-driven and still entertaining hip-hop reference book—a literary category that still needs a great deal more expansion. This is a guidebook of sorts, but it is meant to be more fun than absolutely definitive. In my opinion, the most important thing about *Check the Technique* is that these facts and stories and opinions come from the pioneering artists themselves.

If I have one regret it is that this book isn't two or three times longer, although that might have required some kind of back-support device to carry it around. There are dozens more artists that I would have liked to have included but simply could not, for reasons including: I had to cut the chapter because I was already thousands over my word count for the book; the interview scheduling didn't work out because of timing or publicist ineptitude; or the artist has sadly passed away.

In short, if you know and love true-school hip-hop and you wonder where the chapter on Artist X is: Believe me, I wanted it as much as you did. But if I'm not mistaken, this is precisely the reason sequels were invented.

I am setting this book in front of you for the only reason someone should ever produce a book, an album, a movie, or anything else that can be considered an artistic "product"—because I myself would be first in line to buy it. I hope that I have helped to capture these amazing artists' voices and conveyed them in a way that engages readers as much as the original conversations engaged me.

It is an honor for me to present their words here and to remind hip-hop fans of all stripes that the subjects of these interviews are not just entertainers. They are artists and visionaries. And while they may have a certain image on video screens and in press-junket interviews, *Check the Technique* strips all of that away and talks to them as *people,* with respect and authentic fan-fueled curiosity. This is my way of giving something back to hip-hop, even if it's just a fraction of what it has given to me in the past twenty-five years.

Still frozen, and loving it,

Brian Coleman
October 2006
Commonwealth of Massachusetts
www.waxfacts.com

CONTENTS

CHECK
THE
TECHNIQUE

2 LIVE CREW

As Nasty as They Wanna Be

(Luke Skyywalker Records, 1989)

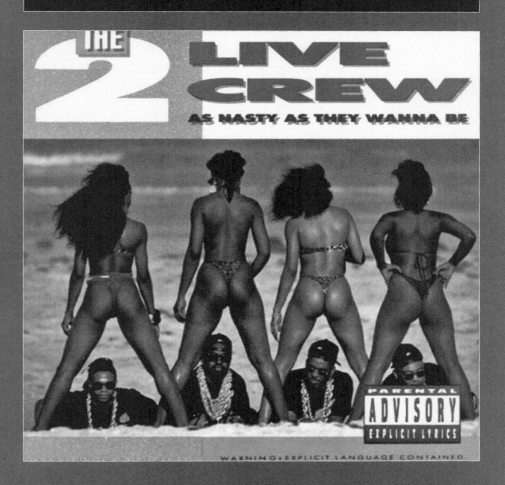

I think a lot of our music got overshadowed by the girls," says legendary DJ Mr. Mixx of 2 Live Crew. That may seem like the understatement of the year, but he's got a point.

In the world of rap there has certainly been no group that did so much to bring females to the front of their lyrics (and the front of their stages). But 2 Live Crew weren't the novelty act that they are all too often remembered as. "The one big misconception about 2 Live Crew was that everybody was trying to make us out to be the nastiest guys on earth," Mixx says. "Before we was doing recordings, I was making mixtapes of the hottest rap records, and I'd just scratch in a Dolemite or Eddie Murphy record in between the breaks. Basically, all we was doing was comedy stuff to a beat. We was Eddie Murphy, Redd Foxx, and Richard Pryor, just as a rap group." The group's figurehead, known then as Luke Skyywalker and nowadays as Uncle Luke, adds, "It was all just comedy, and then all the controversy started and we became misogynists all of a sudden. We was like: 'We ain't doin' this to offend nobody!'"

Back in their heyday in the late eighties and early nineties, the quartet—DJ/producer Mixx (David Hobbs), MCs Brother Marquis (Mark Ross) and Fresh Kid Ice (Christopher Wongwon), and manager/hype-man/first-amendment poster child Luther "Luke Skyywalker" Campbell—were running shit. The group's label, Luke Skyywalker Records, was the first black-owned indie label to have two certified gold records. Master P couldn't have done his thang if 2 Live hadn't opened the door. "When I got in the record business, I wanted to be the next Quincy Jones," Luke says today. "Russell Simmons is still messed up to this day about what kind of money we was making back then, because we were an independent label." Mixx adds: "All this Master P and Puffy praise about them being groundbreaking entrepreneurs is all bullshit. None of them ever sold records to distributors directly. We did. We was a true indie label."

Although 2 Live Crew is still known as a Miami group, its original incarnation (without Luke) was three thousand miles away. The original members met in Riverside, California, on March Air Force Base—Mixx and rappers the Amazing V and Fresh Kid Ice. Mixx recalls: "Me and Ice were in the air force. He worked outpatient records and I was a cook in the hospital on the base. Amazing V was in the service too." Medical records and the military base eventually gave way to an unrelated but similar-sounding pursuit: bass records. The group put out two singles, in 1984 and 1985, on their own Fresh Beat label (distributed through West Coast powerhouse Macola): "Revelation" and "What I Like." Mixx describes their first two wax outings: "The group was marginal on the rap side, but the beats and the scratching was what people really went for."

In 1985, Luke was a hotshot club DJ (his crew was dubbed Ghetto Style DJs) and promoter in Miami, known for making soon-to-be hit records popular in clubs like his home base, Pac Jam on 199th Street in northeast Miami. "My whole thing back then was breaking records," Luke explains. "If I liked a group I'd call up the artist and say: 'Look, I'm gonna make your record hot. Give me three weeks and come down and do a show for me.' The first group I brought down was T La Rock and Jazzy Jay. I would bring guys down and they would have never been on an airplane before in their life."

In 1985, the Cali version of 2 Live Crew was one such group. Luke invited them to Miami in August, where at Pac Jam they played their first show ever. Mixx remembers one extra reason that Luke was inclined to like the group. "There's a lyric in our song '2 Live' [the B-side to 'Revelation'] where Ice says, 'Like Luke Skywalker/I got the force.' When the record started catching on in Miami, Luke told people that it was about him."

Mixx remembers that first show in 1985 vividly: "I had never seen that kind of stuff that [opening act] Ghetto Style DJs did. They'd pull the music completely out and do their own phrases and choruses for songs. They weren't doing any real scratching at all. They'd play all the latest hip-hop and reggae records, but they'd also play old-school breaks. They were really popular. Luke had an amazing sound system too. Twenty-four bass bins and almost no tweeters. Our first show was well received even though we didn't have very much stage presence. My scratching was a big issue back then, though, in Miami. They weren't seeing that in the south then. No one could do that stuff."

The group returned, again at Luke's request, on New Year's Eve 1985 and were again received well. But shortly thereafter, the Amazing V left the group, choosing a safe military career over the less certain hip-hop route. Down to one MC, Mixx knew just the person to fill the spot—a local Riverside rapper whom Mixx had always liked named Marquis Ross. The problem: Marquis had moved back to his hometown of Rochester, New York, after graduating from Riverside Polytech High School. With help from L.A.'s Rodney O (of Rodney O & Joe Cooley fame), Mixx located Marquis and convinced him to come back to California to join the group.

With very little keeping them in California (Mixx had since left the service and Ice was thinking about leaving), Miami became the group's new home by the end of 1986. Mixx says: "We didn't have no kind of angle in L.A., nothing going on, but things were hopping off in Miami, so we went there."

The last music they produced in California was a song that paid tribute to their new patron, Luke Skyywalker: "Trow the D[ick]." Mixx says of the song, which he claims is the first Miami bass record of all time, "['Trow the D'] was a dance at the time down in Miami, and in appreciation to Luke for getting us gigs, we wanted to do a tribute record. We took the dance they was doing and Chris [Fresh Kid Ice] wrote some lyrics. I did the music based on 'Dance to the Drummer's Beat' [by Herman Kelly], which was a break that Luke and them always used to play, and I scratched in some Dolemite stuff. Ghetto Style DJs didn't produce the record, but they inspired it."

Luke tried to convince record labels in Miami, including Pretty Tony's popular Music Specialists imprint, to press the song up, but they wouldn't. So Luke decided to go for self, and the Luke Skyywalker Records empire began. Mixx claims that "Trow the D" went on to sell two hundred thousand records, which would most certainly be a mind-bogglingly large number for a start-up indie. Luke explains how this was the beginning of the true 2 Live Crew era: "Our first real single, 'Trow the D,' kind of started all the sex stuff, combined with the fact that Mixx and I both had a thing for comedians like Redd Foxx and Rudy Ray Moore [aka Dolemite]. In order to be different, we couldn't be coming like Run-DMC and all them New York rappers, so we did the adult comedy thing."

"There was no turning back at that point," Luke continues, "because in the music biz you can't put out one record independently and expect to get your money [from distributors] from that one record. I had to put out another record, because they wanted a steady flow." The label's second release was an answer record to their own label debut, recorded by Luke's cousin Anquette, called "Trow the P[ussy]." "She had never rapped before in her life," Luke laughs. "After those two records I was like: 'Yeah, let's do this.' It was another challenge for me, and I like challenges. I started that label out of my mother's wash house, and those records were sold out of the backseat of a Honda."

By all accounts, early 2 Live Crew shows weren't anything to write home about. The MCs were serious, they did their lines, Mixx blew minds with his innovative turntable skills, and they left. Luke, watching from the wings, slowly went from manager to onstage instigator. He explains: "When I got involved, I didn't really want to be in the group, I was just trying to help them out. Their live show wasn't no different than any other rap group out there; they'd just walk up and down onstage and do their songs. And when I went on the road with them, the shows really started to get boring to me. So I was like: 'All right, let me get up here and start some shit.' So I'd get up there and do what people today call a hype man. Before me there wasn't no hype man."

"Luke came to the front of the stage after a while, since Marquis and Fresh Kid Ice weren't really messing with the crowd," Mixx recalls. "So Luke and other dudes from Ghetto Style DJs would jump onstage when we would perform 'Trow the D' and do the dance and pull girls up onstage to dance with them. That's how the group got to be how everybody knows it now. Eventually Luke or Marquis would pull a girl out of the audience and start humpin' on her, and that always broke the ice with the crowd. A lot of times girls would come up and want to challenge us, thinking they had more game than 2 Live Crew. That definitely made every show unpredictable."

The group continued building on their "adult comedy" niche throughout 1986 and 1987, with continuing fan response. Mixx explains: "All our sex stuff basically came from how the girls were dancing at the parties we'd play, along with the comedy records I had. We were just having fun and reacting to the crowds. For example, they used to do that 'We want some pussy' chant at all the parties, so we just made it into a record [a single off the *2 Live Crew Is What We Are* album]."

The group's first two albums, late 1986's *2 Live Crew Is What We Are* and 1987's *Move Somethin'*, both on Luke Skyywalker, were huge hits in the south and west of the U.S., each going gold (again: on an indie label, with indie distribution). To dispel any misconceptions that all the group wanted to do was pollute the minds of our nation's youth, it should be noted that *Move Somethin'* and *As Nasty . . .* both had corresponding "clean" versions available. Mixx says: "We was the first group to have the parental-advisory stickers on our records, after our first album got in the hands of a fourteen-year-old in 1987. The kid's mother made a stink, called the distributor, Tipper Gore got involved, and those stickers got made." Luke relates a sad fact: "Even after we did those clean versions we still got flack. People said that we were doing the clean versions just so people would want to buy the dirty versions. We couldn't win!"

As popular as their first two albums were, their third full-length, *As Nasty as They Wanna Be,* was the big kahuna both in terms of sales and controversy. As with all 2 Live Crew records, it was recorded quickly, this time at Luke's recently inaugurated Luke Studios, purchased from Miami production legend Pretty Tony. Luke describes the group's basic and effective production dynamic: "I would have an idea about a song and go to Mixx and he'd put the music together, then maybe I'd give [Marquis and Ice] the idea for the lyrics."

Mixx always had a cache of tracks waiting to be matched to a lyric or concept. He says: "I was always doing tracks, so none of our albums took long to record." Samples were never an issue either, as Mixx explains: "Back in the day we never cleared samples [*laughs*]. What ended up happening was that we didn't clear 'em, and then we just got sued. We was selling so many records and making so much money that it was easier to just pay the settlement than to clear that shit in the first place!"

One interesting side note: Contrary to what fans might have assumed, when the group got in the studio, it wasn't a party-time affair. "When those guys got to the studio, it'd be all business," says Luke. "If I was recording by myself in there, it got crazy. You name it, it went on in there. I got a lot of song ideas by stuff I'd see in those sessions [*laughs*]! But with the group, it was boom, boom, boom, knock the tracks out." Mixx agrees: "The studio was the only place where we actually had any real peace, believe it or not. We all had our own friends too, so that was really the only time where we would all get together."

After quick work in early 1989, the *As Nasty as They Wanna Be* album was released in June. It built slowly but surely, driven by the lascivious, bass-driven singles "Me So Horny" and "C'mon Babe," and as the new decade turned, things started to get crazy in a way that no one could have predicted. "We had sold 1.3 million records by March 1990, independently," says Mixx. "And then that sheriff [Broward County, Florida, sheriff Nick Navarro] started attacking the group. He tried to tell stores not to sell our record and even filed a suit against us for obscene material being sold. Not just to minors—just being sold, period!"

The group had fought in court before to protect their right to be as nasty as they chose, but things came to a head that spring of 1990, as Navarro's men arrested Luke, Marquis, and Fresh Kid Ice after a show in Hollywood, Florida. "We went to court about it being legally obscene and we lost," Luke recalls. "Then we performed in Hollywood, Florida, after the judgment and the sheriff said, 'If you perform any of those songs [on the album], we'll arrest you.' We didn't really think they'd do it." Luke and Ice got arrested later that night, driving home in Luke's car. Mixx and Marquis rode in a van with the group's female dancers to hide. Marquis turned himself in the next day. "I didn't get arrested because I didn't say any of the lyrics," Mixx explains.

As much as the controversy helped to sell even more records (Luke estimates that the record has gone quadruple platinum to date: "It's still selling, and it probably always will," he grins), Luke has some regrets, since all the headlines cloud his and the group's important legacy. "In the end I'd rather that all that stuff *hadn't* happened," he says today. "Because I'd be more appreciated as an executive in the record industry. I think I'd be a lot more successful. I would have done my industry a lot more of a service if I hadn't gone through all that. To this day I still get blackballed. But we learned after a while that we couldn't beat the machine. We just had to do our own thing, regardless of what people said that we were."

More than arrests, more than lucrative record sales, and even more than all the ladies that walked through the doors of Luke's compound or onto the group's stages, the 2 Live Crew were about having fun, and that is what *As Nasty as They Wanna Be* is all about. "We were a group that controlled our own destiny," Luke reminds us. "That's the most important part, because [there] wasn't no major label. We could say what we wanted to say, and we sure as hell did!"

TRACKS

ME SO HORNY

Mixx: We was in D.C. recording with [go-go legends] Trouble Funk, and Marquis was watching *Full Metal Jacket* in the hotel on TV. And we saw that part where the girl says, "Me so horny," and he said: "Man, we gotta do something with that shit!" So as soon as we finished the session and got back home, I rented the movie and sampled that [vocal] piece from the girl. I already had the music track programmed, so we put the two things together. That's actually not our biggest hit of all time, even as big as that song was. We're best known for "We Want Some Pussy." That's by far our most recognizable one.

Luke: We really chose to lead with that song [as the first single] because I knew that people would bug out when they heard a song called "Me So Horny."

PUT HER IN THE BUCK

Luke: I don't know who came up with that one. But I'll tell you what—you get me a bottle of liquor and I'll come up with hooks and concepts and all kinds of shit!

D.K. ALMIGHTY

Mixx: That was a Kraftwerk sample on there. I knew the Fearless Four version of that Kraftwerk song ["Rockin It"], but I liked the original better.

Mixx: That was originally supposed to be the first single from the album, and it was the first record we actually did for the album. But once we recorded "Me So Horny" it became a toss-up. Luke went with "Me So Horny" because it had more bite to it. On "C'mon Babe," that's not a porno flick: It's sampled off one of my old comedy records, by this dude Wavy Gravy.

Luke: That was actually a better song than "Me So Horny," from a lyrical standpoint, the delivery and rap style.

DIRTY NURSERY RHYMES

Mixx: We wasn't thinking about Schoolly D when we did that, but Schoolly was one of the few guys from the north that we was cool with. He used to come down and do shows for Luke, and he was a very cool dude.

2 LIVE BLUES

Luke: A lot of the songs from that album were derived from other songs, like rock or reggae or whatever. That one was our blues song. We were just trying to do some different stuff on there, and still keep it on the sex tip.

I AIN'T BULLSHITTIN'

Mixx: A lot of the big tours that went out at the time didn't want us to headline, even though we was sellin' more records than the headliners in some places. But the tours were booked out of New York, and they wasn't giving Luke a fair shake because they didn't take us seriously. We were the first ones to sell records in that kind of volume out of the south, period. They figured it was dance music, not rap. MC Shan came down to Miami early on and would trip out because he was from the land of rap and everyone was paying attention to these so-called country bumpkins from Florida. Most New York guys were like that.

Luke: That's a classic—people like that shit to this day because I was calling people out on that. MC Shan, I don't even remember what he said that pissed me off, but I fucked him up on that record. Everybody was talking shit about us. I mean, a lot of people claim they know all about discrimination and all that, but the people that really know about it are from the sixties, who had to go in segregated bathrooms, go around the corner to get the food at the restaurant they weren't allowed in. We really felt like that with other rappers when we'd meet them or tour with them. Us and N.W.A. bonded together on the road, 'cause we was both outcasts. A lot of people seemed to think that if you wasn't from New York, you wasn't shit.

THE FUCK SHOP

Mixx: I went to high school with white cats and I knew that Van Halen record by hanging out with them. Luke liked that Guns N' Roses guitar riff, so he brought that one in too. We always had rock-oriented records, like "We Want Some Pussy" from the first album and "S&M" from the second.

Luke: I was like, "Let's do a rock 'n' roll song," and I'd like this song or that song and I'd tell Mixx and he'd come back with something great. "The Fuck Shop" was just another name for a hotel. Everybody had their favorite that they'd go in, wherever we were. Whenever we went on the road it became a fuckfest. [*He says this very seriously.*] One thing about us is that we never had to worry about going to jail for raping or nothing like that, because the girls pretty much knew what was gonna happen when they came in the room with us. It could be any hotel, as long as we had a bed to lay on.

Luke: My whole thing as an artist and onstage was that kind of thing, call-and-response stuff, shouting to the crowd. And the other guys in the group would do everything else. All our chant-type songs, that was all me.

GET THE FUCK OUT OF MY HOUSE

Mixx: I was experimenting with house music on that one. The Jungle Brothers' "Girl, I'll House You" came out before that, and a lot of our records would get mixed with that by DJs, since a lot of our records were up-tempo. That was really just us fuckin' around, though, and Luke saying some old bullshit [*laughs*].

Luke: That was me talking about some girl. I had this one chick that was lazy, didn't want to do nothing. So I came home from Chicago and had heard some house tracks and wanted to do something different, some house-styled shit.

REGGAE JOINT

Mixx: Reggae was just big in Miami, and all those songs we sampled on there were big hits in the reggae scene there. Luke used to play a lot of reggae stuff at his jams with Ghetto Style DJs.

BAD ASS BITCH

Mixx: That's Trouble Funk on that one, playing live. It was cool working with them. We was one of the first and only rap groups to use their stuff, aside from some New York cats.

Luke: I was a big fan of go-go, 'cause I stayed in D.C. for a while, back when I was younger. I was out of control and my mother sent me to D.C. to live with my brother, who was in the army. I was going to the Cap [Capital] Center, hearing Trouble Funk and Rare Essence and all that shit. It was great to record with them. I always wanted to put out a go-go record on my label, but never did.

MEGA MIXX III

Mixx: With that third one [he did a "Mega Mixx" on every 2 Live Crew album] I actually had a musical theme to go with, based on [Afrika] Bambaataa's "Renegades of Funk." I found out where he got that chorus from and built off of that. Each one of those Mega Mixxes I did got more complex. They were getting easier to do, though, because I'd line all the records up in advance and just run through 'em.

BEASTIE BOYS

Check Your Head

(Capitol, 1992)

While the learning curve for most groups sets them in full motion after their first album, the Beastie Boys took a bit longer. But this wasn't necessarily a bad thing. In the search for their true group identity, they made some pretty amazing music along the way, like 1986's *Licensed to Ill* (Def Jam/CBS) and 1989's *Paul's Boutique* (Capitol). Even so, it wouldn't be a stretch to say that they didn't truly find themselves until the third time around, six years after their debut.

Paul's Boutique, produced by the Beasties and the Dust Brothers and released on July 25, 1989, was universally revered by fans and almost unanimously jocked by critics. But the group suffered greatly from a lack of label support and low initial sales numbers. In fact, the album wouldn't be certified platinum until 1995. (For an in-depth look at this album, Dan LeRoy's book *Paul's Boutique* [Continuum, 2006] is highly recommended.) Because of their situation with Capitol, the fall of 1989 wasn't as carefree as the trio—who had recently relocated from their hometown of New York to the very different world of Los Angeles—might have hoped.

Adam Yauch, aka MCA, explains: "*Check Your Head* really got under way on the heels of the failure of *Paul's Boutique* [*laughs*], shortly after the president of Capitol Records told us that he wouldn't be able to focus on our album because he had a new Donny Osmond album coming out. He told us that we should just move on, that we should just forget about *Paul's Boutique* and start on the next record." Aside from a very quick promo jaunt, there was almost zero touring for *Paul's Boutique.*

MCA continues: "After that disheartening reaction from Capitol, we just started setting up instruments at Adam's [the other Adam of the group, Adam Horovitz, aka Adrock] place and started jamming. Mark [future group keyboardist "Money" Mark Ramos Nishita] brought over a keyboard and we had a mini setup there." Devoted fans of the group know the three members started out in the early and mid-eighties on the heels of two different punk rock groups: one called the Beastie Boys, one called the Young and the Useless. Each of the trio played an instrument—Yauch on bass, Adrock on guitar, and Mike D (Diamond) on drums—but the three men hadn't played their instruments on a regular basis for years. The jam sessions at Adrock's apartment brought their love of playing together back in quick fashion.

Mike D remembers: "Once we started playing at Adrock's, that was really the initial stuff for *Check Your Head*. This was after *Paul's Boutique* was out, and we all had our own apartments in L.A. We had little drums and little amps, and we just started playing together."

Even though the final product wouldn't hit stores for almost three years, the course had been set for the Beasties. Sampling, the lifeblood of almost all hip-hop groups at the time, would take a backseat to the three MCs actually *playing* (and, truth be told, playing pretty well). Some producers, of course, do rhyme, and some also DJ and play instruments. But few, if any, have done all four with as much success. It was a precedent that has not been equaled or bettered in hip-hop to this day.

Mike says: "I don't know if I'd say that *Paul's Boutique* took the sampling thing as far as it could be taken, but we came close. So we definitely didn't want to jump right back into that same direction." One reason for the change could have also been an economic one. *Check Your Head* producer/engineer Mario Caldato Jr. says that the sample clearances for *Paul's Boutique* were between $200,000 and $250,000, on top of their expensive studio bills. And Money Mark says: "The way I always heard it was that their accountant told them that they couldn't make any money with all those samples, so they tried a different route."

Soon enough, Adrock's neighbors complained about the funky noises coming from his living room, so the group moved to a rehearsal space—Cole Rehearsal Studios in Hollywood. Yauch explains: "We played there for a couple months. And while we were there we'd just set up a couple mics and record onto DAT [digital audio tape]."

At Adrock's and at Cole, another key component to the *Check Your Head* equation, the Brazilian-born and L.A.–raised Caldato, was in attendance. Caldato, a sometime bassist, already had an impressive engineering track record when he met the Beasties in the late eighties. After building the basic but effective Delicious Vinyl Studios in label founder and co-owner Matt Dike's living room (which consisted of an eight-track board, an [E-mu] SP-1200 sampler, and a vocal booth modified from an old coat closet), he went on to engineer all Delicious Vinyl releases in 1988 and 1989. These included multiplatinum albums by Tone-Lōc (*Lōc'ed After Dark,* 1989) and Young MC (*Stone Cold Rhymin',* 1989).

Since Dike was part of the original incarnation of the Dust Brothers (along with John King and Mike Simpson), who produced *Paul's Boutique,* Caldato knew the group and was brought in to engineer the second Beasties album. Caldato produced one song on the album, a skit called "Ask for Janice." He remembers: "Working on *Paul's Boutique* was definitely much bigger for me than the Delicious Vinyl stuff, even though those records had sold a lot. The Beasties were top billin' and they had tons of money. I was getting ten dollars an hour working for Matt Dike, and the Beasties paid me twenty-five dollars an hour."

Mike D explains: "It was a lot of fun making *Paul's Boutique,* but we spent I don't know how many hours and days in all of these fancy-ass studios like Ocean Way and the Record Plant. We were probably paying two thousand dollars a day to work that way, so after that album we were like: 'Okay, that was a lot of fun, but that was also pretty stupid.' "

Caldato says that after *Paul's Boutique,* the Beasties and the Dust Brothers were in a disagreement over money and royalty percentages, so as they started conceptualizing their next record, it was unlikely that the two camps would work together again. Mario opines: "It was a bummer that things worked out that way, because everyone had so much fun making *Paul's Boutique.* But when *Check Your Head* started to take shape, the Beasties just wanted more control."

Caldato, who was still on the best of terms with the Beasties inside and outside the studio, stepped in as co-producer. He says: "After *Paul's Boutique* was out, I was still hanging out with the Beasties just about every day. They weren't from L.A., so they liked hanging with someone who was from here, because they still didn't feel like they were locals." And as for Caldato's new title of producer for the group, he says, "Engineering and production really go hand in hand, in my opinion, so stepping up to that level wasn't a big thing. We all worked really well together."

"By early 1990, things really started to take shape," recalls Caldato. "We'd be listening to a Meters record and they'd say: 'Hey, we should try and do a cover of that.' And so they'd do their own version. From Adrock's to Cole, I was just following them around and recording. Before you know it, the basis for [*Check Your Head* album tracks] 'Something's Got to Give' and 'Pow' are taking shape. By that time, I had gotten my old eight-track board from Delicious Vinyl and would set it up wherever they were. We had the first money for the album budget from Capitol, sixty thousand dollars, and we got a good tape recording setup and a mixing board. That's all we needed, because I had everything else. I wasn't messing with anything related to Delicious Vinyl at that point. I was working full-time for the Beasties."

"We definitely wanted to spend our next recording budget on our own studio, so we could have more freedom," says Yauch. "When you're in a commercial studio, you just have to think a different way, like: 'Let's knock this song out and get out of here.' This time around we wanted to be able to experiment. So after a little while we started to look around for a space, and that's when we found G-Son."

The soon-to-be-crowned G-Son Studios, located at 3218½ Glendale Boulevard in the "uncool" and "weird" Atwater section of L.A. (as described by the Beasties and Caldato), was an old ballroom, and it was to be the Beasties' personal clubhouse for the foreseeable future. Caldato remembers: "G-Son was at one time called the Atwater Community Center. It was

basically a ballroom with a wood floor and a domed ceiling. It had a crazy sound that echoed out in the middle. It was being used as a rehearsal-studio type of place and the guy who rented it to us, Tony Riparetti, had his own equipment in there. [*Author's note: Mark and Mario agree that the owner of the building's name was Bill, and that the Beasties likely subleased part of Riparetti's space.*] We rented the big room from him because he wasn't using it. I think our rent was $1,000 or $1,500 a

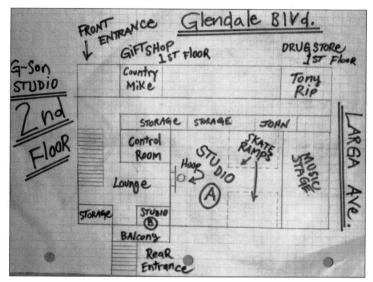

G-Son Studio.
RENDERING BY MONEY MARK. REPRINTED BY PERMISSION.

month. That was less than one day spent at those *Paul's Boutique* studios." The "original" Country Mike, a country music songwriter from whom Beastie Mike D took his country music nom de plume, rented space down the hall.

Yauch recalls that G-Son got its name because the *i* and *l* were missing from a sign on the building describing a business named Gilson. "G-Son was a big, old, open ballroom on the second floor of a commercial space, above a drugstore," he recalls. "The guy who owned it had built a stage at one end of the ballroom, with a small control room off to the side. When we moved in there, we took these two closets that were at the other end of the room, broke down the wall between them, and made it our control room."

"Aside from the main control room and the 'live' room [the ballroom area], we also had a little shitty room called Studio G [also known as Studio B, which is more logical since there were only two studios], which had an SP-1200, a cassette four-track, and some shitty speakers," recalls Mike D. "If someone was working with Mario in the main room, then someone else could work on another track in Studio G."

Caldato adds: "We used the stage to set up the instruments and carpeted it down. And we even built a half-court basketball court in there on the dance floor. That definitely got some good use when we needed a break. More than anything, G-Son was just a big clubhouse."

After stockpiling the equipment they needed under Mario's guidance, the group began woodshedding at G-Son with even greater purpose by the spring of 1990. Interestingly, the usually wordy Beasties didn't have lyrics for any of the songs they were working on. Adrock remembers: "When we first started making *Check Your Head,* it was an even bigger jump, musically, than how it actually ended up. When we first started, I think we figured that we'd just make an all-instrumental album."

Yauch explains what sparked their new instrumental direction: "When we first started playing our instruments again, we got very absorbed in that. I think we were first inspired by all the stuff that we had sampled on *Paul's Boutique.* We played instruments on *Paul's Boutique,* on 'Looking Down the Barrel of a Gun' and 'Hello Brooklyn.' We even played some stuff on *Licensed to Ill.* But it was a different approach when we started *Check Your Head.* Before that, a lot of what we had played was more on the hardcore and rock side."

"Doing an instrumental album for those guys at the beginning was really just by default, because they didn't have any lyrics," says Caldato. "The all-instrumental thing was just a goof. Luckily, at the time they were free to do whatever they wanted and they were just having fun playing. Things evolved slowly. And I think it was just a natural progression after what they had done on *Paul's Boutique.* They were like: 'Let's take a break from all those samples and just sample *ourselves.*'"

One important part of the *Check Your Head* puzzle was their new musical associate, Money Mark Nishita. Mark was a carpenter by trade and a childhood friend (and bandmate, in a group called the Jungle Bugs) of Caldato's. After studying theater at Los Angeles Community College, Mark ended up building backdrops for numerous sets in a nine-to-five gig for Hollywood Center Studios.

The Gardena, California, born and bred Nishita had first met the Beasties in the eighties at Matt Dike's "Power Tools" DJ night and had even taken part in some of the infamous egg-throwing expeditions with the Beasties during their *Paul's Boutique* days. He was brought in to fix a fence at the group's rented "party house," the G-Spot, and the talk quickly turned to music. "There was definitely an instant bond when I first jammed with them," says Mark. "I brought some equipment over there, we hit record on the four-track, and the rest is history."

Aside from the many ultrafunky keyboard lines he played, Nishita's screw-gun-and-nail skills would be equally important to *Check Your Head,* as he built G-Son to the specifications that Caldato and the Beasties needed. Mike D says: "Mark was an excellent carpenter, and his screw-gun expertise was used quite often. He made the 'drum shack' that you can see on the inside of the album." Adrock adds: "I remember one day I was saying how I'd love to have a round guitar amp that I could roll around. Two days later, Mark showed up with a round amp that he had made. It sounded terrible, but it looked very cool!"

Mark says: "As soon as they decided that they were going to build that G-Son space, I was put on the clock and I quit my nine-to-five gig. They needed a carpenter and a keyboardist, so there I was. I was playing guitar back then too, but they didn't need guitar. Once the spot was rented, there was a lot of work to do. I remember we were loading plywood in there for three days straight. As soon as there was some minimal structure in there, we started recording. We were actually building and recording at the same time, so it was a bit of a blurred transition between the two. It was like a kindergarten class: On the first day of school, the walls are bare, but at the end of the year there's all this artwork up there. That's what G-Son and *Check Your Head* was like."

"We never even got around to building proper vocal booths, actually," Mark adds. "It was more important for them to have skateboard ramps and a basketball court [*laughs*]. The ballroom floor was perfect for that."

The group went about recording the album like a job, albeit a casual and most certainly third-shift one. Adrock remembers: "We were there most weekdays for more than a year, but sometimes we wouldn't get anything done for a whole week, because we'd be messing around, playing basketball, playing dominoes [*laughs*]." Yauch adds: "We never really went there during the day because the downstairs neighbor was a drugstore or something, and they'd get upset if we played while they were open. So we'd drive over there at about six thirty at night and hang out until about two in the morning."

Money Mark mentions that he could load in equipment before six P.M., but couldn't start building anything until after that. He would generally build for an hour or two, then the Beasties would arrive and jamming could begin. Mark, of course, pulled double duty, transitioning from screw gun to keyboards. "I was the first one there every day, and the last to leave," he says.

On the subject of the album's songwriting, Mike D says, "Sonically, on *Check Your Head* we put songs together in every type of way. Sometimes it was just us playing, sometimes we cut and pasted parts of us playing together, and sometimes we'd sample ourselves playing a loop and then build something on top of that. We could have done all that in a regular studio, but it's hard to imagine how because of all the time it took. Hundreds of hours went into making that album."

"Each song on *Check Your Head* had its own unique birth and ending," says Mark. "Songs were always mutating. That was the magic of it. You never knew how it would end up." He adds, regarding his self-proclaimed "outsider" contribution to the musical mix, "I was the best musician out of all of us, so it was my job to keep things together when we were all just throwing ideas out there and jamming. I'd hear what they weren't doing and would try to fit sounds into those places. I guess you could say that I was the stealth music director for everyone. And I learned how to write real *songs* from them. I had never done anything like that before."

"Sometimes we'd start to arrange and mix a song, only to put it down and come back to it months later," explains Caldato. "I have about eighteen hours of songs that we went so far as to mix on DAT, stuff we were almost done with. And I'm sure I have a hundred hours of DATs of them beyond that, when they were just fucking around and playing. We recorded *everything*. Some songs would have eight or ten different mixes because they would evolve over time."

According to Caldato, the Beasties had complete creative control when it came to their contracts and, as a result, no A&R reps from Capitol ever came by G-Son. "I think at that point, after a couple years, the label had just written them off," says Caldato. "There was never even a due date for the album from the label."

Aside from bringing the trio's musicality to the front, *Check Your Head* also showed that both Adams in the group could DJ quite effectively, as they claim to have shared turntable duties wherever cuts were needed. (No DJ is listed in the album's liners.) "When it comes to DJing, we have different styles," explains Adrock. "I'm a cutter and a scratcher, and Yauch's a 'terminator'"—a term that the Beasties and Caldato use for what is commonly known as "transforming," most likely a tribute to their friend Terminator X, Public Enemy's DJ. Yauch adds that longtime group associate DJ Hurricane "was only used for our live shows at the time."

There was another DJ angle to *Check Your Head,* as Yauch explains. "Back then we had kind of a battle with different pause-tapes [homemade DJ mixes made without an actual DJ mixer, using the pause and record buttons on a tape deck to simulate a cut-and-paste-style DJ mix] we were making and playing for each other. The tapes we were making would jump around with different styles, just quick parts of different songs. Hip-hop to jazz to funk and whatever else. And in a way, *Check Your Head* ended up being like one of those pause-tapes."

Mario C agrees with the pause-tape description, and recalls, "Every night when we'd hit G-Son, it would be like show-and-tell, because we'd all be trying to come up with the best tape. Eventually, everybody would show up with a whole record bag instead of a tape, and we'd all take turns showing off records we had just found. That album is definitely one big mix-tape, because it evolved from bits and pieces of everything, from them playing live to all the new samples we were using."

"The thing about a pause-tape is that you're only taking the hypest part of any song, like the best two minutes out of an eleven-minute jazz track,"

Beastie Boys (left to right: MCA, Mike D, Adrock)
at G-Son Studios, Los Angeles, 1996.

PHOTO: B+ (FOR WWW.MOCHILLA.COM).

explains Mike D. "While we were making *Check Your Head,* we would constantly review all the tapes of us playing, and then we'd make pause-tapes out of those with the best parts. And even then, a lot of that stuff still sucked [*laughs*]."

1990 and 1991 was an amazingly productive time for the group. Yauch explains the general blueprint of their recording aesthetic: "A lot of times we'd just go in and improvise, and Mario would be running the DAT machine [and recording]. In the control booth at G-Son we had a twenty-four-track tape machine [for more "serious" final recordings] and a DAT player [for better than average sound, usually recorded without having each instrument individually mic'ed]. We'd play for a few hours and it would all be on the DAT, and if there were certain parts that sounded particularly promising, we could build off those parts and actually record them on twenty-four tracks. We tried to keep shit sparse and funky, but frequently we'd just start wailing, and we'd just keep going from there to see if anything good came out of it."

Although group members now say that *Check Your Head* could have been all-instrumental, it still seems unlikely, considering that these were three motormouthed MCs waiting to break loose again. Yauch says: "Towards the end of the whole recording process, we got back into making some hip-hop stuff. That was the last piece of the puzzle for us, once we started doing tracks like 'Pass the Mic' and 'So What'cha Want.' " Mike adds: "When it came to adding more hip-hop to the mix, it wasn't a specific decision, but I do remember that we were playing around and Biz [Markie] came by the studio, and he just rhymed for hours over what we were doing. I think that got us inspired to start rhyming again. We just got back into that mode."

To go along with their laissez-faire attitude toward rhyming on the album, they also downgraded on the microphone side. Yauch explains: "At first we would just plug our mics into a fuzzbox [guitar effect box], and Mario hated that. But he eventually came around to what we were doing and he even bought us these shitty plastic mics at Radio Shack or somewhere."

Caldato, who was indeed initially opposed to using "bullshit" mics, eventually embraced them. "We had a small side studio room that was like a 'B room,' and it had a four-track cassette recorder and a cheap karaoke mic that I had bought, which had effects on it," he says. "The mic could go high or low and do computer voices or whatever. If the main room was being used by someone else, the other person would just do a very rough demo in that side room with the crappy mic. But a lot of times we liked the sound of the crappy mic better. To be honest, we never really used a good microphone on that album."

All the group's jamming and messing around ended up paying big dividends. "We barely did any touring behind *Paul's Boutique* because of the Donny Osmond fiasco, so all the performing that we did during the era after *Paul's Boutique* was really just in the studio," explains Yauch. "For *Check Your Head*, we probably spent three years screwing around and playing instruments and really just trying to get to a new level. We weren't even used to playing them as full songs until we started touring, in 1992."

The obvious difference between *Check Your Head* and *Paul's Boutique*, on paper at least, was in the number of samples used. Caldato says: "Half of the record is instrumental, and a lot of the songs, even the vocal and hip-hop ones, don't have any samples. There are only eight hip-hop songs out of twenty, and even those have a lot of live playing on them. So it was definitely a very unique hip-hop album for the time."

After finishing, in Caldato's estimation, between thirty and forty full songs by late 1991, it was agreed that the album was finally ready. It was eventually pared down to twenty songs, which still made up quite a hearty hip-hop and funk platter. Caldato says: "I really think that the Beasties came into their own on *Check Your Head*. On *Paul's Boutique* they went all out, spending money and living large. But *Check Your Head* is just a real honest record. It's as no-bullshit as you can get." Money Mark also mentions an important fact to think about in that pre–Pro Tools world of recording: With hundreds of hours of DAT and two- and four-track tapes of the group jamming to use for final mixes, all edits were done by cutting and splicing the tapes manually, not with computer-based digital editing. This was complicated and arduous, to say the least.

Mark says: "*Check Your Head* was important for so many reasons. It was the first record that they made on their own, and that was significant. They didn't have Rick [Rubin, who masterfully produced the group's 1986 debut, *Licensed to Ill*] to boss them around, or the Dust Brothers to dictate everything. Mario and I were both strongly dedicated to the fact that everything on that album had to come through the Beastie Boys. They were already written off by Capitol, and I think that was a blessing in disguise. If they had had a firm deadline for the album, it wouldn't have been the same. It's not like they were shy before *Check Your Head,* but at the same time I think the Beasties gained a lot of confidence after that album was finished. They knew they could do anything at that point."

Check Your Head was wrapped up by early 1992 and released on April 21 of that year. Mario says: "I've definitely never been involved in a record like that before or since. I mean, three years to make a record, just a bunch of guys hanging out? We'd hang out when we wanted to and make music when we wanted to. It was all about *inspiration.* There was no pressure, no label politics, nothing bad at all. And after the record hit, we toured behind it and I went and I did the live mix for them. That was really amazing, to bring the music to people and see their reaction. It was the best reward that any of us could have wanted."

The music was so good, in fact, that it brought Mark back from his old hammer-and-nails life a second time. He explains: "All the stuff I did on the record was done before those guys wrapped everything up, so by early 1992 I had gone back to work as a carpenter. They were ready to tour after the album came out, but I had landed a huge kitchen-remodeling job, and so I told them I couldn't go. But after them prodding me and me thinking about it some more, I decided to go on tour and I gave the job to one of my competitors to finish. The songs on that album were so good that I just couldn't say no.

"And," he says, "To this day I still haven't been back to get my tools."

TRACKS

MCA: The album version of that song isn't the one we had originally wanted to put on there. The original version is on the B-side of the twelve-inch of that single. It's all [Jimi] Hendrix samples, and after we finished the song we had difficulty clearing the samples with whoever was controlling the Hendrix estate. So we re-created some of those samples for the version that came out on the album. Then later we got permission from the Hendrix estate so we put the first one ["Original Original Version"] on the single. I like the original version best—that's the way the song was supposed to be heard. I did the DJ cuts on that one, with some editing done to tighten it up.

Mario Caldato Jr.: With the album version, we used some similar, non-Hendrix guitar stuff and added the Cheap Trick [sample on the] intro.

Money Mark: As I recall, that song was written about George Bush Sr., because Desert Storm was going on during that time. Adrock had bought some of those Desert Storm trading cards, with the pictures of the different generals and whatever. And there was one card of the main general, something-koff [General Norman Schwarzkopf]. We were looking at the cards and I took a magic marker and put a big check mark on the general's head. Yauch said: "Check your head!" and that was where the album title came from. [*Author's note: Fans with microscopes will notice an early photo of the*

Beasties with former producer Rick Rubin on the album's liner-note collage, with a Magic Marker check mark on Rubin's head. It has not been confirmed whether this was a coincidence or not.]

PASS THE MIC

Mario Caldato Jr.: That was one of the earlier rap songs we did for the album. Yauch and I did that one, pretty much. It started with that Bad Brains guitar sample ["Big Takeover"], and those were live drums that I processed the shit out of. I remember we made a big tunnel in front of the kick drum, eight or ten feet long, like a long barrel. The bass was from a Ron Carter solo on Johnny Hammond's "Big Sur Suite." Dre even sampled that one [on "A Nigga Witta Gun," from 1992's *The Chronic*]. In the video for that song you can see the skateboard ramps we built in the studio. The ceiling was really high, so it was perfect for that.

Mike D: That was the first video we did for the album, so that song must have been the first single. I remember we did that video in all these different spots [including many shots inside and outside of G-Son Studios] and it took a couple days.

GRATITUDE

MCA: That was a bass line that I had written a long time before, and it had been made into a song by my friend Tom [Cushman] for another band. But the lyrics we had never worked very well with it. So one day we recorded it in the studio and Adrock had the idea to put different vocals on it. He brought the vocals up to where the music was.

Adrock: Yeah, I killed it, son [*laughs*].

Money Mark: That song actually started out as a James Brown thing [*he hums the bass line to the song, and it becomes feasible that it could be more JB–like, with faster drums*], at least at first. Then it became a Latin thing. It just kept mutating.

Mike D: The percussion on there [Juanito Vazquez and Arturo Oliva— Money Mark says that Juanito passed away in the late '90s or early '00s] came about because there was this small Latin percussion store in Echo Park, not far from the studio. We started going there to buy shit and Juanito owned the place, and he'd help us. When you were in the store, Juanito would hold shit right up to your ear, to make sure you could hear it [*laughs*].

Mario Caldato Jr.: Yeah, I remember Juanito. I'd always drive by his store on my way to the studio, it was on Glendale. He was a crazy Cuban guy and he'd play all the instruments in the store to demonstrate how great they were, but he'd do it really fucking loud. I think the first song he played on was "Groove Holmes," and then he did "Lighten Up."

FINGER LICKIN' GOOD

MCA: I don't know if [DJ] Hurricane [Wendell Fite, credited on the song as a writer] was on there; he might have just come up with the idea for the hook. I'm pretty sure that Adrock did the cuts on that one.

SO WHAT'CHA WANT

Mike D: Somehow we knew that we needed just one more banger, and Adam Horovitz had been messing with some part of that song and we started playing over the loop. It was definitely at the very end, like with Eric B. & Rakim: My girl was mad at me and your girl is mad at you because it took too long to make this album. [*Author's note: This is a quite humorous reference to the outro of Eric B. & Rakim's 1987 song "Paid in Full."*]

MCA: Your girl was mad at me?

Mario Caldato Jr.: That was the last song, the one that sealed the deal and let us know that the album was ready. The original of that song is underneath, and the Beasties just replayed it over the top of it [*Mario plays original song over the phone but makes author promise not to reveal what it is*]. That song was recorded on some really bullshit mics. We had one, and I bought two more because they liked to lay their vocals down all together.

Money Mark: I still remember the day we finished that song. The guys flipped out once it was done. They knew they had something amazing. On their greatest hits album [*Solid Gold Hits,* Capitol, 2005], that song is first in the sequence, and my keyboards are the first thing you hear on that song, so that's definitely a huge honor for me. And that keyboard part I did on there was pretty quick. They played the beat, I turned on my shit and belted it out in about thirty seconds. That was a [Korg] CX3 keyboard, run through a Leslie [amplifier/speaker].

THE BIZ VS. THE NUGE *Featuring Biz Markie*

Mike D: Pretty much any time that Biz was around, we'd record it, because there was all kinds of crazy shit going on.

MCA: Yeah, we have a version of Biz singing "Jeremiah Was a Bullfrog" [Three Dog Night's "Joy to the World," which starts out with the line, "Jeremiah was a bullfrog"], all kinds of shit. Biz was just like: "Yo, put on this Ted Nugent joint and I'm gonna sing over it." Biz visited us a bunch of times while we were recording that album.

TIME FOR LIVIN'

Mario Caldato Jr.: That's when they first got into the hardcore mode. I'd just roll the DAT, then whenever they had gotten a song down and they redid it on the multitrack board, they could never do it as well. So we just ended up using the DAT version for that one. I put the DAT version on two tracks out of the twenty-four we had available on the board and I was like: "Dude, you've got twenty-two tracks to use for your vocals [*laughs*]!" So he [Mike D] went into the vocal booth with one of those bullshit mics, grabbed the Sly Stone record [*Small Talk,* Epic, 1974—the lyrics to the song "Time for Livin' " are used, although the Beasties' music couldn't be more different from the original] right from the record racks we had in there, and read the lyrics right off the album. One interesting thing about that song is that if you play it in mono, the vocal disappears. Our tape machine had one track that was out of phase, so it made it turn out that way.

SOMETHING'S GOT TO GIVE

MCA: If I recall correctly, that was one time when we were recording direct to DAT, maybe even when we were still at Cole Rehearsal Studio. We really liked the sound of it, so instead of replaying it on twenty-four tracks at G-Son, we just made loops out of the DAT stuff. The main parts that we sampled were recorded in a pretty shitty way, and we liked that sound.

Adrock: That's actually my favorite song on the record, now that I think about it. I remember putting those samples into the MPC-60 [sampler], and the original stuff was definitely from Cole. I remember that the main groove, aside from the bass, is from a [Yamaha] DX-7 keyboard that we had at Cole. James Bradley did some percussion on there, and on a bunch of other tracks on the album. He played drums for Chuck Mangione on [his smash 1977 jazz album and song] *Feels So Good.* We knew him because he was in a band called Mary's Danish, from L.A.

STAND TOGETHER

MCA: The sax on there at the beginning is sampled from a group called Back Door. The bass is from them too. We were working on that song and

Mark was fixing something in the other room and the sound bled through. We really liked how it sounded, so we recorded it better and put it on there.

Mike D: Somehow what Mark was doing with the screw gun just sounded perfect, and it was even on key.

MCA: With the part on there in the middle where the guitar sounds like it's being cut up, we played it and [sampled] the guitar into loops. I was playing the guitar on there. I think I recorded it in my house on an eight-track. We ran the guitar part through the DJ mixer and then terminated [transformed] the guitar, so that's why it sounds like it's a record being cut up.

THE MAESTRO

Adrock: The main story about that song is about the effects pedal called the Maestro. There was this old used-gear spot in L.A. on Larchmont, and we used to go there, and that's where I first learned about Maestro gear. It was a brand of sixties and seventies guitar pedals.

MCA: Maestro pedals are crazy because they're kind of shitty, but they're also really unique and intense. You could set it so that it sounds like the guitar is playing percussion—or with the one we used on that song, it's playing the guitar effect but it's also playing that bass line. A lot of jazz guys used that effect, running saxophones through it.

Money Mark: There's a Maestro box on the cover of Eddie Harris's *Plug Me In* album, so that always gave it some extra weight to us. I think I had the first Maestro of all of us. There are different models—for percussion, for woodwinds, and for guitar.

Mario Caldato Jr.: The original concept of that song was about the Gibson Maestro effects box, but then we started applying it to people who acted like they were the shit. "The Maestro" is just about attitude, like that kid on the phone message at the beginning of the song.

MCA: Groove Holmes [the jazz keyboardist who passed away in mid–1991] was still alive when we did that song, so it wasn't like an after-he-died tribute. I've always dug that one. Other tracks on the album took a lot more work, but that one was less complicated.

Money Mark: We all loved [jazz keyboard legend] Jimmy Smith, but we were *really* into Richard "Groove" Holmes. He died during the time we were making the album, so it became an homage to him. It wasn't called "Groove Holmes" when it was recorded, but after he passed away we named it that. That might be my favorite track on the album, if I was forced to choose.

LIVE AT P.J.'S

Money Mark: That was the very first song we recorded, I think back at Adrock's apartment. The original version, at least. And the final version wasn't all that different. As I recall, we lost the four-track tape and then just re-created the song at G-Son. With the fake audience sounds on there, that was us clapping, not a sample from a record. I definitely remember that.

MARK ON THE BUS

Money Mark: That was done on one of the nights that I stayed really late, reviewing a DAT of stuff that we had just recorded. I found this little section that I liked and I was delirious and I just sang those vocals over it, at about six in the morning. I did all that in Studio B, the secondary one. I was really the working-class guy of the bunch, so I knew all about taking the bus.

PROFESSOR BOOTY

MCA: [*after being asked if he is dissing 3rd Bass's MC Serch on the song*] I'm not at liberty to comment on that.

Mario Caldato Jr.: If you listen to it, the music changes with each new verse. Each guy brought their own sample to rhyme over, and I threw a beat in there too. Serch was just somebody to pick on—a dude on TV dancing around like a fool. So Yauch just dissed him.

NAMASTE

Mario Caldato Jr.: "Namaste" is just completely mellow. That was one of the earliest songs we recorded, although we added the vocals at the end. I like that song a lot. It's nice, it's sweet. It was a very Zen moment.

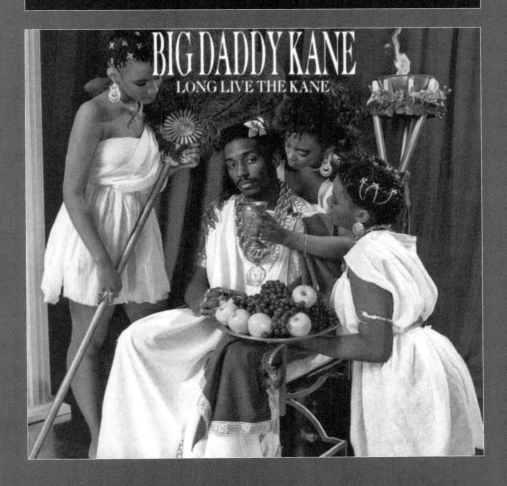

He may be the king of the brag rap, but Big Daddy Kane (Antonio Hardy) actually started out away from the spotlight. "Make sure you mention that I grew up in Bed-Stuy," he says adamantly at the start of our chat. He continues his history lesson, "When I first started messin' with hip-hop, I tried to DJ, but I wasn't all that good. I was writin' rhymes for my cousin Nicole, and I was writing them for myself too. I also had a cousin named Murdoch who started rhyming back then. He was much older and I was a young shorty. I always looked up to him and I'd do whatever he did, so I started rhyming really just to hang out with him. This is like 1982. I basically patterned my style after Grandmaster Caz [of the Cold Crush Brothers], at least when I first started writing."

Introduced into the real rap game by "the Diabolical" Biz Markie, Kane ghostwrote lyrics for Biz's earliest classics: "Nobody Beats the Biz," "Biz Is Goin' Off," "Pickin' Boogers," "Albee Square Mall," and "Vapors." "I really started taking rap seriously when I met Biz," Kane explains. "He started telling me: 'Yo, you're *nice* on the mic!' I met Biz at the Albee Square Mall [in Brooklyn] in 1984. We had a mutual friend, a dude from Central Islip [Long Island]. I also went to Sarah J. Hale High School, which wasn't too far from Albee Square. Biz used to come around a lot, and he'd take me to a lot of parties, like Mike & Dave used to throw back in the day. We'd go onstage and rhyme. Biz would get in lots of spots for free, and lots of them would let us get on the mic. Like Latin Quarter, all the Mike & Dave parties, and spots on Long Island."

Kane's stage name came together in two parts. "At first it was just MC Kane," he says. "The Big Daddy part came from something that happened on a class trip. It was actually a joke that cats was teasing me about. Then they were like: 'Actually, that's kinda hot, you should use that.' The Kane part was from cats teasing me about being so infatuated with the TV series *Kung Fu* [in the series, David Carradine's character is named Caine]. I was that cat at three o'clock on Saturdays in front of the TV for *Kung Fu* Theater. The name didn't always mean 'King Asiatic Nobody's Equal,' not back then. That came later on, when I used it in a song."

Through Biz, Kane met another Juice Crew luminary, Roxanne Shanté. "Fly Ty [manager of most Juice Crew acts and owner of Cold Chillin' Records] asked me to write some stuff for Shanté," he recalls, "and I had a lot of respect for her, so I was like: 'No doubt!' " Kane wrote several hits for her, including "Have a Nice Day." Although he downplays them, Kane did indeed have skills on the turntables back then, and was even Shanté's DJ for the Def Jam Tour of 1986. "After the writing stuff I did, Shanté asked me to go on the road and DJ for her. Cool V [Biz's DJ] knew I could DJ, and Mister Cee [who would become Kane's DJ] knew, but nobody else. I'd be in rehearsal, battling with Marley [Marl] and this other brother named Backspin. I got on and showed 'em my thing, and Shanté thought I was pretty good, so she asked me. I only did one tour. She was paying me a nice amount of money for it, so I had no problem with it."

Kane breaks down his different ghostwriting situations and challenges like this: "Writing for Biz was in a whole different style, so that could be a challenge. But Fly Ty wanted Shanté to have *my* style, so I wrote for her in that way, and it wasn't a problem, of course. Biz had invented this whole different style and wanted to flow like that—he just couldn't always work the words out. So I wrote in that style for him. Because it was different, the way I wrote for him, it didn't sound like nothin' that would come from me, so it was harder to tell. Shanté would always tell people that I wrote rhymes for her. It wasn't a big deal. The Biz thing was something that we kept on the hush. Anybody that was really into the artwork and reading all the credits on albums could put one and one together and figure it out, but it wasn't something we mentioned back then."

After all his backstage success, it became very clear that Kane wasn't meant to be hidden away. The spotlight demanded to shine upon him, with his dashing good looks, calm, strong demeanor, and his inimitable way with words. Juice Crew kingpin Marley Marl knew there was something there. "When Marley found out that I was writin' stuff for Biz, he started wanting to have me record, to see what I sounded like," Kane recalls.

Marley definitely liked what he heard, and by later in 1986 the two were working together. Their first output on wax was Kane's debut single, "Get into It," released on Prism in early 1987. The intro to the A-side featured the already-known Biz Markie, and the B-side was Kane's goofier "Just Rhymin' with Biz" (in addition to the track "Somethin' Funky"). "'Get into It' was getting played," Kane explains. "But everyone thought it was Biz's song, so I wasn't getting no shows." The answer, as Kane says: "I went back into the studio and did 'Raw,' so I could get some shows of my own."

When it came to live shows at the time, Kane traveled with a whole crew who also joined him onstage. "Me and Murph grew up together, went to school together," Kane explains. "He was my sidekick, kind of Jerome to my Morris Day. He decided to become a family man, so he left it alone eventually. And Scoob and Scrap [Lover], they got involved from the Latin Quarter days. I met Mister Cee, my DJ, around 1984. I got down with his crew, the Magnum Force. They were some cats out of LG [Lafayette Gardens, a housing project in Brooklyn]. I started rhymin' with them. One of the members got killed and another one had a bad accident and another one went away to the service. But me and Cee stayed together."

The "Raw" single, released on Prism in late 1987, was Kane's first real calling card: five intense minutes of pure, unadulterated braggadocio, with an incredible Marley-freaked James Brown loop and Kane's unmistakable, testosterone-charged voice. The single took off, convincing the powers that be at Warner Bros. (who were partnered with Cold Chillin', where most of the Marley Marl/Juice Crew output was placed from late 1987 onward) that Kane deserved an album.

The *Long Live the Kane* album was recorded at Marley Marl's home studio in Queens in early 1988, with all cuts done by Mister Cee. "Recording the album went real quick," Kane recalls. "Me and Marley worked together on things. Sometimes I wrote to the beat, sometimes I already had lyrics that fit a beat Marley did. Marley had a gritty feel for music. Regardless of how clean or brand-new the record was that he was sampling, or how light the production may have been, he always gave it a really gritty feel when he sampled it. He always put the 808 to it and gave it a heavy bottom and warm feel." Kane notes that two songs were supposed to be on the full-length but never made it: the B-side "Somethin' Funky" and a newly recorded song called "This Is for Your Own Concern."

Despite the respect he had for his producer, Kane recalls that the two talented artists butted heads often. "Honestly, me and Marley always disagreed in the studio. But then at the end of the day when the song was done and everyone else liked it, everything would be cool. It wasn't beef between us. Two creative minds in the studio are just gonna clash. I think they clashed in a good way." Kane also notes that back at that time, the seemingly tight-knit Juice Crew wasn't spending every minute together, as fans might have assumed. "We became a solid unit at shows, but we all lived our separate lives. Even so, we'd always do shows together, ride in the same limo and all that."

From the minimal Meters loop of the opening brag workout "Long Live the Kane" to the more politically charged final shot "Word to the Mother (Land)," the album is a perfect snapshot of New York hip-hop in 1988. Rap music was getting smoother, but rough edges still abounded. And taking the big picture into account, Marley's unbeatable production and Kane's godlike lyricism still make it one of the most quotable and complete hip-hop albums of all time. "It was my debut, and there's a lot of classic songs on there that I still perform today," says Kane. "A lot of people still remember it, and I'm really thankful for that."

TRACKS

WRATH OF KANE *B-side for "I'll Take You There" single (not on album)*

Warner Bros. wanted to go with "I'll Take You There" for a single, and I didn't want that. I wanted "Set It Off." But they was calling the shots. I wanted a fast-paced song, and they said I could do "Set It Off" as the next single. I didn't want to waste it as a B-side, so I just recorded "Wrath of Kane" for that. I wanted to have something that was street.

RAW (REMIX)

When it came to battle rhymes like that, I wrote that kind of stuff all the time. Like my man Murph would say, "Yo, there's this kid in Bushwick that was talking shit about you and wants to battle." So I'd start writing rhymes like that. We put the original "Raw" out in the fall of '87, on Prism, because Cold Chillin' was then part of Warner Bros. and Warner Bros. was only interested in Biz, Shanté, and Shan at the time. They didn't really want me at first. After they saw that it was doing good they picked it up for the *Colors* soundtrack, and that's when they signed me. Greg Mack in L.A. was bumping it hard on KDAY, and we was finally getting a lot of shows and having the record played in a lot of places. Marley did that remix after mastering, I had nothing to do with it. I wanted the original version on the album, but Marley made a smart call. It turned out for the best. The same day I did "Raw" back in '87 I had [Kool G] Rap with me, and after we finished the song we brought the track back up and just rhymed back and forth for a while until the beat ended. So Marley took some of the rhymes I did on that take and mixed it in on the remix, so there was a few extra lyrics on there. I think Mister Cee must have done the cuts on there [instead of Marley].

That's my favorite song from the album. That's my favorite song of all the songs I've ever made, actually. I just like the adrenaline of it. I wanted it as a single, but Warners was excited about "I'll Take You There." I understand where they were coming from. They were older cats and they saw the relationship between the message and the Staple Singers [sample]. I still perform "Set It Off" all the time.

THE DAY YOU'RE MINE

Andre Booth co-wrote that. He was a keyboard player that Marley used, a real talented dude. He did that "Left Me Lonely" joint for Shan. He also did the "All of Me" joint I did with Barry White. I wanted to do a "Left Me Lonely" of my own. It wasn't written about any specific woman.

ON THE BUGGED TIP *Featuring Scoob Lover*

We were definitely going after the Cold Crush Brothers old-school style on that one. That was the style that Scoob rhymed in anyways. We used the old beat from [the movie] *Wild Style* to try and capture that feeling. That's what I grew up listening to, so I wanted to pay homage. I think I even got those [*Wild Style*] records from Tony Tone from Cold Crush [who was in the film and on the soundtrack]. He let me borrow them, the instrumentals. We went over to Marley's crib, Mister Cee cut it up, and me and Scoob just went for it.

AIN'T NO HALF STEPPIN'

That's the song that I'm most known for to this day, definitely. That was the first single they put out off the album, and we did a video for it. When I look at it now it's funny because that was the suit from my [high school] graduation. It was tight, way too small, but I was still tryin' to do it [*laughs*]. My man Lionel Martin blessed me with a lot of fine women for that video. It was cool, the whole boxing ring thing, it was pretty unique. That was the only video we made for that album, believe it or not.

I'LL TAKE YOU THERE

That was actually the first song I ever did with Marley, before "Get into It" and all that, the first time that he ever heard me rhyme. Marley had the Staple Singers ["I'll Take You There"] 45 and I remembered it from my man Understanding, when I used to be with this crew The Debonair Three. When we heard the part where it says "Big Daddy," I knew we had to use it. We wrote the rhymes and made the track, but apparently Prince owned the rights to all the Staple Singers songs and wasn't tryin' to let no rappers use them. So we put it on the back burner. When I signed with Warner Bros., that was the same label that Prince was on, so then Prince was cool about it. I was trying to paint a picture about paradise, not about religion. It's about being happy and living comfortably. Enjoying life, without any drama or any problems.

JUST RHYMIN' WITH BIZ

I really did the beat for that, over at my man Shim Shom's house. He helped me put it together, with his little sampler, but it was too cheap to actually use for real production. So we had to redo the whole thing over at Marley's place.

> Frick & Frack [lesser-known female MCs from the Juice Crew family] was actually on that one, originally. It was just a two-track I lifted off the DAT tape. That track just happened, when the beat was playing. Kane just started out with, "Check it out, y'all . . ." and it went from there. The levels are fucked up on the track, but it is what it is. Frick & Frack weren't signed to Cold Chillin' at the time so I had to cut their verses off.
> —*Marley Marl, from his interview for* In Control, Volume 1

Those are words from Farrakhan tapes at the end of that track. I felt that he was dropping some serious jewels that a lot of young cats weren't really paying attention to, so I thought that they'd pay attention to a piece of what he was sayin' and would wanna go and get a Farrakhan tape, to hear it. People always asked me what that stuff was there at the end and I was glad to tell them.

BIZ MARKIE
Goin' Off
(Cold Chillin'/Warner Bros., 1988)

A lot of money is given out for albums these days," says Biz Markie. "But it wasn't about money back then. It was about integrity, and about being able to say, 'Yo, my album is *dope.*' That's the reason that *Goin' Off* is the top for me. The hunger was there, and the album had so many different elements to it."

New Jacks who have come up in the rap world past the nineties have had it pretty easy, at least compared to their predecessors. Back in the seventies and eighties, peeps had to pave their own way. And no one showed that more than the diabolical Biz Markie, who brought more humor to hip-hop than it had ever seen. He made heads laugh and dance, but he also made them see themselves. Biz was Everyman. The class clown. The guy in the corner who always had to work harder to get heard.

Biz Markie (Marcel Hall) entered the world in 1964 in Harlem. His family moved to Brentwood, Long Island (home to fellow hip-hop pioneers EPMD), when he was ten, and a couple years later he began honing his MC skills in earnest. "I got turned on to rapping in like 1978 from people around my way in Brentwood," he says. "I've been beatboxing since I was a kid, but I started rapping in '78. I was known as a rapper in Long Island—I had my own dances and stuff like that. I was in contests and doing parties. Uptown, Brooklyn, Long Island. Anywhere I could get on.

"I was always trying to get into crews," he continues. "One of the first ones I was in was from CI [Central Islip, Long Island] called Midnite Express. It was Kevin D, Rapper A, DJ Casper, and Subie Gee. I was seeing live stuff in my area back then, but it was different. The Long Island sound was different than the New York sound, definitely. When we did stuff, at that time it wasn't about shows in clubs. We was doin' house parties, school parties, center parties, going to Bayshore, Long Island, to do American Legion Halls. This was in the early eighties, when I was in eleventh and twelfth grade."

Biz kept active on the party and battle scenes in New York and Long Island throughout the early eighties. But as people who know his legend are aware, his big connection was with Marley Marl's Juice Crew. Biz got in on the ground floor, first meeting the man in 1984. "I wanted to be down with Marley *bad,* all that time," he recalls. "I used to go up to Queensbridge

[Projects] and sit out in front of Marley's house for like six, seven, eight hours. Then he'd tell me to come back tomorrow. My man Phil Rodriguez hooked me up with MC Shan, and when I went to Queensbridge to see Shan one day, he wasn't home. I went into this park and started battling everybody and beatboxing, and I took everybody out. This is when Nas and Prodigy [of Mobb Deep] was little kids, way back."

Marley knew Biz's name from then on out, and from what he heard of Biz's rhyme style, Marley was also warming to his wacky but hard-to-ignore personality on the mic and off. Biz's real entrée into the Juice Crew world was through his work with Roxanne Shanté. "In 1985 I was down with Shanté," Biz explains. "I was her beatboxer because Marley and Shanté wasn't getting along, so he wasn't going out as a DJ for her. Plus he was on the radio [as DJ for Mr. Magic's "Rapp Attack" on WBLS] so he wasn't going out to do shows out of town. I would go out [to perform] with her and do all her records, just doing human beatboxing." Biz's first appearance on wax was on Shanté's Marley Marl–produced "The Def Fresh Crew" single, released on Pop Art Records in 1986.

Around the same time, Biz met another future Juice Crew rapper with whom he would have a long association: Big Daddy Kane. "I met Kane in 1984, in Brooklyn," recalls Biz. "Me and him battled in the street, in front of McQuarrie Mall. I was actually substitute teaching at Kane's school back then, at Sarah J. Hale [High School] in Brooklyn. The kids was so crazy at that time. I was about twenty-one, not much older than them. I wasn't trying to be a teacher—I just had a whole bunch of different schemes back then [*laughs*]. Anything for a dollar."

In '86, after his work with Shanté and after showing talent and determination within the Juice Crew ranks, Biz got his first shot on wax. The result was the Marley Marl–produced *Inhuman Orchestra* EP (Prism), which included the legendary tracks "Make the Music with Your Mouth, Biz" (the song's risible chorus hook was sung in falsetto by his longtime friend TJ Swan) and "The Biz Dance." The EP was loose and goofy, showcasing Biz's sense of humor as well as his rapping and unique beatboxing skills.

"Me and Marley made some great music together," Biz says. "I'd bring in a record and say, 'Yo, can you do something with this?' And he'd hook it up on the drum machine, put this in here, add this, *bah bah bah,* and the beat is done. Marley taught me how to work in a studio and put a beat together.

Everybody to this day thinks Marley was the mastermind. He can definitely hook up a beat, yes. But he usually had to have somebody tell him what to do with the beat. Either way, I learned a lot of studio stuff from him, so it was a good relationship."

The record was a big hit across the tri-state area, and Biz's career was on its way, along with fellow Juice Crew peers Shanté, Shan, and Kane, all of whom Marley was producing concurrently in a swirl of musically incestuous activity. In fact, Kane ghostwrote some of Biz's rhymes back in those days. "For those early singles, I would tell Kane the concept and the subject and he would just write it up," he recalls. "I had him do it because I wanted to get in the game, and he was a great lyricist. It was a trade-off thing too—I gave him the beat for [Kane's single] 'Ain't No Half Steppin'.' Stuff like that."

For Biz 1987 was a busy year, spent performing, guesting on other people's records (like Big Daddy Kane's "Just Rhymin' with Biz"), and releasing his own smash single "Nobody Beats the Biz." And while Marley's Juice Crew, including Shanté and especially Shan, was battling with Boogie Down Productions and DJ Red Alert on wax (with BDP's "South Bronx" and "The Bridge Is Over" and Shan's "Kill That Noise"), Biz didn't get too involved. "It didn't bother me that they were battling because I was cool with Scott La Rock and KRS [One]," he says. "I was like a pope, I was like Switzerland. I didn't have no beefs. And I think that's why my first album was one that hit even more than other Juice Crew records. Everybody liked it because it wasn't a dis record."

In actuality, the Bronx vs. Juice Crew beef *did* reach Biz, and his first single in 1987 was even a result of it. "Back then this group on B-Boy [Boogie Down Productions' label] called the Brothers did a song that said some stuff about me ["You Can't Win," B-Boy Records, 1987]," Biz admits. "I wasn't that mad about it, but I went home and wrote 'Nobody Beats the Biz.' Since my record was so big, no one listened to their record."

In the fall of 1987, Biz's popularity had merited a full-length, and so work on his debut, *Goin' Off,* commenced at Marley's newly built home studio in Astoria, Queens. "It didn't take more than two or three weeks to record everything for that album—it was quick," he recalls. "I had the funk and I knew what I wanted out of the album, so it was easy. The hardest thing was tracking down certain records that I needed. I went to Downstairs

Records a lot for that." Biz's cousin and DJ, Cool V (Vaughan Lee), was, as Biz says, "a main part of that album too. He was there in the studio every day and I'm pretty sure he did all the cuts on there. Fly Ty [label manager for Cold Chillin'] came in and out. Kane was there too. If I needed something written, he'd do it within two minutes, right there."

The album hit in February 1988, and it began the 1988 and 1989 ruling of Marley Marl's Juice Crew syndicate (Biz, Big Daddy Kane, MC Shan, Roxanne Shanté, and Kool G Rap & DJ Polo). "I'm a simple person," says Biz, explaining the appeal of *Goin' Off.* "If the beat is funky with something on top, then that's it, that's all I need. That album was big right away when it came out because I had a couple records out already, and people wanted more. It was really just like I had another single when the album came out. Back then I had to wait until the last single started to die down before I released another hit."

Regarding Cold Chillin's new partnership with Warner Bros. (which began in 1987), Biz says that didn't change anything in his world. "Being on Warners or just through Cold Chillin' didn't make a difference, since I was never that promoted anyways," he says. "I was always my own promoter, since people never seemed to worry that much about me. They put more emphasis on Shan, Shanté, and Kane. It wasn't a big deal. I'd just have to work a little extra harder to get noticed."

TRACKS

I wanted to do a record like that because I knew a lot of people that used to pick boogers. I used to know a kid named Anthony Hussey, and he used to pick his boogers back in the day.

I went to the Albee Square Mall [on Fulton Street in Brooklyn] every day. I used to get food for free, clothes on credit without a credit card. And that was before the song. After the song I paid for everything 'cause I had money then. They loved me there after that song. All my Brooklyn boys in there would look out for me to make sure nothin' happened. I can't really hang out at any malls now. It's like, "Hey, ain't you . . . ?" I guess Laurel Mall, around the corner from my house [in Laurel, Maryland], is one I'd hang out at. TJ Swan was on that song [singing the hook] with me 'cause Swan always used to hang with me at the mall. Swan's great on that track, but I think "Nobody Beats the Biz" is his best song. He was my best friend from around the way in Long Island. I've known him since like 1982. Working with him actually happened accidentally. We would just sit in the car or walk from the train station and he'd just sing while I did the beatbox. Since he was with me through my early struggles in the rap game, I put him on—since he was my boy. And it worked. He had a draw, too, since the girls all liked him.

RETURN OF THE BIZ DANCE

That version was different than the original ["The Biz Dance," from the *Inhuman Orchestra* EP]. The beat that Marley did was so funky that I wanted to do a rhyme to it, and I didn't know what else to do so I did another Biz Dance track. The Biz Dance itself is still the same today as it was back then. I taught everybody the Biz Dance. I can't even tell you how many people.

VAPORS

I wrote that song so I would be like Rod Serling. How he'd have different stories, like on *The Twilight Zone.* I wanted to show four different lives. And I wanted to show the good and the bad in those lives. Every single thing on that song was true. That's still one of my classics, and I still perform that one to this day. I have to. If I don't, they'll fight me. Snoop covered that song and I was always really happy about that cover. "Vapors" was always really big in L.A., bigger than it was in New York. That was probably the biggest record I ever had on the West Coast. It told a story and West Coast loves stories. I love Snoop's version because he still kept the funk in it. Plus he changed the words up. It was a compliment.

MAKE THE MUSIC WITH YOUR MOUTH, BIZ

The first version I had of that, I used the "Pink Panther" beat. But I didn't like it so I didn't use it in the end. I told Marley how I wanted the beat to go. I wanted the 808 bass sound to be deeper, but his button got stuck so it ended up with less bass. Marley did a remix of the song for the album, a dub version of the original. I don't know why he did that. I wasn't there for the mastering of that album. I wanted the "Make the Music" original on the album, not that version. But I had no control at that time. It was my first album. I knew that song would be a big record because people out there was just waiting for something new.

That's a remix, too, different than the single. I don't know why they did that either. The words ain't different, mostly just the way the song starts. I brought in that Steve Miller sample because it was rock and I knew that stuff. I wanted it to just be Steve Miller but Marley had the Lafayette Afro Rock Band sample [for the drumbeat]. As I recall, Marley got the Lafayette Afro Rock track from [legendary Queensbridge DJ] Jappy Jap, but the record itself was really scratched up. So I called all over to get a better copy. I called Bambaataa, I called [Grandmaster] Flash, I called everybody. I think Flash told me the name of it, so I knew that from him. I looked all over and I found a store on Utica Avenue [in Brooklyn] that had African records. So I slept in front of the store and I bought every copy they had of that record when they opened. I brought it back to Marley and he hooked it back up. I think the Wiz [the Nobody Beats the Wiz electronics store, whose jingle is modified for the chorus] might have sued us, but I don't know nothin' about that. They sold my records in their store either way. Marley might have done the cuts on that track.

THIS IS SOMETHING FOR THE RADIO

That wasn't a filler track—I liked that one. It was like three or four in the morning when I did that. I did a version of "Vapors" like that, too, with me talking and not rappin'. I just wanted to act like I was drunk [*slurs speech for effect*]. They recorded it while I was playin' around. And after I heard it, it was cool. I said, "Keep it."

COOL V'S TRIBUTE TO SCRATCHING

We had a record called "Cool V's Scratchstrapiece" that was supposed to go on the album, using all Michael Jackson records. But it never made the album. You gotta hear it, it's incredible. But Michael Jackson wouldn't clear the stuff. It was the second to last record we did for the album. Cool V was an incredible DJ. He was fast, accurate, and he would not mess up. He was like a record. Besides being my cousin, he was just really good. An accurate DJ is the best one you can have.

BLACK MOON

Enta Da Stage

(Wreck/Nervous, 1993)

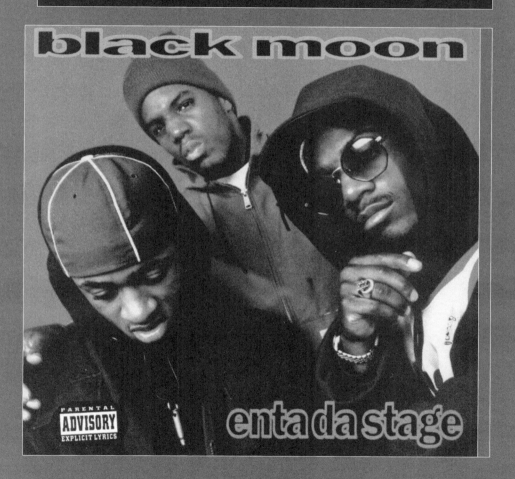

People want to know what makes a dope album, and I'll tell you," says Buckshot, the lead MC of Brooklyn's Black Moon. "It takes persona, energy, character, and vibe. All of them together make a classic album." It's hard to argue his list of ingredients, and if anyone can speak on such things it would be Buck, who, along with fellow MC 5 FT and producers Evil Dee and Mr. Walt, gave the world one of the early nineties' grittiest and most influential albums, *Enta Da Stage.*

Buckshot (Kenyatta Blake), who grew up in Crown Heights and Brownsville, Brooklyn (although he says, "My heart is always on Franklin Avenue, Crown Heights"), came into the MCing game later than some of his peers. You can blame it on his feet. "I first started rhyming through dancing," he says. "Dancing is really my first love. And it's really the thing that made it possible for me to rhyme. I even got into Black Moon because of my dancing. I joined up with them after my dancing partner got locked up for ten years. And the second I got in with Black Moon on that level, I knew I didn't want to dance no more. I decided to put all my energy into my lyrics."

Buck had a great idol to emulate when it came to his MCing. He explains: "Rakim was the first MC who I heard that introduced me to the *technique* of rhyming. He said, 'Eric B. is on the cut, no mistakes allowed.' That shit was *so* important. He was saying that nigga's name *and* telling him what to do. That is *so* gangsta. To me, that was it. Rapping is like a snake traveling up a tree. It's so slitherful."

He continues, bringing his style back to the present day: "I love changing up flows when I rhyme, but it's not always purposefully. I can't control how I rhyme all the time. Because when I hear a beat I *become* the music. I marry that beat in my head before I'm even on the mic. I have like thirty books full of rhymes, and I will go through all of those rhymes and it won't feel nothin' like the shit I just wrote five minutes ago."

As only the hardest-core Black Moon fan might remember, Buck wasn't in the group's earliest incarnation. The original trio was DJ and producer Evil Dee and rappers 5 FT (Kaseem Reid) and Finsta. As Buck recalls: "At the time, Finsta thought that a record deal was taking too long, so he was like, 'Fuck it,' and he jetted. Those guys [Dee and 5 FT] started around '89 or '90 and I became a part of the group in 1991. I knew 5 FT and he introduced me to Evil Dee. I took my leader position by just being an individual and doing it my way or no way."

Aside from Buckshot, the other co-leader of the group is undeniably producer, DJ, and Bushwick ambassador Evil Dee (Ewart Dewgarde). Like many younger brothers at the time, he had to sneak around to get on his older brother Walt's equipment. Evil Dee says: "My brother Walt, who is three years older than me, definitely played a big role in how I started off. I saw Walt DJing at a block party and I got that little-brother jealousy. I could play drums, but the turntables definitely drew me in. Walt had some equipment in the house, and when he'd go to hang out with his friends, I'd go down and turn on his equipment and start trying to DJ. He would catch me and beat me up [*laughs*]. Eventually I got my skills up on the turntables and Walt would keep being mean to me, so I'd practice even more, so I could be even nicer on the decks than him."

By the late eighties, the two siblings had called a truce and starting making tracks together. They eventually worked up to a four-track (still well below the industry standard of twenty-four- or forty-eight-track boards), but started much more modestly on two tape decks. Evil Dee says: "One thing about me, I'm a technical cat, so I always figure out how to maximize any equipment I've got. Walt started out doing two tape decks, bouncing the music as he built up the layers on there. And by the time I started helping him do it, it sounded so clean that people thought we had a full studio in our crib, even though it was just the two decks." In addition to the recording equipment, Evil Dee says they also used the Casio SK-1 sampling keyboard and RZ-1 drum machine.

Walt explains: "I'm the older brother, but eventually I gave in and admitted that you gotta let the little brother shine. Since we started Beatminerz in '92 or '93, we haven't argued once. Well, not about business, at least. Our dynamic is the same today as it was back then. I have more beats than E, and he's the technical guy. I don't have time to learn anything new, so that's on him. Basically, producers always thrive off and build off each other, and E and I are brothers *and* producers, so it's even more intense." Walt points out the difference between the duo's production on both Beatminerz (meaning non–Black Moon) projects and Black Moon albums: "With Beatminerz, I do a majority of the beats. If it's Black Moon, then E does more beats, because that's his group." [*Author's note: Evil Dee describes Beatminerz productions as equal co-productions between him and Walt.*]

Walt says: "Our era, how we came up, was all about using a beat that no one else had used before. In our crew it was that, and then always: 'Whose beat is going to be fresher?' So the competition was fierce. We were doing a lot of the same things that people like Pete Rock, Large Professor, and Q-Tip were doing, like filtering samples. [*Author's note: "Filtering" is a studio process in which an original sample source is EQ'd and then replayed to emphasize the low end and deemphasize high-end (treble) tones, usually to isolate a desired bass line. The modified source song is sampled and manipulated, and sometimes even further filtered.*] If I had to choose a way we were different, it was maybe that we messed with the dark stuff more than other people."

In the late eighties, Walt had one important connection to the music industry that helped the two brothers link up with some of the most important names in hip-hop production at the time. He explains: "I worked at the Music Factory record store back in the eighties, in Queens, on Jamaica Avenue. I was the manager and did all the record-buying." Walt came to know all the classic breaks that DJs used, and also interacted with top-level producers and DJs on the regular.

While Walt continued building his record collection and making connections at Music Factory, younger brother Ewart (usually referred to as "E" by friends) was making his own connections, including meeting Finsta. E recalls: "Finsta was from Bushwick, and we were both in band class at our high school. I played drums and he played sax. I wanted him to play sax over some beats I had, and Finsta was like: 'Yo, I wanna learn how to DJ.' So we'd sit down and work on demos every day. We'd have to finish by six P.M., though, because that's when Walt would come home."

By the early nineties, Walt was building his own studio chops, working on a demo at Studio 1212 in Queens, where the late Paul C—who was murdered in 1989—worked with groups like the Ultramagnetic MCs and Eric B. & Rakim. Walt says: "I was working with a group called Potentially Dangerous, and the rapper was named D.E.A. I was the producer and I was working with Paul C's brother [engineer Tim McKasty]. It was my first taste of the studio, and I'd go there right after work. I basically took all the money I made at my job and put it into studio time." They produced enough songs to make a full album but were never able to interest any labels in D.E.A., who was, as Walt says, "Very complex, way ahead of his time, and he never wanted to dumb it down. I respect him for that."

The work that Walt did at 1212 didn't go to waste, as he built up his production chops and continued to fortify his sampling arsenal. Walt explains: "The 1212 stuff I was doing for D.E.A. wasn't that different from what people heard with Black Moon. I put static on the records, and I still do. It has to be grimy. I was always about the grimy sound."

The earliest glimmer of what would become Black Moon materialized while E was still in high school. As he recalls: "I was putting together a talent show at Bushwick High School, and my friend 5 FT was one of the nicest cats when it came to dancing. I asked 5 to be part of the talent show and he told me that he rhymed too. He also told me he wanted to bring in his partner, who didn't go to Bushwick [High]. So 5 brought the dude to my crib, and it was Buckshot. Buckshot dropped some rhymes right there and I told him we should all start doing some demos. Even I was rhyming back then, and I was wack!"

E continues: "At the time we wasn't even Black Moon, we was called Unique Image [*laughs*]. Oh, man, we are *so* over when people hear that [*laughs*]! Then we used the name High Tech. Walt was using Black Moon for his production company at the time and D.E.A. had a song that was called "The Beatminers" that told the story of how Walt used to go digging for records. So Walt took the name Beatminerz for his productions and we took the name Black Moon."

Walt recalls: "Eventually it just made sense to cut E and Finsta on the mic and just leave the rhyming to 5 and Buckshot. At that time I would just coach them on what to do. I definitely thought they had something, and that it was a solid team effort." E remembers: "Once we did that and got focused, that's when we started getting really serious about it and shopping it. This was like early 1991. Both of those guys [5 FT and Buckshot] just stepped up their game and got nice on the rhymes."

Thus a long deal-shopping journey began, with many frustrations along the way. E remembers: "We had a demo with five songs on it that we had done at our crib. We shopped that demo to everyone *except* Nervous. I was getting a mixtape name at the time, DJing at spots in Brooklyn and also working at a record store and selling tapes there. At the time, A Tribe Called

Quest had just blown up and De La was at the top of their game. Ice Cube was also doing really well, so people at labels were looking for that kind of stuff. But in general, labels were like: 'What is this? It's not hardcore because you're not cursing enough, and it's not commercial either.' They didn't get it."

Their label-shopping luck changed one fateful night, as E recalls: "We were at a party and Buckshot convinced the people putting it on to let us perform there. We got onstage and there was just so much energy, those guys were all over the stage. And I'd always start off our shows with a turntable routine, like a DMC battle type of thing. [Radio legend and sometime industry mover and shaker] Chuck Chillout was there and he said he was doing A&R for a label, Nervous, and he wanted to set up a meeting. We weren't sure about him, and didn't agree to anything at the time, so Chuck said, 'Go ahead and shop to other people, then give me a call.' Everyone said no, so we called Chuck and set up a meeting with Nervous."

Nervous owner Michael Weiss liked the group, but according to E and Walt, it was Weiss's house-music A&R person, Gladys Pizarro, who urged him to sign Black Moon. "Mike didn't really understand what we were about," says E. "But Gladys knew, and she told him he *had* to sign us." The group was signed in the spring of 1992 and given some money to record a single, which ended up being "Who Got Da Props?" They recorded it at Brooklyn's Such-A-Sound studio in the summer of that year.

After his relatively late induction into the group, Buckshot didn't waste much time getting up to speed. The group would always demo songs at Evil Dee's and Walt's house in Bushwick before hitting the studio, and Buck was young and hungry, always going the extra mile to polish his rhymes. Even Buckshot himself noticed a change after the "Who Got Da Props?" single. He recalls: "After that single came out, we were in the studio all the time, and a big bang just happened with me. I really found myself through the creation of that album. I found out who I was, what I do best, and what makes me comfortable."

As E recalls, the recording of their first single was "one big argument. At one point Schlomo [Sonnenfeld], the owner, just walked out, and so I mixed 'Who Got Da Props?' even though I never got credit for it." Things weren't going well with their manager either. Buckshot says: "Chuck Chillout as a manager ended about two songs into recording *Enta Da Stage.*"

After the tension in their studio and business affairs, Black Moon were gratified when "Who Got Da Props?" became a hit after its release in October 1992. "The song just took off in the tri-state, even better than we thought it would," says E. "We were in San Francisco for Gavin [the now-defunct music industry convention], and Mike Weiss said, 'Guys, we're gonna have to record an album.' That was February of 1993, and I said to myself, Okay, I really need to steal some records from Walt now [*laughs*]!"

The recording of the album was definitely a family affair. Evil Dee was at the production helm, but Walt was always looking over everyone's shoulder and contributing. Buck says: "Walt is the guy who taught E how to do everything, and he was a big part of what Black Moon did. If E did a beat and it was wack, Walt would tell him. Everything had to go past Walt to make it to the final stage. The only thing with Walt is that he just don't like to be known, even to this day. We'd have to push him on screen so he'd be in our videos."

E says: "When we got the Nervous deal, I knew that we had to make that record hot, and Walt had the records and could do any kind of beats we needed. I wanted Walt to be like the captain, to make sure everything was sounding okay. We collaborated on a lot of tracks, and we both mixed each track."

Another key member of the Black Moon team was a young Nervous Records employee named Dru Ha (Drew Friedman), who would go on to be co-founder, with Buckshot, of Duck Down Records and Management. E remembers: "Dru came in when we did 'Who Got Da Props?' because we had just fired Chuck Chillout. We had no way to get to a show we had in Philly, so Dru took his mom's car and drove us there and back." Dru and Buckshot formed Duck Down in 1993 to manage Black Moon and Smif-N-Wessun while Dru was still a Nervous employee.

Buck says that the *Enta Da Stage* album took about half a year to record: "Six months, every day, constant work. Pure rap. Eat, sleep, shit, smoke, sleep, and wake-up rap." Buckshot remembers the album budget being $40,000, and Evil Dee estimates between $60,000 and $100,000. But, Buck says, "I wasn't thinking about the amount of the budget, I was just thinking, How much can we get so that we can put out the best album we can?"

Black Moon started recording the album at Calliope (songs included "Powaful Impak!," "Niguz Talk Shit," and "Buck Em Down"), but E says they had problems with the owner. They finished most of the album at the soon-to-be-legendary D&D Studios in midtown, on a referral from DJ Premier, who had just started making it his own home base.

All parties agree that things really started to click once the four Black Moon members got to D&D. At the time, the Dewgardes were still in Bushwick, Buckshot was in Crown Heights, and 5 FT was living in East New York's Pink Houses. E remembers: "We would just have Brooklyn in the studio every night. It was great, because I always loved that neighborhood feel." He says that there could be upward of forty people there at D&D on any given night: hanging around, lending an ear, and lending voices to choruses, in addition to smoking, drinking, and carousing.

E says, about the D&D atmosphere: "That studio is when I started really gearing up with my style. I started getting really into pitch-bending and pitch-shifting. Swift [Leo "Swift" Morris] engineered the whole album because we stole him from Calliope, and he was playing around with an Ultra-Harmonizer [vocal-processing unit] and showing me how to use it. That was also when Buckshot started to really shine. He went from being dope to the realm of 'Oh shit! He's getting crazy with it!' I always thought that he was freestyling when he was there, but I think he had just memorized lines before he got to the studio."

Evil Dee's newfound confidence led the tech-savvy producer to explore deep new techniques that continued to place him in a league with peers he admired, like Pete Rock and Large Professor. E says: "I was always the technical guy—I figured out how things worked. And the thing with me and making beats is that I could never just do a loop. If I do a loop, I'll do it by taking the kick and snare out [of the original sample], and put them over the different track parts again to beef the sound up. It's still the same loop, but you can take parts in and out of it, expand sounds, and make the whole thing thicker. Maybe it's because with breaks, I always wished that I had played drums on those records I was sampling [laughs]!"

Walt points out another interesting sonic situation on *Enta Da Stage* that contributed to the fuzzy, grimy sound of the tracks. "We never brought *records* to the studio. Everything we sampled was off cassettes. That's why the album sounded like it did. It's not like we consciously tried to do it that way, but we borrowed a lot of the music we sampled, taping it from other people."

For those paying close attention to the album vocals, on the MC tip *Enta Da Stage* was a very one-sided affair, with Buckshot taking ten tracks as a solo MC. It wasn't a matter of pushing 5 FT to the side, but merely a situation brought on by time constraints and work habits. Buck explains, "5 FT was always my partner—he gave energy to everything Black Moon did. But if I heard a beat that night and it was hot, then I gotta finish that song *tonight.* I can't wait until Tuesday. If you don't have your lyrics ready when I do, then I'm going, I'm laying three verses and that's it. 5 needed to take a lot more time for his shit, and if he wasn't ready to finish a record when I was, then it was just me. 5 rhymes on more tracks now, but back then he didn't."

Didn't 5 FT mind? "Of course he minded!" Buck says. "He even left Black Moon after the 'I Got Cha Opin' single. He felt that he should get everything equal to me and I felt different. I was up onstage bustin' my ass for an hour, sweatin', and you're gonna do two lines and the backup and then get half?" The two are still friends and groupmates today, of course, but the Black Moon studio days of 1992 and 1993 were obviously a supreme example of the saying, You snooze, you lose.

E gives his take on the MC dynamic in the group: "Buck and 5 were both the MCs of the group, and one was supposed to do a verse, then the other would do a verse, like Smif-N-Wessun or Run-DMC. But Buckshot is a workaholic, and if you give him a bunch of beats, he'll try and write to everything. Buck worked fast and 5 would take his time, and basically Buck just outworked him. If 5 wrote faster, it would have been a nicer balance. 5 was definitely pissed, but it was no one's fault but his."

On the record-label front, by all group members' accounts dealings with Nervous were not rosy and eventually led to a court battle to extricate them from their original deal. Buck says: "We never got paid at all for all the sales we had on *Enta Da Stage,* which sold more than four hundred thousand copies. So there was no way that we was going to do a second album. From day one, dealing with that label was just total shit. It took me until 1997 to get out of that contract."

Evil Dee says: "We didn't need the label to do anything for us—we always knew what had to be done to promote our own records. We was at the office all the time, doing our own mail-outs. We'd make radio calls, go to stores, and make sure that our stuff was in stock." Walt is fairly Zen about the whole business aspect of their Nervous deal: "Really, you have to ask: 'What record label is great?' The answer is: None of them. So if Nervous hadn't done that, someone else would have."

To make matters more awkward and artistically questionable, after the group refused to submit a second album, Nervous put out *Diggin' in Dah Vaults,* which was not authorized by the group and contained no newly recorded tracks. Buckshot says: "That album was everything that didn't make *Enta Da Stage.* Nervous went back and bootlegged our shit! We didn't want people to hear our practice sessions and our demos. It's a good thing that people respected us enough that they bought that album and didn't stop listening to us after they did."

Nervous-bashing aside, Buck says of Black Moon's debut: "That album was just an example of a vibe, and it turned out like it did because of the love and energy that went into it. It wasn't planned. We was just *one* when we did those songs. It was before I started Duck Down with Dru Ha. Dealing with all the business stuff now, I miss just being an MC like that."

Walt muses, "People say different things about how it went down, but technically *we* were the ones who brought hip-hop back to the East Coast at the time. Us and Wu-Tang—not Nas and Biggie. In '92 and '93, 'Who Got Da Props?' and [Wu-Tang's] 'Protect Ya Neck' came out and really blew everything up. It set the stage."

E says: "The main thing about *Enta Da Stage* was that none of us were trying to make a record that sounded like anybody else's. I just wanted to make my interpretation of hip-hop, the theme song for cats around my way who were out hustling at three in the morning. Everybody in the industry had seen us, but they still couldn't figure out exactly what we did. And in the end, it was perfect, because I didn't want to talk about what we did, I just wanted cats to *hear* it."

T R A C K S

POWAFUL IMPAK!

Evil Dee: That was just a bunch of samples from different hip-hop records. I even showed Premier how [Gang Starr's] "Just to Get a Rep" was in there, and he was impressed. I made that record to try and fool everybody by sampling hip-hop. Like: "We can flip *anything.*"

Mr. Walt: That beat is just E saying to the world, "I'm trying to get on." On that one he sampled the "open" parts of the hip-hop tracks, where there were no vocals. So they were closer to the original samples, in a way.

NIGUZ TALK SHIT

Buckshot: That was the second song we did. 5 FT's on the chorus. All the songs we did, I didn't want to be on the chorus, so I'd get everybody in the booth. I had fun with that song. That horn on there is just from mine and E's love of jazz.

Evil Dee: That was a perfect example of Buck's style, speaking calmly about rugged shit. He wasn't as much about actually doing thug shit all the time, but it was what was going on all around him. Either way, you'd never want to fuck with him. 5 FT, on the other hand, he *was* wildin' out. He was the ill nigga out in the streets.

Evil Dee: We already had that instrumental when we got signed, but didn't use it until we decided not to use a song we had called "Female Hood" as our single. Buck pulled the instrumental out and said he was going to write to it. A couple days later he was like: "Yo, man, everybody wants props, so we should call it 'Who Got the Props?' and it'll be telling people that *we* got the props." Originally we recorded that in my basement on a four-track, then we took it to the label and told them it'd be the first single. Mike [Weiss] was still iffy, but Gladys [Pizarro] loved the song. So we went to a studio called Such-A-Sound with this guy Schlomo. He was an asshole. With "Props" the thing was that there was no bass line in that song. The beat was all about vibes, and there were two drum loops: Skull Snaps and the other was "Sport" [by Lightnin' Rod]. I wanted the "Sport" drums to be the mids and the highs, and I wanted the Skull Snaps [drums] to be the bass. So when you put them on top of each other it would sound rugged. Then the strings, the Ronnie Laws. If you took the mids and the highs out of the strings, it would fit right into it. So you had highs, mids, and bass. Schlomo wasn't having it. He said, "You can't make records like that."

That record is one of the only ones where I'm on the hook with the other guys. Finsta was even on there too, on the hook. He was hanging out at the time—he had his own record deal by then. I really wanted it to be loud on radio, because radio is all compression, and compression squeezes the bass. So when it's loud and clear and not much bass, then it'll sound very loud on radio. Mike [Weiss] and Schlomo did a mix of that song which I hate to this day. The twelve-inch had both versions. Everybody played my version except for Red Alert—he played theirs. But Uncle Red is Uncle Red, so who am I to say?

We knew that song was going to be a hit because we were going to the Philly Greek Fest [an annual black college party] in July of 1992, and Walt's friend had a Sidekick or Pathfinder with what I called "the bass system of death." He had a tape of the "Props" instrumental and he put the tape in his ride and we was driving through Brooklyn and we'd just stop and everyone was just bobbing their head to the beat. We passed by Spike Lee's store and Spike was outside, bobbing his head. So I knew it would be a hit. Everyone who heard it knew that beat was crazy. One time I bumped into Pete Rock and he was *the* man at the time, and he said, "Yo, I had that Ronnie Laws record and I tried to fuck with it so many times, but I just couldn't get it to do what I wanted." And that was it . . . I made a beat that Pete Rock couldn't do!

Buckshot: That was the first song we ever did. It took longer, like two days in the studio. We had to struggle and fight for that song to get on the radio. The first time I ever heard it out was on the radio: [DJ] Premier played it. It definitely took about two months after it was out to start catching on.

Mr. Walt: That's the track when I realized that E had really stepped to the next level. I was just blown away.

ACK LIKE U WANT IT

Evil Dee: I made the beat to that one—Walt added the horns. 5 was on it, and that one wasn't on the wax, just the CD and cassette. It was the B-side to the "How Many MCs" single. I filtered the shit out of Lee Michaels on that one, just to show cats how I could do it like that.

BUCK EM DOWN

Evil Dee: There's a *lot* of filtering on that song. I would always discover shit at my house, but someone else would do it on record first. So I discovered filtering at my crib, and put extra bass on stuff all the time. Pete Rock did the same thing, just at Greene Street [studios]. Lots of my tracks had filtering, but that one probably had the most. All I wanted to hear was bass! That was one of my favorite remixes of all time [from the twelve-inch single]. We recorded the original at Calliope, but the SMPTE codes didn't match. I took the original two-inch reel and stripped it down to just the drums. I kept the two drum loops and scratched the bass line over it. It was all on turntables and it took like three hours. I wanted to remake it as a DJ record, so that's what the remix was. With something like that, it was cool because I could re-create it in a live show.

Buckshot: That was some Brooklyn love shit. I mention my man Butta from Coney Island at the end of that. He was a wild nigga, but he was real cool. He got killed riding a motorcycle. I had found out about that about a month before I made that record.

BLACK SMIF-N-WESSUN *Featuring Tek & Steele*

Buckshot: I'm from Little Jamaica, Franklin Ave., so I always grew up with reggae and had that influence. That's an old reggae record we sampled on the chorus. We used it on "Powaful Impak!" also. That was the first time people got to hear Tek and Steele. I was always tellin' people how dope those guys were. They were from Brownsville, and that was their first thing ever on wax as a group.

Mr. Walt: To me, those are Tek's best lyrics. His approach and the way he sounded on there were amazing. When we'd be doing stuff for [Smif-N-Wessun's debut album] *Dah Shinin* I'd tell Tek, "We need 'Black Smif-N-Wessun,'" because his rhymes on there were so good. Tek and Steele, to me, are up there with EPMD and Run-DMC in the sense that both MCs are great and you can't say who is really better. Most groups are unequal.

Evil Dee: Buck knew Steele and would always talk about how dope he was. He had even had a record out already as MC Steele. And when we started doing shows, Tek and Steele would open for Black Moon. They'd wear ski masks and come out and freestyle over the [Dre and Snoop] "Deep Cover" instrumental. Steele was very influential on Buckshot. When he walks into a room you just feel his presence.

SON GET WREC

Evil Dee: That was 5 FT's only solo cut on the album. 5 was always crazy on the mic, but you only really heard him on three tracks. For that one, I looped up a Lyn Collins song, and 5 loved it. But when I listened back, I thought 5's verse sounded better than the beat I had done. I had a girlfriend at the time and I was at her mother's house and her mother had mad records, so I found the same record that Q-Tip used for [A Tribe Called Quest's hit] "Scenario." Right after the part he sampled there's another great part, and that's what I ended up using for "Son Get Wrec." I stole that record from my girl's mother! I pitch-shifted that one too. I made it faster because I didn't want anyone to know that it was the same song as "Scenario."

Buckshot: I obviously had done a lot of songs, so we wanted 5 FT to get a solo record. They gave him a beat that I had wanted, but that was cool. That was done probably the third month into the album.

MAKE MUNNE

Mr. Walt: That was my beat, and those lyrics were true, in parts. Buck was a little booster dude back in the day, and that always stays with you no matter how famous you get, how old you are, or how many kids you've got. I chopped up a Sly and the Family Stone thing from a bootleg record. Michael Weiss didn't want to clear the sample, so we brought a million people into the studio to replay it, but it was never the right vibe. And after all that, we ended up going back to the original loop. It was a bootleg to start with so we wasn't worried, but Michael was sweating it.

Buckshot: That was just how niggas on my level gotta get money—by taking money. I was rappin' and a big star, but I wasn't gettin' no bread [from the label] even when the album came out. So I still had to do what I still had to do. I did a lot of shit, legal to illegal, but I kept it smart and in balance.

SLAVE

Evil Dee: That was really just an interlude. Buck did one verse and that was it. But people liked it so much that we put it on the CD and cassette. It was just a loop with a filter on it. [The group] 9th Creation got us [sued us] on that one. It was a sample off the same album as the [9th Creation] song "Bubble Gum."

Mr. Walt: That was E's track, and I remember he used a cassette [for the sample source] for that. I'm credited on the album for that but I didn't do it—E did the whole thing. For me, that's my fast-forward song on the album, but every MC that I know *loves* that song.

I GOT CHA OPIN

Buckshot: We had a hardcore version of that and a remix [the "hardcore" original appears on the LP], but we put the remix out because I knew the hardcore version wasn't going to be as commercially successful. People had never heard a hardcore nigga rhyming over Barry White before. I guess I'm so pure and real with it that it just got accepted. I love both versions. 5 FT was in jail when we were recording that shit [the remix]. He's been in jail more times than I've put out albums [*laughs*].

Evil Dee: Walt did the original of that one, and we filtered it like crazy. I did the remix, and that was actually the biggest radio hit on the album. Buckshot just loved Barry White, so we had to use that for it. Buckshot still loves Barry White! He begged me to flip that one, but I didn't want to, because everyone knew that song. Finally I just said: "Fuck it, give me the record." I was in D&D [studios] and I just listened to that track for like two hours and then I sat down and did the beat. It might sound like I just looped it, but if you really listen, you can hear that I took a kick from one part and a snare from another part, and laid those down. Then I chopped up the record and put it back together. If you listen real close you can hear the chops. Then I also filtered everything. I did that because I wanted to be able to make the drums stronger, and give the record more depth. Honestly, I thought that Walt's original was the craziest track, I just loved it. So there was no way I was gonna remix it with the original music. I had to do a whole new track to it.

Mr. Walt: I like Buck's flow on the remix, but not the music. For the real hip-hop heads, they had the original. And the newcomers or radio people, they could have the remix. One corny dude I knew from our neighborhood didn't like the album because the remix wasn't on there, and I just laughed at that.

Evil Dee: That was recorded at D&D almost towards the end of the recording sessions; it was a Dennis Coffey loop ["Whole Lot of Love"]. I just loved those drums, I used them on three different records. I always wanted to use "California Soul" but Pete Rock had used it for A.D.O.R. [an artist he produced]. Then I saw that Marvin Gaye and Tammi Terrell had a version of "California Soul," so I took that one and tuned it down so that it wouldn't sound like Pete's. Then Swift [the engineer] tuned the keys sample to the bass line, and I did the same with the horn sample. That song is definitely my most musical one on the album. When I did it, I was saying to people, "Yo, this is what I'm bringing to the game. I'm bringing *music*." That was definitely the first time I had done anything that complex musically. It went over everybody's head, but people appreciated it when I explained it to them. My goal was to take samples and have them blend together musically. That's what that song is. The keyboards were from "Riding High" by Faze-O, but through a pitch shifter. And the horn was "My Love Song to Katherine" by John Klemmer, pitch-shifted up.

Evil Dee: That sample was a John Coltrane track, on 45. I don't think we ever cleared that sample. That was Walt's "Bomb Squad" record. We loved the Bomb Squad [Public Enemy's production team]—those were our heroes.

Mr. Walt: Yeah, that was my Bomb Squad song, I agree. Those guys were the reason that I made beats in the first place. I was just dibbling and dabbling on production until I heard [Public Enemy's 1988 masterpiece] *Nation of Millions.* Back then I wanted to be a DJ more than a producer. After *Nation of Millions* all I wanted to do was make beats. That was the second to last track that we did.

Buckshot: I included lots of the album song titles in my rhymes, just trying to do some different shit.

Buckshot: That was the last song we recorded for the album. One day I was going through my room and the album was supposed to be turned in already and I found the tape [for the instrumental] on the floor. I played it and was like: "Why'd we never use this shit?"

Evil Dee: Walt did a majority of the work on that one. I just added a little bit. I added the horns to the track, and the weird noises [*makes high-pitched "blip" noises*]. That track was our underground core record. That "Mind tricks the body, body thinks the mind's crazy" thing [lyric], that was just Buckshot back then. If you didn't know Buck, he would kind of talk to you in riddles. I'm telling you, Buck has a shoebox somewhere under his bed, with my first beat tape in there and all the rest of them. I had definitely forgotten about that track, and he made us like that beat when he rhymed to it.

Mr. Walt: Buck wanted the Grover Washington ["Hydra"] on there and I didn't have a problem with that, because it was on some beat shit. Erick and Parrish had used it, maybe King Tee also. But my whole thing with samples was always, If they didn't rock it in the park back in the day, then I'm not looping it up. I never heard Barry White in the park, but I heard Grover Washington. E said he added the horns? Okay. If not, then I'm taking his credit back [*laughs*]. Or I'll just give him a wedgie or something [*laughs*].

U DA MAN *Featuring Tek, Steele, Havoc, and Dru Ha*

Evil Dee: Buckshot and [Havoc's group] Mobb Deep just had an ill bond. If you look at the credits for the first Mobb Deep album it says, BLACK MOON AND MOBB DEEP FOREVER. At the time, Mobb Deep had been dropped from 4th & Bway and Prodigy was in the hospital for sickle cell. That's why Havoc's the only one on there. Dru Ha used to rhyme a little—I produced one of his first demos. He was nice, he was the ill Caucasian [*laughs*]! Buck told him to go in there and rhyme even though we didn't think that we'd actually keep Dru's verse. But it was dope, so we did.

Buckshot: That was the second to last song we did. That's why everybody's on it. We definitely knew there would be more collaborations with those cats afterwards. I knew Havoc from way back, before I even had a record deal, back when he wasn't even using the name Havoc.

BOOGIE DOWN PRODUCTIONS

Criminal Minded

(B-Boy Records, 1987)

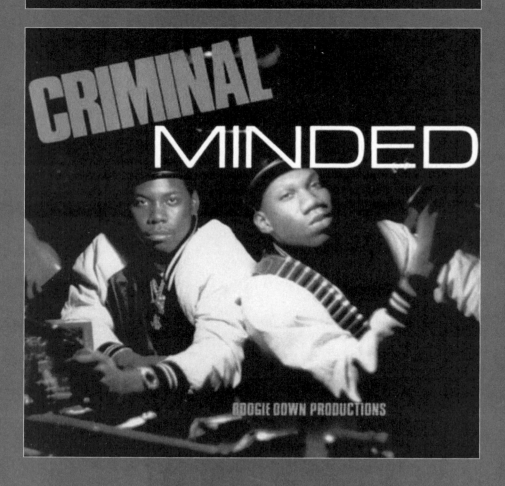

*A*s you'll notice, this is in a different format from most of the chapters in the book. Essentially it's a selective oral history of the life of KRS-One (aka Kris Parker) from elementary school until about age twenty-two, culled from a three-hour interview I did with him on March 25, 2002. These are all his words.

As you'll also notice, not all of this is in chronological order, since Kris skipped around while telling his story. For the sake of order, I've tried to break things up into subject headings where applicable. And when he's talking about a specific song from Criminal Minded, *I've bolded it.*

EARLY YEARS

I had three starts in hip-hop, and all of them were significant. Take it back to 1973. My mother moved from Manhattan to Harlem, a place called Lenox Terrace. I was attending the Charles B. Rushworm School. It's still there, directly across the street from Lenox Terrace. Then my mother left an abusive husband, my stepfather, and moved to the Bronx, to 1600 Sedgewick Avenue, Cedar Park. It was across from 1520 Sedgewick, where Kool Herc lived with his sister Cindy. I started to experience these block parties, or better yet, jams. I didn't know that it was Kool Herc at the time. Nobody knew it was even hip-hop. It was just a fun time. That was my first experience with it.

Skip ahead some years to 1977 and I'm in Brooklyn now. Flatbush. 170 East Thirty-fifth Street, at Church Ave. In 1977 there was a blackout in New York, and that night I felt an overwhelming desire to say something to society. Me and Kenny [Kris's brother] was there in the apartment, waiting for my mother to come home. The lights go out and everybody was breaking into stores, stealing TVs, cars are crashing into each other. It's complete madness. And I remember this weird feeling. Wanting to say something right out of the window, something that would stop the people from looting and robbing. When my mother came home that night I said, "Mom, why are they doing this?" And she said, "When there is no light, there is chaos." And I never forgot that. It just struck me. I saw people reducing themselves to savages, if I can use that term. And I didn't like it.

So I started writing poetry from that day forward. Poems about social injustice and about how I felt about living in Brooklyn at that time. I would write them to my mother and she would grade them for punctuation and grammar. Not so much on content [*laughs*]. That was my second break into hip-hop.

By then, of course, block parties were prevalent, live tapes were out. You'd go into a basketball court and somebody would have a big box and they'd be blasting a homemade tape of someone kicking rhymes over "Love Is the Message" [by MFSB] and "Sing Sing" [by Gaz] and all these breaks. I fell in love with it at that point. I knew what rap was and I knew what MCing was, and I just wanted to be a part of that. I was growing up in that.

I didn't link my poetry and MCing together back then. Back then hip-hop had other components to it. For instance, I was a master skully player. It's a street game that you play with bottle tops, and you go from one to thirteen knocking out other tops along the way. Soda-can tops or milk-carton tops or whatever. I mean, that was as big as breaking or graf or MCing back then. It was huge, and so was double Dutch. It was all just part of the culture. You didn't separate anything. MCing was a different kind of poetry, a different mentality.

In 1977 my poetry was just to my mom. It was my first attempt at making words rhyme. I don't remember explicitly what my early poems were. My first record, "Advance," although there are three MCs on it—Jerry Levi [Levi 167] and MC Quality also—I wrote the record. I had three verses and I gave them each one and took the last verse. That rhyme that Levi 167 says was the closest to my earliest poetry. It said stuff like: "The quick sensation/Can only lead the mind to destructive creation." That was the type of poetry that I started writing in 1977. Later, rhythm and color and style were given to it. Some of the words are even the same. That might have been right after the blackout. Most MCs keep their first rhyme in their head. It's like their seed rhyme for all their other rhymes.

NO TURNING BACK

Then rap music came out around 1979. Fatback Band had a 45 out on Spring Records. My mother copped that for us. "King Tim III, Personality

Jock." I was ecstatic. I was like, "Those guys are finally doing what the streets is doing." And a few months later "Rappers Delight" [by the Sugarhill Gang] came out, and at that moment I made my mind up. I am an MC, that's it. Sometime around 1980 I linked up with a crew in Brooklyn—we didn't even have a name for the crew. I was called Larry G [Kris's given first name is Lawrence]. Kenny wasn't into any of this at the time; he was studying to be a basketball player. And there was this guy named Money Mike and a guy named Neville T and me, Larry G. And we put together rhymes and routines and that type of thing. We used to rhyme over Dr. Jeckyll & Mr. Hyde and the whole Sugar Hill catalog. Those records used to come out every week and we were there like clockwork, purchasing all of them. That wasn't really even much of a start, more of an influence.

What crystallized it for me was in 1984, maybe 1983. I was at a group home in the Bronx. By now I had left home. I told my mother, "I'm an MC, I'm going to study philosophy." She was pissed off and thought I was crazy, since I had dropped out of school. I was probably about seventeen years old. And everybody was rappin' in this group home, beating on the tables to make a beat, and people would kick their rhymes. But I had put MCing on hold during this whole time, because I had hooked up with this guy named Zore who was down with this crew DB, Down to Bomb. He turned me on to graffiti art and I got *hooked*. We used to go down to the 2 and the 5 yard, the Jerome Avenue layups, Sixth Avenue [subway] line in the Bronx. Later I would go to the bus yards on Tremont Avenue in the Bronx. And I made a little name for myself. I wrote KRS.

THE NAME, THE BOMBING

My name Kris started as a joke, as a pun. When I had left home I had spent maybe a year on the street, and then I went into a shelter. The Men's Shelter, down on East Bowery. And down there the Hare Krishnas used to come down and feed the homeless. And just before they'd start they'd say that if anyone wants to help feed the homeless they would get a free book, the *Bhagavad Gita.* And I was gassed, because I was studying philosophy in the public library, so I was like: "Wow, the library ain't got the *Bhagavad Gita,* so let me get that." I'd offer to help and I'd hang out with them and they'd tell me all about reincarnation and the divinity of Krishna. And I'd go back to the shelter and everybody'd start laughing at me, and my nickname in the shelter became Krishna. I couldn't tell them that calling me the name of a Hindu god was bad—they wouldn't understand. That's like calling me Allah or Yahweh. I couldn't escape it, so I took it on as a name.

When I left the shelter and went into the group home, the Bureau of Child Welfare system found out that I was too young. So I ended up at Covenant House for under-twenty-one-year-olds. From there—where I met Just-Ice, by the way—the Bureau asked me my name and where my parents were and I told them that my name was Krishna Parker. And that became my name, Kris Parker.

Once Zore opened my whole mind to this world of graffiti, I started writing KRS and bombing Soundview and Bronx River [Projects], and that's when I got into hip-hop for real: when I'd go around to Bronx River to see Afrika Bambaataa in the Bronx River Housing Projects throwing parties. Stevenson Park. I actually caught Red Alert and the Jazzy 5 doing "Jazzy Sensation" [*sings part of song*] in the park one night. Other people started writing KR and KS and KRESS, so I started to add the ONE. Which isn't a new thing, to put *One* after your name.

By the end of my group-home stay I was twenty, and rap had exploded by then. And I had this skill. I went to the School of Visual Arts for about three months. It was a wasted opportunity, because the Bureau of Child Welfare was paying for my education. Somewhere around 1984 I'm bombing KRS-One, rap is big, Run-DMC, LL, Whodini. Those groups were the epitome of rap music, nothing like what you have today. Run-DMC were the messiahs when they were out. The epitome. Period. Taking their lead, I picked up the mic.

METAPHYSICS, MARTIANS, AND MORALITY

My poetry at that time was heavily into religion and philosophy, while I was in the group home. A lot of metaphysics. But poetry wasn't a priority. Once I got into graffiti art I just got engulfed in that. Then after that phase I picked up the pen and the mic again. And it happened kind of haphazardly, battling other MCs in the group home. And by doing that, I realized that I had some talent.

When I said my rhymes, other people would look at me like I was a Martian because I was talking about nuclear war, police brutality, and stuff like that back then. I was bringing in all the philosophy that I was reading, and biblical stuff too. Morality. Ethics. Especially after 1982, when Melle Mel came out with "The Message." My style of rap was crystallized at that point. I knew exactly what I was going to do. I would somehow try to add a biblical twist to what he was doing. In battles it was ruthless, because I would rhyme like the Bible, with "Thou" and "Thy," and it would give the appearance of being in an authoritative position. I didn't know that at the time, it was just my style. By that time I was twenty and figuring out what I was doing. So I went back to my original love: MCing.

I got kicked out of the group home on my twentieth birthday, in 1985. I went to the YMCA for three months and after that I was supposed to get a job. Of course I jerked all the money and wasted my time and they kicked me out of the Y, so I was homeless again. So I went back to the Third Avenue Men's Shelter on the Bowery and they shipped me and a bunch of other guys on a school bus up to 166th Street and Boston Road in the Bronx.

ENTER SCOTT LA ROCK

I was in this shelter, and about two months after that walks in this new social worker, with a briefcase and everything. And we knew that he was a nerd; he was not part of the cool clique. I went to him to get subway tokens, to jerk the money or whatever. The shelter used to give you two tokens [per day] and you'd sell them, go and buy some herb or some OE [Olde English] 800 or some Chinese food. So I went to this guy, Scott Sterling, and we started arguing over these tokens. We went back and forth with this until I finally said: "You're one of those handkerchief-head house negroes, tap-dancing for the white establishment. You ain't got nothing to do with us black folks, you're a sellout!" And he stood up, all angry, and said: "You don't even know me. You don't know who I am!" And he started saying: "All you homeless blacks who want to sit on your ass, you're lazy and you're wasting your life." And we went back and forth. I was the lazy homeless guy and he was the sellout. We argued for about an hour until security kicked me out of the office.

Then about a week later, I went to Ced-Gee's [from Ultramagnetic MCs] house. He had a four-track in his house. I met him through another graffiti artist named Funkmaster, who used to write with a guy named Pre-Sweet. They were bombing all over the Bronx. They were a crew, TR, the Rascals. They were an older clique. Funkmaster was a security guard in the shelter, so he'd hear us rhyming and he took us over to Ced's spot. We'd all be piled in there, and then two weeks went by and in walked Scott Sterling. And I'm like, "Yo, how'd your nerd ass get in here, with all us MCs, us true hip-hoppers?" and he's shocked, he's like, "You homeless, broke-ass, no future . . . how are *you* here?" So we went into the corner after he heard me rhyme and we both sat there feeling pretty stupid. That started our friendship.

Scott asked me to come down to Broadway International—or Broadway RT is what it became. Broadway Repertory Theater. On 145th and Broadway. So, lo and behold, I get into this place and it was like Moses in front of the burning bush. It was an epiphany. First of all, it was my first club experience—ever. I get there all dirty, I get in for free, and people are dancing and the clothes are outrageous and people are breakin' and doing the Whop. It was like walking into another world. And I look to see the source of the music, and it's Scott Sterling. I was blown away. I was humbled and embarrassed.

I went up to the DJ booth and some big security guy blocked me. Then Scott gave a nod and the hand disappeared and I get a chance to walk into the DJ booth. Back then the DJ booth was sacred. He gave me drink tickets, I got some rum and Cokes, and I'm feeling great. He was scratchin', people are screaming for every record he plays. We went back to the shelter and I was like: "That is *it.* That's me, that's it. I have no other purpose in life."

So Scott would just invite me down and I'd go there every week for a month or so. And one time this MC group was up there and Scott was in the booth. And the record he was playing kept skippin', so the group was getting messed up and they blamed Scott even though it was their DJ's fault. So I'm like: "You're dissin' *my* DJ?" Scott had never said he was my DJ or anything like that. But I felt such an allegiance to him; he was Morpheus in my world. So I jumped onstage and smashed all five of these MCs. We went line for line and of course I had all these styles backed up in my head for years. So I battled and smashed them. I don't even remember who it was. We were all just locals.

And that's when Scott was like: "Yo, we gotta make this a group." And he called the group the Boogie Down Crew. It was really more like a gang. It was me and Just-Ice and ICU, Jerry Levi from the shelter, this guy named Castle D. He knew MC Quality, who would eventually introduce me to Ms. Melody. And Scott used to DJ for the breaking crew called BIA—B-Boys in Action. So all of us got together as the Boogie Down Crew. There were about twenty of us at the end of the day, with friends and all.

EARLY DAYS ON WAX

Out of that group we recorded this demo called "Advance" [by Scott La Rock & the Celebrity Three], with these lyrics that I had written, three verses that I used to say by myself. After that, Scott took us to a place called Zakia Records. He knew about them from Eric B. Scott and Eric were close friends, they used to buy gold together. They'd buy these big chains, and I used to dis Scott with that, like, "What are you doing?" But that was him. We was so different it was like night and day. So we signed this record to Zakia, "Advance," and we didn't get no money. I wonder to this day if Scott got any money. I remember what I got out of the deal was a pair of blue Air Jordans. And I was happy and satisfied. So it came out and it didn't really do anything, but it was out and we had a record and it felt good. By then I was going to the Roxy [club]. The Roxy was a whole other experience unto itself.

As for the Boogie Down Crew, Levi 167 became a crackhead, Castle D—who wasn't really part of the group, but was a side MC and used to travel with us—he went to Philly and robbed someone and went to jail for like two years. One day we just didn't see him anymore. MC Quality's mother felt weird about her being in an all-guy group. We were definitely the first Fugees-type group, with two guys and a girl.

After that first group didn't work out, me and Scott went to Sleeping Bag and met with a guy named Will Socolov. This was one of the greatest record companies ever. No one ever got paid anything, you got paid in marijuana. But it was a great label. We learned about them from Just-Ice. One day he left the shelter and never came back. And next time we heard him it was "La la la la la LaToya," with the original DMX. And we knew it was him. So we went over there [to Sleeping Bag] to try and get the same deal. We came out on Fresh Records [Fresh is a part of Sleeping Bag] as a group called 12:41, and the song was "Success Is the Word," using the *Gilligan's Island* theme. Of course we got no publishing, nothing—maybe we got our names credited on the record. The group was named from the time when we finally finished mixing the record. It was really that simple.

So the 12:41 record came out, and Mr. Magic spun it one time on WBLS. The clubs were spinning it a little. A guy named Kenny Beck produced the record, who was a pretty big dance producer back then. He put his brother in the group, and it was me and Scott with him. It was the only time that Scott ever really rhymed on a record, his only MC appearance. Except for the end of "Dope Beat." We showed up, he [*Author's note: probably Will Socolov*] gave us two hundred dollars each, we rapped on it, and signed something that took all rights away. And that was it. Will and Ronald Resnick [from Sleeping Bag/Fresh] were great. I really love those guys, even though no one ever got paid. Just-Ice got paid. He'd go up there every week and they'd just give him money.

Then we got rejected by Will Socolov. He said he didn't have the room to sign us as artists. We went over to Spring Records and Van Silk was doing A&R there. By then we had our demo, with "Advance," "Success Is the Word," and I had just recorded a demo of the record that would become **"Elementary"** and also the song **"Criminal Minded."** We took those songs everywhere. We recorded those songs in a studio on Broadway and I think Seventy-ninth Street. It was a little setup in somebody's house and was about twenty-five dollars an hour to record. There was one other song on the demo, I can't remember the name. It never came out anyways. We took the demo to Spring, Polygram, Sony, everywhere. And everyone rejected us.

ROCK CANDY AND B-BOY RECORDS

One day we was walking home to the Bronx from Manhattan, we had no money, we had just came back from Tommy Boy, who also dissed us. They were on Ninety-sixth Street and we walked from there to the Bronx. So we were walking across the Willis Avenue Bridge and Scott had a newspaper and he sees an ad on the back of it: ROCK CANDY RECORDS AND FILMWORKS, LOOKING FOR

NEW TALENT. So Scott calls them up on a pay phone and they said to come right over. So we went over and met Jack Allen, Ray Wilson, and Bill Kamarra. And they said: "Let's do it. You can have your own label, we'll put you out." They were in the Bronx, 132nd Street and Cypress Avenue. We thought we was large.

By then, in 1986, we were calling ourselves Boogie Down Productions. Because we said we would never be MCs, we'd be producers. Because we thought that no one wanted to hear conscious rap, and no one wanted to hear hardcore thug stuff either. The party-style rhyme is what was prevalent then. We wanted to start a label and get some other acts. So I drew the label logo while Scott was talking to those guys [at Rock Candy]. The little b-boy character, holding the radio. I did that with a pen on a piece of paper. So B-Boy Records was born. It was just me and Scott.

With contracts, Scott didn't actually know what he was doing, but he knew more than me. I was just green. With Rock Candy we signed a contract that signed away all our rights [*laughs*]. Before we started with these Rock Candy guys, they put a demand on us. They wanted us to make an anticrack record. And I'm all for it, because I've always been socially conscious. I was running around calling Ronald Reagan a drug dealer and people thought I was crazy. So we did this record called "Crack Attack," which was our contribution to fighting the crack epidemic. They put it out and it didn't go anywhere.

ON THE ATTACK: "SOUTH BRONX"

There was an engineer named Frankie D who worked at Power Play Studios in Queens. And Rock Candy had us go into Power Play to re-record stuff from our demo. I did "Elementary" and Frankie liked our stuff and wanted us to meet with Mr. Magic. Even though we had a label, we went back and tried to meet with Mr. Magic by basically bombarding his session. And he was working, so he was like: "Get outta here!" Then Frankie D must have played him something when we were gone, and he came back and said, "I played it for Mr. Magic and he said it was wack." We was like: "What? Are you crazy? MC Shan is wack, not me." And I went home and wrote **"South Bronx."**

I performed it for Scott, he played the "Funky Drummer" and started in on the song, and it blew his mind. So we ran over to Ced-Gee's house and were like: "Yo, Ced, we need that SP-12 [sampler]." Keep in mind that at that time Ced-Gee was the only person in the Bronx with an SP-12, and he was the absolute man. So he lent us the sounds, the kick, the drum, the snare, the hi-hat. Scott took his records over to Ced and Ced sampled them and made the beat for "South Bronx," and Scott did the drums and Ced chopped it up. I wasn't paying no attention to the beat, it had no significance to me at all. I was strictly about the lyrics.

So we went to this studio in Queens for twenty-five dollars an hour and recorded it in two hours. Fifty dollars on eight tracks, one take. I must have practiced it once and then recorded it, because Scott was like: "All I got is fifty dollars!" I think the guy at the studio kept the master and gave us a cassette of it, and we ran out of there.

Scott was on his way to see Mr. Magic with the song and he ran into Marley Marl. Scott was such an entrepreneur that his whole plan was to go to Mr. Magic and say: "Okay, we'll do a track dissing you, and then Shan can come out and dis us." Back then the answer records were real big, with Shanté and UTFO and Spyder-D and Sparky-D. We went to them [Marley and Magic] because they was the kings of the battle record. But Marley was the one Scott met with, and Marley basically said: "We don't need you, we're the Juice Crew." So we pressed the song up and put it out on B-Boy. We took D-Nice down to that same studio in Queens and recorded **"The P Is Free"** [D-Nice does human beatbox on the original track]. That was another one-take record.

In between this time, in 1986, I had met Ms. Melody, who lived in Brooklyn. And I was living in a freezer under the offices of B-Boy Records. They had a garage that had a freezer, like a walk-in meat freezer. Two people had actually died in there—they had suffocated—so they couldn't do anything else with the building. I was still homeless at the time and was going from house to house. ICU's mother had given him an apartment in Millbrook Projects, so he asked me if I wanted to stay with him, but my pride wouldn't let me stay there continuously. So if I was at the Roxy too late and couldn't get in the shelter, I'd crash at ICU's, or at Ced-Gee's, or sometimes at Ms. Melody's. But I said to Bill Kamarra that I wanted money to get an apartment. He said, "No, but you can have the freezer downstairs."

So I took it. It was either that or be in the street. I remember I had to keep a big brick by the door because if the door slammed I would suffocate and die. So I kept the door open and slept on sixteen crates put together with a mattress made out of clothes and newspapers. And that's where I was staying when "South Bronx" came out.

I remember that I went to Latin Quarter, which had just opened, and Red Alert had already been battling Mr. Magic—Red on Kiss 98 and Magic on WBLS. They had a record out called "Duck Alert" [by Marley Marl] that was dissin' Red [and Chuck Chillout], calling him Red Dirt [*KRS imitates part of "Duck Alert"*]. So Scott, who was friends with Red Alert, gave him "South Bronx." And of course on that record I had shouted out Red Alert, I had brought back the history of the Bronx, the Zulu Nation, the Rock Steady Crew. This was street history that I was chatting off. So Scott brought a test pressing of the record to the Latin Quarter and Red Alert threw it on, and that place erupted. I've never felt a chill in my body like that. Everybody stopped dancing and just looked up at the DJ booth. Red Alert played it three times, one right after another, without even mixing it. [*Author's note: Red Alert says that fellow Latin Quarter DJ Raoul was the first to play the test pressing consecutive times, and after that he gave the test pressing to Red to play on his radio show.*] He'd just pick up the needle and play it again. And I remember Just-Ice turned to me and said, "You got a hit, you out the shelter now." The record started getting really big in the clubs.

I used to go to the clubs and nobody knew who I was. At the time Scott La Rock was the biggest name, like "Scott La Rock and that 'South Bronx' song." No one could even pronounce my name. It was such a weird name for people. As Roxanne Shanté said, it sounded like a wack radio station! And that it did [*laughs*]. Scott was rising in prominence and I was happy because for me Scott was Morpheus, and I would do anything for him. I was like: "You're the one that saved me." So I was basically defending my DJ everywhere we went, which was a prominent theme of that era. We became the kings of the Latin Quarter; we could do no wrong there. And that place was huge too. If there was a Class of 1986 or what is called the Golden Age, then the Latin Quarter was the school. That was the place that housed the Class of 1986.

I remember somewhere along at this time I got a job mopping floors at a children's nursery in Brooklyn. Twenty-five dollars for each time I mopped the floor. I'd do it twice a week, and if I got lucky I'd get to do it three times a week. And I was happy. I'd take the train down there and catch a quick [graffiti] tag along the way, of course. One day while I was mopping, "South Bronx" came on the radio and I was buggin', with that mop in my hand. I had just put the Mop & Glo down and the record came on. And the chill went through my spine again. But I still didn't realize the impact of it. It was a huge hit record. Red Alert played it on Kiss.

ON THE ATTACK, PART TWO: "THE BRIDGE IS OVER"

From there on out, Scott started to ask Rock Candy for money. We started getting six hundred dollars and I would get three hundred. At least I was told we was getting six hundred dollars. And out of that three hundred each we had to give D-Nice fifty or a hundred out of what we made. Three weeks later after we was on the radio, MC Shan answered with "Kill That Noise." And that hit *hard.* I heard that [*imitates Shan's voice*] and I was like, *Whaaat?* When that came out, Mr. Magic played it on a Friday night, and by that next Friday I had **"The Bridge Is Over."** I wrote the beginning part [*he sings: "Come on in the dance, with a spliff of sensi . . ."*] first, after we met Mr. Magic. But I threw it aside, 'cause I said, "Nah, nobody's gonna mess with this style." Then I wrote "South Bronx." But then, when Shan answered us, I said, "Let's do this."

So I ran back to Ced-Gee and said, "Yo, Ced, let's get this on." So Ced came down to this studio on Forty-seventh Street between Eighth and Ninth Avenues, a place called A&R Recording. And we recorded "The Bridge Is Over" in forty-five minutes. It was crazy. Ced was buggin' that I did it in only one take. I didn't pay no mind to it because in my mind you was always one take. To this day I'm like that. I did the beat for that song; I played the piano too. Scott had nothin' to do with that record. It was like a surprise—I was tryin' to do it for him. Scott was somewhere else, probably out buying gold with Eric B. [*laughs*]. I remember Ced-Gee sampled "Eric B. Is President" [which Marley Marl had helped produce], the kick and the snare. We threw it in the SP-12 and I did the beat [*he imitates the beat, "boom boom bap bap, boom bap . . ."*]. Not too much brainwork for that one. It didn't take too much talent.

At the time there was a record by Super Cat called "Boops" and it had the bass line I wanted, so I had the piano that was free in the studio. It was a real piano, and I played it live, one take, for the whole song. If you listen to the original [of "The Bridge Is Over"] there's so many mistakes, like at the beginning. That's just me tuning up, trying to get my timing together. We laid the beat down one time, then I played the piano one time, then I got on the mic and recorded the whole record one time. And Ced-Gee mixed it one time. The only overdubs were where you hear the kicks and snares double up. Ced did that live, while we were mastering it [*laughs*]. Ced's overdubs went directly to the master at the same time! I made a cassette of it, came back and gave it to Scott, and he was blown away. He gave it to Red Alert and Red played it off the tape, and it was just *on* in New York City.

After that we started to get flack—people said we was just a battle group, that we couldn't write actual songs. Because that's all that we was doin' at the time. "The Bridge Is Over" came out by itself, but when it came out as a single, we went back in and did a clean radio version to it. Instead of "Shanté's only good for steady fuckin'," it became "steady pumpin'." We had shout-outs at the end of the record. Those were added later. Then we recorded **"A Word from Our Sponsor"** [which came out as the B-side to "The Bridge Is Over"].

"MANY PEOPLE TELL ME THIS STYLE IS TERRIFIC"

After "The Bridge Is Over," MC Shan never responded, and neither did Marley or Mr. Magic. That was pretty much the end of the battle. So we was going around battling other crews. That was our thing, that was what we did. And I had a style that's mostly forgotten now. I had a quick style, like when I said, "That's it, that's all, solo, single, no more, no less" [on "Poetry"], and that was new.

The whole idea of hip-hop reggae was new too. I mean, Run-DMC did the first rap-reggae collaboration with "Roots, Rock, Reggae," so historically they had that record, with Yellowman. But it still wasn't what we was doin'. They were rapping and Yellowman was doing his Jamaican patois. My style was to incorporate Jamaican patois language over hip-hop beats. Oh, man, the damage we used to inflict on these groups, it was just crazy. We'd go into these clubs and they'd set up the battle and I would just start rhyming, and it wasn't just the Jamaican lyrics. It was *how* we battled. We battled like a Jamaican sound system. You played one record, then you'd rewind, and the crowd would go crazy. I had the biggest record out in 1986, and here I come with this cocky, arrogant attitude. I was the Teacher, so in each battle I was scolding the MCs. I was teaching them how they were wack and why they needed to get better. It was just an unstoppable style.

But the battle-MC reputation bothered me and Scott. Me more than Scott, because I was the writer. I was like: "Yo, I got songs." But Scott said that nobody wanted to hear messages. He said that to me early on. He knew we had to come out with the hardcore style, as we called it back then. So I started writing about themes that appealed more to the street. In a way, around 1986 and '87, Run-DMC, LL, Fat Boys, and others had gotten so big that there was a whole other audience that was being alienated. These people respected those artists, but those artists also weren't considered "street" anymore. They had videos and were on MTV.

THE ALBUM: *CRIMINAL MINDED*

We appealed more to that alienated audience, the audience that felt that rap was getting too commercial. So I wrote this album called *Criminal Minded.* The purpose of the album was to attract a thug-type audience, so we could teach them later on. That was the whole point. We wanted to make intelligence a cool thing. And so we wrote up these records that I personally didn't think was too hardcore. In fact I kind of thought that *Criminal Minded,* the album, was corny when we finished it. I said, "Man, we're going to get dissed for this. I mean, 'Listen to my nine-millimeter go bang'? Who's going to listen to this?" No one at that time was even thinking about that sing-song kind of style back then. The closest was Doug E. Fresh and Slick Rick. They, too, were battle MCs, and that was what you did when you battled. You took a familiar tune, which was also a Jamaican thing, and you turned it into a battle kind of thing. So I said: "I'm going to go from writing records to writing *songs,*" and I wanted to position myself as the teacher of hip-hop. I wanted to start to distance myself from being just a battle MC.

We touched up the original "Criminal Minded" song from our demo. We had "Elementary" touched up too. The beat may have changed or maybe Scott added some cuts. We completed the *Criminal Minded* album at Power Play in Queens in about two weeks. We didn't have time to be in the studio, loungin'. We got to the studio on time. And we just kicked out the rest of the songs: **"Poetry," "Super Hoe,"** the new version of "Criminal Minded." When the album came out, I guess I had never realized that it was an album. That was just not part of my mentality. I thought that the album was corny. After all those battle records we did, here I am now, making myself into an artist. I thought I was throwing away a very comfortable position that I was holding in the hip-hop community at the time. It was like facing your fears. You want to go, but you don't. I was recording tracks—I didn't think about an album. Scott's the one who named it *Criminal Minded.*

On the original vinyl for the album, there's a typo, and **"Dope Beat"** was actually called "Hope Beat." Scott La Rock and Ced-Gee brought in the AC/DC sample on that one. I don't know which one of them actually did it, but Scott was heavily into rock. He was a big Led Zeppelin fan—he had everything they ever did. He had all the AC/DC stuff, Iron Maiden, Whitesnake. He'd rock that right along with P-Funk. To this day I don't know why AC/DC didn't sue us for that song [which samples "Back in Black"]. That's all samples. I'm probably incriminating myself, but nothing on *Criminal Minded* is cleared.

It was Scott's idea to remix "The P Is Free." He did it with Ced-Gee. Scott was big into reggae too, just like I was. I think he took Michigan & Smiley's "Dangerous Diseases," which was a huge record back in the eighties [*Kris imitates the chopped, stuttered beginning of the song*]. That intro is what makes me think it was Ced-Gee, because that was more his style. I wasn't there when that beat was made. I think the lyrics are mostly the same as the original version.

I always loved the track "Super Hoe." That night up in Rochester [mentioned in song] was crazy. And Scott La Rock *was* the Super Hoe. We were completely opposite as people. I'm this shy, reserved seminary student. I was even afraid of girls. I was definitely not the player type, and I'm still not. And Scott was the *e-pit-o-me* of the player type. I was basically just making fun of him on that track, and he was just laughing in the studio [*Kris sings chorus*]. WDKX is a real radio station in Rochester, New York, and I think Scott had slept with one of the DJs or somethin'. He was famous for that.

Rochester was our first paid gig outside of New York City. The first time we traveled to a place to do a show. But we got there and didn't get paid, and we were stranded. The promoter ran off with the money. And somehow Scott got this girl, who I think worked at WDKX, and that's how we got a place to sleep and something to eat the next morning. She might have even paid our way back, or drove us back or something. That was probably the first time that men were referred to as hos, in that song. Scott was proud to be a ho. That record was a celebration of our oppositeness. We respected each other's position. In a way we balanced each other out.

THE ALBUM COVER: 9MM GOES BANG

The cover of the album was pretty crazy. Some of that artillery [Kris and Scott are armed with various weaponry, including guns and a hand grenade] we already had, and the rest of it was from this ex-marine. Like the grenades and the shoulder rounds. On a side note, we used to get our guns in the Bronx from ex-military people who would come there with brand-new guns, and we used to buy from them. That's part of a whole other book, if you decide to write it. *The Origin of Guns in the Ghetto.* But there was this ex-marine guy that the Rock Candy guys knew. They brought him in. Every day back then we was packin', with .38s and whatever. We had all kinds of .45s and so on. And we'd go on the roofs of the projects and shoot at cans. That stuff I was wearing, and the grenades and the guns on the table, that was all this ex-marine's stuff. The gun I was holding was mine, and I think the gun that Scott was holding was ICU's. I can't remember exactly.

We wanted the most shocking album cover that we could find, and that was what it ended up being. We wanted to set a precedent that we was real, this is real, this is where hip-hop is going. From fantasy to reality. And that's exactly what happened. I wouldn't say that we were the only ones, because Eric B. & Rakim's *Paid in Full* assisted that image as well, and Schoolly D was out of control with "P.S.K." That was a huge record back then. But in terms of pictures, posing, how you posed, Eric B. and Rakim on the cover with the Dapper Dan jacket and the big gold, that's how you came to the club. We were all part of the same movement that wanted to show the street mentality.

We wanted you to think that we was the most ruthless crew on the face of the earth, and if you even thought of battling us, you was gonna get a buckshot. And we suffered for that too, in a lot of different ways. To this day I'm not proud when people say that *Criminal Minded* was the beginning of gangsta rap. That's not something I put on my résumé. But it was true. No one else was coming out like that, or did what we did.

R.I.P. SCOTT LA ROCK

And then we suffered, because on August 26, 1987, Scott La Rock gets a call from D-Nice that some guy was threatening to kill him or shoot him. Because D was allegedly talking to this guy's girlfriend. Scott said: "Let's squash this beef. You can't run all your life." So Scott went over to where the beef was, in the Bronx River Houses. Scott showed up and actually squashed the beef with D-Nice and this guy. But then somebody starts shooting from across the street, out of a window. They was ambushed. The Jeep was packed with people, but only Scott got hit, behind the ear.

I was in Brooklyn then—me and Ms. Melody was renting a house in Canarsie—and I got the call from D-Nice, he was screaming on the phone. "They shot Scott, yo, it's fucked up! Oh God, they shot Scott!" I thought he was kidding, 'cause D-Nice was a jokester. Then he started cursin' at me and I knew it was real. I got in a cab and went all the way up to the Bronx, to where Scott was staying at the time. He was staying with this girl named Dee Dee. And she was there and was hysterical. So we jumped in another cab and went to the hospital. I don't remember which one, it was on Grand Concourse. I didn't even want to go upstairs. I was deeply immersed in metaphysics and spiritual thought and I said, "Nope, I'm going to remember him alive. I don't even want to put the image of Scott being dead in my memory." And I stayed downstairs. I remember that MC Serch [from 3rd Bass] was the first person I saw on the scene there.

I remember later on in life, Serch asked me why I had a smile on my face on that sad day. And it was because I was like: "Scott's in a better place now. We are now going to win. Because half the crew is in the spirit realm and the other half of the group is on earth. We can't lose now." No one knew what I was talking about; no one cared. There was grief and there was finger-pointing.

The city was in an uproar, it was all on the news. I remember Connie Chung, she came and said [*imitates uptight female voice*]: "Don't you think that your album cover incites violence?" And I was like: "No, this is how people are livin' every day. Does John Wayne incite violence?" So afterwards I had to answer all these questions about violence.

It was wild because we had already started to write *By All Means Necessary* [Boogie Down Productions' second album]. I had already written "Stop the Violence" and "My Philosophy." Scott wanted to cut up "Sister Sanctified" [by Stanley Turrentine, sampled on "My Philosophy"], and I had those rhymes. I had just battled Melle Mel at the Latin Quarter and I was trying to turn those rhymes into "Still #1." So we was already doing this other album because the point was to come out like the thug and then turn back and say, "But wait, you can go from this to that."

LOOKING BACK

When I look back on *Criminal Minded* now, first of all I'm very proud of it. It's probably one of the only records I'll ever be remembered for. But if you don't know KRS-One, that was the beginning of what's now called gangsta rap. It wasn't gangsta rap then—it was basically telling the reality of the street. That's all it was supposed to be. We wanted to pose with guns because that was the reality of the streets at the time. If the reality of the streets at the time was the Mister Softee ice cream truck, we'd have posed in front of that. We was trying to tell our story, and the mainstream didn't hear you unless you were shocking. So if there's anything to come away from it, I would say that you would have to look at *Criminal Minded* all the way up to my latest release, *Spiritual Minded*. To go from being immature to being mature. From boys to men.

Today we take rhyme styles for granted. On *Criminal Minded* those rhyme styles you hear were original. They hadn't been heard before. The album had originality and we lack so much of that today. It seems that if one rapper comes out with a style, twenty others come after him. Hip-hop now, what it has become, is just not what we intended it to be. When *Criminal Minded* came out, Big Daddy Kane had his own style, Rakim still has his own style, Kool G Rap, Biz Markie. We've lost cultural continuity because hip-hop has gone from being a culture to being a product. And that's one of the things I've devoted my life to, to correct it.

If there's anything to convey to the public, in my opinion we cannot allow corporate America to validate us and to dictate what hip-hop is and what hip-hop isn't. And *Criminal Minded* was that stake in the heart of corporate America at that time. All respect to Run-DMC, LL, Whodini, Fat Boys, and Kurtis Blow. But when they were doing it, they was called sellouts in the streets. They was the mainstream rappers, they was MC Hammer. And we were pretty much fighting against that. That's what *Criminal Minded* stood for. It stood for hip-hop Kulture with a *K*. It was like: "You think this way, but *blaw!,* it's *this* way." We was conscious of what we was doin'. It wasn't a mistake.

And we weren't the only ones. There was the Class of 1987. You have to include Eric B. & Rakim's *Paid in Full* too, because they're really the same album. It was all one album, and it was Biz Markie's *Goin' Off,* Big Daddy Kane's *Long Live the Kane,* Public Enemy's *Yo! Bum Rush the Show* too. These albums were collectively one album, and we all picked a different topic to address from the streets. We all hung out together. We sampled Eric B. & Rakim's drums to make "The Bridge Is Over." Those were Marley Marl's drums. Even though we were battling at the time, there was still this family thing going on. And big up to all the Juice Crew, because without them I literally could not exist. If Shan and Marley hadn't answered, I would not have had all the other records I've done over the last fifteen years. If Shan had not followed the rules of hip-hop, it would have been different. But the rules are that if you respect the rapper that is challenging you, then you answer the challenge.

BRAND NUBIAN

One for All

(Elektra, 1990)

Brand Nubian, one of the most influential acts of the early nineties, boasted four unique members: MCs Grand Puba (William Dixon, often listed as Maxwell Dixon or Grand Puba Maxwell), Sadat X (Derek Murphy, also known as Derrick X), Lord Jamar (Lorenzo De Chalus), and DJ Alamo. They claimed New Rochelle, New York—a town right outside of the upper reaches of the Bronx—as their home base and brought a pro-black, sometimes-controversial Five Percent Nation of Gods and Earths doctrine to the masses in a way that was funky as hell and impossible to ignore. Their debut, *One for All,* was a unanimously jocked masterpiece with serious social commentary, incredibly well-constructed beats, and Puba's unique brand of female-chasing frivolity.

Sadat X describes his early years: "I was born in the Bronx and lived in Concourse Village, Melrose Projects, Jackson Projects, and Park Avenue. I moved to New Rochelle when I was about ten years old, and in elementary school I'd still go down to the Bronx on the weekends. I'd go to block parties and see groups like the Cold Crush Brothers, Afrika Bambaataa, the Fantastic Five. And in New Ro [New Rochelle], groups would perform at the Remington [Park] Boys Club there."

Sadat's entrée into the hip-hop game was through DJing, but rhyming wasn't too far behind. He says: "I was doing hip-hop for real, at least as far as I was concerned, going back to fifth grade. My first rhyming partner was this kid Wiz. I had two mismatched turntables and a mixer, and I'd DJ and we'd both rhyme. In high school, Wiz got into trouble frequently, so a lot of times I'd just end up doing it by myself. My father and [DJ] Alamo's father grew up together in Harlem, so I knew Alamo from my youngest days."

Sadat continues: "New Rochelle had a hip-hop scene, despite what some people think. New Ro isn't *that* different from the Bronx. They got projects and crack there too. They had local crews in town, and Puba came before us. He was always an integral part of the scene. He lived in the projects and Jamar lived on the other side of town. I knew both of them years before Brand Nubian started. The rhyming community in New Ro was pretty small, so we all knew each other. I was trying to do production back then too. We all were. But Puba was way ahead of us. He was the one who brought me to the studio for the first time."

Grand Puba was the undisputed leader of the group because of his wide-ranging talent—combined with the fact that he was several years older than the rest of the Brand Nubian crew. In his early teens he was a DJ who rhymed on the side. He had equipment and rocked neighborhood block parties.

As fans may remember, Brand Nubian wasn't Puba's debut in the hip-hop world. His first group, Masters of Ceremony (with Puba's cousin Dr. Who and DJ Shabazz), had music out as early as 1985. Their wax debut was a Teddy Riley co-produced single called "Crime" on the small M-Low label. DJ Shabazz was originally from East Elmhurst, Queens, but had moved to New Rochelle, so they were one of the first groups from the town to make any noise in the rap game.

In 1986, the group put out the Puba-produced single "Sexy," featuring MC/toaster Don Baron, on Jazzy Jay's Strong City label. A third single, 1987's "Cracked Out (Remix)," also on Strong City, was another midlevel hit. The latter two singles were produced by Puba, and it was clear that the group was on to something good. As a result of their steady success, they were signed to a major and their debut (and only) full-length, *Dynamite,* came out on 4th & Bway/Island in 1988.

Chiefly produced by Puba with three tracks done by Shabazz, *Dynamite* was an underrated record at the time, combining funky samples, intelligent lyrics, and occasional reggae-infused toasting by Don Baron. But sales weren't what they could have been. Puba says: "Most people never heard *Dynamite,* unfortunately. 4th & Bway didn't do anything with us. They didn't even give us a video. We did the 'Sexy' video on our own, before we even signed with them."

For many reasons, the Masters of Ceremony trio didn't last past their 4th & Bway tenure. Puba recalls: "By 1988, Dr. Who and Don Baron wanted to do their own thing, and then I started my own thing, with Sadat and Jamar. We were all pretty much from New Rochelle. Sadat and Alamo were close friends [not cousins, as is sometimes incorrectly stated]. I'm a little older than those guys, about three years, but I've been knowing them all since we were small."

While many groups in New York at the time were banding together in or-ganized cliques (Native Tongues, Blackwatch), Brand Nubian were loners. Puba says: "After we started the group we pretty much kept to ourselves—

we wasn't really with any particular clique. We were still cool with a lot of other groups, though."

Puba says of his post-Masters work: "Once I had left Masters of Ceremony, I started doing a solo project and I was producing Jamar and Sadat as solo artists. I was trying to get them deals, but everybody was frontin' on them. So we, as a group, said: 'Let's put it all together and make somethin' happen.' "

Sadat X remembers the pre–Brand Nubian demo days: "Puba was producing a demo for me and one for Jamar, both at the same time. Sometimes we'd even split a session. I think that if you want to pinpoint it, Brand Nubian started when Jazzy Jay [likely with Puba's co-production help] made a track and put all three of us on it. It was called 'I Ain't Goin' out Like That.' Jay did the beat, and that's the first time that we had ever rhymed together. This was in 1988, maybe early '89. That track was in the same vein as other stuff on the album, but the song just never made it on there."

Puba remembers the track in question very well: "The hottest track I think that we ever did never came out. It was on our first demo, and it was called 'I Ain't Goin' out Like That.' It had the hottest James Brown sample, of 'Super Bad.' I don't know why it never came out. We always ask ourselves that question to this day. I think those were the hottest rhymes that all of us ever said."

Puba explains his concept of Brand Nubian (who were called Brand Nubians on their first single) at the time: "We were raised in a conscious way, so it was natural for us to include that [mentality] in the group's rhymes. I was raised in the BLA [*Author's note: I assume he means Black Liberation Army*] and I participated in all that as a young man. Basically it was just the coming together of our minds and the social conditions of the day to give us the subject matter that we were talking about. We talked about the struggles that we were going through. And that wasn't anything new for me, since my days with Masters of Ceremony. 'Crime' and 'Cracked Out' were socially conscious songs. That was part of the reason why the group broke up, because Rocky [Bucano, the group's executive producer] wanted more party records like 'Sexy.' "

Sadat remembers the deal-shopping process once Puba had the demo in hand: "Getting a deal didn't take that long, probably within a couple months of us coming together. I think Puba had three or four songs and he took it downtown to a couple people, and that was that."

The quartet's early demos, none of which made Brand Nubian's first album, caught the ear of one A&R man who would be important in bringing the group to wax: Dante Ross. In 1989, Ross was riding high on the success of De La Soul's *3 Feet High and Rising* at Tommy Boy, for which he had been Production Supervisor. He was also on the verge of leaving the label for more lucrative A&R pastures. Puba recalls: "Dante was at Tommy Boy and was about to leave, so he said: 'Listen, I'm about to go over to Elektra, I'll sign you there.' So we waited. He had always wanted to sign me as a solo artist, so when I brought him all the stuff with Sadat and Jamar on it, it was already a done deal."

Dante Ross says, simply, "That first Brand Nubian record is my favorite record that I've ever been involved with, no question. Puba taught me a lot and showed me a lot of records that I didn't know. A lot of people forget about it, but he's the original producing MC." Ross knew a thing or two about producing since he was a beatmaker himself, producing tracks and remixes for Shazzy and Shinehead before Brand Nubian, and later with 3rd Bass (on their 1991 *Derelects of Dialect* album) and KMD. Ross ended up producing two album tracks on *One for All.*

Ross adds: "There were so many people jocking Puba, even before *One for All,* and afterwards everyone knew how dope he was. I actually had even wanted Puba to produce a lot of the first Queen Latifah record when I was still at Tommy Boy. Puba disappeared for a couple months after the Latifah stuff [in 1989], and then he caught up with me and told me about these kids the Brand Nubians. The demo that Puba played me had only one song on it, called 'I Ain't Goin' out Like That.' I heard Sadat and I loved his voice. I loved their group style, because I've always been a fan of Run-DMC, the Beastie Boys, Cold Crush Brothers. Anytime you have more voices, you can do more with them."

He continues: "I was heading to Elektra and I wanted them to be my first signing. Tommy Boy was ready to give them a fifty-thousand-dollar album deal and take half their publishing. Monica [Lynch, at Tommy Boy] knew about Puba and she pursued him after I left for Elektra. Things were definitely a little tense in my last days at Tommy Boy, because Monica didn't want me to sign Brand Nubian to Elektra, but I told her that I was going to. I had zero support there at Elektra when I got there, though, since it was Crackerville and very un-hip-hop. But I signed them up as soon as I could."

Ross recalls: "I signed them to a single deal with an album option. The album budget wasn't too much—about sixty thousand dollars for the recording and their advances." He adds: "Recording that album was amazing. The album ended up costing seventy-eight thousand dollars, which seemed like a lot since I had just come from Tommy Boy. But I didn't realize that that was like Metallica-taking-a-fart money [i.e., nowhere near a rock-star album budget]. So the label was happy."

Brand Nubian released their first single, "Brand Nubian" b/w "Feels So Good" (the latter was their first video) in 1989. "We were out for a year before the album hit," Puba says. Dante Ross recalls: "That first single didn't really connect like I thought it should have, and it had the world's worst video. It was a rocky moment for a minute, but my champ, DJ Red Alert, came through and started banging it. It started to connect, although just in New York and maybe the Bay Area."

The single might not have been a smash hit, but it connected enough for Elektra to green-light an album, and they were off. The group got down to work in the studio and were all business when they got there, knocking the album out within a couple months at Manhattan's Calliope Studios, with other work at Jazzy Jay's studio in the Bronx and Chung King in Manhattan as well. Skeff Anselm, who had worked with Masters of Ceremony (and who would produce later tracks by A Tribe Called Quest, among others), engineered the majority of the album.

The album officially credits Grand Puba Maxwell & Brand Nubian for production. Grand Puba says: "Whoever brought something to the table, that's what got used. All of us would bring stuff in. When we came with music, it wasn't like: 'This is *my* beat.' It was more like this is *our* beat. Then again, we didn't really know about the money situation back then [*laughs*]."

As for Puba's membership in the Islam-derived Five Percent Nation (aka the Nation of Gods and Earths) and his simultaneous talk of "getting skins," he explains: "There wasn't any problem with me on all those levels. I was human, I was positive and negative, left and right, up and down. If you're serious all the time, it's too boring, too preachy. I'm the same dude that hung out in the streets all night, drinkin' 40s, smokin' weed, and everything. But when I did those things, the serious stuff was on my mind. Like: 'Why are we in this condition?' I wasn't going through all that shit blindly."

Puba says that Sadat and Jamar were also members of the Five Percent Nation, and, he adds, "Alamo was freelance [*laughs*]."

Sadat says: "Puba mixing serious stuff with sex talk was great, if you ask me. That's just what his life was about. Me and Jamar didn't talk about skins, but we damn sure got skins! It just never came up in our lyrics. We were all part of the [Five Percent] Nation at various points during the first album. If you really listen closely to the lyrics, Puba and Jamar were really on the Gods and Earths stuff more than I was." Dante Ross adds: "Puba was just that dude who was caught between the Koran and the street."

On the vocal side, there were several tracks on the album where only one member appeared on the mic, and Puba claimed most of these. Sadat explains: "He was the founder of the group and he had the most experience, so I don't think anybody had any problems with him having more solo joints. He was the leader." Dante Ross says: "Somewhere in the middle of the record, Puba decided that he wanted to do solo records, so he just started doing them by himself. Tracks like 'Step to the Rear,' 'Who Can Get Busy Like This Man . . . ,' and 'Puba, Positive & L.G.' Those just weren't Brand Nubian records. And I don't care what he or anyone says, he was already making a solo record at that point. There was tension between he and Jamar about it. Puba just felt entitled. Like: 'I put you on, and I can do what I want.' "

With visionary tracks that presented serious pro-black and Afrocentric topics with a mix of Native Tongues–style musical finesse, *One for All* changed many things in 1990, and with likeminded (and even more serious) groups like X-Clan and Poor Righteous Teachers, real issues were being slammed down on the hip-hop table. This was, of course, after Public Enemy and Boogie Down Productions had set that metaphorical table in the late eighties. Sadat says: "I never called my style 'political' or whatever, I never labeled it like that at all. It was all just *rhyming* to me. We was all into a similar lyrical zone, so we all just influenced each other."

The album's legendary status was always about influence rather than sales, since the album, unjustly, never reached gold status, a fact that bothers Puba to this day. But, he says, "When you've got an album with controversial songs on it like that, you're not going to sell a gazillion records. They're not going to want the whole world to hear that."

Dante Ross says that the album sold around four hundred thousand copies at the time, but adds, "Apparently it's gone gold through catalog sales by now." He also notes that the album sales, even as relatively modest as they were, were the definition of a "slow burn": "That record was *so* slow to catch on. But it was one of those records that sold for like a whole year. I knew it was going to be big when I went to Virginia Beach and I heard it being bumped on the beach several months before it was even out. When it came out in May [of 1990], it was a regional record, really just moving in New York and the Bay Area. Then eventually it was doing ten thousand a month."

Ross adds: "Since the budget was low compared to other Elektra albums, the label was happy and I got green-lighted to do what I wanted to do there for a little while. Without Brand Nubian's success, I would have never gotten to do KMD or anything else afterwards."

Puba left the group after *One for All* to pursue a solo career. He explains: "I already had my album [*Reel to Reel,* which came out on Elektra in 1992] half done by the time [Brand Nubian's] 'Slow Down' was a hit. I just had different ideas and concepts that I wanted to do. I got them [the other members of Brand Nubian] in the door. They couldn't get a deal before that and now they were the hottest group in New York, so my job was done."

Sadat remembers: "When we finished recording I thought we had a good album, but rap albums were still kinda new then, so I didn't have too much to really measure it with. I definitely realized the impact of the album years later. That first one is definitely my favorite Brand Nubian album, though. We were all young and it was just a cool time." He adds: "I first knew that it was blowin' up when I saw the bootleggers with it. It was bad that we was losing money, but it was good just to see that it was one of the albums big enough to be bootlegged. It was a weird kind of good, I guess."

"Not to sound conceited," Puba says, "but yeah, I thought that the album was a classic when we finished it. It was bringin' something to the game that cats wasn't doing yet. The way we used samples, the way we used singing on the chorus of certain songs. It was definitely different."

TRACKS

ALL FOR ONE

Grand Puba: That's one of my favorite tracks on the album. I did that one, and I got that James Brown record ["Can Mind"] out of my girlfriend's closet [*laughs*]. I thought for a while that "All for One" was gonna be our biggest record. Then after a while I knew that "Slow Down" was gonna be *big.* You'd hear "All for One" on mix shows, but it wasn't on regular rotation and played every day like "Slow Down" was. We did a video for that one, and it was like all our videos back then—just helter-skelter, no format or nothin'.

Dante Ross: I thought that song was going to be the big hit on the album, not "Slow Down." That song was just amazing to me. The loop is all crusty and it was a James Brown joint that nobody really knew. Puba grabbed [sampled] it and separated it and took just the left side of it [through stereo separation]. What Puba did on production was always just real ill.

CONCERTO IN X MINOR

Sadat X: I remember we said we'd all do a solo track on the album, and that's just the one I chose. That wasn't on my own demo that Puba produced—it was new. None of those songs we did on my demo ended up on the album.

Grand Puba: I really love that track, and I had nothing to do with it. Sadat, Jamar, and Alamo did it. I wish that would have been a single too. Mood-wise, it always just put me in a different state of mind. A positive mood, with a different energy.

Grand Puba: Skeff Anselm produced that. He did some stuff for Q-Tip and A Tribe Called Quest too. The title came from the saying: "Yo, rag that, tear it up." It was time to tear the mic up. Those were basically just freestyle rhymes. That was one of the last tracks we recorded.

Sadat X: Skeff worked in Jazzy Jay's studio. He was the engineer there and he made beats too, so we ended up using a couple of his.

DANCE TO MY MINISTRY

Sadat X: That was all Jamar. I was in the studio when he did that, but it was his track. Mixing wisdom with funky music is definitely something that Brand Nubian brought to the game back then. It wasn't like that was our main goal, but it's definitely something that came out when we made tracks.

Grand Puba: Jamar's dropping serious science on there. You can definitely dance to it and learn at the same time. Basically Brand Nubian was a group thing, but when people wanted to do a solo joint, it was like: "Aight, go ahead," and everybody used their methods in the way they wanted to do it. There wasn't no animosity or nothin' when one guy did a solo track, at least not with me.

DROP THE BOMB

Grand Puba: I produced that one, with that Kool and the Gang loop [*he sings the chorus*]. There's a lot of "devil" talk on that, and I think people took it wrong sometimes. We don't hate anyone. The devil is any color; it's a mind state. It can be a black man doin' it worse than a white man. Our anger was always towards society, the environment we were in, not a specific color necessarily. And I never understood why it was bad for us to express ourselves. If you have hostility, are you supposed to hold it in?

WAKE UP (STIMULATED DUMMIES MIX *AND* REPRISE IN THE SUNSHINE)
Both versions appear on album

Grand Puba: The original version of that ["Reprise in the Sunshine," which Puba produced] was the one that we did the video to, with the Ray, Goodman & Brown loop [*"Another Day"—Puba hums tune*]. DJ Sincere [the group's second DJ] gave me that record. He was always just part of the clique, to add to our game. Dante Ross [who produces under the name Stimulated Dummies, with John Gamble and John Dajani] must have stuck that remix on the album because he needed something to do. [*Author's note: Puba seems annoyed that the Stimulated Dummies version was placed first in the album sequence.*]

Dante Ross: That was the first single off the album when it hit, and I was definitely close to that one. I did the first of two versions [in the sequence] on the album, with the Niteliters ["Tanga Boo Gonk"] sample. We did that one first and then they [Brand Nubian] went and did the other one and I was really mad. But then when I really listened to it, I knew that it was really good. It was always tough to compete with Puba. And I don't know how I got to produce two tracks on the album. I guess they just thought my shit was bangin'. That video was fucked up, because MTV actually banned it, even though Fab Five Freddy [who hosted MTV's *Yo! MTV Raps* show] directed it. In the video they had a black dude in whiteface and devil horns. But aside from the video problems, that song was big in the streets, and at that point I knew something good was going to happen.

STEP TO THE REAR

Dante Ross: We were working on another song, but the group decided that they couldn't write to that. So my old [production] partner Johnny [*unclear whether he means Gamble or Dajani*] pulled out a disk that had the Mar-Keys on it, and he popped it in. Puba loved it and wanted us to hook it up. He started writing [lyrics] to it and I pulled out an Allen Toussaint drum loop. Then Shane Faber, the engineer, chopped something up [on a sampler] and tuned it, the little piano change-up. We did the track in like an hour, while Puba was writing to it. The other Stimulated Dummies were tired and left, so me and Puba stayed there all night, drank some 40s, smoked some weed, and we finished it up. He did his rhyme A-to-Z, he only punched in twice, and those were on purpose. I remember that Melle Mel walked in on that session to say hello and after that, Puba was doing Melle Mel impressions all night. That shit was cracking me up.

Grand Puba: That's one of the most famous tracks on the album and we didn't even do that one. Dante [Ross] did. We didn't mind having his stuff on the album at all. He trusted in us when we were working on the album, so we liked working with him.

Sadat X: That's just Puba on there, and to this day that's one of my favorites.

SLOW DOWN

Sadat X: I remember that I had the record [Edie Brickell's "What I Am"] for that one. I had seen her video on some show and I went out and bought the record. We tried [to sample] it at first and it didn't really go down; the sample wasn't loopin' up right somehow. So then we put it on the back burner, and as I recall that was the last song we finished.

Grand Puba: That was definitely our biggest hit. Sadat brought that Edie Brickell loop to the table, then we all threw in pieces. Alamo brought that Ohio Players drumbeat underneath. I came up with the concept and wrote the chorus. That was probably our biggest group effort on the album, and that theme, about crackheads, was just something that was on our minds back then. That's really the only track with any swears on it. The more hostile you are with the situation, I guess the fouler your language is gonna be. That was also the only record that got non–mix show radio play, really.

Dante Ross: Sadat did that song. He kept asking me about getting his own studio time, so I gave it to him, and when I did, he first did "Concerto in X

Minor." I walked into that session and he was looping up the Ohio Players drums that got used on "Slow Down" and he had the Edie Brickell shit he wanted to sample, but he got a girl to sing on it instead. That song was all his vision, one hundred percent. And that wasn't an Edie Brickell sample, that's a girl who re-sang it. Her name was Jetta.

GRAND PUBA, POSITIVE AND L.G.

Grand Puba: L.G. was like the official Zulu Nation DJ for Bambaataa, along with Jazzy Jay. He made that beat. I knew him through Jazzy Jay but more through Positive K, who was my rhyme partner [Puba produced Positive K's 1988 hit "Step Up Front," on First Priority] from way back. I think I met him through Lumumba Carson, also known as Professor X [of X-Clan], who was managing him at the time.

Dante Ross: L.G. produced that song, even though Puba said it was his at first. L.G. called after he read the album credits so he could get paid for it.

DEDICATION

Grand Puba: I had thought about doing that track for a while. Nobody had done something like that before, and I wanted to shout everybody out who had influenced me. Those people I mention on there made it so that we could do what we did.

COMMON (SENSE)

Resurrection

(Relativity, 1994)

In recent years, Chicago has exploded onto the hip-hop map. But through the nineties, MCs and producers from the Windy City had one hell of a time getting any love from New York, L.A., and even their hometown on occasion. Nevertheless, the city always had a thriving scene with many talented acts, and Common (formerly known as Common Sense) is the one who first made the country give Chi a serious look.

The man himself, born Lonnie Rashid Lynn and raised on Chicago's South Side, recalls: "I really first got into hip-hop through break dancing. My first time actually writing a rap was in about seventh grade, in Cincinnati, where I would go in the summers [to visit relatives]. I was attracted to hip-hop because the culture was really revolutionary and it was relevant to our inner city life. I really decided to be an MC around 1986, when I was fourteen, when Rakim came out, and then a year later with EPMD. With those guys, I saw a whole new branch of hip-hop. Rakim gave me a whole new twist to what the art form was. I started making demo tapes at that point."

Common's main partner in crime for much of his earliest work was DJ-turned-producer and sometime MC No I.D. (Ernest Dion Wilson). He wasn't always a hip-hop guy. As for most young, hip Chicagoans, house music loomed large on his musical horizon. He says: "Because I'm from Chicago, I was really into house music when I was in my teens. I was a DJ and was producing house tracks back then, before I did hip-hop. Back in my house days I also used to break-dance, so that's how I came into hip-hop, because it's what we used to dance to when we were outside. There wasn't any clubs playing rap at the time, so it was pretty hard to hear it."

No I.D. continues: "It wasn't until I got some [DJ] Red Alert tapes that I started to hear more about real hip-hop, and Rakim is definitely the reason that I got into it at all. When I started rapping, I wasn't even doing beats— Twilite Tone [friend and future production partner Anthony "Tony" Craig, aka Ynot] was doing them. I did some beats here and there, and the main reason was because I needed something to rap to." He produced songs with Tone, mostly house music, and their production group was called 1015, named after the address of legendary house DJ Frankie Knuckles's club.

Common's first attempt at a hip-hop group, CDR, involved No I.D. (then going by Dion, later known as Immenslope) and also a friend named Corey

(*C* for Corey, *D* for Dion, *R* for Rashid). Common recalls: "One of our friends had DJ equipment and a [Roland] 707 [drum machine], and No I.D. would make really simple beats for us. Dion was just always gifted as a musician, a genius on production even at that point. I would write the lyrics in that group for me and Corey." No I.D. says of those early days: "I knew Common since grammar school, and we both went to Luther South High School. We both lived in the Eighty-seventh Street neighborhood, Stony Island."

Up until 1990, Common Sense went by his middle name, Rashid, and also the Black Poet Kadin. No I.D. humorously recalls the origins of that early alias of his, Immenslope: "That was me being silly and trying to prove a point. I had a theory that you could have the dumbest name ever and if your music was hot, your name would become hot. Immenslope was a word that I just made up by combining two words, *immense* and *slope.* My theory was never really proven, though, because I was more popular after I changed it. Some people still call me Slope, though."

Common says: "With CDR, we would take our tapes up to a college radio station and get play on there. WHPK 88.5. [WHPK was the University of Chicago's radio station. The hip-hop show was hosted by DJ Chilly Q at the time.] I remember looking for the address in a phone book in a phone booth and driving out there to find the studio, which was pretty janky. Our first song was called 'CDR in Effect,' in 1988. WHPK played it, and it just felt so good to know that you're on the radio." The song was tape-only, never appearing on vinyl, and, according to No I.D, never for sale.

"We were really just fucking around with CDR, as far as I was concerned," says No I.D. "Having a record deal was kind of unthinkable back at that time. Even in house music, it was all indie. Our main goals were just to get some tapes out locally and do some shows." In 1988 the group got local exposure by opening up for Big Daddy Kane, N.W.A., and Too $hort at Chicago's Regal Theater. "That was most definitely a highlight of our early years," recalls Common.

Interestingly, Common and his crew weren't ever an integral part of the eighties Chicago hip-hop scene that he calls "very underground" and "not very united." He remembers: "Twista was around doing his thing, and the Blue Gargoyle was the club that used to do a lot of those shows. But I wasn't really part of the hip-hop scene in town too much. I just kinda hung out with my homies."

No I.D. adds: "There was a whole history of Chicago hip-hop that we kind of jumped over. And a lot of the people in that scene would say that we was commercial once we got some recognition, mostly because we weren't at those events. We never got much recognition from the relatively small hip-hop community in Chicago, because we never battled and paid our dues."

I.D. continues: "Even after the first [Common Sense] single, 'Take It EZ,' got big and was on a national label, we still didn't get any love in Chicago, except on WHPK, and that's only a college station. We didn't really care that much, though, because we weren't part of the scene anyways. Plus I was converting into hip-hop from house. The house scene would have like three or four thousand people at a party, and a hip-hop party would have fifty people and none of them were dancing. It was a big difference. Tone was a house DJ, too, and he took what he got from the house scene and started his own hip-hop scene. His crew was called Dem Dere [a play on Chicago's famous accent, no doubt]. Their whole crew was definitely the predecessor to what Kanye became. They did parties where girls would come and you could dance, and they'd wear nice clothes."

"It was an advantage being in Chicago when I started," explains Common, "because I could step away from the influences of living in New York or L.A. and come up with my own formula, my own sound. There wasn't ever a resistance to anything from Chicago, it was more like people just weren't paying any attention at all." He also expounds on his vision of the "Chicago sound": "The difference is in the dialect and the mentality. It's a bit slick, trash-talkin', maybe a little pimpish. But with a very realistic approach to life. Most of the people there are just common folk who work blue-collar jobs. That reality has always soaked into a lot of my music."

After Common finished high school, he headed to college in the fall of 1989, all the way to Florida A&M in Tallahassee. He says: "I wanted to go to a black college and they had a good business program. I was in business administration and writing raps on the side. I used to get drunk and then just rap out in this place on campus where people hung out. I went there for two years, then I got signed and I left. My mother was like: 'You need to stay in school.' And I was like: 'I'm in a new school, the school of hip-hop!' "

In 1989, No I.D. enrolled at Southern Illinois University but returned to Chicago after only three semesters, collegiate ambitions unfulfilled. He says: "After a year and a half of doing nothing but writing raps, I decided that I didn't want to pursue that route, so I came back home. Back then, Tone and another guy had a group named 1213. Common wasn't really in the picture at the time; he was second in line to anything I wanted to do with 1213. A little bit after that I helped Common with his demo, but I didn't get more involved until I started doing my own demo. That's when Common started using all of my beats. But he had the money to go and lay the demos, so I let him have them. He basically got his first deal using my demo beats. That first one had six songs on it, and not all of them appeared on the first album."

In 1990, as Common continued to make demos and give college a shot, he traveled to New York to attend the New Music Seminar. It had a big impact on him, as he relates: "That was the first time I ever got to see KRS-One, there in New York. My heart was beating, because those guys were like TV characters to me. They were my heroes. I also saw Brand Nubian and Leaders of the New School there. And at the same time, I was like: 'I can do this, it ain't that far away.' "

Common caught the ear of Relativity Records on the strength of one song: a demo that No I.D. and Tone had produced in early 1991 while Common was in Chicago on break, "Take It EZ." I.D. says: "Twilight did the original beat and I ended up taking his music out and putting a new sample to his drums, so it was a co-production. This was in 1991, when I was out of college. I had gone down to Florida and was staying with Common since my mom didn't want me sitting around at home with no job. So we were basically working on the first album at that point, even though we weren't signed." He adds: "Common used to rap like Tone Lōc until the 'Take It EZ' demo. Then he started using all the punch lines."

"Take It EZ" was never on wax, but it earned the prestigious honor of being featured in the Unsigned Hype column in *The Source* magazine, written by journalist Matty C (aka Matt Life). It was enough for the newly formed Relativity Records to throw a contract at the young business major in late 1991. Common remembers: "I was still making demo tapes and in college when I got that Unsigned Hype. We got an offer to get signed when I was on my way back to school, and once I hit Florida I just turned right back around."

Aside from writing about Common in *The Source,* Matty C explains his role in Common's signing to Relativity: "We were working on an Unsigned Hype album with Relativity at the time, which would have had then-unknown artists like Common, Notorious B.I.G., Mobb Deep, and DMX. But the deal that Relativity was offering each artist wasn't good enough for guys like B.I.G., so it didn't go through. And out of all those demos that [Relativity A&R contact] Peter Kang heard for that compilation, Common's was the one he liked best. I remember that demo. The sound was incredible, much better than most demos at the time. I always liked No I.D.'s style."

Common Sense's debut on Relativity was *Can I Borrow a Dollar?*, released in 1992. Common says it was officially recorded in two weeks, produced by No I.D. (then Immenslope) and Ynot (then Twilite Tone). No I.D. recalls: "Common got signed as a solo artist, and I got signed on to produce. [*Author's note: Presumably Tone did as well, since both are credited with co-production on the album.*] And then Relativity heard me rap on some of the songs on the first album and offered me my own deal. But I worked on Common's record first. Most of my tracks on the first two Common albums were originally supposed to be for me, but he would always take them. In later days, if I wanted him to use a beat of mine, I'd pretend like it was for me. Because most of the time if I made a beat for him specifically, he wouldn't want it. So in a way, once Common got a deal, I stopped MCing and focused on producing."

According to No I.D., most of the recording time spent on *Can I Borrow a Dollar?* was preproduction, and it was done in Chicago. He says: "We did tons of stuff to get the tracks ready to go, and then we went into a studio in New York and laid down all the songs in like three days." Overall, he says that the first album cost about eighty thousand dollars to record.

Common has mixed feelings about *Can I Borrow a Dollar?* "That album was basically a compilation of my demo songs with a couple of new songs we added to it. We re-recorded a lot of the songs that had been in demo form, but they were still older, lyrically and musically." Common was the second hip-hop artist signed to Relativity, which was a division of the rock/punk label Combat Records. The first artists on Relativity were the Beatnuts, who would be very influential and helpful to Common and No I.D., and with whom they would go out on their first tour, along with Artifacts and Organized Konfusion.

Common continues: "Overall, that era was a slight introduction for me as an artist. It didn't get the whole world to turn their heads, but a lot more people became familiar with me. [Getting even a small amount of recognition] made me want to get heard even more, and to work even harder for my career in music. The first album sold about a hundred thousand copies, and I definitely wasn't satisfied with that. It gave me more inspiration to try and push on, even though my mom still wanted me to be in school. But school to me didn't feel like an option, because I had this dream right in front of me."

The difference between Common's first and second albums is a dramatic one, and there are many reasons for this. One was the fact that the MC was only twenty in 1992. He says: "When I got to when we were working on [the second album] *Resurrection,* it was the first step in me becoming an adult. I could feel the growing pains. I was young and ignorant on the first album, but my second was a first step into awareness."

Common adds: "With *Resurrection,* I had definitely found a new place in music where I wanted to be. I became aware of jazz music. I was listening to a lot of Last Poets and Coltrane, and understanding that I wanted to make some pure, timeless music." Common didn't produce anything on the album, per se, but was still always involved in the music. He says: "The closest I ever came to producing was picking out samples."

No I.D. saw the transformation as well. He says: "With that second album, our whole goal was just to make good *songs.* [*Author's note: No I.D.'s definition of "song" in this sense means tracks that were more collaborative and planned out, versus simply having a rapper rhyme over a beat that was provided.*] There was no 'This is gonna be the single,' or 'This will be great for radio.' It was all just making music without worrying about what would happen when it was done. It was also so strong because it was the way that albums should be produced, with two main people working on the whole album. The first album didn't count because we really didn't know what we were doing. I mean, it was more like a demo which just happened to come out [*laughs*]."

With what they had learned from their triumphs and mistakes the first time around, Common and his production partners No I.D. and Ynot (now no longer Immenslope and Twilite Tone) went about getting tracks ready for the second album with a renewed sense of purpose. During late 1993 and early 1994 they would gather frequently in Battery Studios in Chicago to work on tracks. As Common remembers: "I would always write after I got a beat, and write to that specific music. At the time I was also still working on different aspects of my delivery and mic technique."

No I.D.'s musical approach also changed between albums: "The most important thing for me back then was meeting the Beatnuts [Psycho Les and Ju-Ju, who were both producer/MCs]. I'd go to their sessions and I learned a lot, like about digging for records. I also started making beats the reverse way that I did on the first album. I would get a sound [like a horn or a bass line] first and then build the beat around it, rather than just getting a beat and putting stuff on top of it." He was also making $1,500 per track this time, versus $1,600 for his entire part in producing *Can I Borrow a Dollar?*

Common performing at Unity, Hollywood, 1995.
PHOTO: B+ (FOR WWW.MOCHILLA.COM).

During the *Resurrection* recording process, Common started to gravitate toward No I.D.'s beats more than he had in the past. Common says: "I would always want to get to those beats he had before he gave them away, so I'd write right away. His beats inspired just about every song I wrote on that album." No I.D. remembers as well: "With *Resurrection,* Tone was really supposed to be producing Common, and I was really supposed to be producing myself for my own album [which would become *Accept Your Own and Be Yourself (The Black Album),* released in 1997 on Relativity]. Common would always try and get stuff from me when he heard my beats. And at that point, me and Tone never did beats together. It was a competitive, internal thing with us."

According to No I.D., "Common and Tone would argue a lot about beats, and at some point, Tone just stopped doing what Common wanted. That's why most of my beats are on *Resurrection.* I didn't mind Common taking my beats at the time because even though I had a record deal, I didn't really want to rap anymore. I realized that I was a producer, not a rapper, and even though it wasn't exactly structured the same way, it was a group, like Gang Starr [which features DJ Premier as the only producer, and Guru as the only rapper]."

Did the new "playing favorites" situation create tension? No I.D. says: "It was kind of an uncomfortable thing, sure. Tone was on the first album a lot on production and he was also the hype man with Common on stage. And there was always tension after that. But I didn't want to debate anything, I just wanted to make great records."

All in all, the maturity heard on *Resurrection* is in part due to the learning curve that Common and crew went through in 1992 and 1993. Common says: "Recording *Resurrection* was easier, because the recording time was more spread out and it was more of a cultured style of recording. My voice was even still developing at that point."

"It wasn't even about making a hit back then," Common says. "That just wasn't realistic. It was more like, 'Let's make some cold-blooded stuff that can get played with A Tribe Called Quest.'" The album definitely accomplished that, with Common's less battle-centric style and a decidedly more pensive, jazzier vibe. *Resurrection* as a group effort stood strongly alongside peers of the day like Pete Rock & CL Smooth and Tribe.

After basic tracks were laid down in Chicago at Battery, the final mixes for songs were done at Mirror Image in Huntington, Long Island, in the span of a couple weeks. The engineer was Troy Hightower. "It was a twenty-minute drive from New York," says No I.D. "It was good to get out of the city to record."

No I.D. adds, "We would never go into the studio without ideas. We always knew exactly what we'd be doing once we got there. And no matter how high-tech things got, almost everything always started with me putting a beat on Common's answering machine. He'd listen to it, make a copy of it, and write to it. Then we'd finish it up in the studio."

Resurrection came out in October 1994, and although it only sold in the neighborhood of two hundred thousand copies (according to Common), it was still a success. "There were a lot more concepts, and Common brought a lot more reality to a fun hip-hop sound," says No I.D. "The first album was more punch lines over a fun hip-hop sound." He adds, "We didn't get a ton of sales, but we did get respect. In a weird way, I think that a major thing in our minds was on making something that would prove to all the Chicago people that we were good. Just having a good record, proving that we could do it. We wanted respect in our city."

Common says: "It was really fun doing that record, even if I look back on some of those tracks like, 'Oh, man, did I really say that?' But I'm very proud of it and I'm glad that the hip-hop community recognized it. That was big to us."

"Back then it wasn't even a producer and rapper relationship, it was just us being friends," says No I.D. "*Resurrection* is probably the only album I've ever worked on that was purely about making great music. Marketing plans and sales had nothing to do with how we made it. And because of that, it might be one of the most innocent albums in hip-hop history."

T R A C K S

Common: That was one of two singles off the album. I really felt like I was being born again to people who weren't familiar with me. I felt like I was coming up from the dead, the dead of not being heard.

No I.D.: I think that was the second single. The video for that one was black-and-white, with some projects in there and gang signs. It was definitely the first time that some of the grittier parts of Chicago culture were put into visuals like that.

I USED TO LOVE H.E.R.

Common: That song got big love on the mix shows, but Relativity was definitely hoping it would be a bigger radio hit. I was really disappointed with the whole Ice Cube beef. [*Author's note: Ice Cube, apparently thinking that he was being dissed in "I Used to Love H.E.R.," responded to the song on Mack 10's track "Westside Slaughterhouse" in 1996.*] He was one of my heroes, an artist that I looked up to. I didn't want to be beefin' with the dude, and I wasn't even trying to dis the West Coast on that song. I was just talking about how hip-hop had evolved and was doing everything gangsta at that point in time. I saw some artists on the East Coast trying to imitate artists on the West Coast and I saw everything starting to be an imitation instead of being pure. H.E.R. stands for "Hip-hop, in its essence, and real." I was just feeling frustrated with the state of music, and I [personified hip-hop as] a girl and told the story that way. I'm glad we said all we wanted to say on records [including Common's reply record to Ice Cube, "The Bitch in Yoo," from 1996] and nothing turned violent.

No I.D.: As for the content of the song, I always thought it was interesting, the balance between trying to earn hip-hop and street respect without turning into your average gangsta rapper. Most people did it the gangsta way. I did that beat and the one for "Communism" [also on *Resurrection*] back to back. There's something about guitars that I've always loved since I was a child, that George Benson–ish sound. I think Common and Tone both came up with that concept. We actually shot a first version of the video for that, and it was really bad, so we wasted all the money we had for the budget. The director didn't really understand what the song was about—he thought it was more of a love song to a woman, so he had a pretty girl in there. We used some of the footage of her in the final version. But after the first one, we had to spend like five or ten thousand dollars on another version. We took what we had and put some camcorder and 8mm footage together.

WATERMELON

Common: That wasn't a freestyle—I didn't really freestyle on that album much at all. But I love doing songs like that, with no particular subject matter. We titled the song that way because of No I.D.'s sample that he used [a man's voice saying "Watermelon"].

BOOK OF LIFE

Common: That's definitely one of my favorite tracks. That was one of the first songs we did for the album. It was about me realizing that I was becoming a grown man, basically.

IN MY OWN WORLD (CHECK THE METHOD) *Featuring No I.D.*

No I.D.: I remember that track was done at the last minute. It was an internal battle and respect thing [with Ynot]. I wasn't trying to rap too much at that point, but I figured I should have at least one verse on every album. And Common never really wanted to put other people on his albums [as guest MCs], but he thought it would be a dis to not offer it to us. I didn't really like MCing too much, but I guess I just did it because I could.

ANOTHER WASTED NITE WITH . . .

No I.D.: That was a real answering machine message from that guy Moe Love, not anything that was planned. That guy was pretty funny.

NUTHIN' TO DO

Common: That wasn't originally on the album, but during mixdown [No I.D.] played me two new beats and I wrote those lyrics after hearing it on his Walkman. The other one was "In My Own World." I wrote them in the car going to the airport, I think. We did a remix to that, but it never came out. And it was banging, too. We sampled [Kool and the Gang's] "Summer Madness." [Ynot] did the remix and he just freaked it. Man, it was just dope. We were trying to push for it as a single but they [Relativity] wasn't seeing the vision. They were like: "The album has sold what it's going to sell and we're straight."

No I.D.: That's one of my favorite tracks because it painted a perfect picture of Chicago. I loved the nostalgia on there, but even despite that, it didn't get any love in Chi.

WMOE

Common: That was this guy Mohammed Ali on there [as the radio announcer]—he worked at Relativity. He was the head of marketing and promotions or something. He was one of the hardest-working brothas I have ever met. He was a great people person.

THISISME

Common: I was starting to be more introspective and I was saying, "This is what I'm putting out and I'm not trying to be nothing but *me.*" I ain't no gangsta, I'm an average cool cat who grew up on the South Side of Chicago, and I've experienced a lot of the same things that you have.

No I.D.: That song definitely summed up what Common was about at that time. It was the first time, on that album, that he was talkin' about him and Chicago. The first album didn't really have anything like that.

CHAPTER 13 (RICH MAN VS. POOR MAN)
Featuring Ynot, on production and as guest MC

Common: Ynot has always been a genius with the music. He produced some of my first demo with No I.D. His vocals were excellent. Great rhyming and great, clever stuff to say. He just didn't rap a lot back then.

No I.D.: I didn't love that record, and not just because Ynot and I were competitive. I just felt like it wasn't in the vein of the rest of the album. But I understood that Ynot had to have stuff on the album. Plus it was also important to have a break from it just being Common all the time. The album was so much of Common's voice that everyone just needed a break. I thought that song was too complicated, though, like it was two peoples' vision on one song.

SUM SHIT I WROTE *Produced by Ynot*

No I.D.: Now *that* song was Common and Tone hitting it perfectly. I thought that "Chapter 13" was a Tone record with Common on it, and "Sum Shit" wasn't like that at all. I remember the original verses Common had on there might have been the worst start-off ever [*laughs*].

Common: I had a whole other rap to that and I remember specifically my boy named Moe—the guy on the answering machine on "Another Wasted Nite With . . ."—was like: "Yo, that shit is wack!" So I went back and rewrote it. It was real good to have buddies around who weren't just like: "Yeah, that's fresh" to everything. They always gave it to me straight.

POP'S RAP *Keyboards by Lenny Underwood*

Common: I invited my dad to the studio just so he could see what we was doin'. His talks with me on the phone were always really potent to me, so I said, "Pop, why don't you get up there and say somethin'?" So the keyboardist just replayed the music from "Thisisme" and we let my pops talk. First he was just sitting there in the studio, eating pizza, then he's on the record [*laughs*]. He lived in Denver at the time—he was just visiting Chicago.

No I.D.: That was the first time he ever did one of those [after *Resurrection,* there is a "Pop's Rap" on each Common album]. Even though I grew up with Common, I never knew his dad, because he was living in Denver. That might have even been the first time I had ever met him. We never planned to do that song, but if Common feels something in the studio, he'll just do it. So I was like: "Fine, but I'm not doing a new beat for it." It was probably one of the last things we recorded for the album. Lenny Underwood is on there. He's a keyboardist who played on a lot of disco records from the seventies that I liked. He's from New York, and he was on the first album, too, on the intro. There was some sample that we couldn't use, so we had him replay it, even though he was the guy who played it on the original in the first place! I think it was Eddie Kendricks's "Intimate Friends." Lenny came into the studio and was just playing us all the old songs he did. But the weirdest thing is that we didn't even ask for him specifically. The label brought him in somehow. It was a pretty crazy coincidence.

CYPRESS HILL

Cypress Hill

(Ruff House/Columbia, 1991)

Our favorite groups back then weren't selling platinum, they were more in the 150,000 to 300,000 range," says now-legendary producer and DJ Muggs. "We loved artists like Boogie Down Productions, Tribe Called Quest, Ultramagnetic [MCs]. So we figured that's where we would probably be. We thought hip-hop heads would like the album, but we never expected it to sell like it did."

Muggs and any of Cypress Hill's detractors were proven equally wrong in 1991 when their self-titled LP took the country by storm, eventually reaching double-platinum status. "Our style was everything that we were about on our block," says Muggs, reminiscing about the group's earliest days. "We sold weed, we hung out, we gang-banged, we listened to funk." Broken down like that on paper, it seems pretty basic. But the group's L.A. masterpiece was anything but.

Cypress Hill might have come to represent the darker side of L.A. (alongside the N.W.A. family tree, of course), but their leader wasn't a native. Lawrence "Muggs" Muggerud grew up in Queens, New York, and didn't hit L.A. until 1984, when he journeyed west to live with his mother. "It was a huge culture shock," he recalls. "I came out here from New York to nothing. Everybody's gangbanging, smoking PCP. They had bald heads, white T-shirts, and khakis. And if anyone out here was listening to hip-hop back then, it was [Afrika Bambaataa's electro classic] 'Planet Rock' and they called it funk. I'd go back home and I would bring stuff back from New York before anybody had it. The only person who had the stuff that I had was [KDAY radio's head Mixmaster] Tony G."

Upon his arrival in L.A., Muggs also started his DJ career and picked up the art of turntablism fairly quickly, eventually working his way into local and even national DJ competitions like DMC. He won the DMC West Coast crown in 1989, as well as many other local contests. "DJing was an education for me, for when I got into production," Muggs explains. "I think at a certain point in the later eighties I had taken DJing as far as I could take it, before getting disillusioned with competitions like DMC. I saw these kids doing all this shit and all they got was a jacket and some spray paint and a gold turntable. Those competitions exploited the DJs and made millions of dollars. Being a DJ you can only go so far. I mean, I got fifteen hundred dol-

Cypress Hill (left to right: DJ Muggs, B-Real, Sen Dog) in Highland Park, Los Angeles, 1996.
PHOTO: B+ (FOR WWW.MOCHILLA.COM).

lars on my first production job, making a beat that took me five hours."

Cypress Hill's lead voice, B-Real (Louis Freese, sometimes written as Freeze), was born and raised in L.A. and got into hip-hop through break dancing, where he met brothers Sen Dog (Senen Reyes) and Mellow Man Ace. He remembers: "Watching Sen and Mellow rap definitely influenced me to start writing my own stuff." Like Sen, B wrote his raps in Spanish and English, realizing that it was not only a tribute to his heritage but a selling point. "What really got us signed to Columbia were the songs that were in Spanish," B-Real says. "Nobody was doing that much at the time."

While Muggs's reputation as a DJ and producer continued to grow, the three-member Cypress Hill unit was formed around 1988 out of a multi-member crew called DVX. The name derives from the block on which they lived in L.A., Cypress Avenue. "It started and it kind of went up," explains Muggs. "And we all lived on the part that was higher, the hill."

"They had like seven rappers in DVX," recalls Muggs, who points out that KDAY radio DJ Julio G was a DJ in the crew. Sen Dog and Ace were a duo within DVX, and Julio was their DJ. B-Real was also in the crew, working as a solo artist. Soon after they met, Muggs and B-Real started working on a demo together.

Along the way Muggs also helped Mellow Man Ace get his big break. He remembers: "I told Mike Ross at Delicious Vinyl that Ace rapped in Spanish, and I could see the dollar signs in his eyes." Interestingly, Ace didn't really rap in Spanish at the time—his brother Sen did. Muggs says: "Mellow went home that night and his mom and Sen helped him write a Spanish song. He did a demo in my house and a week later he was on Delicious Vinyl."

Ace's single "Do This" came out on the label in 1987 before Ace was signed to Capitol, who put out his *Escape from Havana* album in 1989. Michael Ross was executive producer and Muggs produced two tracks. Once Mellow Man Ace was off as a solo act, Sen joined the newly minted Cypress Hill, which became the trio that the world knows today.

"At one time I was just going to be the writer of the group," says B-Real. "I was pretty good at it, and I wrote all the time. I would just take an idea and draw on it from a real experience I had had on the streets. I had to work on my mic skills to be more of a part of the group's performance. And fortunately I stumbled onto the nasal thing."

The "nasal thing" is B-Real's rap style, which is one of the most unique in hip-hop. He explains: "Sen brings a different energy to the group, and his voice is so strong. It's powerful. Mine is high and annoying. But it all blends together. The nasal style I have was just something that I developed. My more natural style of rapping wasn't so pleasing to those guys' ears, so they wanted me to try something different, and it just stuck."

At the same time that Cypress Hill was forming, Muggs's DJ skills landed him his first group exposure with fellow NY expatriates 7A3 (with brothers Brett and Sean Bouldin). The group already had a single out at the time, 1987's "7A3 Will Rock You" (on Macola). Muggs met them at a party in L.A. and was in the trio for a two-year ride. The group went on to release the album *Coolin in Cali* in 1988 on Geffen and achieved perhaps their greatest success with the song "Mad Mad World" on the talent-filled soundtrack to *Colors* that same year. They toured with groups like Salt 'N Pepa and Kid 'N Play, but the group was short-lived.

While Muggs was exploring the 7A3 gig, B and Sen were waiting in the wings. B-Real recalls: "It was frustrating to wait, but in the end it turned out to be the best thing for us. We polished what we were doing and formulated our sound. We had our own niche, with our production and vocal sound and also the Spanish thing. It's good we didn't rush, because if we had, we might have blown our one big shot."

B wasn't the only one who was frustrated at the time. Muggs was tired of being behind the scenes and having no say in the artistic outcome of 7A3—he was never even credited on any of the group's singles or albums. "I was DJing for those guys and I had all these ideas for songs and all the samples, and somebody else came in and basically produced all my ideas," says

Muggs. [*Author's note: The "somebody" he is talking about is probably Joe "The Butcher" Nicolo, 7A3's main producer.*] "I wanted things to sound another way. But I got to go in the studio and saw how things worked and I was like: 'Oh, that's *it*?' I got a little bit of money, bought a drum machine, and started doing the Cypress Hill demos from that point on."

Muggs left 7A3 in 1989 and was now ready for the group he realized that he had wanted to be with all along: Cypress Hill. "7A3 was basically a crash course education in rap, and they wanted to do R&B stuff and work with Teddy Riley, that type of shit. And that's when I knew my next group had to have its shit together, otherwise we'd have some forty-year-old guy filling in the blanks and telling us what we had to do."

Fortunately Muggs, Sen, and B-Real had been working on demos all the while, and now their work went forward with a definite purpose: get their shit together and get signed. In fact, Muggs says the first album was "a collection of three years' worth of demos." Joe "The Butcher" Nicolo saw Muggs's production talent, so the group was an easy sell to his still-young Ruff House label, based out of Philly and distributed by Columbia.

Muggs wasn't messing around about having a plan. He says: "When we finished our demo we had everything structured, everything ready to go. We had our look, our style, our image all ready." According to Muggs, they were signed in 1990 and recorded the album that winter. Their self-titled debut was released in August of 1991.

"We got about a sixty-five-thousand-dollar budget for [recording] the first album, and about ten thousand each in our pockets," says Muggs. "We recorded it in L.A. on a four-track and then fixed and mixed most of it at Studio 4 in Philly (Nicolo's home base). It only took about ten days because we basically already knew everything we needed to do." Also notable is the insular nature of the proceedings: There was not one guest on the album. "If you're a great rapper," says Muggs, "you're going to make a great album all by yourself. Anybody can make an album with fifteen guests on it. We were in our own little world, with our own slang and our own style."

The mixture of ultra-real depictions of gangbanging with an oddly glib view of life and death was powerful. Muggs explains: "The thing about Cypress Hill compared to N.W.A. was that they was hard, in-your-face motherfuckers. We did the same thing, but we'd pull the gun out and laugh at you, then make a joke about shooting you." He continues: "N.W.A. was shocking to a lot of people, I guess, but the stuff they were talking about was just shit about guys that I grew up with. Guys in my neighborhood like Big Hub, Madman, Baldie. That was their lifestyle. To us it was like: 'Oh, that's just gangbangers rappin'.' "

Featuring Muggs's gritty, ultra-funky tracks, Sen Dog's lower-register growl, and B-Real's distinctive delivery, Cypress's self-titled debut hit softly when it was released, but quickly gained momentum when their driving, dark "How I Could Just Kill a Man"—the B-side to their "Phuncky Feel One" single—took hold. Interestingly, B-Real says: "Our first shows were actually in New York. We kept all our shit under wraps in L.A. We knew we had something different and we didn't want it to get out. In L.A. we did shows with other names. We might have done one talent show as Cypress Hill."

The sonics of the eponymous album are dense, dark, complex, and multilayered. "My favorite shit was Ultramagnetic [MCs] or Public Enemy," says Muggs. "And with PE, there was just always something going on with their music. There were sounds that only happened in the chorus or different verses, sounds that would happen for two bars in the second verse that didn't happen for the rest of the song. That kind of influence was where I came from."

The group also had a clear purpose when it came to their visuals. Muggs says: "We didn't want to show our faces anywhere, but the label made us after a while. We believed in the air of mystery, because mystery lasts. It lets your imagination figure things out. That kind of got lost along the way with us, but we used it at the beginning. We just loved Led Zeppelin and Black Sabbath album covers—they had a big effect on us."

The result of all the group's work was a groundbreaking album that ultimately became a commercial success as well. "In the midst of MC Hammer and all that, it showed that you could be underground rappers, real rappers, and blow up," says B-Real. "When we sold a million records, we were pretty fucking surprised. But it proved that you could be yourself and do that. I think that changed the game in a lot of ways."

Muggs remembers emerging from a New York club at the time. "I came out and somebody was bumpin' 'How I Could Just Kill a Man.' I looked over to see who it was and it was Erick Sermon [from EPMD]. We was buggin' the fuck out. Apparently they had a promo of the album before it even came out and were on it very early. That was one hell of an honor."

Muggs beams: "Since that first album blew the fuck up, everything for us has been: 'What do you guys want to do?' When that album came out, hip-hop was like it is now: real glitzy and poppy. Cypress Hill brought grit back into the game."

TRACKS

B-Real: I've always been fucked with by the cops, more when I was younger, whether I was doing something wrong or not. So I figured I couldn't do anything, I couldn't take them to court or nothing, so the only way I could lash out at those fuckers was with a song. It was a form of therapy for me.

Muggs: That song was originally three times as long. We ended up cutting it down. B-Real was talking about the pig and his "pork chopper" and all this shit. It was kind of nursery rhyme–ish.

HOW I COULD JUST KILL A MAN

Muggs: That was done two years before it came out on the album. We just kept adding layers to it. Songs like that got a chance to mature naturally. After the first album we started rushing tracks more. We wanted that track as the A-side of our first single with "Hand on the Pump" as the B-side, but the label put "The Phuncky Feel One" on the A-side and "Kill a Man" on the B-side. We were on tour with Naughty [by Nature] and had a day off so we shot the video for that. *Yo! MTV Raps* was playing it like two or three times a week. Then the movie *Juice* came out and that song was in the climax of the film. Things just came together to make that such a huge single. B-Real wrote his first verse to that song and it was like thirty bars long, and in the middle of it he said, "How I could just kill a man," and I said, "That line is *dope,* man! Let's cut it here and make that the chorus." That track was originally called "Trigga Happy Nigga."

B-Real: That song was comprised of like three different songs. I took the best lines and pieced them together into one. The label put out "Phuncky Feel" on the A-side of the single because it was more radio-friendly, but they found out that people liked the more aggressive of the two.

HAND ON THE PUMP

B-Real: We were all pretty much a bunch of thugs running around as kids, but I was a bit deeper in my involvement with gangs. I was doing all kinds of bullshit. Some things were fucked up and I learned from them. I wouldn't change it, but I wouldn't encourage it for nobody either. I chilled out after a while because if I had kept fucking around with gang shit, I would have blown it for all of us, all that we had worked for.

Muggs: That's definitely one of my favorite tracks on the album, but I didn't like that track at first when we recorded it at the house. Once we recorded it in the studio it came out ill. I had never heard anything like that. The style that B-Real kicked on there was brand-new—no one had ever heard anyone kick it like that.

HOLE IN THE HEAD

Muggs: We had [L.A.'s Samoan hip-hop group] Boo-Yaa T.R.I.B.E. on that track, singing background vocals. Other than that we didn't have any guests on our album.

LIGHT ANOTHER

B-Real: Some people thought we were just potheads and couldn't talk about anything else, but that's just who we were. We weren't hiding anything. If you listen to the album, there's deeper shit on there than smoking pot, so we weren't really that worried about it.

Muggs: That was just what we did, that's why we talked about it so much. Then, later on, we took it to a higher level with our NORML [National Organization for the Repeal of Marijuana Laws] associations. But in reality we was just carrying the torch that Bob Marley had left when he died.

THE PHUNCKY FEEL ONE

Muggs: That was the A-side of our first single, and it was an older song of ours, from probably like 1988. There were so many layers on there. Complex, layered shit.

REAL ESTATE

Muggs: We did that shit the first time back in late 1987, early 1988, in B-Real's living room, with a radio. We plugged the mic right into the radio and did the vocals in one take. We did that track the way it sounded like on the album a couple years later, in 1989. That was probably the first demo that we did that actually sounded like a "real" record. Then after that we did "How I Could Just Kill a Man," "Phuncky Feel One," and "Light Another," and that's what got us the deal. All the breakdowns and extra sounds on there were added as time went on. Mellow Man Ace actually wrote the lyrics to that one.

B-Real: We did one live performance in L.A., a contest, before the album came out. We went there to fuck around more than anything, and we played "Real Estate" and started breaking tables and shit. We didn't win, but we made an impression. Sen jumped up on the table where the judges were sitting during our set, and the table broke right in their laps.

STONED IS THE WAY OF THE WALK

Muggs: At first B-Real didn't want to rhyme on that track, but Joe [Nicolo] said that we needed some more songs. B originally wrote the lyrics for

"Stoned Is the Way of the Walk" to the music for "Hole in the Head," and vice versa. So we flipped them around and it ended up fine.

SOMETHING FOR THE BLUNTED

Muggs: I just had all these samples hanging around, so I made a little collage about getting high. That was the closest to a DJ track I had on the album. I really didn't have a lot of cutting on the record—I just didn't want to. Everything was about scratching back then, and I was even roommates with [legendary L.A. DJ] Aladdin for three years, so I wanted to take it a different way. I wasn't trying to showcase me as a DJ, I was just trying to do what was right for the song.

LATIN LINGO

Muggs: We recorded that in Philly, right at the end of doing the album. Sen and B-Real wrote the lyrics for that together, side by side. I had that sample for three years, but it all came together there at the last minute. Back in the day, Sen would do all the Spanish rhymes at the house parties, way before [his brother] Mellow [Man Ace] even rapped in Spanish. The style that B-Real kicked on the album, the nasal style, was something that Mellow actually invented on a song called "Rhyme Fighter." When you're in a clique everyone just borrows from one another.

B-Real: There were rappers of Latin descent but no one was rapping in "Spanglish" or even all in Spanish. Mellow [Man Ace] capitalized off it first, then we got our deal. The record company wanted to capitalize on the Latin market. Even though it was smaller back then, they wanted us to give it a shot. We wasn't trying to force the issue, but it was fine with us.

Muggs: That was a rhyme that Sen had for about four years, and he would kick that at all the Spanish parties. It was a tale about fucking a girl all over the house. It was X-rated and everybody would bug the fuck out when he did it. He got kicked out of a few parties because there were older people there that didn't like it.

DAS EFX

Dead Serious

(East West, 1992)

Whether you love it or hate it, there is no debating the influence and originality of DAS EFX's vocal style, which took the rap world by storm in the early nineties. Dray and Skoob, produced by talented unknowns from their 'hood and under the guidance of EPMD, briggity-brought a stutter-step to their rhymes that was unique, catchy, and rode perfectly over the hard-rock, midtempo jams that were custom-made for their bouncy style. They jumped from topic to topic, always keeping fans guessing. Drayz explains: "Lyrically, nothing really followed any logical pattern with us. We definitely went overboard with that."

Dray (Andre Weston, aka Krazy Drayz or Drayz) was born in Jamaica ("You know, the island"), and came to the United States as a child, living in Union City and Teaneck, New Jersey. He was, like many artists his age, brought to hip-hop in his younger years through the radio hits of the early eighties. "My pops would buy me the Sugar Hill baby-blue-colored records, like the Sugarhill Gang, [Grandmaster] Flash and the Furious Five," Dray says. "I never saw any of those groups live, but I'd hear it at the roller rink on the weekends. My friends around me weren't trying to be rap stars, so I wasn't surrounded by that mentality. When I started, I did the hip-hop thing for fun."

Unlike other MCs, Dray never DJed or produced; he always focused on rhyming, starting to write raps on paper as early as 1980. He continued throughout his high school years (1984 to 1988), competing in local talent shows. "I took my stance on the mic from an early age," he explains.

Once he graduated from high school, Dray, wanting to attend a black college, headed south for school, matriculating in the fall of 1988 at Virginia State University in Petersburg. He was an English major, completing three years at VSU before pursuing his hip-hop career.

Skoob (William "Willie" Hines) was born in Bushwick, Brooklyn, but was raised for most of his life in the nearby Crown Heights neighborhood. He rhymed in high school with an MC named Tony, who was future DAS EFX producer Derek Lynch's brother—but Derek was actually their DJ first, before he started producing. Skoob says: "We all just had a knack for doing music back then, so we went with it."

Skoob also enrolled at VSU in 1988 and was rhyming with other MCs at Virginia State before he met Dray. It was more for fun than as a career path—a sorority party or two here and there, and some student union throwdowns. Dray and Skoob met during their freshman year through a mutual friend, on a road trip to a party at another college. Dray remembers: "Me and Skoob were both rhyming in the car to this guy who was sitting in between us in the backseat. I didn't know Skoob at that point. At one point the guy kind of leaned back so that we could hear what the other guy was saying, and that was the beginning of it all. We were impressed."

Dray continues: "I ran into Skoob that next Monday at school and he suggested that we enter a campus contest that was coming up. We didn't even have a name for the group back then. But we won the contest and we were a pair from there. By sophomore year we were known on campus as entertainers because we did so many talent shows at sororities. People around campus definitely knew we could rap."

A big reason for DAS EFX's unique lyrical style came from the Virginia location of the group's genesis. Dray says: "The whole DAS EFX style came about because we weren't able to turn on a radio in Virginia and hear New York rap. We used to go home to the city on breaks and you'd get some New York mixtapes and then go back to school. But except for Brand Nubian, we weren't influenced by what was going on in New York. Basically we wanted to be different and we wanted to be dope like Brand Nubian. We got big into wordplay. So instead of saying, 'I got a lot of balls,' we'd say, 'I got more nuts than a Baby Ruth.' Shit like that."

Skoob says: "When I got to Virginia, it definitely made it that much harder to get recognized, because everything was happenin' in New York back then. And maybe being away from New York radio helped. We just wasn't exposed to that many styles at the time, so it helped us form our own. Aside from Brand Nubian and N.W.A., I was really influenced by KRS-One and Rakim, too, of course. All the old-school cats who stepped it up lyrically."

With their first talent-show win and other performances they did back in early 1989, they still didn't have any of their own music. Dray says they would just rhyme over popular instrumentals of the day. But by later that year, they started working with two Brooklyn-based producers who would help them bring the whole package together: Chris Charity and Derek Lynch, who used the name Solid Scheme Music. The two were friends of Skoob's from his high school days and had started building their production résumé as they themselves were going to school. Chris went to a community college in Brooklyn and Derek went to Morgan State in Maryland, heading home to Brooklyn on most weekends.

Skoob says: "Our early demos, lyrically, were real primitive, man. We were just starting to find ourselves, getting into that style, trying to stay away from what everybody else was saying. We were trying to make a serious statement but not do it so seriously. We would take something gangsta and put it into cartoon terms, for instance. And the production on our early stuff didn't come up to par until 'Klap Ya Handz.' That song was the last homemade demo we did before things got really serious. Dexx, who produced 'Klap Ya Handz,' was from Crown Heights too. Aside from that track and 'They Want EFX,'" which me and Dray produced, Chris and Derek did all the rest of the music on our first album."

By 1990, the two MCs realized that they needed a name to use for bookings, and, they hoped, for recording contracts. Dray relates: "The name as it ended up was mostly Skoob's idea. People were always like: 'Where's Skoob and Dray?' And that got to be 'S.A.D.' And the 'EFX' part came from how we would always want some reverb on our vocals, like: 'Yo! Wet up my vocals!' [*he imitates an echo effect on the last word, a 'wet' sound in studio parlance*]. So it was Sad EFX for a minute, but that didn't really make much sense, so we changed it to DAS EFX."

DAS EFX (left to right: DJ Dice, Dray, Skoob) in West Los Angeles, 1992.
PHOTO: B+ (FOR WWW.MOCHILLA.COM).

In early 1991 the duo got their big break in an unlikely place—a spot called Club Tropicana in Richmond, Virginia, which Dray refers to as a "hole in the wall." Dray remembers: "We had won campus talent shows, but we still never figured we'd ever get any kind of break at an Amateur Night at the Apollo Theater kind of thing. But we heard on the radio that this talent show was going on and it was going to be hosted by EPMD, so we knew we had to do it. It was like a meant-to-be type of thing."

He continues: "We got there early, about eight p.m., before anyone else was even there. And the DJ at the club knew everyone else there except for us, so everything was against us. He called us 'Doctor EFX' or something. We were the ninth group out of ten to go on, and we only had about five people there supporting us. But by the time we got to the chorus of the song, people were already singing along."

The song they performed that night was "Klap Ya Handz," which they had already recorded as a demo (and which ended up on their debut album two years later) with Skoob's friend Dexx. In fact, the two rhymed over the actual demo version, lyrics and all, because they didn't have an instrumental version of the music.

Dray explains the fortuitous twist to the evening's outcome: "We had the highest score in the talent contest up until the last group, and that group did well, but it seemed like the crowd was still with us at the end. We had a 25 and they got a 24, I think. The prize for the contest was one hundred dollars. So Parrish [Smith, half of EPMD] stopped the announcer, whispered in his ear, and then the guy announced that the other group had won. There was dead silence for a second, and the whole club was like: '*What?*' Then in the midst of all the confusion, when the other group came up to get their prize, Parrish came over to us and said: 'Yo, what would you guys rather have: a record deal or a hundred dollars? Meet me in the back of the club in five minutes.' "

Erick Sermon (EPMD's other half) and Parrish met with Dray and Skoob in the club's back room and asked them to play the tape of "Klap Ya Handz" for them again. In fact, the duo liked the song so much that they asked to have the tape. It was a risky move to give their tape to two of the biggest producers in hip-hop with minimal copyright protection, but it was a chance they had to take. Dray recalls: "Parrish said: 'If you can get us nine more songs like the one you just performed, we can get you a deal.' "

The duo kept in touch with EPMD during their junior year and finished the school year in May, heading back to the tri-state, still without a contract.

Their production team of Charity and Lynch had also been hard at work, woodshedding new music for the duo since they had heard about the talent-show win in January or February. "Klap Ya Handz" was one of twenty songs that the duo had completed through the end of 1989, albeit the only one that had not been done with Charity and Lynch. But all concerned knew that their vocals on the song were their best by far, and they had to make new material to impress EPMD.

Dray says: "Erick and Parrish definitely thought that 'Klap Ya Handz' was the best song of all our earliest ones. We were definitely conscious of being different at the time. I mean, people thought 'They Want EFX' was weird when it came out [in 1992], so imagine us ten songs before that. Our earliest shit was even weirder."

Upon returning to the New York area in May of 1991, Dray and Skoob stepped up their efforts to complete their new demo, which they hoped would contain enough songs for an EPMD-backed album. They were signed to EPMD's GMC Productions production and management company, and the company paid for their studio time. The group worked at Firehouse Studios in Brooklyn and also at EPMD's production home base, Charlie Marotta's North Shore Soundworks studio in Long Island.

Dray remembers: "We really wanted to blow Erick and Parrish away, because we wanted to make sure they didn't regret trying to get with us. We'd finish tracks and then send them to EPMD because they were on tour all that summer. We basically went back and forth like that until we had enough songs."

Many people assume that their debut LP was produced by EPMD, who were executive producers, but Dray says, "In the studio back then it was just me, Skoob, Chris, and Derek, and that was it. EPMD didn't produce us, we were just with their production company. A lot of people forget that." Sadly, Chris Charity passed away in 2000. "He was the brains of the operation, definitely," says Dray. "He was definitely the boss and the real executive producer of the first album. We'd have meetings at his crib in Brooklyn and he was running things."

DAS EFX were finally signed in late 1991 to Atlantic subsidiary East West Records. Dray says that influential DJ Clark Kent was in the A&R department at East West and was very enthusiastic about the group, who were also courted by Jive Records. EPMD shopped the deal through their lawyer, and were also managing the group through GMC. And since the two MCs were hot on the trail of their hip-hop dreams, both Dray and Skoob gave a pass to their senior years at VSU. "We both told our parents that we were just taking the first semester of our senior year off," says Dray. "I think we got signed in October, so there was a lot of tension in my house before that."

The album was released in March of 1992, according to Dray, and broke the prestigious platinum sales mark in 1993 on the strength of the singles "They Want EFX" and "Mic Checka." They breezed into their success relatively easily, even though their rep in New York was low-key. But, as Dray explains, "Whether we had been in Virginia or not, it didn't matter, because we were both from the New York area originally. Plus, coming through the EPMD situation, the foundation was already laid."

Dray continues: "EPMD had shit to do, so they took us and Redman and K-Solo [the first three artists that EPMD produced and managed in the early nineties] out on tour with them. It was crazy. We was like: 'We weren't doing nothing a month ago, and now we're in Texas, and they're singing along to all of our songs.' "

"Being with EPMD back then was so big for us," says Skoob. "A lot of cats don't come up under guys who have been on world tours and know how to handle crowds and how to deal with certain situations that come up. At first I didn't even want to perform live. I wasn't that dude. I just wanted to make records. But since we had to do it, I figured we might as well learn from the best.

"Back then a lot of rappers were doing the same thing, and what we were doing brought a twist to the game without watering anything down. If you were only hearing our radio stuff, you had one impression of us, but if you got the album then you realized there was a lot more depth there."

TRACKS

MIC CHECKA

Dray: I'm not sure if people know us more for that song or "They Want EFX." I love that song and how it turned out, but it was definitely tough to get done. It was really more of a club track. We had it done, but we had about ten different hooks for the chorus. We put [samples of] Slick Rick and Ice Cube in there and just couldn't get it right. We left it for about three weeks and were just calling it "that song." Then one day Chris had a brainstorm and he just sampled one part of Skoob's verse from the track itself, and that gave us the song title too.

Skoob: That's one of my favorites, because we paid so many dues with that song [*laughs*]! You don't understand what we went through to get that song right. We probably started that song right after we got the deal, and didn't finish it until the album was supposed to be handed in. If we had just used that hook that Chris came up with from the beginning, we definitely would have had a lot less gray hairs [*laughs*].

JUSSUMMEN

Skoob: I liked the style on that one. It's different from everything else. There wasn't a lot of 'iggity' in that song. The beat was lovely. It actually had a different beat originally, before Chris came up with that [final] one. The original was a little less spacey and it didn't have as much bang to it. With all the TV stuff we talked about [lyrics on the song reference everything from the Thundercats cartoon to *All My Children*], it was just a different approach to get my point across. It was stuff that people could relate to, and they'd chuckle about it as well.

Dray: Instead of just saying, "I'm the best MC," we were more about putting some adjectives in there and being creative with it. Like: "Fuck *what* he's saying. It's the *way* he says it." So we had a lot of TV references thrown in that song with everything else we were rhyming about, whether they related or not. It was just a part of the way we rhymed. Gunplay rhymes weren't big then; talking about ice wasn't big. It was always just braggadocious. That's where rap came from.

THEY WANT EFX

Skoob: We did that track with a cat named Kevin Birdsong. He sent me the beat but I didn't like the way he looped it.

Dray: That was the first single, and we were still in Virginia at school when we did that. I remember we loved that sample, but the loop was too long. So we took the record [James Brown's "Blind Man Can See It"] to the studio and looped it up ourselves. For whatever reason, Chris and Derek couldn't be there. What we did was pretty simple, 'cause I'm no producer. We just told the engineer: "Loop that part right there." That song got leaked to the streets before it was out on wax and the people at the label were really pissed. I was in a rent-a-car coming from Jersey and I heard [radio station] Hot 97 or Kiss, I can't remember which one, doing it as a Pump It or Dump It. They played the song, and the people dumped it! So I was like: "Oh, shit, it's over for us." Slowly but surely, though, we started hearing that people were digging it, so the label hurried up the production [of the album]. That was probably January or February 1992. The single ended up coming out a month before the album.

LOOSEYS

Dray: Yeah, that was a pretty fucked-up concept [telling different "I crapped my pants" stories]. But it shows that we weren't afraid to have fun.

If you're going to talk about going to the bathroom, why not make it funny? Would we ever do a song like that again? I doubt it. But Ice Cube and them did that song about going to the clinic [presumably referring to Ice Cube's "Look Who's Burnin'," from 1991's *Death Certificate*], so what we was doing wasn't *that* far out.

DUM DUMS

Dray: That song was definitely more mature than other tracks because you could follow what we were saying. It was a story. We did that later in the album, and we were growing up, thinking of concepts. It was more serious to us towards the end [of the album recording process]. We were growing out of the "bump figgedy bump" phase already.

Skoob: Listening to the groups we grew up influenced by, we were always well-rounded, and we never wanted to make every song into a party song. It was important for us to tell stories and use actual topics sometimes, not just bounce around.

EAST COAST

Dray: We were impressed by Ice Cube and N.W.A., and we wanted to show how *we* do it. We were like: "Damn, y'all are impressing us, so let us impress *you* now." We were fans and students of West Coast rap, so it definitely wasn't a dis.

IF ONLY

Dray: There are some DJ cuts on there. DJ Dice became our DJ, but he wasn't at that point. On that track it was either Dice or DJ Scratch [from EPMD]. I can't remember which one. On the road, Scratch might have done one show with us, and Redman used to DJ for us a lot of the time too.

BROOKLYN TO T-NECK

Dray: That definitely has some EPMD flavor on there, although they didn't have anything to do with it. I do distinctly remember that Chris and Derek wanted to impress Erick [Sermon] and show him that they could do stuff in his kind of frame [style]. So that's how that one came about.

KLAP YA HANDZ

Dray: We did that one with another producer from Brooklyn that Skoob knew, and it was on one of our early demos. That's the song that we performed at the talent show Erick and Parrish were judging.

STRAIGHT OUT THE SEWER

Dray: I don't remember the first song we recorded, but that was definitely the last one. We were in the studio, we were high, and we were tired because it was an early-morning session. And it just started coming out like that [*sings chorus*]—I don't know exactly why it was the sewer. Probably just an early-morning haze, some dribble-drabble on the mic. But Chris and us, we felt like we was coming from the underground, and the sewer was definitely, literally, under the ground. So there you go.

DE LA SOUL
3 Feet High and Rising

(Tommy Boy Records, 1989)

Nineteen eighty-nine was a hugely transitional year for hip-hop. With strong albums by artists like Public Enemy, Boogie Down Productions, N.W.A., and various Juice Crew members, things were beginning to break wide open. And in that crucial year there was no album more unique, groundbreaking, and important to the game than De La Soul's debut. Three Long Island teenagers—Posdnuos (Kelvin Mercer), Trugoy (David Jolicoeur, now going by Dave instead of Trugoy), and DJ Maseo (Vincent Mason)—and their wily, open-eared producer Prince Paul (Paul Huston) blew a lot of minds before the decade came to a close.

"I still stand in amazement at how timeless that album feels," says Pos. "It was a capsule of our innocence," adds Dave, continuing, "I can hear four individuals who didn't give a damn about the rules and just went in and had a good time." Tommy Boy founder and owner Tom Silverman agrees: "That album is so important because it threw out the rulebook. At the time, hip-hop was starting to define itself as being one thing, with all the bragging, the way people dressed, even the sound. These guys said: 'No, you don't have to sound like that.' They were the start of the third generation of hip-hop."

Although born in Brooklyn (Dave and Maseo) and the Bronx (Pos), all three De La members were raised through their high school years in Amityville, Long Island, about twenty miles to the east of New York City's five boroughs. Being close enough to have contact with hip-hop as it burgeoned, but also far enough away from the urban congestion and stress, they agree that their geographical situation made all the difference. "Being where we were, there was just more room for you to try different things," explains Pos. "It's a different mind state. In LI you had your own four walls that weren't attached to anyone else's four walls. There wasn't the city congestion." "Hip-hop was something that we had the opportunity to digest from afar," says Dave. "If we had all grown up for all our years in the Bronx, De La Soul definitely wouldn't have been the same."

Dave and Pos first hooked up together in a local Amityville group called Easy Street around 1985. Neither of them were up front as MCs: Pos DJed (as DJ Soundsop—Posdnuos is that name reversed) and Dave (going by Jude, his middle name) beatboxed. "I was in tenth grade and Dave was in eleventh," Pos recalls. The group didn't last long, but it cemented the artistic partnership between Pos and Dave. "Even back then, me and Dave knew that regardless of what happened, we'd still be working together," says Pos. Dave remembers: "Pos and I clicked personally, and we were more serious than the other guys in that group, so we broke with Easy Street and got down with Charlie Rock, who was a good friend of mine. We didn't have a name—we were just starting to put music and concepts together."

Charlie was a well-known DJ in town, and Dave and Pos learned a great deal from him. More important for their future, though, Charlie brought someone else into the fold: DJ Maseo. Maseo was a more recent Amityville transplant, having moved from Brooklyn about two years earlier. Even within that short time, he had made a name as one of the best DJs in town. Charlie, who was busy on the party circuit, saw the chemistry that Mase had with the two ex–Easy Streeters, and soon enough the De La Soul trio was set in stone. "By 1986, De La Soul was in place," says Pos. "We had performed at high school functions and people around town were starting to know the name a little bit."

The final piece of the puzzle was just as important: Amityville's most popular DJ and a budding producer at the time, Prince Paul. Aside from his local rep, Paul—who was one year older than Dave—was also known for being part of the groundbreaking hip-hop band Stetsasonic. "Paul did a lot of house parties around the way and was a great battle DJ," says Pos. "But I never even knew that he produced. I just knew that he DJed a lot and that Stetsasonic were incredible."

"I knew those guys from around the [high] school, but I didn't know them as De La Soul," says Paul, of their first official introduction. "The one I really knew was Maseo, because he had a big family in Amityville and I saw him at a lot of parties. I first worked with Mase in '86 or maybe early '87, when I did some programming for a single by this guy that Mase was DJing for, Gangster B.

"After that Gangster B thing, Mase said to me: 'Hey, I have a *real* group that I DJ for, called De La Soul,' " remembers Paul. "And he gave me their demo and asked if I had any thoughts about what could be added. That demo was a rough sketch of the song 'Plug Tunin',' and I really liked it. I did a two-tape-decks thing where I overdubbed some beats and added other things to what they had done originally. Then Mase brought Pos and Dave over and I recognized them immediately. I was like: 'Wait . . . you rhyme?' [*Laughs.*] And eventually I realized that they were even nerdier than I was, which was amazing."

Paul did have dreams of producing, but he wasn't getting heard on that front in Stet, who were chiefly produced by the group's leader, Daddy-O. When Paul heard De La's rough demos, a lightbulb flashed. Paul's budding genius behind the boards was just waiting to be unleashed, and he put it to work in his role as "mentor." As Dave says, "Prior to Paul even becoming involved, we had already made songs like 'Potholes in My Lawn' and 'Plug Tunin'.' When Paul came on, he just added on to what we already had. Paul could really stretch records out. We'd let him add just one more thing, and it was always the cherry on top. There was never a time when Paul didn't make a song better, where he didn't find exactly what was missing."

"With Stetsasonic, a lot of the ideas I had for production were just too juvenile for them, since they were more serious," explains Paul. "De La was more my age, more my style. And on that first De La record, it was a situation where I felt in total control for maybe the first time. So the next thing in the plan was all about how we could get a real demo recorded. We put our money together and went into Calliope [Studios, in Manhattan]. The whole goal was to jump right over the homemade four-track stuff and do it for real, then shop it. I definitely felt *that* strongly about what they were doing."

Paul and the trio worked on a three-track demo including the songs "Plug Tunin'," "Freedom of Speak," and "De La Games" [which would eventually turn into "Daisy Age"] in 1987, and brought De La through a bidding war and into the arms of Tommy Boy Records. "We had three songs and—literally—a book full of ideas," Dave says.

"Daddy-O [from Stet] and us were both shopping our stuff at the same time, but the labels were having more interest in De La than in Daddy's stuff," recalls Pos. "That's when Daddy-O started to come more on board with De La. It was all pretty surprising—we couldn't believe it. Pretty much anyplace that Paul and Daddy-O took our demo to was interested in giving us a deal." Dave says: "We went with Tommy Boy just for the comfort of knowing that Prince Paul was there [as part of Stetsasonic], and the enthusiasm was also a bit greater there as well. [Tommy Boy second-in-command] Monica Lynch saw our vision and was down for it. Tommy Boy gave us a lot of love from the start, and gave us room to do whatever we chose to, creatively."

"I don't want to dis Daddy-O, but I think he got a lot of credit for taking the group to Tommy Boy, and that's not the whole story," says Paul. "In reality, the guy who actually convinced me to take them to the label was a guy named Rodd Houston, who worked there. He was the guy who pushed us to take Tommy Boy seriously. I really didn't want them to go there at first. In the end it was cool, though. They let us experiment and they trusted us."

Dante Ross, aka "Dante the Scrubb" (as he was referred to by the group; he was also made famous in the album's "liner notes" cartoon, where he is portrayed as a featherless duck), who was "production supervisor" for the album, also remembers his first encounter with De La's music: "I had just had my interview at Tommy Boy to do A&R for them, thanks to Daddy-O, who got me in there. I was there in the office and Monica Lynch mentioned that there was a new group that Prince Paul was producing. I knew Paul, but I had never heard of De La Soul, so Mo [Monica] played it for me and I loved it. She said: 'That's good, because we just signed them.' And once I started, she was like: 'De La is your first project, so get busy.' I thought De La were the best thing that I had heard since Slick Rick. Rick was the only thing that I could equate it with, because it was quirky like that."

The group signed with Tommy Boy in the fall of 1987, a couple months after Pos had graduated high school (he was already enrolled in Five Towns College in Dix Hills, Long Island, where Prince Paul also took classes), and, as Pos says, "started work right away." Their first single, "Plug Tunin'," was released early in 1988, followed by "Potholes in My Lawn" a couple months later. Both singles did well, and Tommy Boy green-lighted them for a full album. "After the second single ["Potholes"] did well, we booked Calliope Studios for four to five days a week for maybe two months," says Ross. "They basically made that record in the studio because they didn't own their own equipment yet, so they couldn't do much at home except brainstorm ideas."

"The album didn't take that long to record because a lot of the ideas were already gathered in our minds, even before we got signed" says Pos. According to Tom Silverman, their recording budget was twenty-eight thousand dollars, which included all recording costs, sample clearance fees, and their own advances. "They got lower advances," says Tom Silverman, "but after

De La Soul (left to right: Pos, Maseo, Dave/Trugoy)
in New York, 1996.

the album blew up they got paid massive royalty checks. They bought houses for all of their parents after that."

"Whatever idea was brought to the table, we'd all just expound on it," says Dave. "It didn't matter who brought it. It could have been us four, it could have been my sister. It was all about enjoying music and enjoying creating more music." Dave adds, about production roles on the album (Paul is listed as producer and De La Soul as co-producer): "I didn't have a concept of what a producer was until I learned more about the game. The way I was introduced to production was with what we did. From the start, with us, it was like every man puts in their ten cents, and let's make this into a dollar."

Many times the unexpected turned into fodder for whole songs. "Prince Paul taught us that you need to leave open the surprise of a mistake, because it could turn around and be great," recalls Pos. "Paul's a genius that way. He's not afraid to scrap a record and start from scratch and try something else totally different. A lot of ideas came from us just joking around. I'd crack a joke and next thing you know we're doing a game show. We learned, mostly from Paul, that you don't always need to map things out. You can make mistakes. And the zaniness of the album, overall, definitely came from Paul."

"There are definitely a lot of mistakes on that album, and that's okay," Paul explains. "Because of the way I was sometimes treated in Stetsasonic, not being fully trusted to work out my own ideas, I never wanted to treat anyone else that way. So it was like: 'Whatever y'all want to do, let's just try it. We can always erase it.'"

And although Paul was the group's "mentor," he had a dirty little secret that he never let on about. He explains, with a smirk, "All those early sessions were literally the blind leading the blind. But I never let those guys know that I didn't really know what I was doing, because I thought that would make them more comfortable. My job was to take whatever they wanted to do and make it a reality. I'd be like: 'Not a problem!' and then I'd turn around and say: 'Hmm, how do I do *that*?' [*Laughs.*] In the process of figuring everything out, it just made all those sessions that much more fun. Those *3 Feet High* sessions are still probably the best recording experiences that I've ever had."

"Making that record was just a magical time for everybody involved," recalls Dante Ross. "The list of people who came by the studio when they were making tracks was insane. Biz Markie, the Beatnuts, the Jungle Brothers, Ultramagnetic, even Melle Mel. Hip-hop was a smaller, tighter community back then, and everybody didn't know everything yet. Hip-hop was still the next big thing—it wasn't bona fide yet. I can't remember one iota of bad vibes anywhere when that album was being made."

After their studio lockdown, De La and their mentor had something amazing to give to the world: *3 Feet High and Rising*. Dave recalls: "I would say that we probably had ideas for six or seven more songs than actually made the album, too. We probably created twenty-eight or thirty altogether. There are a lot of songs that have never been released—they're still sitting on tape."

"The record was done at the start of the third quarter [fall] of 1988, and we waited until the winter [early 1989] to put it out," Ross recalls. "That was a genius move, because during the fourth quarter [of 1988] we wouldn't have gotten rack space or as much airplay."

Critically acclaimed across the board and eventually platinum-bound, the album was a phenomenon to say the least. Samples from early Johnny Cash songs to well-known Hall & Oates tracks informed the musical landscape they created, and lyrically they traded between lines that were sometimes serious and sometimes so abstract that they didn't make a whole lot of sense to people outside the group. "Maybe it was our warped character, but we didn't really want people to understand it all," chuckles Dave. "Sometimes we were trying to make it difficult, because it would make people always want to know more."

"I knew that the album was either going to do absolutely nothing or it was going to be really, really big," Tom Silverman recalls. "It was just so different that it couldn't possibly land anywhere in the middle. I loved it when I heard all the tracks, and when they did the *final* version, when they put all the interstitial pieces in, it made it even more of a masterpiece."

There was one major turning point once *3 Feet High and Rising* was released, and it came to be both a blessing and a curse for the group: the smash single "Me Myself and I." "Originally the attention on the album, which was a lot, was from press and college radio, which will only give you so many sales," explains Silverman. "Without 'Me Myself and I' it's very clear that the album wouldn't have done more than one hundred thousand units, instead of the platinum-plus that it achieved. We needed a focal-point single for radio, and that song was it. We needed a spoonful of sugar to help the medicine go down."

According to Dave and Pos, group members eventually came to dislike not only the "Me Myself and I" single but also the hippie image that they had inherited, partially because of the way that they were sold to America. "To call them hippies wasn't overly accurate, really," says Silverman. "But it was an easy way to explain to people why they were different."

"I think [depicting De La as hippies] was an incorrect way to portray them, and I also think they did overreact a bit," says Paul. "Tommy Boy definitely pushed the hippie thing, especially with the album cover. The guys [in De La] always dressed differently, and there was a bit of a sixties vibe, so I see why Tommy Boy did what they did with the marketing. But it was hard when the guys had gigs, because people would always test them. I didn't go on the road with them, so I'd get calls like: 'De La just beat up some guy in Alabama!' They got kicked off of tours because they'd house people who gave them shit about their image."

In short, there was a reason why their second album was called *De La Soul Is Dead.* "We were really sick of all the hype after a while," explains Pos. "When we handed in the album to the label, we were already elsewhere musically. And *3 Feet High* was in the marketplace for so long. We were really just tired of it, and that's why we reacted like that."

The group, of course, still looks back fondly on the album. "*3 Feet High* is art to its fullest," says Dave. "It's the record that I'm most proud of." And Pos beams, "That album was just a great stepping stone for us, and I'm so happy to know that someplace in our career we made something that was so timeless and had such innocence."

"When De La Soul came in the game, there was just a changing of the guard, and they knew it," says Ross. "KRS-One had started it, because Run-DMC was old at that point—they weren't as relevant. The gold chains and the macho shit just wasn't all that anymore. Lyricism and the music was the thing. People had stepped up, and no one stepped up more than De La and Paul at that time."

"We were definitely amazed at how well the album sold, and how quickly," says Paul. "I would always be a good coach and tell them that I was sure it would go gold, but did we know it would be huge? No way. That was the nicest surprise of all. To do something so original and have it be so well received."

"Aside from the U.S., that album was also important because it was the first hit hip-hop album on the international scene," Silverman says. "It was the first album to do more than five hundred thousand units in Europe, way more than even Run-DMC. Musically it was just more accessible to people over there who were rock 'n' roll fans. It just wasn't seen as a dark, American rap record."

Prince Paul gets the final word, stating, "That was just an album of total sincerity. We went in there to have fun and experiment, and with De La, we could literally do *anything*. I hate to bring religion into it, but if there was ever a sign of the existence of God, De La Soul would be that proof to me. I mean, how perfect was it to put all of us together? I've never had such a perfect fit in any other production situation. We had a mutual respect for each other, and after we'd finish tracks, we'd just look at each other in awe."

TRACKS

INTRO

Pos: The game show concept was one of the last things we did, during the mixing phase. I think Paul might have come up with the idea. [Game show announcer] Al Watts was just one of the engineers where we were mixing. We were doing skits back when we used to make tapes back at the crib, before we even met Paul. So we just fell right into that.

THE MAGIC NUMBER

Pos: The name of the album came from a Johnny Cash tune called "Five Feet High and Rising," which we [sampled], when it says, "Three feet high and rising" right at the very end of that track. Dave's father had that record.

CHANGE IN SPEAK

Dave: That was the album version of "Freedom of Speak," which was the B-side to our first single ["Plug Tunin' "]. It was definitely a declaration about us, like, "We've landed, we're here." But it wasn't boasting, like, "We're the shit." It was more about letting people know that there's room for a change, and this is what we're all about.

Pos: The music on there was from a Mad Lads record, and then we used that Cymande ["Bra"] thing in there. I pretty much put that song together, I guess. We weren't as aware as it might have seemed about what ground we were breaking lyrically.

Pos: That was on our second single, and we used another 45 from my father's collection on there. I looped it up on a pause-tape. That single was really more of a double A-side, with "Potholes in My Lawn" on the other side. We didn't want "Potholes" on a single alone, because we thought it was too slow. But we did the video for "Potholes."

Dave: Derwin [mentioned in the song] is a friend of ours who we used to crack on because he never got no girls. He loved the song, of course. It put him on the map [*laughs*].

GHETTO THANG

Dave: Being more serious, like we were on that song, was just part of what we've always done. We've always touched on serious topics here and there, whether it's [later songs like] "Millie Pulled a Pistol on Santa" or "Baby Phat," as much as people might not think of those as serious records. In the midst of the fun, we always talk about important stuff as well.

TRANSMITTING LIVE FROM MARS

Dave: That's the one that the Turtles sued us for. It startled us at the time, because we were clueless about how severe it could get. The attacks [lawsuits], especially the Turtles one, started coming after the record went gold. Steely Dan sued us too.

Tom Silverman: That Turtles suit cost Tommy Boy about a hundred thousand dollars total, and De La had to bear about fifty thousand of that amount. We had some "errors and omissions" insurance which helped for some of it. The problem was that although we cleared thirty-five samples on the album, the Turtles one wasn't on the list that the group gave us, because it was one of the interstitial pieces. It wasn't even a real song, just an interlude. That was a bad situation, and demoralizing.

Prince Paul: We're still going through sample hassles with that album to this day. When we finished the album we gave Tommy Boy all the samples and they just cleared the ones [on songs that] they thought would be popular. I'm not surprised it didn't get cleared. When the lawsuit came, it didn't bother me too much because I hadn't made any money on the record yet anyways, and with Stet I wasn't used to making money on records. So it didn't come out of my pocket!

TAKE IT OFF

Prince Paul: I love that song! We'd always bust on corny people, so we made a song about it. They had the hook and there were a million people in the studio, so that became a million people in the [vocal] booth. I think all the things they talked about on there were written down, and we just went down the line.

Dave: Lyrically on that track it was like, "Clear the way, let's gravitate towards some newer things, let's evolve, let's turn the soil over."

TREAD WATER

Dave: When I heard the music, I just thought of that concept. A story line with animals just strolling down the line. And I used that happy-go-lucky rhyme style.

POTHOLES IN MY LAWN

Dante Ross: That second single did really well—everyone in New York played it. After that it was definitely a lock that people were really digging the group, so we knew we were on to something.

Tom Silverman: We did an eight-hundred-dollar video for that song. It was done with a handheld 8mm camera, and they were on these motorized scooters.

Pos: That was another single off the record. It sampled Hall & Oates's "I Can't Go for That." We never met them [Hall & Oates], but I was like, "Yo, if you need me to come and explain it to them, I will," in case they had trouble clearing it. Because I was just a fan of theirs. "Say No Go" was one of my favorite records on the album. I put most of that together, and Paul and Mase added some things.

Dante Ross: I love Hall & Oates. They used that sample because they felt it, not because they were trying to blow up. The way it was done was really creative.

PLUG TUNIN' (LAST CHANCE TO COMPREHEND)

Pos: "Plug Tunin' " was on our three-song demo that we shopped to labels, and it became our first single. The arrangement was always the same—Paul added the Liberace record on top. With that track, we had always had the rhymes and the routine. I had found the music for the main part from an old 45 of my father's, I paused it up on a tape [prepared it ahead of time as a pause-tape], and had my rhyme and the chorus already mapped out. We took it to Mase and he put the drum pattern to it. When Paul heard it and we decided to deal with him, I was really concerned with what he was going to add to it. But he added the "Night Themes" beat [Manzel's "Midnight Theme"], the main looped beat that Cypress Hill used for "How I Could Just Kill a Man." He added that James Brown cut, the Billy Joel piano. Definitely the things he added to it made it 120 percent better than what we did.

Prince Paul: I added the Liberace record on there. We were mixing at a place called Island Media, in Long Island, and there was a Liberace cassette in there, so of course we giggled about it and wanted to see what was on it. We thought that intro was hilarious, so we just threw it on the beginning of the song. Like everything else we did, there wasn't much rhyme or reason to it. And we never got sued by Liberace, thankfully.

Dave: We didn't always know that "Plug Tunin' " would be our first single. It's the first thing we did and it was almost all we had when we got signed. Tommy Boy was so excited about it that they just wanted it *out*. It was an era when groups were still doing singles, so an album wasn't even talked about at that point.

Dante Ross: That first single took off right away. I walked it right over to [Kiss FM DJ] Red Alert once I had it, and he played it that night. De La met the Jungle Brothers through Red [who was group member Mike G's uncle]. After that single did so well, Tommy Boy exercised the option to do the second single, which was "Potholes in My Lawn."

BUDDY *Featuring the Jungle Brothers and Q-Tip*

Dave: I recall just being in Mase's den, sampling something on a little keyboard, and I started doing that "meanie meanie meanie meanie meanie" thing. Then we just thought of the word *buddy* instead of the word *body*. We didn't get specific about what we loved on a woman, so we just kept it vague. Then we was in the studio and just wanted to invite some people on there. The closest people to what we was doing at the time was the Jungle Brothers and Tribe [Called Quest]. And Latifah [heard on the twelve-inch remix] was a labelmate on Tommy Boy. It just became a family affair.

Prince Paul: That video was definitely the most fun because everybody was in it. All the people who helped with the vibe of that album got to be on there, and I definitely loved that.

I CAN DO ANYTHING (DELACRATIC)

Dave: That's Wize of Stetsasonic on beatbox there. I don't know why I didn't do it. [*Dave started out as a beatboxer.*] I was probably too shy.

Pos: That song was the second to last record we made for the album. After the first two singles, we realized we had to put "Me Myself and I" out. We were like, "It ain't my favorite song, but people seem to be gravitating towards it, and Tommy Boy could get a lot of things done with this song. So let's do it." We put it pretty far back in the album sequence, though.

Dave: When Mase played the track, I came up with what the song would be about right away. I actually wrote Pos's first eight bars. The vibe was just like, "I'm being me. Enjoy the music. If you like it, then don't worry about how I'm dressed."

Tom Silverman: I loved that song when I first heard it, but I can't even say that I knew it would be such a huge hit. I think that video pretty much encapsulates the entire message of that whole album. The anti-gold-chain sentiment. Maseo claims responsibility for that record being made. Paul didn't even want it on the album. It was so commercial, and they didn't want anything that obvious. Using that [P-Funk] "Knee Deep" sample on that track really helped De La Soul get over on the West Coast when not many East Coast groups were getting over back then.

Prince Paul: I always liked that song! Dave and Pos were the ones who didn't like it. Mase came up with the "Knee Deep" sample and I thought it was a great idea, so we put it all together. Pos and Dave came up with using the rhyme style from [the Jungle Brothers' song] "Black Is Black." So we really did it to please Tommy Boy, more or less, by using a popular loop. But I liked that song—Mase and I both loved it. After all that work, if we just had to do a radio record to get the album put out, then that was an easy decision.

Pos: I just realized, talking to you, that that song was the last track we did for the record. For a long time I was thinking it was "Me Myself and I." Right when ["Me Myself and I"] was done I went back and tried to put that together because I was like, "Yo, we don't have nothing, in my mind, that sounds 'street' or whatever. We got all these crazy-ass songs that we love, but is anyone gonna really *like* any of this?"

DIGABLE PLANETS

Reachin' (A New Refutation of Time and Space)

(Pendulum/Elektra, 1993)

If we had tried to make that album like it ended up, it wouldn't have worked," postulates producer and MC Ishmael Butler (aka Butterfly, aka Cherrywine) of the Digable Planets. "The best results always happen when things just go down instinctively."

Instinct definitely played a part in the Digable story, and fate may have stepped in as well. In many ways it's a miracle that the group ever came together in the first place, since each member of the trio—which also included MCs Doodlebug (Craig Irving, aka Cee Knowledge) and Ladybug (Mary Ann Vieira, aka Ladybug Mecca)—came from a different city. But the Digable Planets did come together, and they blew up on the strength of their originality and laid-back jazz cool.

The first part of the Digable puzzle starts with Butler. Raised in Seattle's Central District, he wasn't part of the hustle and bustle of industry centers like New York and L.A. He recalls: "I pretty much started writing raps when I first heard 'Rapper's Delight' [by the Sugarhill Gang]. Morning, during school, after school, at night. When I was in tenth grade I got more serious and formed a group with some other guys in town, and we'd perform at school talent shows or at the local Boys' Club. There was rap everywhere in Seattle back then. Sir Mix-A-Lot was really big in town when I was younger. He was in these housing projects over on Yesler [Way], and he'd DJ at the Boys' Club where I played basketball. We had a good time back then, bumping Ice-T and Too $hort tapes and all that West Coast stuff. My parents were divorced and my dad was in New York all the time, so I'd go and visit him most summers. From that, I had a proper mix of East and West Coast shit."

Attending the University of Massachusetts at Amherst on a basketball scholarship, Butler got his first taste at creating hip-hop in the dorms. He recalls: "I never made tracks before I got to college because I just never had access to equipment. But in my second semester freshman year, a guy in my dorm had a keyboard and a ministudio, so he let me get on there and I started putting beats together." For better or worse, his college days were short-lived. "I wanted to play basketball, but I just didn't have the discipline to keep my grades up," he explains.

After leaving the bucolic confines of Amherst, Butler made his way to hip-hop's epicenter: New York City. He had no money and no concrete plan, but that wasn't going to stop him. "I always knew how to hustle," says Butler, "and if I had a plan, I knew I could use my street smarts to survive. My dad's girlfriend's mother lived in New York and ran a boarding house. She had an open room, so I got a job and was staying in Brooklyn."

He might not have been living the high life, but he was soaking in all the music he could and making baby-step power moves, which included winning an internship at one of the best indie labels of the era: Sleeping Bag Records. "There was just so much amazing stuff going on over there at the time," he recalls. "EPMD, Nice & Smooth, Mantronix. I was working in the mail room, handing out flyers, running errands, doing whatever needed to be done. I was there simply to learn how to make a record, and that was it."

During 1989 and 1990 he started thinking more seriously about making his own music. At the time one album in particular, De La Soul's *3 Feet High and Rising,* pushed him over the edge. "When that came out, it sparked something in me," says Butler. "Coming up, my dad was really into avant-garde jazz, so from a musical standpoint I always knew that you could be original and succeed. Then De La came along, and a lot of stuff I was thinking about starting adding up very quickly."

Butler's father, Reginald Butler, was a Black Panther and a history professor who was originally from Philadelphia. "Jazz was big there when he was younger," says the younger Butler. "It was the hip-hop of his day. He was more on the revolutionary tip, too, so he loved Sun Ra, Albert Ayler, Coltrane, Andrew Hill. Any revolutionary music. When I was young, that's the music that I heard. My dad was down with a lot of hard-core guys. Black Panthers, gangsters. People who were well-rounded, who were from the street but who were down with communist principles." In addition to the obvious influence of jazz music to Digable's future sound, George Clinton had a lot of sway. Butler says: "My uncles were big P-Funk fans. That's where I got a lot of the space and planetary stuff."

Even in the earliest plans for the group, Butler imagined Digable group members as insects. "They work together for the good of the colony," he explains. "It was a socialist, communist thing that I was talking about. Nobody really got what I was doing with Digable before it became a hit. It wasn't a joke, but it wasn't far from funny to a lot of people. Even if they were digging it back then, they wouldn't admit it." Doodlebug recalls: "I was confident in the concept and how original it was—I just didn't know how the rap world would take it. But, as we learned, sometimes it's good to be an outcast."

Like Butler, Craig Irving (Doodlebug) took a roundabout way to see his rap dreams realized through Digable Planets. He recounts: "I'm from North Philly, a section called West Oak Lane, around Mt. Airy, uptown. And I fell in love with DJing. That was my first foray into the hip-hop world. I had a paper route and I'd go and buy 45s with the money I made, so I'd DJ all my junior-high parties. I used to run home and grab my mom's turntable and records before she got home from work."

DJing was fulfilling, but celebrity appeal turned Irving's attention to rhymes. He says: "Once I got to high school, the rappers were getting the honeys at that point, so I started writing rhymes. And by the time I got to college, I was all about rapping. At first I was influenced a lot by local guys like the Fresh Prince (Will Smith), MC Parry P, and the Grandmasters of Funk. I was MC Cosmic C back then, because I was always influenced by outer space and cosmic shit."

Irving attended Howard University in D.C. for two years, and added "show promoter" to his résumé, bringing acts like Salt 'N Pepa and Just Ice to campus. "My major was partying," he laughs. "I was really being stupid. I was even on academic probation for a while." Back then, Irving also became the first member of Digable Planets to release anything on wax: DJ Trouble Trev and Cosmic Cool's "Here Comes Trouble" (on Dynasty Records), which came out in 1989. Irving was Cosmic Cool. "I've still got the record downstairs—it's funny as shit [laughs]."

The final Digable Planets member came into the mix during Irving's years in D.C. He says: "I first met Ladybug when she was a sophomore in high school, around 1987. She was from Silver Spring, Maryland, and her crew would come to some of our parties. They had a little dance group, and whenever a group like Leaders of the New School would come to D.C., they would use her crew as backup dancers." Eventually Irving and Ladybug became a couple.

After his money ran out in D.C., Irving headed home to Philly, where he met Butler. "His grandmother lived right around the corner from my grandmother's place, in West Oak Lane," Irving explains. "This girl I was dating was best friends with this girl that he was dating. We went on a double date once and he and I had so much in common that we weren't even talking to our girls [*laughs*]. We exchanged numbers and whenever we were both in Philly, we'd hang out. He was living in New York back then, interning at Sleeping Bag. But he'd come to Philly and that was the magnetic force that ended up bringing us all together."

"Me and [Irving] would go to New York, Philly, D.C., and Baltimore, all the big parties on the East Coast, but not together," recalls Butler. "And we'd just keep running into each other. He was real fly, always dressed well, with cool dreads. It just kept happening and we developed a rapport. I knew what he was doing with all the parties he was promoting, but I always kept kind of quiet about what I was doing." At the time, Irving was in a Philly group called Dread Poets Society. "It was a Native Tongues vibe," Irving says. "It wasn't on a level of what Butterfly was doing, but it was similar."

Although the three members had connected at the time, the earliest incarnation of Digable Planets did not involve Irving or Ladybug. Butler recalls: "Early on, I was saying that Digable was a group, even though it was just me for a while. I did my demo at a guy's studio in Queens who I knew from Sleeping Bag. There were nine songs and it was just me on vocals." After briefly working as Digable Planets with an MC named Katrina Lust and Butler's friend Michael Gaber Keaton, Butler was back on the hunt for the right people to complete the crew. "I intended for the original two members to be in the group, but it just never happened, so they went their respective ways and I stayed." Craig says of the pre-signed days: "There was definitely a little buzz on the group. Right before [Ladybug and I] became the new members of the group, the old group did a couple of live shows and they had some people talking."

Butler continued to perform in New York and to work on his demo, even though his imaginary band was still just that. Labels called and demos were sent (including one to Pendulum in 1989, two years before the group was signed). The final demo that got them the deal was actually a combination of work that Butler had done on his own and some of Craig's work with Dread Poets Society. One DPS song on the demo actually included the basic music for the group's future smash hit "Rebirth of Slick."

By 1989, Irving and Butler began working on music together at Irving's grandmother's house in Philly. "Ladybug would be quietly writing rhymes while we'd be rehearsing," Irving recalls. "And eventually we prodded her to let us hear what she was doing, and after four or five tries, she gave us a

sample. We was like: 'Oh shit! She's got skills!' Up until then it was looking more like a duo with me and Ishmael. But by the time we started recording in real studios, Ladybug was in the group."

Butler recalls: "In 1991, after a lot of recording and shopping I did on my
own, Pendulum Records was interested and they said, 'Okay, we want to
see the group.' But I still didn't have a group. I ran into [Doodlebug] one
time at the mall [in Philly] and I told him about Pendulum. He probably
didn't take it that seriously, because everyone back then was trying to get a
record deal. I had always wanted to have a female in the group and Ladybug was dope, so I wanted to get her in the group too. She came up to New
York and we all did a showcase for Ruben Rodriguez [at Pendulum], and
that was it."

And so, after years with an on-again, off-again (and sometimes imaginary) group, the Digable Planets were finally a reality. "I was definitely surprised when we got the deal," says Butler. "It's all very surreal when it's
going down, because even when you get the deal you still never know what
will happen. I think the whole budget we got from Pendulum was thirty
thousand dollars. But then again, we recouped pretty quickly." Irving says:
"Basically, Pendulum's whole idea was for us to be a college group, and that
was about it." They were signed by early '92 and started recording right
away.

Irving recalls: "Once we connected with Pendulum, we needed new
songs for a production demo for the label. And Ishmael was like: 'Why
don't we use that one song you had?' He was talking about 'Skin Treatment.' I talked to the guys in Dread Poets and they didn't care. Obviously
they didn't know it was going to become a Grammy winner [*laughs*]! So we
put that together, along with another song called 'Brown Baby Funk.' "

The Digable Planets' sound—in the early-nineties demos and also as it
came to be in 1993's Grammy-winning form—was a potent mix of jazz cool
(and samples) and some of the more laid-back elements of funk get-downs.
If you were cynical you might have even thought they were just capitaliz-
ing on the jazz hip-hop trend of the time. But Butler claims that was far
from the real deal: "When it came to stuff I would sample, it was all about
resources, really, nothing more. We didn't have no money, even after the
deal got signed, so when it came time to go and sample records, I just went
and got the records that I had around me. And a lot of those were my dad's

shit, which was lots of jazz. The whole concept of 'We're a jazz group' didn't go down like that. Except that DJ Premier was a big influence, and he sampled a lot of jazz."

Irving adds: "When we got in the game, James Brown had gotten looped to the point where it was like: 'Is James Brown real, or does he only exist as something to sample and make a record out of?' When we came out, we tried to be as creative as possible, like De La Soul and A Tribe Called Quest and all them. That kind of stuff inspired us."

Irving continues: "In the early nineties we were college age, and back then communal living and socialist ideas made a lot of sense. It was some rebel shit. It just wasn't easy for a group like Digable in that era [the late eighties]. Ultramagnetic MCs was out and they were weird, but they were still a hardcore rap group. We were peace and love and we were supposed to be insects [laughs]! We were from the same 'hoods as a lot of rappers, but we went a different route with how we expressed ourselves. We was definitely more Daisy Age."

The group, still new to each other as a fully functioning trio, agreed that production work started with Butterfly. "On the first album I was pretty hands-on because I had pretty much developed our sound and most of those songs," Butler says. "The second album [1994's *Blowout Comb*] was more collaborative, musically."

"I brought more of a hardcore hip-hop thing to the table, a street influence," says Irving. "And Ladybug was from Brazil, so she brought an international mentality to the group. We all brought different things. There was a foundation and we would add and make the building what it was. But Ishmael was definitely the production supervisor, and we followed his lead. He was the Q-Tip of our group, and we allowed him to take the lead that first time around."

Irving remembers: "We had to come up with insect names, and I created Doodlebug because I was like: 'If I'm gonna be an insect, I'm gonna be a cool insect.' I remembered the movie *Cleopatra Jones,* and Antonio Fargas was Doodlebug. So I went with that. The original other guy in the group was called the Termite [laughs], but I wasn't going to take that one."

Lyrically, the group was a wide-ranging but certainly complementary mix. Butterfly's verses were sometimes cryptic and abstract, but always rooted in experiences he had or saw. Doodlebug tended to be more down-to-earth, since he had started out on the mic in his early days with a party and battle style. Ladybug was somewhere in between, adding an important strong female voice to the mix.

"I always loved Butterfly's style and I always dug what he was saying," says Irving. "Today you can spit somebody else's rhyme and get away with it, but back then you'd be a biter [i.e., a copycat] if you did that. Originality was serious back then. And I had never heard anyone rhyme like Butterfly did. One thing that I think was overlooked was that Butterfly's rhymes were rooted in the 'hood. It was just a smart way to say it and relate it. He definitely inspired me to get more eclectic with my own rhymes."

For the recording of most album tracks, the members of the group, who had all moved to Brooklyn (Irving and Butler were roommates) for the summer of 1992, headed out to Shane Faber's Sound Doctor studio in Montclair, New Jersey. Irving recalls: "We'd catch these dollar vans from New York to New Jersey, where the studio was above a dentist's office. It was a job for us. We'd get up early as shit in the morning and be there until six at night, then go back to Brooklyn and do it again the next day."

Faber and Mike Mangini engineered and co-produced the album. Butler recalls: "We found those guys just because we read all the names on some of our favorite records. They were very professional and I'm sure my ideas were pretty raw to them. They didn't come up with any concepts, but they just made things sound great. They were pros and that's just what we needed."

"It was just such a blessing to make a record," Butler says of *Reachin'*. "That's all I had thought about doing for years and years and it had finally happened. Just putting a record out was everything to me back then." But merely putting out a record wasn't all that happened to Digable Planets. The album's first single was the now classic "Rebirth of Slick (Cool Like Dat)," released in the fall of 1992 and blowing up in early 1993, when the album was released. *Reachin'* went gold, and the group won a Grammy in early 1994 for Best Rap Performance by a Duo or Group.

Despite the runaway success of the first single, Irving says, "People who went to our shows always knew the album cuts, the deeper ones—they sang all the words along with us. So I didn't ever really feel like our big hit defined us or held us back. And despite all the success, we never really hung out with mainstream cats. Whenever we weren't at an awards show or something, we'd be chilling with people who appreciated the vibe and the content of the album. People like Talib Kweli and Mos Def, back then, before they were known. Guys like them always kept us grounded."

Butler says: "The whole cool thing wasn't an act, but we never thought that we were bigger than anyone. We knew that success in the music business is an illusion, and no matter how abstract we might have been, all our music was from the 'hood. Because at no point in time when we were recording that album did any of us have any money. So that's where we were—in the 'hood."

"I think that whole album cost us thirty thousand dollars to make, maybe fifty thousand," says Irving. "People today get that for just one sixteen-bar verse. It still blows my mind to think about that."

TRACKS

PACIFICS (FROM THE SOUNDTRACK TO THE MOTION PICTURE *N.Y. IS RED HOT*)

Butterfly: When I was living out on Linden [Boulevard, in Brooklyn's Flatbush neighborhood], it was a neighborhood that was real wild. It was mostly West Indians, and it was like an open market out on the streets, all day and all night. On Sunday I'd get up early or be coming home late from a club and it would just be wild like that, just like the song says. That song was never on a soundtrack to anything, I was just trying to be creative with the title.

Doodlebug: That was Ishmael's idea and it's really a solo song for him. We're on it, but mostly just on the chorus.

WHERE I'M FROM

Doodlebug: That was the third single we put out off the album. It was a song that we put together back in the day when me and Ishmael were both in Philly. We found that KC & the Sunshine Band sample ["Ain't Nothing Wrong"] and thought it was hot, and we were all from different places, so the theme made a lot of sense. We both wrote our parts separately and really liked them, but we didn't record the song until we got the deal with Pendulum. Shane Faber helped us put it together, and we found this other jazz sample that was mad tight, and that was the remix of the song. Ladybug talks about "bandits" on there ["People think they canned it/Rap is not by bandits"], because when rap started getting real popular, musicians started hatin'. They was like: "Yo, this shit ain't real music, you're stealing our shit." Which is kind of true, but it wasn't like we was in ski masks, robbing people on the street. We were people that loved music and wanted to make music, but there weren't music programs in inner-city schools. Kids couldn't learn guitar or bass. All we had was records and turntables and we were creating our own sound.

Butterfly: It might seem like we were speaking about a specific place with each of our verses on that song, but we weren't. We were trying to talk about every place. Having a double meaning, a universal meaning. It was just trying to find commonality with everybody.

WHAT COOL BREEZES DO

Butterfly: When I say, "If they call it a fad, we just ignore it like it's pork" on that song, that was more about hip-hop than about the jazz hip-hop trend. At that time, even then, some people were still trying to say that hip-hop wasn't going to last, which was crazy.

Doodlebug: Oh yeah, about the "jazz fad" stuff. Using jazz was our backbone, that was what we were all about. So it was either you accepted it or you didn't. The jazz thing wasn't just about samples. We consciously wanted to build an album concept that was about the correlation of rap music and jazz culture, to put it all together. We wanted to do it in a jazz and bebop type of form. With something like Guru's *Jazzmatazz,* that was more of an album where he liked jazz, but I don't think he put the whole concept together.

TIME & SPACE (A NEW REFUTATION OF)

Butterfly: That song title was part of the title of the album. It came from [Argentine author] Jorge Luis Borges. I was reading a lot of his stuff at the time. He has a short story called "A New Refutation of Time and Space."

Everything he wrote was real metaphysical and circular, and things didn't always happen for any reason. Time and space are conceptual, and it can only relate to you as an individual. "Reachin' " in the album title probably just came from all those old jazz albums, how they were always, like, "Cookin'!" or "Smokin'!" We used it to talk about trying to get to a new place.

REBIRTH OF SLICK (COOL LIKE DAT)

Doodlebug: The original beat for that was off an old demo by my original group from Philly, Dread Poets Society, called "Skin Treatment." It had that Art Blakey sample [*he "replays" horns from Art Blakey's "Stretchin' " by singing lines*], the horns, and the bass. Once I started to become more involved with Digable, then it worked its way in that direction. With Dread Poets, we never went to a studio—it was all old homemade demos. Recording in studios costs money, and we didn't have any. I remember that the group didn't think "Rebirth of Slick" was going to be the hit. I think the label chose it as the first single and we went along with it. Any of the songs would have been fine with us. The single came out in September or October of 1992, and then Giant Step [a popular, jazz-informed dance club in New York, which later became a record label as well] got behind the single and that helped a lot. Maurice Bernstein [of Giant Step] was very helpful. Right before the end of the year, Ruben Rodriguez called us to the label to meet somebody, and that person was Rosie Perez. She chose the groups who would appear on *In Living Color* and we were like: "Oh, hell yeah!" So after Christmas break, we flew to L.A. and filmed that episode. When it aired [on January 3, 1993], [sales of the single] just went crazy. The album was released early in 1993 [February 9] and we started touring, and it was over after that. That song got to the point where it was just everywhere, on the radio every five seconds.

Butterfly: We actually thought the song "Brown Baby Funk" would be the hit, and that one didn't even make the album! We were definitely shocked when that song started blowing up. *In Living Color* is what pushed it over the edge.

Doodlebug: When we first won the Grammy in 1994, there was a bit of a backlash. The next day in the newspaper they interviewed other rappers and KRS-One dissed us. He thought a hardcore group should have won the Grammy. We were up against Dre and Snoop, Cypress Hill, Naughty by Nature. It was all the powerhouse groups of the time, and I loved all of those groups. When they called our name I just couldn't believe it. The backlash with KRS bothered me a bit, and it bothered Ladybug a lot. It was too bad, because I really respected KRS as a rapper. But then again, I was there at the Grammys, at the after party with Juliette Lewis, hanging out with Rosie Perez, so I wasn't that mad [*laughs*]!

Butterfly: There's no way I thought we'd beat Snoop and Dre [who were nominated for "Nuthin' but a 'G' Thang" off Dre's *Chronic* album]. I don't know how those decisions are made and maybe we got it because we were more friendly to the public. I think we had a good record, but for impact it wasn't bigger than Snoop and Dre, and it wasn't better than Cypress Hill either.

LAST OF THE SPIDDYOCKS

Butterfly: That was a term from when my dad was growing up, and it meant a real jazzhead type of person. You dressed a certain way and listened to a certain kind of music. It was just a type of socialite when he was young. I can't remember how we used those live players [trumpeter Steven Bernstein and bassist Alan Goldsher are credited] at the time. I think what I did was instead of clearing the Art Farmer [sample], I credited it to someone playing it live, so that I didn't have to pay for the sample. Back then, sample clearances was a motherfucker. I think that's why we didn't put the song "Brown Baby Funk" on the record, because it was a George Duke sample and they wanted some astronomical amount to clear it. I talk about classic jazz cats on there and the sadness of the drug abuse that a lot of them went through.

Doodlebug: At the time I was definitely going to more hip-hop shows than jazz shows. We went to Nuyorican [Poets Café] and Giant Step shows, but we weren't tight with the jazz world. Ishmael's father had the jazz hookups. He wasn't living in New York at the time, but he'd visit the studio and bring a famous jazz cat with him, or one of his friends, and they'd sit down and talk with us.

JIMMI DIGGIN CATS

Butterfly: With that, we originally had a sample of Jimi Hendrix talking about a cover tune, and he said: "We really dig the cats and we really dig this song," but we couldn't clear it. It was a live recording of him.

LA FEMME FÉTAL

Butterfly: My favorite vocal artist in the world is Jalil from the Last Poets, and obviously that style there is just a total bite of his style on [the 1975 Last Poets album and song] *Jazzoetry*. The concept of that song was just some personal shit. I was the only one on it because I think it was just complete when I did it. It didn't need anything else.

ESCAPISM (GETTIN' FREE)

Butterfly: The hook in there was originally supposed to be from [Parliament's] "P-Funk (Wants to Get Funked Up)," but we couldn't clear it.

APPOINTMENT AT THE FAT CLINIC

Doodlebug: I was supposed to rhyme on that song, but it was like school, and I didn't do my homework. I had been partying, having too much fun the night before, so I had had to think of something really quick and I was reading the liner notes to a [avant-garde jazz legend] Roland Kirk album. Basically, what I said on that song in my "announcement" was my interpretation and updating of those Kirk liner notes. I was rolling a joint on the record and looking at it and listening to the record and I said, "Damn, this shit is ill." After I finished my joint I did my version.

Doodlebug: That was another single and that one did really well too. We weren't worried about how it would do after the first single blew up. It was more like: "If they liked that, they'll like this too." The theme of that song was us being college weedheads, but we wanted to talk about it using music as a metaphor instead. Instead of going around the corner to get a nickel, we're giving you a nickel bag of *funk*. So we did that in our own cool, eclectic way.

Butterfly: When I was in Philly I worked at Reading Terminal, which was like a public market with restaurants and shit. I was a prep cook down there and I used to work with this lady named Hannah. Whenever a guy came by that she and this lady Jill thought was nice-looking, they'd say, "Swoon units!" So I got that from them.

Doodlebug: I guess it's fair to say that that song was our version of [De La Soul's] "Buddy" [*laughs*]. We were down at Washington Square Park [in New York] one day and the women walking by us were just off the meter. That was our little joke—they'd walk past us and not even give us the time of day and we'd be like, "*Swwwwooooonnn unittttssssss!*" That was one of the last songs we did, and Ladybug didn't want anything to do with that one [*laughs*]. I mean, she's saying, "swoon units" on the chorus, but she didn't rhyme on there. That was a song about girls and she just let us do our thing. When we signed for the album, she and I had agreed to remain friends but not go out. And that was one of the smartest things we ever did, considering how popular we got. If we hadn't done that, we would have hated each other!

Butterfly: I was talking about a lot of societal stuff on there in an abstract way, but I never really worried about whether people would be able to understand too much of what I was saying. Miles Davis said in a book I read that the duty of a revolutionary is to relate and educate, but to also raise the standard of art at the same time. I wanted to be abstract. You might not learn more than what you knew, but you could at least learn something different. Elevate, relate, and enlighten. As to whether that track accomplished that, I can't really say.

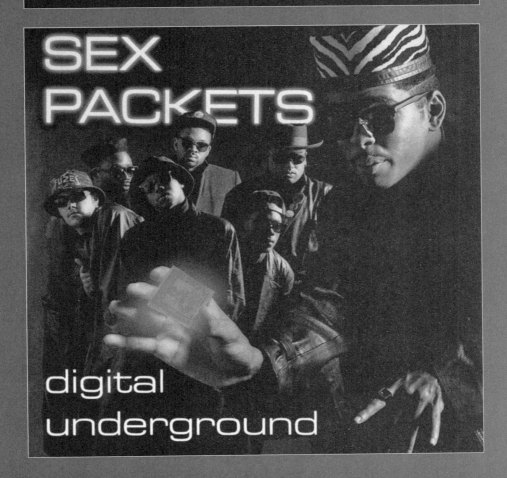

W e were a serious act at first, trying to be this techno, pro-struggle type of thing," blurts Digital Underground prime mover Shock G. For those who remember the first time they heard group singles like "The Humpty Dance" or "Doowutchyalike," *serious* isn't necessarily a word they would use to describe Digital Underground. The group—consisting of main rapper and producer Shock G (Greg Jacobs), rapper Money B (Ron Brooks), DJ Fuze (David Elliott), and singer Schmoovy Schmoov (Earl Cook), with some contributions from original member Chopmaster J (Jimi Dright)—was constantly morphing, and that was what always kept their fans guessing (in only the best way).

Shock moved to the Bay Area from Tampa in 1986 after traversing the U.S. map in his early years. He says he was born in Brooklyn, spent many years in Tampa because of his father's job, went back to junior high at PS 180 in Queens ("That's where I really got my hip-hop schooling," he says), and then spent a brief stint in L.A. He played keyboards, bass, and DJed in addition to his loose-tongued MCing. In short, Shock was a never-standing-still one-man band.

The seeds for Digital Underground were sown around 1987, after Shock met Chopmaster J. Shock was working at a music equipment store, in the keyboard and drum department, and J was a jazz drummer who was trying to set up a production studio at his house to make hip-hop. Shock explains: "Jimi had a MIDI setup and a lot of credit, so I sold him *my* dream setup. But he didn't know how to work any of it, so our deal was that if I made a couple house calls to set stuff up, he'd let me finish my demo on his equipment." At the time, Shock says, he already had the blueprints for the songs "Your Life's a Cartoon" and "Underwater Rimes," but he didn't have the money to go to a studio and actually record them.

Chopmaster J loved Shock's demos of the two songs and had a friend in L.A., Atron Gregory (who was road-managing N.W.A. and J.J. Fad in 1988), who wanted to put the two songs out. Shock agreed to put Jimi in the group if he was able to get the deal locked up. And thus Digital Underground's "Underwater Rimes" single was born, released in 1988 on Gregory's T.N.T. Records through L.A.–based indie powerhouse Macola. Shock says of the B-side, "Life's a Cartoon": "That was us when we were trying to be black-beret, Black Panther rappers. The lyrics were about how society makes fools out of African Americans, messing with their heads and making them want to be European. It was preachy and arrogant."

The single purportedly became a hit in markets around the world, according to Shock charting in the Top 20 in the UK and reaching number one on a chart in Amsterdam. ("I don't know how," Shock says with a smile. "It just did.") Shock says: "Even though we sold about twenty thousand copies of that single, the label's books showed that we owed *them* money. We never made any cash on that record, but it did get us to the next level."

As with many new bands, Digital Underground's early years were times of constant change as they shaped their image and style. Shock recalls: "Back in 1988 we used to wear berets and shit—that was the style for 'Your Life's a Cartoon.' Then when Public Enemy came out we were like: 'Damn, they did that to the fullest, way better than we were even thinking about.' So then we decided to include humor in what we were doing, and that's why we did 'Underwater Rimes.' We decided we'd be this hippie-oriented band. Then De La Soul came out. Everything we tried, someone else did it, and usually better than us. So we were like: 'Fuck it, we're gonna be on some Parliament-Funkadelic shit, and do all kinds of different songs and wear different hats all the time."

After the moderate success of the first single, the buzz reached Tommy Boy Records in New York, home to heady funkateers like De La Soul and pro-black spacemen like Afrika Bambaataa. The label was impressed by the group's intelligence: Label owner Tom Silverman says that *Sex Packets* is his favorite Tommy Boy release of all time and calls Shock "a genius, maybe the most talented artist that I ever worked with." In early 1989, Digital Underground were signed up for a single to test the waters.

"It was the humor element that caught Tommy Boy's attention," recalls Shock. "They thought that 'Underwater Rimes' was brilliant and weird and they wanted to know if the rest of our stuff was brilliant and weird. The first thing we recorded for them was 'Doowutchyalike.' That kind of laid the groundwork for the whole party vibe, and I guess that's what we did best. We had our own identity with that."

After Shock had presented Digital Underground as a full-fledged group—when in reality D.U. was Shock G doing almost everything, and a couple friends helping out—some hiring needed to be done. "Tommy Boy wanted to see a group," says Shock, "so I had to get one going! I always wanted Digital Underground to be this big supergroup, but we didn't have all the true characters yet. Basically, most of the time if I had a vision of a kind of guy we needed, I'd just *be* that guy."

Shock started auditioning local DJs for the group and came across DJ Fuze. "Fuze was definitely the hottest one we found," says Shock. "And the fact that he was white gave it a nice touch of novelty. But regardless, he was the best. He had a real knowledge of hip-hop history."

Rapper Money B was easy to get on board, since he was already partnered up with Fuze in a group called Raw Fusion. B's style brought an important balance to the mix, bringing some of Too $hort's pimp essence and a dash of N.W.A.'s gangsta roughness. Originally from Philadelphia, Money B mostly grew up in Oakland and Berkeley.

B explains: "My original rapping style was a mix of party and street stuff, with some humor in there. I was definitely a product of the Too $hort tapes era. When I got with Fuze, who was using Goldfingers as his DJ name in 1986 and 1987, he gave me ideas to broaden my subject matter beyond just what I knew in the neighborhood." Before Raw Fusion started, Money B also worked with another rapper named Mack-Mone, and their group was called MGM. After Mone got locked up, Money and Fuze, who both went to Berkeley High School, kept moving forward.

Money B, who is the son of Black Panther Bobby McCall, remembers meeting Shock. "I definitely thought Shock was weird when I first met him," he chuckles. "I still do [*laughs*]! Raw Fusion were doing talent shows, and Shock and Jimi were doing some of the same shows we were, so we know them from that scene. And I didn't have a problem with being part of Digital Underground, because Shock always explained it to us that we were a group inside of a group, and that Raw Fusion would always get a chance to do what we wanted. In the early days, me and Fuze would always open up Digital Underground shows as Raw Fusion." Raw Fusion's first single, "Throw Your Hands in the Air," wouldn't appear until 1991, on Hollywood Basic Records.

Another piece of the strange musical puzzle was Shock's roommate Earl Cook, aka Schmoovy Schmoov, who was a part-time vocalist and full-time freak. "We had P-Funk in common," says Shock. "He was a Curtis Mayfield type of singer, like that Neptunes dude [Pharrell]. Me and Schmoov used to experiment with all kinds of shit on the weekends. Mushrooms, Ecstacy, coke, all kinds of craziness."

Perhaps closest of all group members to Shock was guest MC and group pervert Humpty Hump. This is because Humpty was, of course, Shock G himself, with a Groucho Marx nose and a blatantly bitten Slick Rick flow. Although Shock now admits that he and Humpty are one and the same, for years he did everything he could to keep people guessing. "There were those that didn't care, there were those that swear we're two different people, and there were a few who actually knew," Shock says. "We kept people guessing the whole time by using body doubles on stage, just to keep the fun in it. I remember a George Clinton interview from when he was younger where he said that characters live on longer than human beings do. They don't burn out as quickly. So that was an inspiration."

Shock points to George Clinton's Parliament-Funkadelic universe as the one major unifying aesthetic that went into putting Digital Underground together as they got ready for their Tommy Boy partnership. "P-Funk was theatrical, operatic, feel-good African-American music," he says. "They were the Grateful Dead of the black world. Their concerts were more like rituals. And we wanted to tap into some of that and pay tribute to it. You could always just feel the party that was taking place in the studio when those guys recorded albums, and that went into what we were doing as well."

Money B agrees: "Shock was always so eclectic—he was such a free spirit. I was more straight-up hip-hop, more of a b-boy, but Shock's thing was always more on the Parliament-Funkadelic tip. Before I worked with him I thought that rap songs were always supposed to be the same thing. Three verses, some hooks, just rapping. But Shock showed me about song structures, bridges, melody. Doing songs in a more *musical* way."

"Digital Underground was always Shock's vision," B continues. "But people could always add things. He was in control, but he was still open-minded. I was eighteen when I joined, and Shock was twenty-four or twenty-five, so he was the older dude with the vision. My main role with the group, and the album, was just to help write lyrics and work on the words more than to actually perform them. I didn't write verses for Shock, but I would make suggestions about certain things because I was more of a traditional hip-hop MC. Shock would be the first to admit that his rhymes are pretty old-school, and we wanted to be as current as we could."

When Digital were signed to Tommy Boy, their demo was no more than four tracks deep, including songs that would make the final album like "Doowutchyalike" and "The Way We Swing." Their deal stated that if the "Doowutchyalike" single passed the eighty-thousand sales mark, then they would be green-lighted for a full album. The single (and video) hit in August of 1989 and the group continued to record new songs as well as beef up their local performance résumé. It surpassed eighty thousand and the group's upward trajectory continued, with their promised album deal in hand.

Money B remembers the album's late-1989 recording process: "My manager and Digital's road manager, Neil Johnson [aka Sleuth], had a house, [*Author's note: presumably in Oakland or Berkeley*], and Shock and Chopmaster J lived there sometimes. So basically that was the Digital Underground's headquarters—it was like the clubhouse. The door was always open and we'd always be working on music there. We'd sit up on the roof and just write shit. The house was a mix of crazy and serious. When it was time to get down to business, we were ready to work, and when we partied, we definitely partied!"

Shock was a free spirit in those days, a characterization that also related to his housing and recording locations. "Back then, in 1989, I was sorta homeless, just couch surfin', with this girl or that girl, in this hotel or that hotel for a couple days," says Shock. "My two keyboards and my drum machine would usually stay at the last studio or person's house that I recorded at. From the time that 'Underwater Rimes' was out, I was always tinkering away at a new song or two in my spare time until it was time to actually record the album. So at that point I had plenty of roughs, scraps, and four-track cassette versions to pull from and put the album together. By the time Tommy Boy said, 'Here's the budget, finish the album,' it only took two or three weeks to re-record everything in a pro studio."

After a quick recording process at Richmond, California's Starlight Sound, *Sex Packets* the album was released in February 1990. Money B says: "At the time that the album came out, everybody was so tough and serious. Grab the mic, hold your dick, act hard. And we weren't like that. We were just cats who liked to hang out, kick it, and do what we liked [*laughs*]."

Fun was what Digital Underground came to be known for, but the group was serious about the idea that gave the album its original concept: sex packets. Purportedly an idea developed by Shock's roommate Schmoovy Schmoov, sex packets were pills that were supposed to help men and women control the mental images that gave them wet dreams. Far-fetched, maybe, but as Shock explains: "Schmoov actually had, in his briefcase, the plans to do research going for these things. He was trying to get a grant from the government to develop them!"

Sonically, the vibe on the album was pure funk, with plenty of live playing and also great samples from artists ranging from P-Funk (of course) to Jimi Hendrix and Donna Summer. Shock says: "I like the fact that we was using these cheap little Casio samplers and these old-school metallic drum machines to make that album. It had a crusty, tinny sound to it that we didn't have on later albums after we upgraded. But in the end we didn't really want to upgrade, and it took us years to get back to that sound. Probably until 'I Get Around' that we did for Tupac [in 1993]."

Money B says: "Shock is just so creative and artistic as a musician and also an artist. He did all the visuals and the album artwork, everything, and we as a group had a lot to say in all of our videos too. His vision was so strong that he didn't need any help from a label or a video director. That's pretty rare in the rap game."

Considering all the aliases and strange stories that went into the album, fiction mixed with earthly honestly is likely *Sex Packets*' legacy. Shock says: " 'The Humpty Dance' was a strange oasis on the album, because it's the only time that anyone talked about *themselves.* That was outside of the concept. 'The Way We Swing' was just battle raps. But the rest of the album is about engaging people in broader thought, bringing boundaries down, or getting wild. It's an album that's not conscious of self. It's more about ideas than it is about *us.* Humpty could brag all he wanted because he was a cartoon character." And Shock adds another reason for the blurring of fantasy and reality: "There are a lot of 'shrooms and Ecstasy that went into some of the thinking on that album, too. I even wrote some of that stuff on these mescaline 'yellow giggle drops.' "

Money B points out: "Back then, before [Dr. Dre's] *The Chronic,* a lot of the samples people were using were James Brown and all the break beats that everyone already knew. Shock brought the P-Funk stuff into the game more than anyone else had up to that point. And we weren't just sampling George Clinton—we literally *were* the next P-Funk generation, with all the alter egos and all the funk. That's just what the Bay Area is all about. There are all kinds of different people, and everybody just does their own thing. Our thing was P-Funk."

"All of us tugging in different directions made it a really rich gumbo album," says Shock of the platinum debut. "We were freestyling and just riding that wave and the vibe around us, more than we even realized at the time. As soon as you know what you're doing, that's when things can fall apart. That album was classic in a lot of ways that were completely outside of hip-hop, and that's why it still sounds good."

TRACKS

Shock G: The whole Humpty thing wasn't from any kind of master plan—it just evolved. I actually played the bass line on that. The album was almost done when we recorded the song. That's why there's no picture of Humpty on the album cover, because when the cover shot was taken we hadn't even written that shit yet! Humpty's like a nerd version of a pimp nigga, with a little perv mentality from Benny Hill, some Morris Day, and Groucho Marx's sense of humor. The image of Humpty really started to evolve with the "Doowutchalike" video [in the fall of 1989]. At that time, I wasn't really trying to sell Humpty as a separate person yet. It wasn't until we were editing the footage for the video shoot that we realized that it's more powerful when the nose goes with that voice. Fooling around with the Humpty voice was like doing hip-hop ventriloquism, putting a spin on Slick Rick, like a skit. I started the myth of Humpty during a college radio interview. I said that he was my brother from Tampa, an ex–lounge singer who got in a grease accident in the kitchen. He stood as a hero for all handicapped people around the world, because you can overcome anything. And people were buying that shit!

My first experience meeting George Clinton was because of "The Humpty Dance." I sent the four-track demo of the song to Tommy Boy to tell them they had to add it to the album, and when I called them up about it, Monica Lynch just so happened to have George sitting in her office, dealing with the [De La Soul] "Me Myself and I" sample rights [De La's song sampled Funkadelic's "(Not Just) Knee Deep"]. She put him on the phone with me and I couldn't believe it was him. In fact I *didn't* believe it was him. But I eventually did realize it, talking to him, and I was speechless. I knew I was on the right path when George Clinton said that he thought "The Humpty Dance" was cool. That song is an American classic. It's in karaoke books!

Money B: I'm not sure that we knew it would be a hit like that [the single went platinum], but we definitely all really liked it. Me and my brother contributed to the actual Humpty Dance itself, and I was on that song, on the chorus. We really thought that dance out. It was right at the time of the San Francisco earthquake [October 17, 1989], so that had some influence on the dance, like when you started off doing the dance you were almost like bracing yourself 'cause the ground is moving. We recorded the song maybe three or four times, actually. The demo of it was really hot, and we kept trying to re-create it but just couldn't do it. That eight-track version might still be the best version ever made. Fuze and Shock were fucking around with the song, and they were like: "What's missing?" And I figured it out. It was Hennessy! So I went to the store, got some Hennessy, got Shock drunk, and then Humpty came right out, just like magic.

THE WAY WE SWING

Shock G: DJ Goldfingers was just DJ Fuze, his alter ego. Fuze was the serious DJ and Goldfingers was his James Bond super-scratch side. He would wear a tuxedo, dark glasses, a long overcoat, and gold gloves.

PACKET PRELUDE

Shock G: That's me playing on there, as the Piano Man. Two or three years before Digital Underground, I had put my microphone down for a while and played keyboard in some jazz and funk bands. I was in a band in L.A. called Onyx that used to do Prince-style Minneapolis funk.

SEX PACKETS

Shock G: That song samples Prince's guitar solo from "She's Always in My Hair," from the B-side of "Raspberry Beret." George Clinton was never that hung up on sex—he was more spiritual—but Prince really got into the eroticism. He ruined a lot of us, turned us into a bunch of pervs. I had the music to the song for about a year before I met Schmoov. I put lyrics and the idea to the riff and that song was born. We printed up fake hospital pamphlets warning against the use of sex packets, as if they already existed. It said that they were developed by NASA at Stanford. It said: PACKET MIXING: BE CAREFUL and SEX PACKETS: A TRUE ALTERNATIVE TO SAFE SEX IN HIV TIMES, OR A DANGEROUS STREET DRUG? It was a three- or four-page folded pamphlet, and we made up several thousand of them. We had friends in New York and L.A. that actually put them in hospitals, and in the bathrooms at different clubs. It got so far that right around when the album was coming out a journalist called NASA and they answered no, they weren't real, and an article ran in *USA Today.* NASA's denial made it sound even more real.

FREAKS OF THE INDUSTRY

Shock G: We never released that as a single, except as DJ-only wax that was never in stores. I didn't go into things with the ladies with the "I just want to fuck you" vibe. I brought the perv tone: bolt the doors down, lock people out, get the whipped cream and the cherries, and let's make a night of it. At that time, lyrically there wasn't anything romantic in the rap world, for the girls. I wanted to bridge the gap between Prince and hip-hop, a European hip-hop vibe like with [Prince's] "Under the Cherry Moon." We were like: "We eat pussy, and we admit it." That was a *big* deal at the time—we even had a meeting in the studio about whether we should say it or not. We said: "We don't need it, we just eat it." We knew women would love that, of course [*laughs*].

Money B: That's probably my favorite song on the album. I wasn't even going to be on that song originally. That's why Shock's verses are so much longer than mine. We were writing them together for him to do, and at the last minute he was like: "Do you want to be on this?" So I wrote my verse real quick. I was drinkin' a 40 in the outer room of the studio, so it was just a quick thing. And I went in there to the vocal booth just thinking I was doing a test, to get my mic level or whatever, and Shock was like: "Okay, we got it." It was already recorded. We ended up doing that song a couple times as well, because we couldn't clear the samples. At first it was Diana Ross, then we had George Benson, but he wouldn't clear it because he's a Jehovah's Witness and he didn't want rappers using his music. Then we did the last version when we literally had one more day to hand in the album. We ran all over San Francisco to find that Donna Summer ["Love to Love You Baby"] to sample. That was definitely the last song recorded. Lyrically that one was groundbreaking. People had always made sex records, like "We Want Some Pussy" or whatever. But we were some of the first to say that we wanted to please the woman.

UNDERWATER RIMES (REMIX)

Money B: I didn't know the original version of that single before I joined the group, but they played it for me when I got in there, and I dug it. We did a different version of it for the album because people really liked the original, so why not include it?

THE NEW JAZZ (ONE)

Shock G: Chopmaster J is on drums there on that song. He was a jazz cat trying to make the transition to digital music and he just never quite made it. [*Author's note: Chopmaster J also went on to produce demos for a young Tupac Shakur, who also started out in the Digital Underground posse, after Sex Packets.*]

RHYMIN' ON THE FUNK

Money B: That one was interesting because Shock wrote my rhyme and I wrote his rhyme. We just wanted to do something different. On there, we was just talking about all the P-Funk influence that we had. That's actually probably my longest rhyme on any of the tracks on the album, except for "Gutfest '89," which is only on the cassette.

Shock G: The influences on there were X-Clan on the production and programming side, and De La Soul's sense of rhyme flow. You can hear we damn near bit their style from "Me Myself and I." We weren't trying to hide the homage.

Shock G: That was one of the four or five songs on our original Tommy Boy demo tape. That rhyme style on there is my true, undiluted style. The four-track original version of that got college play out here in the Bay. With that song we knew we had to represent that serious side of us, even though the humor and sci-fi side of us was more prominent on the album. We wanted to keep a door open where we could be serious commentators if it ever leaned that way again.

Money B: That's one of my favorites. I didn't write any of that stuff, but Kenny K was on there. He was a DJ and an MC, and he was down with Shock from before Digital Underground. Kenny actually passed away right when the album came out. He was on "The Way We Swing," too.

Money B: When I first heard what Shock was doing on there, I didn't really like it. It might have not had enough bass in it for me or something, because I was really into the [Roland TR-] 808 drum machine sound. So I didn't really want to be on it. But Shock had me do some stuff on there. We did one video for that one when it was out originally [in 1989] and then added some stuff from our album-release party when the album came out in 1990. I definitely grew to like that song. Seventeen years later, I obviously appreciate the fact that people still like it!

Shock G: That was released as our first single for Tommy Boy, before the record. The video for "Doowutchalike," which we directed ourselves, actually got *tons* of play. It sold ninety thousand, which was ten thousand more than Tommy Boy wanted to see for us to get an album going. The video was supposed to be like an insane party, which is what the lyrics were sounding like. We went to a party store and got all these accessories for the video, like the Groucho nose. Shark noses, pig noses. Later on, the Humpty stuff paved the way so much that we rereleased "Doowutchyalike" again, with a remix and new video. Now that we had the world's attention, we wanted to give it another shot.

EPMD

Strictly Business

(Fresh/Sleeping Bag, 1988)

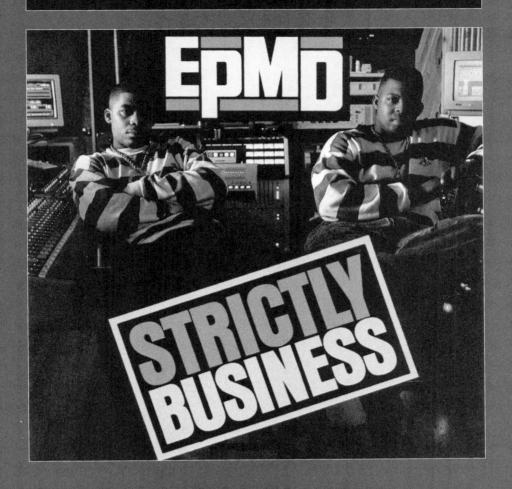

A little-known fact: If things hadn't worked out on the rap side, Erick Sermon might have been a landscaper and Parrish Smith could have been on his way to the NFL. Luckily for music fans, a higher power intervened. Says Parrish: "*Strictly Business* was God's way of taking two average kids and letting them express their hearts through music and rhyming."

In 1987, both talented young men were just out of high school in Brentwood, Long Island (a "big, crazy, multicultural community," Parrish says), about one hour to the east of New York City. Although Erick and Parrish (aka PMD) knew each other in junior high (Parrish says they first met in eighth grade), they became much tighter in high school. "I was always into sports," Parrish recalls. "But after school everybody would meet in the foyer and that's where the rhyming sessions and the breaking would go down. I was a DJ from a young age, but I really started MCing in high school, when me and Erick started colliding in the hallway. The more I started getting into rapping, the less I DJed."

"Parrish didn't start rapping until I had already been rapping," Erick says. The two bounced rhymes and ideas off each other, enjoying and building upon the collaborations. "We never wrote rhymes for each other, but our rhymes were always related," he continues. "PMD would write something, and I would want to write something better than him. That's what made us dope, because we had a friendly battle between us. It made us better."

Parrish, an Eagle Scout, graduated high school in 1986 and started college that fall, studying communications and business and landing a scholarship spot as punter and receiver for Southern Connecticut State's football squad. But even while he suited up, he stayed with the music, working on rhymes and staying in touch with his rhyme partner E on the phone. Erick, starting his senior year in the fall of 1986, continued working on his style. "I had to rhyme slow because I had a lisp," he says. "One day I got to school and these kids said, 'Erick, some kid named Rock Wind has a record out and he sounds just like you.' People who knew me knew I rhymed slow like that."

Rock Wind was actually fellow Long Islander Rakim (from Wyandanch), who, with Eric B., had released the radical hip-hop juggernaut "Eric B. Is President" b/w "My Melody" in 1986. The confusion told Erick and Parrish that even if they weren't on wax yet, they were on the right track. "Rakim had melody and EPMD had melody," Erick explains. "That's why we shocked the world." Parrish also notes both the artistic camaraderie and the influence of Rakim on their sound. "Rakim was the first to record a rhyme slow, but we brought the smoothness too."

But let's go back to the early days for a second, because although EPMD was new to the world in '87, Erick and Parrish weren't exactly greenhorns. Back in the early and mid-eighties, Parrish's older brother (he's the fourth of seven siblings) Smitty D was a promoter who rolled with Afrika Bambaataa and the Zulu Nation, and even released a Tommy Boy single, "Facts of Life," in 1985. Parrish, then aka DJ Easy P, was his DJ. "When I was like thirteen my brother Smitty was bringing Bambaataa to town for block parties, so I was already around real hip-hop from a young age," Parrish says. Smitty eventually became a member of the Brentwood police force around 1987.

Back in the day, Erick didn't have to go into New York City to get his dose of the real hip-hop; he just had to step outside. "It was real hip-hop where I grew up, in Regis Park. If I didn't know better I would have thought that hip-hop was started in Brentwood," Erick says today. "It was real heavy." PMD remembers Regis Park as well: "I used to go over there. It was a little hectic in Regis, though, so my father bought me turntables for Christmas when I was fourteen so I didn't have to go all the way to that part of town."

Around 1985, Erick moved over to another part of Brentwood to live with his grandmother. Her house was one street over from Parrish's, so at that point they knew each other from the neighborhood and also from high school. Parrish was one year older. His side of town wasn't quite like Regis Park. "It wasn't like where I came from," says Erick. "It was just Parrish doing hip-hop on that side of town." Erick also says that although the Smitty D record was on wax, it didn't have much impact. The big stars from town were an up-and-comer from Noble Street, Biz Markie, and also Disco Richie from the Brooklyn-based group Divine Sounds.

Flash forward again, now to the summer of 1987, with Parrish lacing up for practice with Southern Connecticut State's varsity squad. He began to do the math, looked into his heart, and says today, "I started looking at the football game and I thought, What would be easier: to get on stage and rip a show, or practice five days a week, with film on Sunday? So I was like: 'Yo, I'll grip the mic.' " And a rap dynasty was born.

"When I came back from college in the spring that first year [1987], Erick was still in high school," PMD remembers. "I'd go into the high school and sign E out like he had a dentist appointment, then we'd drive to New York in my '68 Camaro and start shopping our demo. We already knew what was out there and we was like: 'We can do better than this. If we get a chance we're gonna make it happen.' "

That spring the two had recorded the demo in question, which included the song "It's My Thing." Shopping wasn't a very scientific matter. "I wrote down all the record labels for stuff in my crate, and Sleeping Bag was one of them," Parrish remembers, "because 'Latoya' by Just-Ice was hot at the time. We went to four labels with our demo and Sleeping Bag ended up saying yes." They were signed to the label for a single deal (with their other demo song, "You're a Customer" on the flip). "It's My Thing" was re-recorded with important help from Teddy Tedd and Special K, aka the Awesome 2, released in the late summer. It proceeded to blow up on New York's ultra-competitive airwaves.

"When we got that first single deal with Sleeping Bag, we got fifteen hundred dollars total," Parris says. "When we got the first check we split it fifty-fifty. Erick took his and went shopping, but I had to take my half and put it back into my school money, since I had used that money to do our demo. I got it right in time so I could go back to school. Once the single sold eighty thousand copies, they called us in to do an album." Erick recalls: "Everything we did in those days ended up going on *Strictly Business*. When we was in the studio back then we didn't have much money, so whatever we made, we kept!"

Recorded in less than a month at Charlie Marotta's North Shore Soundworks studio, *Strictly Business* blew up airwaves and video screens from Brentwood to Burbank, with singles like "You Gots to Chill" and "It's My Thing." The sound was deep and the samples (from artists like Eric Clapton, Zapp, ZZ Top, and Steve Miller) were both recognizable and massively funky. "The samples we used are well-known now, but back then they was more foreign to hip-hop," Erick explains. "People also thought we was from L.A. because we was so bass-line driven."

Using easily identifiable samples was a double-edged sword, since the artists whose riffs and grooves formed the basis for EPMD's throwdowns were easily tipped off to the song use. "We never cleared any samples on the first album," Erick chuckles. "People would just come after us after they knew we had sampled them. Eric Clapton wanted ten thousand dollars,

EPMD (left to right: Parrish Smith, Erick Sermon) performing at Catch One, Los Angeles, 1993.
PHOTO: B+ (FOR WWW.MOCHILLA.COM).

Roger Troutman wanted five thousand. They didn't even sue us back then—we just paid them and that was that."

Erick and Parrish were, of course, very hands-on with the music on the album, unlike some peers who stayed on one side of the producer-MC wall. "When we came in the game we just thought that every MC produced and wrote their own music," Parrish explains. "So that's the way we came." Erick agrees: "We thought everyone who had records out did that—we didn't know that some people were just producers. We didn't even know what a producer was. So I guess we became producers."

One provocative item that goes against hip-hop's unwritten history is Parrish's contention that Erick—now rightfully respected as one of the top producers in the game—wasn't the main producer for the group's first two or three albums [which credit the production to the group, not specific members]. "Everybody now is using the music I produced, and the whole hip-hop industry is under the impression that E produced it," says P. "With the first three EPMD albums, I did most of the production and Erick just wrote his rhymes. He did one track on [the group's second album] *Unfinished Business*. I was already connected to the turntables, so it was natural for me. I'm not bitter about people thinking Erick did most of it, not at all. It wasn't even about who's gonna do what back then. It was about 'Let's just get the job done.' "

Erick rebuts this contention, adding that neither of them *produced* their earliest work as much as their important and invisible third group member, engineer Charlie Marotta. "In the beginning, everything was both of us [Erick and Parrish]," says Erick. "PMD brought the 'More Bounce to the Ounce' sample for 'You Gots to Chill' because his father played Zapp records at parties. My dad was a big musical influence, too, just like Parrish's. He played records all the time, tons and tons of albums, so I just knew what good music felt like. The rest of the songs were just taken off break beats [records like the *Ultimate Breaks & Beats* compilations, which contained famous and often-used breaks of the day, compiled in multiple volumes]. We both put our minds together and it was a collaboration. We collaborated a lot on the first three records."

"And either way," E continues, "neither of us knew how to make records back then. Charlie Marotta knew. Neither of us did anything technical on the first couple of records. We just got the records and gave them to Charlie. Charlie spliced all those samples in, because none of us knew of any machines that sampled for that long back then. But it wasn't as time-consuming as you might think. We'd take a loop and we'd splice it on quarter-inch tape and then record it back to half-inch."

"We used to call Charlie 'MacGyver' because he did it all, no matter what the situation," PMD laughs. "We had no idea how that stuff worked. All those loops were spliced. We had quarter-inch tape looped around pencils and chairs in the studio!"

In the end, it was the down-to-earth quality of EPMD, aside from their witty brags and occasional tough talk, that endeared them to fans. "When we toured and came through different states, a lot of people were pissed off at the artists who were there before us," Parrish explains. "They had their noses in the air and were disrespecting the audience. We were no different than the dudes next door—we just made dope music and rhymed. We had no aura or façade. We came straight out of our house, grabbed a mic, and wrecked it."

"It was just two kids who heard wack stuff on the radio and wanted to do better," adds E. "We wanted to make records and we just happened to make classic material."

TRACKS

Parrish: I brought that Eric Clapton sample. And that's me cutting on that track, too [*makes noises imitating scratches*]!

Erick: Yeah, Parrish did the cuts on that. He was nice! That was a one-bar sample, real short, and it was just dope. The concept was just dope. EPMD was making *music,* but we didn't even know that we were making actual music. While the world was sampling James Brown, we was over here venturing out on something that was *other.* We sampled some other type of shit.

Erick: I think PMD got that Aretha Franklin record from his mom's house.

Erick: That's probably my favorite verse on the album [*he raps the first eight lines a cappella*]. It was like taboo to say your name in a rhyme back then—you just didn't do that in rap! But that's how real we were. "Yo, I'm saying my name, Erick Sermon." The echo was heavy on that track. We brought that from the street. If you went to any type of house party or block party, the echo chamber was the main attraction [*imitates effect*]. It was Run-DMC, or Nice & Smooth. It was the essence of hip-hop. It was important.

Parrish: That was the first video we did for the album, and definitely my favorite video from back then. We never did a video for the first single. The "You Gots to Chill" video was done at an ice factory in Brooklyn—somebody at Sleeping Bag found it. I remember we had to stay out there because we did a show for Patrick Moxey. We had a beat-up limo that took us to the video shoot, but it got us there. That's K La Boss cutting on that track, not me. He was one of the dopest DJs from Brentwood. Diamond J was with us before that. Then after K La Boss, Jam Master Jay introduced us to DJ Scratch. My father used to hang with this guy Mr. Roy, and he was a DJ. They'd go on a break and let me on the tables and that Zapp ["More Bounce to the Ounce"] was my favorite song to cut. We use a ton of echo-chamber effect on that track, because that was always big. You gotta write about the echo chamber, please, for hip-hop. There's a lot of essentials missing in the game right now. I had two echo chambers myself. After we finished the song in the studio, Charlie [Marotta] showed us the button where the echo was and we could put it where we wanted. We were ODing on it, using it all over the place.

IT'S MY THING

Erick: We didn't know how to invent and write a chorus, so we owe that to the Awesome 2. After that record, we knew how to make choruses. They added that drum stutter too. The original demo was just the beat playing all the way through, with no horns or drum roll. The sound that we had back then was amazing. "It's My Thing" was like the groove of life! Red Alert was the first person to play that track on the radio. We was over at Parrish's father's apartment and it was like eleven forty-five and all of a sudden we heard helicopters [which are heard at the beginning of the song], then it started. It was just pandemonium in the house after that.

Parrish: We did that track when I came home after my freshman year in college, in May of 1987, when I had a break from football. When we first did the song, on our demo, I took the main sample off a scratchy break-beat record. It was dope, but the loop was scratched. So Will Socolov from Sleeping Bag got in touch with the Awesome 2 and they got us the clean copy we needed. They added some accents too, like extra drum rolls. Stuff we didn't know to put in there. They didn't know how to get out to us in Long Island so we had to pick them up in front of the Latin Quarter and bring them back to Charlie Marotta's studio. I knew "7 Minutes of Funk" [by the Whole Darn Family, sampled in the song] from my brother's Jazzy Jay tapes that he'd bring back from the T-Connection and from Bronx River parties in the city. That was always the number-one song on a tape to get the party jumpin'. So I didn't just get that out of the blue. My family was around it. I had to go back to school for football camp in the summer and I was there when "It's My Thing" first started getting played on the radio in August. We could barely get the station in, 98.7 Kiss, but we heard the helicopters and it was *on.* I'm pretty sure Red Alert was the first guy to play it. I knew Red from way back, through my brother.

YOU'RE A CUSTOMER

Parrish: That was the other song besides "It's My Thing" on our demo, so that's why those two tracks were on the first single. That song took about four hours to record, and it was actually a mistake. I got that sample from ZZ Top's "Cheap Sunglasses" and I was playing around in the studio and muted out the ZZ Top to where just the bass line and drums were left. So I left it like that. Sleeping Bag didn't even listen to that song at first, but I made Virgil Simms check it out by asking him to describe how it sounded to me. When I called back later they said, "Yo, come in." Diamond J was our DJ then, but he didn't have any cuts on that song. We just shouted him out. He started touring with Prince after he left us. With the rock influence on there—I went to Southern Connecticut State University and it was a melting pot. You had white and black in the dorms and a lot of mornings I'd wake up and they'd be playing "Cheap Sunglasses" by ZZ Top. That Steve Miller ["Fly Like an Eagle"] was like, when I was in the Boy Scouts, on campouts dudes would be drinking Southern Comfort and listening to Steve Miller and Phil Collins.

Erick: Even though it was on the B-side of the "It's My Thing" single, which was big, that song was the one that really banged them out on the streets when the single hit. It took off even bigger than "It's My Thing," even though they were both strong. There was just something about that record! That Steve Miller song, the real full version, is a *serious* record.

THE STEVE MARTIN

Parrish: That was based on the Stezo dance that our man was rocking in the "You Gots to Chill" video. Even to this day, anyone who brings up that video has to bring up Stezo. We were just out there trying to take it a little further and show Stezo some love. We didn't have a name for the actual dance, so it just became the Steve Martin.

Erick: That was a record we made for our dancer, Stezo, and it was the last song we made for the album. It was weird, because people *loved* that record. EPMD could do no wrong, the Steve Martin was big! And no, I never did that dance.

GET OFF THE BANDWAGON

Parrish: That's another hot one [*imitates bass line*]! We didn't do that at Charlie Marotta's, but at the place where we took the cover photo, Island Sound in West Islip. Back then we weren't talking about albums when we were talking about people biting our shit, we were talking about our demo tapes. One time my roommate took one of my tapes and tried to bring it back home with him and I chased him down on I-95 to get my tape back, for real. Our music wasn't out yet and we didn't want to take any chances. We was tight with our music because we knew we had something that was cutting edge. I played that music on keyboard. I don't know how to play keyboard even to this day, but I know how to play what I want to hear. I did the bass line for "You're a Customer" too.

DJ K LA BOSS

Erick: K lived around the corner from Biz Markie, near Noble Street [in Brentwood].

Parrish: All three of us went to the same high schools. I went to Sonderling and he and Erick went to Ross. We were overseas on a tour and something happened and La Boss had to fly back to the States, so we had to finish up like seven dates by ourselves, and we never used him again. We're still cool with him, though. He DJs for Puffy sometimes, and does mixtapes.

JANE

Erick: That was based on a story that I kicked to Parrish when I first met him. I had "Jane" and a song about Bernhard Goetz and I had them both memorized. I never recorded the Goetz one. When I first made it up, it wasn't called "Jane"—it didn't have any name at all.

Parrish: We definitely never thought we'd do a "Jane" on every album, no way. But as life goes on and as you get older, you start writing about the girl you don't know, the girl that doesn't exist. After all that shit, though, now there's a real Jane. I ran right into her. Her name isn't Jane, though [*laughs*]. That was the last track we did on the album—it usually is. That's how we know we're done, when we do a "Jane" song.

ERIC B. & RAKIM

Paid in Full

(4th & Bway/Island, 1987)

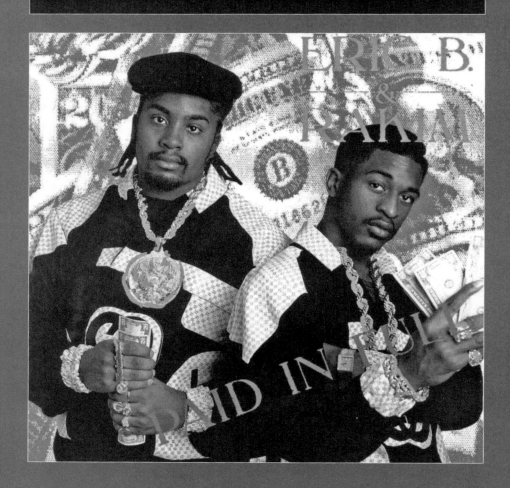

came in the door, I said it before/I never let the mic magnetize me no more."

When you hear those first lines, your whole body starts to shiver. You're instantly transported to New York, 1986. The verses are so ill that your mom could say them and they'd still move a crowd. And they don't stop for the duration of Eric B. & Rakim's unsinkable classic, "Eric B. Is President." A song like that only comes along maybe twice a decade, and few of them stay with you like the duo's master tome. Eric B. and Rakim set off a lot of things in 1986—an onslaught of raids on the James Brown sampling archive; a rebirth of anti-party, pro-scientific lyricism; and a 500 percent rise in purchases of dinosaur-choking gold medallions from Bushwick to Bangkok.

Interestingly, William Griffin Jr.—the youngest of three Griffin brothers and better known to hip-hop as Rakim—didn't figure their booming single (first released on Zakia Records, B-sided with the also mind-blowing "My Melody") would change hip-hop the way it did. "I had no idea it would impact like that, but maybe that's because I'm my own worst critic," Rakim Allah says, adding, "I had already been rhyming for so long at that point that I wasn't looking to pursue a recording career. To be honest, at the time I was hoping to play football at Stony Brook [University, in Long Island], since my cousin had a scholarship there. I played quarterback and had met with the coach there. He told me to get my grades up and we could talk." Luckily for hip-hop fans, fate turned Rakim away from the gridiron and gave the duo a monster hit.

Although he had deep family roots in Brooklyn, William Jr. was born and raised in Long Island's Wyandanch, New York, and came up through an established hip-hop scene that wasn't as flashy as New York's—though skills were most certainly required at the door. "Wyandanch played a big influence in my life," he says. "There was always block parties and DJs at the park. DJs like Pleasure, Nelson PR, DJ Motor, and DJ Maniac. These guys were around—like, back when I said in 'Microphone Fiend' that I was too small to get on the mic. There were a lot of parties in the school gyms. We had a lot going on." He adds, talking about his New York experiences, "I had lots of family in Brooklyn and cousins in Queens, so I used to go to their cribs and go to the park in Jamaica [Queens]. I'd also make sure I always saw the Cold Crush Brothers. [Grandmaster] Caz was a big influence on me. We'd go to DJ battles in New York all the time, like Mike & Dave Productions. I remember joining in on a rap convention back then, I think it was on 127th Street. Biz Markie was there, I remember that."

Aside from his cousins and local friends who introduced him to the hip-hop life, he also had an important musical influence in his family: his aunt, legendary R&B vocalist Ruth Brown. "She used to keep her eye on me, babysit me," he says, also adding that he saw her perform on several occasions in his youth. "Being in that environment, watching her do what she do, that kept me grounded once I got on for myself." Did the music legend approve of her nephew making hip-hop? "Once she heard my first record she called me up to let me know how much she liked it," he says. "She told me to keep doing my thing and to stay focused. She definitely appreciated it, because what I was doing was about poetry and rhythm. She respected that."

Back in his earlier teens, before he picked up a mic and started dropping supreme knowledge, young William flexed behind the turntables as Kid Wizard (he says he started using Rakim in late '84 or early '85). "I started DJing before I was rapping. I didn't know which one to do, so I did both. Back then you had to do everything. You had to break-dance, beatbox, all that," he recalls. "But after a while a lot of crews were trying to recruit me on the mic, even when I was too young to even hang out. Plus it was always easier to get on the mic than it was to get on somebody's turntables. Once I started rapping, a lot of people forgot I could even DJ. They started realizing that I had more skill than anyone in the area, and they wanted me.

"Melle Mel was always using big words and ill rhythms, but he'd break it down and get a little political, too, like 'White Lines' or the joint he did on *Beat Street,*" Rakim says, discussing one of his biggest influences on the mic. "He was scientific with it. Kool Moe Dee and Caz [from Cold Crush] were conscious and lyrical with their skills, and witty, too. I knew that Melle Mel and Caz and Moe always put something into their work, and every time I sat down to write a rhyme I always wanted to make sense and show that I went to school and I took language and social studies and that I knew how to write a book report. That's the way I took my rhymes, because of those guys. Listening to them coming up was the best thing that could have happened to me."

Around 1985, as his MC skills were beginning to hit full stride, he made an important trip to the crib of DJ Maniac (a friend of his older brother Stevie). "I went over to his house and made a tape, so when I went to college and cats start yappin' off about how great they were, I could put in my tape and shut all that talk down," says Rakim. "I had ninety minutes with different beats and me rapping on the whole thing, all the way through." That tape was soon heard by an up-and-coming DJ and producer named Eric Barrier through a mutual friend—future record exec Alvin Toney, also from Wyandanch. Eric B. was engineering mobile broadcasts for New York's WBLS-FM at the time. "Eric was looking for an MC, and Alvin brought him to my crib and we played him the tape that me and Maniac made," Rakim recalls. The rest, as they say, is history.

"I told Eric that I wasn't really interested in the rap game, but I said that if he popped something off I'd be a special guest," Rakim explains. Eric wasn't so casual about what might go down. He knew they had chemistry and something big could be made of the situation. As such, he started shopping rough demos around, and literally didn't have to go far before he found their first home: Robert Hill's Zakia Records. "I think that's the first place that Eric took our music to," Rakim says. "Zakia was right around the corner from his mom's place. She lived on 124th Street, and Zakia was between 124th and 125th on Adam Clayton Powell Boulevard in Harlem. They liked what they heard and we did a deal with them." With Zakia behind them ("Robert Hill ran the label and took care of studio costs," Rakim says), they went in the studio and the duo was born—the single even reflected Rakim's request for "special guest" status: "Eric B. *featuring* Rakim."

The Marley Marl–overseen single (technically and nominally Eric B. produced it, but Rakim claims that Marley's sonic input truly made it what it was), was recorded in late 1985 and hit streets in early 1986. It straight-up sideswiped the hip-hop world, boasting a new sound, a slower tempo, and Rakim dropping quotable line after quotable line. "Whenever I heard a slow track, what would click in my head was that I could put more rhythms and more words into it," explains Rakim. "I could triple up on words, take the rhythm, syncopate it, and take you where you've never been before. That was my little trademark. When a track is fast, there are only so many rhythms and so many words you can throw in four bars."

After the single's success, it wasn't hard to find suitors for an album deal. "4th & Bway kind of bought Zakia," Rakim explains about the biz angle back in '86 and '87. "It was kind of a joint venture. Robert Hill ran into some . . . [*pauses*] . . . business problems; he got into some trouble with the law. But whatever he was doin', it didn't affect me. So our deal with 4th & Bway was nothing bad for my career. Either way, sometimes you don't need a major label to get you where you need to be."

The group also benefited from running with a talented crew back in '86 and early '87. "At first we was running with the Juice Crew," Rakim says. "We was doing shows with Shan and Marley, and Fly Ty was booking us. Eric knew Mr. Magic from WBLS and Kool G Rap used to live around the corner from him in Queens, so that's how we got in with them at first. The Juice Crew guys kept me on my toes. When you hear some hot shit, like what Kane and G Rap was doing back then, you can't wait to go home and try to top it."

As anyone who recalls from promo shots and album covers back in the day, Eric B. & Rakim, like many of their peers, wore gold on a level just below Mr. T. "Me and Eric never really competed with wearing gold, because we knew if one of us bought something, the other one would go up the block and buy something too," Rakim laughs. "If I came through with a piece, he'd go out and get another piece. Eric was getting a new piece like every two weeks. The biggest piece I ever bought was like fourteen thousand dollars back then. A necklace, with diamonds in it. Someone went into this shop and ordered it and then got locked up. It was like eighteen thousand dollars but they were stuck with it, so I got it for less."

After 4th & Bway signed off on a full album, the duo quickly dispatched eight more classic cuts (six vocals and two DJ workouts) and the ultimate classic *Paid in Full* was born. "That album to me was like experimenting," Rakim recalls. "We went to the studio, we laid the beat down, I took the notebook and did the rhymes right there. And that was a wrap. Today I like to perfect and shape it a little bit more. But back then that rawness was what was good about it. We just went in there, we wasn't shootin' to do a single, we wasn't trying to cross over. I was just going into the studio doing what I would do before going to a block party. Give me a beat, I'm gonna write some rhymes to it and I'ma say this shit tonight. Everything now is more like tunnel vision. If you ain't talkin' about what everyone else is talkin' about, it's a different language."

As untouchable as the group's first classic was, Rakim states, "Those were just beats and rhymes that I would always do out in the park." He also says that although Eric B. got album credit as sole producer, Rakim did a decent portion of the work in the studio. "Most of the tracks on the first and second albums, I done those myself, no question," he states. "Back then Eric B. wanted to be the businessman, so I said, 'Okay, you can take care of business, I'm going to stick with this notebook right here.' So by not getting involved, he was right there telling them [at the record label] to print whatever he wanted them to print on the album cover. That was my mistake. If we did ten tracks on the album, I did like seven of the beats myself. A lot of times they was just old park records. I had a record collection, I had turntables, I had all the break beats." Regardless of how the credits on the album were given, Eric B.'s musical input was undeniably a big part of the album's success, and his DJ skills were some of the most innovative heard on wax during that era.

Even though Rakim tends to downplay the depth of the first album, when pressed he will admit to its lyrical importance. "Lyrically I took things from the nursery-rhyme frame of mind, writing things that rhymed and sounded good, and put the ghetto on it," he explains. "I just wanted people to see what I was talkin' about, wanted them to see the scenery. So they could put themselves in my place and live out what I was saying. The things I spoke about was things we did in the street, and we wanted people in the street to relate to them."

He adds, casually, "I wasn't planning on the rap game, but after the first single, the door opened and I walked in."

TRACKS

I AIN'T NO JOKE

That was the first single we did for the album itself, and the first video we ever did, too. That sample was just another James Brown record that I used to rhyme off. At first we was going to sample more of it, but then we decided to have Eric just scratch [the horn riff] in. I used that song a long time before I met Eric, so that's another Rakim banger right there. With the drum programming on the album, our engineer Patrick Adams did a lot of that. I just spoke with him the other day, actually. He's a real talented cat. I'd basically just take my break beats and ideas in, and he'd sample it up and put the [Roland TR-] 808 on it. Patrick was the guy who first turned me on to the 808. We'd dress up the beats. I titled the song that way because that's how I wanted people to perceive me on the mic. Back then I tried to think of slogans that somebody would want to put on the side of their car, or say all day. So that was like the ultimate thing you could say.

MY MELODY

That was the first song we ever made. We did that one and Marley Marl made it sound like it was supposed to sound. He played a big role in that record. I always used to rhyme off "Standing on the Top" so we used that. [*Author's note: Rakim likely means Keni Burke's 1982 R&B hit "Risin' to the Top."*] We replayed it on keyboard, Marley did a lot of scratchin', Eric did some scratchin' too. MC Shan helped engineer it when we finished the mix at the crib. After Marley's help on that first single, we took it and ran with it. If you notice, that song was like five verses and they was like twenty-eight bars long. Those was all just different rhymes I had, and most of them was on that tape I made with DJ Maniac back in '85. So I took 'em and put 'em on one joint. Then I wrote one more verse in the studio, the one with "Marley Marl synthesized it." But those were some of my favorite older verses and I took them and shaped them into that track. That version on the album is a little different than the single that came out on Zakia. I guess back in the day they would change the single up and remix it for the album so you'd buy both. It was a squeeze play. "Eric B. Is President" definitely got more play than "My Melody" because it was more of a dance track. "Melody" was more of a listener type of track. But I've got more love for the lyrics on "Melody" than "President." When I see people in the street today, they always talk about what I said on "Melody." I say, "Writin' my name in graffiti on the wall" on there. I wrote KID WIZARD or WIZ KID or whatever saying was hot for that week. Graffiti always just amazed me. Back then we covered all the elements, and graffiti was an important part of it. I used to write my rhymes in graffiti, fucking up the school hallways and shit like that.

I KNOW YOU GOT SOUL

Eric B. brought in that drumroll [Funkadelic's "You'll Like It Too"] and I always used to rhyme off that James Brown track [Bobby Byrd's "I Know You Got Soul," produced by Brown]. Those drums Eric brought were a real good idea because that just set it off.

MOVE THE CROWD

My brother Steve did the music for that track. My oldest brother, Ronnie, played piano and Steve played sax and some piano. If I wasn't sampling something, like on there, we would play it on keyboards, and Steve was my keyboard player. That beat I think was Chick Corea "Return to Forever" and the horns were James Brown. We put it all together. My family's musical background at the crib was crazy. My mom played jazz all day and my pops played smooth shit. My mom sang in Brooklyn sometimes, opera and jazz. She was definitely a big influence on me.

PAID IN FULL

When we got the deal with 4th & Bway, we got the check and it said PAID IN FULL on it, so we was lookin' at it and Eric said, "Yo, that's what we're gonna name the album." I wasn't sure about it at first, but that idea definitely worked. It was a statement. With that track, I always used to rhyme off that Dennis Edwards ["Don't Look Any Further"] in the park. Eric put that beat up under the bass line. I think that was Patrick Adams [their engineer] re-playing the bass line. I really dug the [Coldcut "Seven Minutes of Mad-ness"] remix of that song [which appeared on the twelve-inch release in 1987]. When we did [the original album version], it wasn't even sixteen bars—it was kinda plain. I was gonna write another verse but Eric was like, "Yo, that's it. You said it all right there." But when they put the remix on it, it added a bit of flavor to it, and they put the universal sound in there, so I was feelin' it. The remix was done in London. We didn't hire them to do it, they just did it, and we ended up using it in the end.

AS THE RHYME GOES ON

We did that in between, after the two singles were done ["Eric B. Is Presi-dent" and "I Ain't No Joke"]. I used to say that rhyme over a more up-tempo beat, then I added more to it when we recorded it. But that's just an old freestyle that I used to rock.

CHINESE ARITHMETIC

That's all Eric B. cutting on there. Eric did most of the turntable stuff, of course, but I did all the cuts on "Musical Massacre" [from 1988's *Follow the Leader* album].

We laid "My Melody" down and then Marley was like, "We need a B-side." I went home and played with a little something on my turntables, got the "Funky President" [by James Brown] out, did the rhymes to it, and it was ready. I used to always rhyme off of "Funky President" back in the day, so I grabbed it off my mom's shelf. That woman's voice at the beginning [of the album version] was just a stock record with different sayings on it, like they used for the London [Coldcut remix of "Paid in Full"] record. That was a cool way to set it off on the album version. We put that track way at the end of the album because that single had been out for a long time—people had already heard it. I remember the first time I heard that song on the radio I was walkin' home one night at about ten o'clock, to get ready for school the next day. And this kid was sitting in his car and the song is playing and the kid is nodding his head. Back then people used to always steal my tapes, so I went over to the car and I said [*his tone gets more aggressive*], "Where the fuck you get that tape from, man?" And he looked at me and said, "Yo, this shit is on the radio." He didn't know who I was, and he was an older motherfucker on the block and I was running up on him. But I had the best walk home that night. We knew that track was larger than life when they started playing it on the radio during the day. Back then we didn't have hip-hop all day on the radio, so prime-time was when they played a joint from noon to one. We jumped in the car one afternoon to drive to New York and we heard it on the jump-off. That let me know, *All right, Ra, it's getting serious.* Frankie Crocker [WBLS's legendary program director and personality] played it. Shit like that. That song is still one of my favorites to perform live. Everybody gets their whop [dance] on—it's still a classic joint. I always try to save that towards the end of a show, if not last.

FUGEES

The Score

(Ruff House/Columbia, 1996)

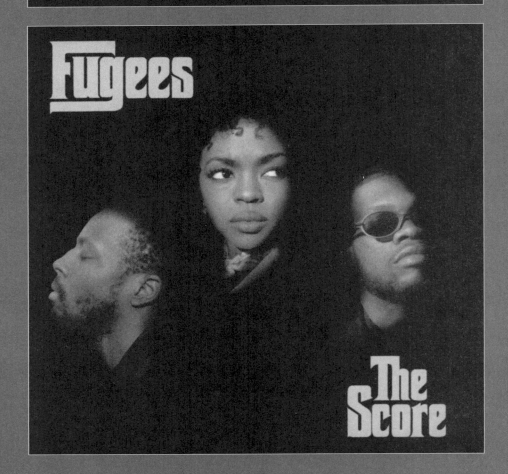

I think we were one of the last groups in hip-hop to be *developed*," says Pras (Samuel Prakazrel Michel), who, alongside Wyclef Jean (Nel Wyclef Jean) and Lauryn Hill, made one of the most influential and popular hip-hop albums of all time: 1996's *The Score*.

The Fugees, who exploded out of the then-burgeoning northern New Jersey scene around Newark and South Orange (fellow hip-hop peers included Redman, Queen Latifah, and Naughty by Nature), were a trio with vastly different experiences, ages, and talents. Wyclef, the eldest, was Haitian-born and Brooklyn-bred since the age of nine—moving to Jersey in the early eighties—with a knack for music from an early age. South Orange's Hill, the youngest (six years younger than Clef, three years younger than Pras), was perhaps the most stunningly and undeniably talented, with a powerful voice and a deep R&B schooling. Pras had Brooklyn roots as well, arriving in New Jersey in the mid-eighties with an ear for the streets and a mind for the hip-hop game.

"I've been in this business since I was a kid," explains Wyclef, who says that his first recording session, produced by the legendary Kurtis Blow, predated *The Score* by a decade. The session, recorded with the five-member group Exact Change, was never released. Clef, who was fifteen at the time, recalls: "I was writin' all the rhymes for everybody and doing all the arrangements, and Kurtis came and checked us out. He was fascinated because even at that age I was rhyming in different languages. English, French, and Spanish. Kurtis said we should call it Translators because of all the languages. The single never came out so we broke up, but that's when I first started being known as the 'Rap Translator.' "

Exact Change wasn't the only pre-Fugees session that Wyclef would be a part of. He claims that he was signed by Craig Kallman of Big Beat Records (now the president of Atlantic), and put out a single in 1987 called "Out of the Jungle." [*Author's note: He could be referring to Nelson "Paradise" Roman's single "Out of the Jungle" featuring Afrikali, from 1990 on Easy Street. Wyclef is not credited or mentioned on the single, although Roman did put out music on Big Beat later on.*] "It was a club record," he says today. He sang on the record instead of rapped, and he didn't produce it, but it wasn't bad for a high school kid from out of town. "I was only seventeen, in my senior year of high school, when that came out. It's still a cult record to this day. At the time I was going to Vailsburg High School in Newark, and early on I even went by my first name, which was Nel. People knew me as Nelly Nel. I'm the original Nelly [*laughs*]! Wyclef is my middle name. I started using Wyclef at the end of high school."

Pras was born and bred in Brooklyn, moving to the Maplewood–South Orange, New Jersey, area in 1984. He and Lauryn went to the same high school. Pras was hooked on hip-hop from a young age: "I used to run home every day after school at three thirty and watch Video Music Box. I listened to Mr. Magic and Marley Marl on WBLS all the time. I was just living hip-hop." He knew of Wyclef as soon as he got to New Jersey through Wyclef's group Exact Change. Pras recalls: "I wanted to start a group too, but I wanted it to be me and two girls. I knew this girl Marcy from my class and she introduced me to Lauryn, who was probably eleven years old at the time. Back then, around 1988, I wasn't producing at all. We were working with a producer named Khalis Bayyan [aka Ronald Bell], who was the writer and producer for some of Kool and the Gang's big hits. That's pretty much how we got on. Working with him was our first introduction to a real studio."

Wyclef recalls: "I met Pras because my dad was a minister in the church, and we had the hottest church band in the ghetto. Pras wanted to be in the band and said that he played trumpet, but when he played something on the trumpet it was the worst we'd ever heard. But we kept him around, and we all became cool. He went to Columbia High School [in Maplewood, a suburb of Newark]. I was in the 'hood high school in Newark."

The original version of the Fugees included Pras, Lauryn (who didn't rap at the time, only sang), and the aforementioned Marcy, who lost interest and left after their first recording sessions. During the same time, Wyclef, whose local reputation preceded him, was called in to help bandage the hook on a song they were recording with Bayyan. "That song never came out," Wyclef remembers. "It was a horrible song called 'The Enforcer.' The song was bad but the melodies worked." Nonetheless, Wyclef knew there was something going on that deserved some exploring. He says: "When I did that hook for them, there was definitely a chemistry with all of us."

When it came to joining a group with artists who were much younger and less experienced than Wyclef, it was definitely the vibe that made it happen. Clef says now: "I was already the biggest thing in my community at that time. I couldn't get any bigger locally. It was time to get out of the community and be heard by the world." Wyclef was decidedly impressed with the South Orange–raised Lauryn Hill, who was only in her midteens when they worked on their first tracks together. He says: "She was an incredible singer and an incredible poet. When I met her she was singing, not rhyming. So I started teaching her how to rhyme. She doesn't even rap that much on the first records, because she was still working on her style, getting it to where it was going to end up."

The group's 1993 debut, *Blunted on Reality* (Ruff House/Columbia), was recorded at House of Music Studios in West Orange and produced by Bayyan. It was, by all accounts, a failed effort. Before the group settled into the soulful, laid-back, and highly musical formula that made them international superstars, they had some growing to do. "On that first album, I'm screaming most of the time, sounding like Onyx," Clef explains. "I guess we was just influenced by that sound—it was hot at the time." Pras adds: "We were figuring ourselves out as artists. It was just a reflection of how we felt when we recorded it. It wasn't successful, but it was all a part of us feelin' our way, figuring ourselves out as artists. It had to be what it was in order for us to evolve into *The Score*."

The group was most certainly at a crossroads stylewise, but they're very clear about what went wrong. "The only tracks that were calm on that album were the ones where Lauryn came in," says Clef. "She smoothed things out." Another huge influence on the group at the time was producer-to-the-stars Salaam Remi, who was brought in to work with the group on a remix of their single "Nappy Heads," from *Blunted*. Wyclef says: "Working with Salaam was part of our grooming process. He said: 'Don't scream your rhyme, you've got a microphone right in front of you. Just say it [*laughs*]! Recording was a whole different thing than performing live, and we hadn't really adjusted to that yet. When the remix to 'Nappy Heads' that he did came out, that was when people started responding and we started understanding where we were going." Remi went on to produce *The Score*'s hit lead single, "Fu-Gee-La," as well.

Even with mediocre sales on the first album (Pras says it sold around 100,000), Ruff House heard potential in the Fugees sound, and gave them the advance they needed to make a second album, hoping this time would bring more artistic and sales returns. Wyclef says of Ruff House's wise ruler: "Chris Schwartz is into good old-fashioned artist development. It was like three

Fugees (left to right: Wyclef Jean, Lauryn Hill, Pras)
at Ellis Island, New York, 1996.
PHOTO: B+ (FOR WWW.MOCHILLA.COM).

strikes, and we only had one at the time. Artists never get multiple chances like that today."

"We got $135,000 for the second album," recalls Pras. "So we took that money, kept a little advance, and bought studio equipment with the rest." The results: a top-of-the-line home studio in Wyclef's uncle's crib in East Orange. They called it the Booga Basement, and without it, *The Score* wouldn't have been what it was.

"When the first album was out, we had never had a chance to really produce ourselves," Clef says. "But when we'd perform, we'd pull out the guitars and sing and people would say: 'Wow, why don't you guys record that on a CD?' By the time we got control and were making *The Score,* we were definitely ready for that direction."

After hooking the new equipment up and teaching themselves how to use it—with important help from Wyclef's cousins Renel Duplessis and Jerry "Te Bass" Duplessis (aka Jerry Wonder)—they started recording, and the rebirth of the Fugees had begun. "I couldn't believe that I could actually go in and produce myself," says Clef. "It was very liberating. I could be in there as long as I wanted because it was in my uncle's house and I was living there at the time, since my dad had kicked me out. Every week Renel would bring something else in there and me and Jerry would have to learn it immediately, since there were no engineers to help us along."

Regarding the production duties on *The Score,* Wyclef says, "Creatively, it's clear that the album was produced by Wyclef, Lauryn Hill, and Jerry Wonder. If you look at everybody's body of work since that album you can hear it. [*Author's note: Wyclef and Pras were publicly feuding at the time these interviews were conducted in 2003 and 2004, so take this with a grain of salt.*] Pras was more of a business head. At the time, me and Lauryn didn't know what an executive producer was." (Pras is listed as "Executive Producer" on the album; Lauryn and Wyclef as "co–Executive Producers.")

The Score was recorded during a six-month period in 1995 at a relaxed pace. Wyclef says: "It was done calmly, almost subconsciously. There wasn't any pressure—it was like, 'Let's make some music in the basement.' And it just started forming into something amazing. It sounded like a feel-good hip-hop record to us, and it was different than anyone was doing at the time. It was honest. It was three kids from an urban background expressing ourselves."

"After the first album, we just started making songs that would work without compromising what we believed in," says Pras. "We had to be on a mainstream level, without being pretentious about it. We wanted to capture a vibe and give it a little relevance about what was going on in the world."

The Fugees' masterwork was released in February 1996 and took the world by storm, eventually blown up by "Killing Me Softly," a song that wasn't even a commercially released single. Mixing Caribbean fire with Hill's R&B power pipes and centered around a hip-hop heart, the album appealed to music fans of all ages and races, eventually being certified sextuple platinum by the RIAA, and, Pras says, almost three times that many worldwide. "Making *The Score* was a great process for me," Pras says. "I'm part of history, and being part of that album was incredible. Also, working with Clef and Lauryn at the time was great too. They're both geniuses in their own right. Our strength was in being three individuals who blended together perfectly. Clef brought the musicality, Lauryn brought the soulfulness, and I brought the roughness and a little flash. When it meshed together, it was perfect."

Wyclef explains: "You had three different points of view from three different worlds on that album. I'm from the Caribbean, Pras listened to a lot of rock stuff, and Lauryn had the soul. Three into one, a fusion. That hadn't happened on *Blunted on Reality.*"

Pras remembers: "We just wanted to go gold at that point, and all the success of that album was just because of us. Ruff House didn't totally believe until it started blowing up, of course. But they at least believed in us enough to write that second check."

TRACKS

RED INTRO

Wyclef: DJ Red Alert was just someone that we all looked up to, because he was the king of radio in New York. Having him do that intro on our record just solidified the hip-hop we were doing, because he was the king of hip-hop for us.

HOW MANY MICS

Wyclef: That was the first song that we recorded in the Booga Basement that actually ended up coming out on the album. It's definitely one of my favorite few tracks from *The Score.* I'm a hook man, so I always start off with that, like the "How many mics do we rip on the daily?" That whole thing is just a basic cipher track. Like the best out of three going at it on some freestyle stuff. Right there, right away, we already sounded different from the last record. We put that track on the B-side of the "Fu-Gee-La" single because we knew that record would go commercial. We wanted to put that on the flip to make sure that the hip-hop side of us was still there.

Pras: Shawn King was the guy who actually made that beat originally [he is credited as a co-producer, along with Wyclef and Lauryn]. We took it and produced it and made it what it was. I think Clef did the chorus on that one.

Wyclef: The original for the chorus was the Delfonics, and the sample on there was an Enya thing. Whenever you hear any kind of soul stuff, classics like the Delfonics, that's all Lauryn. That's her world. She brought the soul vibe.

Pras: That's one of my favorites on the record, definitely.

Pras: Lauryn brought that doo-wop song ["I Only Have Eyes for You"] in.

Wyclef: The police problems we're talking about on that track were just in the neighborhood, all around. I didn't get any extra hassle from them because I was Haitian—just because I was black.

Pras: The guy playing the Chinese dude at the very end of that is a friend of ours named Talent. We was just fucking around and it sounded funny so we kept it in.

Pras: That was the first song we produced for *The Score.* We recorded that with Salaam Remi, and after that everything was recorded in the Booga Basement. He played the beat for "Fu-Gee-La" for us and we fell in love with it. Lauryn and Clef heard it first, then we went in there and recorded it. The single came out in October of 1995. We did that video in Jamaica. We couldn't go to Haiti because it was too crazy there, so Jamaica was the next best place.

Salaam Remi: I had already done "Vocab" [a remix from *Blunted on Reality*] for them in May of 1994, and I was working on songs for Spike Lee's movie *Clockers* back when they approached me about working with the Fugees again. During that time I had this track that was originally going to be for Fat Joe, but Joe didn't like it. I played it for the Fugees and Lauryn wasn't feeling it. She thought it was the same thing as "Nappy Heads" [Salaam's remix, presumably]. So during the *Clockers* sessions, Wyclef was there and he just jumped up at one point and shouted: "We used to be number ten, now we're permanent one!" And that was his first line. They ended up coming around to that beat and using the music, and that was that.

Wyclef: We definitely had no idea that "Killing Me Softly" would be a hit, so we figured that that song would probably be our big shot from the album. We shot that video in Jamaica, and we were trying to re-create Jimmy Cliff's [1972] movie *The Harder They Come.*

FAMILY BUSINESS

Pras: John Forte is on that one. He was a friend of Lauryn's—she brought him in the camp. Omega [who is also on the track] was a dude that just happened to be around the Booga Basement. Forte brought that dark vibe to the track.

KILLING ME SOFTLY

Pras: I love that song! That was the one where I was most involved on production. I brought the record [Roberta Flack's "Killing Me Softly"] to the group and put the Tribe [Called Quest] beat [from Tribe's 1989 hit "Bonita Applebum"] underneath it. We knew it was going to be big, but you never know what level. We did a video for the song, but it never came out commercially in America. It sold millions of singles in Europe, though. We didn't release the single in America because we didn't want to interfere with album sales. Lauryn came up with the idea for that video.

Wyclef: I really didn't have a clue that that song would blow up like it did. It was never even a single. But once people started playing it and once it started blowing up, we had to do a video for it. We performed that with Roberta Flack a couple times back then, which was amazing. Just to be near her and work with her, she's such a professional, such a great person.

THE SCORE

Wyclef: That was near the end of the recording of the record, and we had always liked Diamond D [who produced], so we wanted to bring him in and get him involved.

Pras: Diamond D kept comin' to us like: "Yo, I gotta get on the album!" He played us that track and we liked it.

COWBOYS *Featuring the Outsidaz*
(Pace 1 aka Pacewon, Young Zee, and Ra Digga)

Wyclef: We always loved the [Outsidaz] but it never seemed like they ever got their chance to shine. So we put them on there. All of them were great.

Pras: [John] Forte brought that track to us. The younger cats on there [Pacewon, Young Zee, Ra Digga] was just guys that was around. They were like, "Yo, let me rap," and so we said, "Okay, go ahead and rap." They had talent so we put them on.

NO WOMAN, NO CRY

Pras: I think that was the last track we recorded for the album. That was pretty much all Wyclef, just by himself. Forte might have helped out with the drum programming.

Wyclef: One night I think I just went down and started strumming that song, and it started to take shape. Lauryn was in the booth, I remember, and we just made that track. Being in Booga Basement made it that much more relaxed, so we could just do something like that spontaneously. I think that song definitely shows how relaxed the situation was.

MANIFEST/OUTRO

Wyclef: That's another one of my favorite tracks on the album. I always just liked the stories on there, how they all came together. Everything there was definitely very personal. There's a Poor Righteous Teachers sample on there. They're from Trenton. New Jersey is the place!

Pras: DJ Scribble is doing cuts on there. He was someone who always supported us, so we was like: "Come and get down with us." He gave us love before *The Score,* even if he didn't have as much of a name back then.

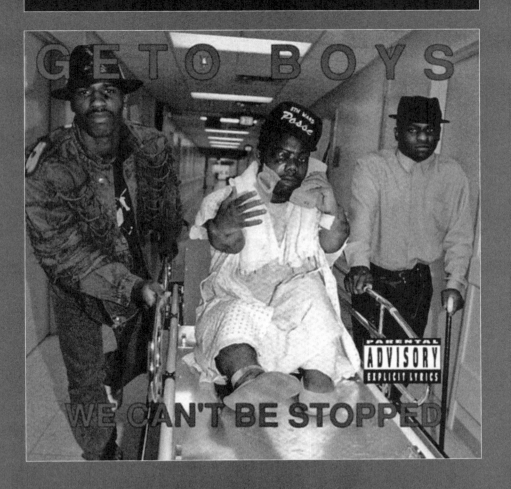

GETO BOYS

We Can't Be Stopped

(Rap-A-Lot, 1991)

I f you think that Eminem is rude and DMX is tough, then you might not be giving enough props to their forebears, the Geto Boys. Rampaging out of Houston's notorious Fifth Ward, Scarface (Brad Jordan), Willie D (Willie Dennis), and Bushwick Bill (Richard Shaw) were like nothing that hip-hop in the early nineties had experienced before.

Their 1991 single "Mind Playing Tricks on Me" was one of the most unique and influential hip-hop songs of the decade, going gold within a couple months of its release. And while many fans figured they were new to the scene, the Geto Boys were far from an overnight success. In fact, the trio that eventually hit platinum with *We Can't Be Stopped* had very little to do with the original Geto Boys.

Formed in 1985 by manager and Rap-A-Lot Records owner James Prince (then known as James "Lil J" Smith), early editions of the Geto Boys (initially spelled Ghetto Boys) included producer/DJ Ready Red and MCs Raheem, K-9, Sire Juke Box, and Prince Johny "C," with Bushwick Bill originally hired on as a dancer. The group released singles like 1987's "Car Freak," 1988's "Be Down," and the 1988 album *Making Trouble* (all on Rap-A-Lot).

Willie D says: "James Prince was the man who started it all—he was the whole foundation. He brought everybody together, he picked the members, and he was integral to the development of the Geto Boys. He was definitely very hands-on with all aspects of the group."

Bushwick Bill illuminates the group's early years: "Juke Box was from the Third Ward, and Johny and Red were originally from Trenton, New Jersey, so I was the only guy from the Fifth Ward in the group. In the early years it was just us doing hip-hop, but the problem was that the group was trying to compete with Run-DMC, even though we were from the South. Our earliest stuff was a lot like Run-DMC, lots of call-and-response type of stuff. Everybody was loving us and they thought it was really strange at the same time. It was a love-hate thing that people had with us.

"My opinion," Bill continues, "was always that we should talk about southern stuff, instead of trying to pretend we were from the East or West Coast. We should deal with the situations that were all around us. Once Face [Scarface] and Willie got in the group, that's when we started talking about how we was raised and what the neighborhood was all about. They were right on time with the stuff I was saying, stuff that the other guys before them just couldn't feel. We took the foundation that the other guys and James Prince laid, and brought it to the next level."

Before the trio lineup that most people know, the group was frequently in flux in the early years. Stories differ as to why Juke Box and Johny "C" left the Boys in 1988 after the *Making Trouble* album. Willie recalls: "A couple of the band members felt like the lyrics was just too edgy—they thought the whole thing was too raw. Stuff like 'Do It Like a G.O.' and 'Fuck the KKK' [the latter is from Willie's 1989 solo album, *Controversy*] and shit like that. They thought it was too raunchy, too hard. So James [Prince] gave them an ultimatum. He said: 'You need to say this shit or get out of the group.' And they chose the latter. Ready Red stayed longer than the other guys."

Bill says: "I don't think that those guys left because the lyrics were too hard. Johny and Juke Box left because they were tired of makin' records that they felt were goin' nowhere. We had toured in California, Texas, Ohio, but they couldn't put up with the struggle that it was going to take to make it. They thought it was a waste of time." Still, Bill admits not having a problem with their departure. "I was in there with the Geto Boys since 1985 and I could always rap, but they never gave me an opportunity," Bill says. "I guess they didn't feel that me being short [as fans know, Bill is a person of small stature] and being a rebel would be a good thing. I got my first opportunity to rap when Sire Juke Box and Johny "C" quit, because at that point it was only me and Ready left, before Face and Willie came in."

Willie recalls: "The day we started recording [the group's second album] *Grip It! On That Other Level* was the first day that I met Brad [Scarface]. Brad was a DJ first—he called himself Akshen—and then he became a rapper. I was already a solo artist on Rap-A-Lot before I was in the group, so at that point my own solo tracks became Geto Boys tracks. I was definitely excited about joinin' them, because they had street credibility. They was the only group in Houston who was doin' anything in the rap department. Hell, they was really the only ones doing much in music in Houston, period. And if you want to give credit, I have to say that the whole Geto Boys sound that came out at that time was all due to Ready Red. That's where it evolved from. He created it. He did a couple songs on *We Can't Be Stopped* too [Red is not credited]. Even so, when he left, there was no delay, we just kept moving. James Prince was the executive producer on the records—he didn't produce any of the music." (Prince is credited as a producer with seven other people including the three rappers.)

Willie says, regarding what different members of the newly annointed *Geto* Boys trio brought to the table, "I brought social and political awareness, but I also was the straight-up rebel. I just didn't give a fuck about nothin'! Brad [Scarface] brought the code of the streets to the game, and the playa type of angle. And Bushwick brought the character and the comical side. He was the guy that made everybody laugh. He also had a manic side, too, a split personality. You never know which Bushwick is gonna show up. That's just who he is and we love him for it. Overall we all just respect one another. That's always been the main thing."

In 1990 the group, buoyed and guided by Ready Red's hard, early N.W.A.–influenced production style, finished the album that was alternately known as both *Grip It! On That Other Level* and *Geto Boys.* (Each contains roughly the same songs, but in a different sequence.) Considering its mix of explicitly violent street tales and graphic storytelling ("Mind of a Lunatic" details murder, rape, and even necrophilia), the original distributor, Geffen Records, refused to release it. Saved by Def Jam Records founder and Def American owner Rick Rubin, *Geto Boys* was eventually released through Def American's Geffen-free distribution. The album received as much acclaim as it did parental concern.

"With the Geffen bullshit, that was a wake-up call about how people viewed us in the industry," Willie says. "I was majorly impressed with Rick Rubin in all of that, too. I always thought Rick was a musical genius, so it was great to be associated with him. When Geffen decided that they weren't going to manufacture the record we gave them because of the content, I just felt like they were the biggest hypocrites in the industry. How can you promote Andrew Dice Clay [his album *Dice* came out in 1989, ironically on Rubin's Def American label, which was part of the David Geffen Company at the time] on one hand and then dump the Geto Boys? They already knew what kind of music we was doing, they had heard our other stuff. They just punked out."

After the success of *Grip It! On That Other Level,* including an eyebrow-raising five-mic score in industry-leading magazine *The Source,* the group wasn't planning on stopping their momentum. Among other things, they experienced a flourish of touring that brought their arc of influence farther from Houston, creeping toward both coasts. Their next record was another step up, sonically, and it also kept the controversy level high. Fans, of course, expected nothing less.

"*We Can't Be Stopped* took about six weeks to record, maybe a month," recalls Willie. "It never, ever took us long to record any of our albums. I never understood the whole thing about recording a hundred songs for one album and then not releasing them. If you know what you're doing, you go into the studio and get out and then go promote the record. Easy as that." Bill remembers differently: "That album only took about two weeks to record. We was very hungry, basically. We knew what we wanted to do and we did it."

As mentioned, original beatmaker and DJ Ready Red left during the recording of *We Can't Be Stopped*. Willie says: "He just had personal reasons why he left. He found God or somethin'. Bushwick said that he might have lost God after that, 'cause he wanted to get back in the group later [*laughs*]. It was tough at the time, but it just seemed like the best move for everyone. Things just weren't working out personally. But it was no bad blood." Bill, remembering a bit differently, says, "Red left after he finished working on the album [*We Can't Be Stopped*] because he got married and felt like he couldn't be a Geto Boy and be a married man. After the record got big, his wife left him and he wanted to get back in the group."

When it came to working in the studio, Willie says: "Our goal was always to make the best music that we could possibly make, so we all brought ideas to the table, and it was always majority rule. One big thing about the people around us was that we trusted them—they was always honest. If it didn't sound right, they'd say so."

The group had a dicey public image, and this couldn't have come as a surprise, considering their lyrics. But they didn't always help their own cause, either. Willie remembers a live appearance from 1990 that went awry: "We had a show opening up for [the R&B group] Troop. Basically the promoter wasn't selling enough tickets so they put us on the bill, and then the show sold out. But they cut our set short when we was on-stage, and all hell broke loose. Equipment got torn up, stagehands got beat down, and Troop's manager got roughed up too. A near riot broke out because the people were there to see us, not fuckin' Troop. After that, word got around that you shouldn't book the Geto Boys because they're just out to tear your shit up. That was bullshit, because that was the only incident like that we ever had. But you know how people always want to believe the worst."

After the album was mastered, Bushwick Bill was shot and nearly blinded during an altercation with his girlfriend. The incident played a major part in the album's legend: four days after the shooting, Scarface, Willie D, and the Geto Boys management team of James Prince, Tony Randle, and Cliff Blodget went to the hospital, yanked Bill out of his room, and photographed the trio in the hallway. The shot included Bill's severely injured eye exposed for the world to see. It was a chilling image, and proof about how "real" the group was.

Willie recalls: "We had just wrapped the album up and Bill got shot, and we was in a situation where we had to get the record out. We hadn't done the album cover yet. And I don't know who introduced the idea, but somebody said: 'Shit, let's just go down to the damn hospital and shoot it there.' It was for real, the whole situation. That really is what his eye looked like [on the front of the album]. People thought it was some artwork thing, but that was the real deal."

Bill expresses regret about the cover shot. "It still hurts me to look at that cover because that was a personal thing I went through," he says. "I still feel the pain from the fact that I've got a bullet in my brain. To see that picture only brings it back more so. I think it was pretty wrong of them to do it, even though I went along with the program at first. I really didn't understand why that picture was so important for them, important enough to take the IV out of my arm and endanger my life by taking the patch off my eye. I could have been blinded for life. And Face was against it the whole time. That's why he has that look in his eye in those pictures."

Controversy sells, and the Geto Boys did too, fueled also by the tremendous success of their "Mind Playing Tricks on Me" single, which charted even on non-rap stations and drove the album platinum by 1992. The group also toured more than ever before in 1991 and 1992, with hip-hop marquee acts of the day like Public Enemy, Naughty by Nature, Too $hort, Ice Cube, and Queen Latifah.

"It took a lot of perseverance to get to that level, especially comin' from the south," says Willie. "We still don't get any real respect from the mainstream and the industry, just from rap historians and real hip-hop heads. But to get into the mainstream and get that much radio play at that time with 'Mind Playing Tricks on Me,' that was something huge. We went from being known by our family to being known all over the world. Everything in our lives just got magnified."

Bill explains: "On that album, we left no stone unturned lyrically. It was important in that era. We were talking about shit that no one else would. I have no regrets. And even though I have my disagreements and discrepancies with how money was taken care of and how everybody got paid for their accomplishments, if it wasn't for all of their contributions, there wouldn't be no Bushwick Bill. Those guys all believed in me and they gave me an opportunity to expand beyond just [being] that short guy walkin' down the street that people would have pointed at and made fun of. I want to thank them for giving me a chance."

Bill ends with this: "May God bless us all, and keep rap alive!" Amen to that.

TRACKS

WE CAN'T BE STOPPED

Bill: The lyrics on that were about how we were banned by Geffen for the previous album [*Grip It! On That Other Level*]. It was bad enough that we was comin' from the south and people didn't believe that we could do what we were doing and be successful. Then to be banned by a major distributor, that was really fucked up. In the end, though, it made us stronger.

CHUCKIE

Bill: I was watching the movie *Chuckie* [*Child's Play,* with main character Chuckie] with [Houston rapper] Ganksta N-I-P, and me and him put that song together. I was still pretty new to the writing thing, so I needed some help. I could write poems, but I didn't really know how to translate them into real raps yet. The point of the rhymes was easy: Chuckie was short and I was short. I could relate [*laughs*]!

MIND PLAYING TRICKS ON ME

Willie: That was a song that couldn't be denied. It crossed all racial, social, and economical lines. Gender, age, you name it. Take that track off the album and it's just a cult classic instead of platinum. We was on the radio for seven or eight months with that song. To tell you the truth, I didn't think the song was that amazing when I first heard it. I thought it was cool, but what enticed me was that it was different. I don't usually like to write to songs like that. There was some radio station in L.A., it was an R&B station, and I remember they despised rap. I can't remember the call letters, but they broke their format just to play that song. That's when I knew it was gonna be huge. We did a video for that song too. It was basically just following the lyrics. I think Brad [Scarface] brought the music and the concept for that one. He already had his verse for it, I remember that.

Bill: That was originally a Scarface song—it didn't have Willie or me on it. That's why he's got two verses on there. That could have easily ended up with just him on the *Mr. Scarface Is Back* [Scarface's first solo album, from 1991], and that would have been a pretty different story, wouldn't it [*laughs*]? I consider it a privilege to have been a part of that song.

I'M NOT A GENTLEMAN

Willie: We sampled Queen Latifah on that song, at the beginning, from [her 1989 single] "Ladies First," and then later in 1991 we toured with her. She was really cool—she knew that our lyrics weren't anything personal. My wife, who was my girlfriend at the time, gave me that idea. She used to tell me that I wasn't a gentleman [*laughs*]. And I was like: "No, I'm sho' not." She liked the song because she was like: "Yeah, that's your ass all right." She liked the artistic side of the song, but she wasn't with the side that was disrespectful to women. Whenever I make a song like that, I always think about how she's going to react. But this is what I do. I have to be free to make whatever music I deem necessary.

FUCK A WAR

Bill: My cousin Tommy was in Desert Storm and Willie D had an uncle that was in the army. Between my personal feelings and Willie D's knowledge of being in wars, that song was written. Lyrically it was a collaboration between us, but he did a majority of the writing on it. He asked me for footnotes of an opinion, but I would say he carved out the novel by himself.

Willie: That was the second single off the album. We did a video for that song too.

Bill: Willie D wrote that whole song and Face and me just rapped the lyrics that he gave us. That was definitely Willie D's.

PUNK BITCH GAME

Bill: Believe it or not, Salt from Salt 'N Pepa was instrumental in how that song ended up. She was down here in Houston and we were rehearsing somewhere and she came by the studio. We were really bad at crowd participation, and she was like: "Why don't you say something about the ladies and involve them? It should be more well-rounded in the audience." So it goes, "Don't call me punk, bitch," and then, "Don't call me bitch, punk." If it wasn't for her there would have been no female point of view in there. She didn't want any recognition for her input. I think we first did that live in Greensville, Mississippi, and I had just seen *Mississippi Burning,* so I'll never forget that. That was when I first met Mannie Fresh [of Cash Money Records fame]. He was with a guy called Ice Mike and another guy, and they opened for us.

THE OTHER LEVEL

Bill: On that song, I was the first rapper to talk about one guy fucking two women. After I did that song, it happened all the time. It's definitely been like that ever since I did that song, so I can't complain!

TROPHY

Willie: That was a reaction to the basic disrespect that industry people have towards the Geto Boys. We've never been recognized in this game. *The*

Source gave us an award for Best Song back in '91 for "Mind Playing Tricks on Me," but other than that we've received no accolades. Normally when you have the hottest record of the year, that should garner some kind of attention. They could have at least tricked us and *nominated* us for a Grammy. It's on the fans' minds. They know it's bullshit. We thought that the fans needed a voice at those award shows. It's just such a political game, and you've gotta have people in high places pulling strings. It's hard to get a fair shake.

ICE-T
Power

(Sire Records, 1988)

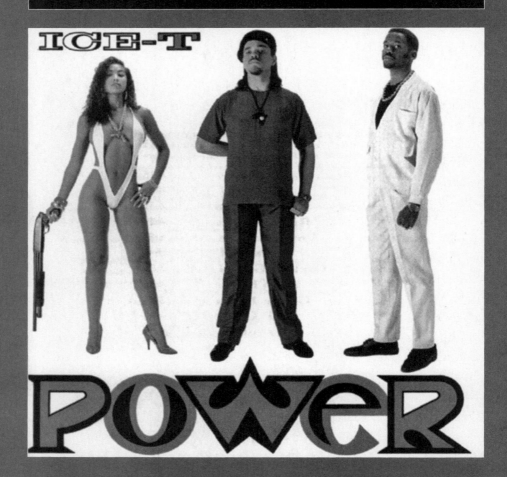

Ice-T is one of rap's true originals. And although he wasn't born in L.A., he certainly came to embody the flashy West Coast lifestyle to the fullest—first in his real life, and later in his rhymes. Throughout the early eighties he built wealth on the down low while he built his rap reputation across Southern California, and by the close of the decade he approached platinum every time he hit the studio—with no radio play.

Born in Newark, New Jersey, Ice (Tracy Marrow, sometimes incorrectly listed as Morrow) grew up in nearby Summit, where he attended Summit Junior High School. His earliest years were normal ones in a nice suburban town, but drama hit before he entered his teens. "My mother died of a heart attack when I was in the third grade, and my father died when I was in the seventh grade," he says. "When my father passed, I moved to Los Angeles to live with his sister. After that I never went back. I had no family, no connections, no friends. It was gone."

Ice lived in the View Park section of L.A. when he arrived at his aunt's in the early seventies. "It was a nice upper-middle-class area," he recalls. For school he was bused to Palms Junior High, a mostly white school in Culver City. "At that point in time my life hadn't gotten traumatic," he says, despite the fact that he had, of course, lost both of his parents. "The drama started in high school."

"When I got to high school age, I decided that I didn't want to be bused anymore," Ice continues. "I wanted to go to Crenshaw, which was one of the roughest high schools in L.A. I went there just because I didn't want to take the bus. I wanted to walk, and to go to a local school. But in my neighborhood not that many people went to Crenshaw, so I was basically going to school by myself. That's when I got introduced to the gangs, mostly for survival."

"When I got to Crenshaw, the kids in my grade were already cliqued up," he recalls. "So I got in with these kids from the Avenues, the flatter area of L.A., the more dangerous area. I had to connect with them and roll with whatever was rolling, because I was a one-man team coming into school, with no backup. This was right when the Crips was jumping off, the beginning of the era when the L.A. gangs were *really* getting going."

Ice doesn't glorify and doesn't seem to exaggerate his gang activities back at that time. "To put actual work in for a gang, that meant you had to kill for them, but I never went out and did that," he states. "I was more what I considered a 'gang affiliate.' I wore my colors. My main allegiance came with some kids in the forties [Avenue numbers], who really didn't gangbang. They were hustlers more than anything."

When Ice graduated high school in 1976, he went down a decidedly non-hustlerlike path: joining the army as a Ranger (an elite combat-trained force within the armed services). Why? He answers, with no hint of humor, "I did it because I wanted a black beret."

"When I got out of high school I had a kid, so going into the military was my attempt to try and get some stability in my life," he explains of his military service, which lasted four years. "I got jump status and I went to the 25th Infantry. Schofield Barracks in Hawaii. Overall it wasn't a good experience. The military is crazy! It was interesting, I guess. Maybe it made me more structured in my life."

By 1980 he was a civilian once again, and he figured that DJing parties might be a good way to make cash since he was a music fan. "Back then I wanted to do parties," he explains. "I had bought all this equipment and everything. But my friends picked me up at the airport after I got back, and at that point they were doing a lot of heavy crime. So we started making moves on jewelry stores and doing all kinds of robberies. In a little while I was able to obtain a lot of wealth. Within a year I think I had close to a million dollars. That's when I built my street reputation, being a flashy character in L.A."

Even though he was doing just fine on the crime side, he still gave the party circuit a shot. "I started giving parties, but I didn't like carrying all the equipment," he recalls. "This is around when 'Rapper's Delight' was out and rap was starting to break out all over the place. So I tried my luck on the mic. And even though I was wack, I was still better than everybody else [*laughs*]. I found that I could make more money and enjoy myself more by going from party to party, just rapping." And thus a side career was born, which he undertook each weekend on the party scene, in clubs, and at house parties.

Often he was aided by another upstart rapper from L.A.: Kid Frost. "Once me and Frost started to get known, our names would just start popping up on flyers whether we had said we'd be there or not," Ice says. "So we'd just bum-rush parties that had our names on flyers, anywhere we could. When we'd show up, the promoters' eyes would open up, 'cause we was actually there, and that meant they'd have to pay us. We were jacking promoters like that. On any given Friday or Saturday night we could run from party to party and make a thousand or fifteen hundred dollars. That was a lot of money in the rap game back then."

After a couple years on the scene honing his skills, Ice put out his first single, "The Coldest Rap," on the Saturn label in 1983. "I didn't make any money from that, or from any of those early singles I did," he explains. (This includes his second single, "Killers," on Electro Beat from 1984.) And even though he was making decent money on the party scene, his hustling ways continued. "My illegal hustle didn't really stop until I got my first record deal [in 1987]," says Ice. "All throughout those independent records there was no money. I was living a certain lifestyle back then, and a rap record wasn't going to change my life. I never thought I'd make a career of rap—it was totally just for fun. I mean, how could I think about it as a career? Nobody had even bought a car from rap money back then."

Rap also served another purpose for Ice: "I looked at rap as a way of covering my [illegal] game. Hip-hop was a front for me. It was my way of having the things and telling people that I got this Porsche from rapping. But that stuff I had on my album covers, I never could have bought that jewelry and that stuff from rap. So I had to use it as a cover-up."

One place that Ice cites as a major influence on his hip-hop game was a hipster club in downtown L.A. called Radio (later known as Radio Tron). "It was an underground European hip-hop club, run by a guy named Alex Jordanov and this guy KK," Ice recalls. "It was all white kids, because it was a Russian club, and because there were really no hip-hoppers in L.A. back in '82 and '83. Alex was a Russian motherfucker by way of France, by way of New York. They were graffiti artists and brought [Afrika] Bambaataa in, Grandmixer D.ST, Rocksteady Crew. That place was way ahead of the curve."

"Back in '83 I had [one of] the only record[s] out in L.A. at the time ["The Coldest Rap"], and they were playing it every night at that club," Ice recalls about his first experience at Radio. "They booked me for a show, so I went down there. There wasn't a black face in the joint—it was a totally different crowd than I had ever been in before. I walked on stage and everybody in the audience knew every word of that record. And it was the first time I had even heard of this place! I hung out there a lot after that."

Ice, in fact, went on to be, as he calls it, the "stage manager" of Radio in 1984 and 1985. "I went back to that club every weekend, and I'd bring more and more friends, all my hustler buddies," he says. "Eventually, anybody who wanted to perform at Radio would have to come to me first." Among those he put onstage there were a not-yet-famous Madonna. ("I take credit for telling Madonna to show more cleavage," he beams.)

More important, he met one of his crucial future collaborators at Radio: New York DJ and producer Afrika Islam (Charles Glenn). Islam was the touring DJ for the Rocksteady Crew at the time and a high-ranking member of Afrika Bambaataa's Bronx-based Zulu Nation. "I remember meeting Ice at Radio back then," says Islam from his home in Germany. "It was right before he and Egyptian Lover did 'Breaking & Entering.' [*Author's note: He's referring to the instrumental music that Ice-T rapped over in the movie* Breakin'; *the music was never commercially released, only pressed on acetates, and subsequently bootlegged.*] I didn't know much about Ice-T, just that Afrika Bambaataa had met him before and said that I should also. Ice and I were both concerned with the dance floor. He did it with his raps and I did it with turntables."

Ice and Afrika hit it off and agreed to stay in touch. When Ice's 1986 single "Dog 'N the Wax" (with its B-side, "6 in the Mornin' ") came out on Techno Hop, he sent a box of the singles to New York, asking Islam to spread them around. Instead of just handing the singles out, Islam convinced Ice to take a trip to New York City to meet the city's hip-hop cognoscenti himself at clubs like Union Square and Latin Quarter. "I got a cheap ticket and flew to the South Bronx," Ice recalls. "I was staying with Afrika on 156th. And because Islam is the man, he introduced me to New York City hip-hop from the top down. Scott La Rock, Chuck Chillout, Red Alert. All the top people."

"When Ice came to New York that first time, it put him in a position where he was around a lot of legends, like Melle Mel and Grandmaster Caz," Afrika explains. "Before Ice came to New York, L.A. didn't exist to them. 'Dog 'N the Wax' was a good track, but '6 in the Mornin' ' was the one that really had the impact in New York. It set the pace and it gave him acceptance." Ice concurs: "Sound-wise, '6 in the Mornin' ' is definitely more of an East Coast–style record. Less music, more beat."

"Ice played the Prospect Theater in 1986," Afrika continues. "It was unheard of for a hip-hop concert to go down in a South Bronx movie theater. He did '6 in the Mornin'' and Rakim was there, KRS and Scott La Rock were there. It shocked people when he said: 'We beat the bitch down in the goddamn street.' Back then, people didn't associate Los Angeles with 'hood stories. We thought it was all Hollywood and Malibu Beach. So when he came to New York saying rhymes that dealt with violence, it was all new. So that's where Ice got his merit badge from the Bronx."

Ice impressed locals not only with his rhymes and beats, but also with his style and panache. "New York loved me," he brags. "They could see I had paper. I was a half-assed rapper, but I had a Porsche Turbo, and they were trying to figure that out. They wanted to know how to get the money, and I wanted to know how to be a rapper. The only resistance I got was from Kool Herc. He didn't like the fact that I cursed [*laughs*]. He still doesn't. I respect that, but that's all I know how to do!"

Ice returned to New York frequently and continued to build his rep on both coasts. He also appeared on an Afrika Islam–produced single on Posse Records later in 1986: "Cars" by the Zulu Kings (with Melle Mel and Bronx Style Bob). In 1987 an opportunity came that changed both Ice's life and his hustle. Afrika's friend Ralph Cooper knew Sire Records

Ice-T at home, Hollywood, 1992.
PHOTO: B+ (FOR WWW.MOCHILLA.COM).

president Seymour Stein though Cooper's father, who managed the famed Apollo Theater. "This has actually never been written about before, but Ralph presented a compilation-album concept to Seymour Stein," says Ice. "The compilation was supposed to be me, Melle Mel, Grandmaster Caz, Donald D, and this guy Bronx Style Bob, who was down with Afrika."

Islam says that the "compilation" album in question was actually supposed to be an extension of the Zulu Kings single, with many of Islam's Bronx associates and Ice as well. "I was DJing at the Roxy back then and Madonna [who was Sire's biggest star] was always performing and hanging out there in her earlier days," Islam recalls. "So when Ralph Cooper walked us into the office, Seymour Stein knew exactly who I was. Madonna even knew Ice-T from Radio in L.A., so everything came together. Melle Mel couldn't get out of his contract, so they said, 'Ice, we'll sign you, and Afrika, you produce it.' So we walked out of there and we were signed."

Ice adds: "By Seymour Stein just saying, 'Fuck it!,' that got me in the door. He didn't even know much at all about hip-hop. He told me it sounded like Bob Dylan to him. Mine was the first rap record on Sire, the first on Warner Bros., and one of the first on a major label. I got forty thousand dollars for the record budget, with no video. And that's when we did *Rhyme Pays*."

Ice and Islam got right to work, recording the album in about thirty days in New York (contrary to the listing on the back of the album, which says it was recorded in L.A.). "We mixed it in one night, at Secret Sound in New York," Ice recalls. "We got the forty thousand, bought an SP-12 [the E-mu SP-1200 sampler/drum machine], and fucked off some of the money. The record probably cost about twenty-five thousand dollars to make, total. We made that whole album with one drum machine, the SP-1200, using the sounds that were in the machine."

"I had never used an SP-1200 before," says Islam. "I knew all the beats that I'd have to program—I knew all the loops because I was a DJ who was down with Bambaataa. My supply of material was infinite. I just had to learn how to translate it onto that machine."

Islam adds, regarding his production approach with his new musical partner, "With *Rhyme Pays,* the big difference for me was that I was writing to a lyricist. I knew all these legends, like Kool Moe Dee, Melle Mel, and Grandmaster Caz, and I realized that whenever an MC takes a breath, that's what establishes their rhyme pattern. I knew Ice's rhyme pattern. I think that's why those records worked so well for us, because all the beats were matched to him specifically. He wasn't a party rhymer, he was more of a lyricist. So you had to write music that was dedicated to the lyrics more than making music for the dance floor. I would start writing the music directly from his rhymes. I'd finish the beat and he'd press the button on the SP-1200 and he'd rap over it, and that was it. I don't think the album actually took more than two weeks, really. It was as basic as you can get."

Even though they were learning as they went along, both men still knew the gravity of the situation. "An album was serious shit, and I knew it had to be good," states Ice. "You always want to get to the next album. I came out with the best I could do at the time. I also knew that I had to rap in a lot of different ways. I couldn't rap the same way each time, because I hated when other rappers did that. I knew I had to have different cadences and different topics. Street shit, some politics, some sex shit. Public Enemy's album [*Yo! Bum Rush the Show*, from 1987] came out at that time and it was dope, but it was just one thing. I knew that if I went that route, I'd never be able to tell a joke or to have fun with the audience."

In addition to the single "Somebody's Gotta Do It (Pimpin' Ain't Easy)," the album was solid top to bottom, with Ice's array of approaches: sex ("I Love Ladies" and "Sex"); politics ("Pain"); street reality ("Squeeze the Trigger"); and good old-fashioned partying ("409"). Ice, the savvy, flashy L.A. player, knew that the album cover would be important. For that he enlisted one of hip-hop's most important photographers from that era, Glen E. Friedman. "Glen gave me that album cover for *Rhyme Pays* that made me stand alongside the big cats," Ice says.

The image was certainly a powerful one: Ice scowling from behind the wheel of his purple Porsche, with a fine female standing tall in the passenger seat, DJ Evil E in the back, and a palm tree hovering strategically above their heads. "[Glen] made sure that we got the girl, the Porsche, and the palm tree in it," Ice says. "He said, 'The palm tree is the most important thing in this shot.' L.A. was very important to the image I was getting across."

Rhyme Pays, released in 1987, went gold [Ice claims that sales were around eight hundred thousand] with no video and very little national radio airplay. It was an impressive feat, and one that did not go unnoticed at Sire.

Ice's DJ for most of the eighties was Evil E, the brother of fellow New York Spin Master (their DJ group, which was very popular in L.A. at the time) Hen Gee. "Those guys came into the fold way back in the Kid Frost days, really," Ice says. "When I started doing clubs, they was in the party scene already. They was from New York, so they called themselves the New York

City Spin Masters. When I first broke, Chris 'the Glove' was gonna be my DJ, but he didn't want to do it. Henry [Hen] started becoming more of a manager and Evil and I just started doing routines. E was so eager to make money that I could call him up for any party and he'd always be glad to show up."

Even though Afrika Islam was a talented DJ in his own right, Ice explains, "Me and Evil was always a team." So Afrika stuck to producing, and Evil was behind the decks. "We talked about it many times, about who should be the DJ, but we decided that it should be Evil, because he had been there in L.A. with Ice," explains Islam. "I was from New York, not L.A., so I was there on stage with Ice on the mic [as his hype man], giving him the Zulu Nation's endorsement."

When 1988 rolled around, things couldn't have been better for Ice. Aside from a gold record with *Rhyme Pays,* he was also featured on the soundtrack to the film *Colors* and convinced Warner Bros. to release the Rhyme Syndicate compilation album *Comin' Through* in early 1988. [*Author's note: Ice says the* Colors *soundtrack went platinum, although currently the RIAA has only certified it gold.*] With all this swirling about, he and Afrika Islam were on a serious roll, and they walked directly into their next major work: Ice's *Power.*

"By the time I got to *Power,* I was aware that people were listening," Ice says. "With *Rhyme Pays* I didn't even know if people were going to listen or buy it at all. But with eight hundred thousand fans it's a whole different thing. I knew *Power* had to be more serious, and that I had to get some points across."

The recording of *Power* was different from *Rhyme Pays* in many ways, except for the amount of time it took. "The recording was fast," Ice recalls. "I pretty much record every record in a matter of a month, maybe two at the most. It's better that way, because you can stay in one mental set. We did *Power* in L.A., on a fourteen-track Akai machine in Evil E's back house. That was Syndicate Studios West. The board was connected to the biggest system we could build that resembled a car stereo system, so we could check how it sounded when real people who would buy our tapes listened to that shit. Big woofers and all that. We had a little bitty closet where we did the vocals."

"I was out in L.A. for the recording of *Power* and I definitely understood the whole premise of the album by that time," says Afrika. "We were making money, but we were still getting disrespected at venues where we were performing. N.W.A. and Public Enemy were also out at the time, so things were even more serious. But he was still Ice and so he still had to do a song like 'Let's Get Butt Naked and Fuck,' and his crime stories as well. He had to write even better, and I had to come up with beats that matched him. When I got there to L.A. after *Rhyme Pays,* I just learned by watching. I played Ice close because I wanted to get *his* opinion, about how *he* saw L.A. I wasn't trying to stay there. To me, that place was always La-la Land. Ice showed me the dark side of L.A. and I understood. It was all pretty surreal for me."

Islam continues: "We recorded at Evil's place, in the back, but I probably actually wrote most of those tracks at my apartment. At the time I had two SP-1200s and a [Roland] 909 drum machine, and that was about it. Doing it at Evil's was good because we didn't have any time constraints. Evil had a bigger place than Ice or I, so we could bring more people over there. I didn't want all those people at my apartment! And we could also get loud at Evil's, because we had the vocal booth in a closet. There wasn't anything too complicated—it was all very natural. We didn't take too much time to record our albums because rap back then was topical. You were writing a song and you were making a statement."

The album's eleven main tracks are another tour de force for Ice, and they again explore a wide range of topics, moods, and approaches. As with *Rhyme Pays,* Ice's most important approach may have been the one for which he was most misunderstood: his descriptions and subsequent condemnation of the gangbanging lifestyle. Tracks like "Drama" and even "I'm Your Pusher" are morality tales that start posh and end badly for those who choose that way of life. "When my dad would teach me lessons, he would never just say: 'Don't do it,' " Ice explains. "He would tell me stories and he would get me into it. It would be like: 'He was about to get a million dollars, but that night he OD'd.' So I always used that technique. Because I *do* really, truly come from the game, I can't write a story about the hustle where the dude doesn't end up in prison or dead. Because all the real stories do. If I'm rhyming and I shoot somebody, I'm on the run in the next verse."

Despite Ice's allegiance to L.A., he never got involved in any battles with New York, even despite the Big Apple's frequent resistance to West Coast rap in the eighties and early nineties. "Back then I had a Syndicate meeting and said, 'Look, New York is always going to have a resistance to West Coast stuff,' " he recalls. "So I took a pen and I circled New York, Philly, and New Jersey on a map. And I said, 'Okay, they can have those. But the West Coast starts *right here* and I was pointing to everything outside of the circle. Because a motherfucker from Detroit doesn't give a fuck if you're from New York or L.A., because he's from neither. I knew we could sell a million records with or without New York. We could just take the rest of the country.

"I never really played the East-West game," Ice says. "My thing is that I'm from Earth and I'm playing the whole map, and I go anywhere. I rep L.A., but I gotta be down with New York. For me to rep the West and dis the East would make me a fake, because I was born in the East. Plus Islam put me on, so I could never dis New York."

"Ice definitely knew that things were serious with *Power*," Afrika says. "He was also trying to come as an adult with more awareness. He said a lot on *Power*. It was like a kid getting to college after graduating from high school. With that album we were definitely leaps and bounds ahead of ninety-nine percent of the rest of the game and the rest of the country with what we were saying. Ice knew more about the pimping and West Coast life and gang situation, and I knew about the East Coast [Black] Panther type of situations because of the Zulu Nation. And that's where our nucleus was, as a team."

Power neared platinum by 1989 and has passed that mark by now. The album cemented Ice's rep as a top draw and also as one of rap's most creative provocateurs. And now that Ice was making money legally, his illegal hustle was a thing of the past. "It was really nice to be the hot shit back then," he recalls with pride. "My star definitely banged from *Power* right until around *OG* [his 1991 Sire album]. When I look at the magazines now and I see all the new guys, I'm like, 'Yo, they deserve that, because we had it.' There was a time when motherfuckers had to look at us every day and they probably got sick of it, too [*laughs*]."

TRACKS

Ice-T: That song never appeared on any of my albums—it was only a single and on the *Colors* soundtrack. I don't know why I didn't include "Colors" on the *Power* album. It was probably just timing. I never really thought about it, to be honest. I love that song, that's the one that I close my show with even to this day. "Colors" was never actually intended to be a record. They were gonna use my song "Squeeze the Trigger" on the soundtrack to that movie and I saw a screening of the film and knew I could do the title song to it. The Rick James song on there ["Everywhere I Go"] was supposed to be the main song, but I was like: "Rick, I can handle this." We went in and took the beat from King Sun's "Mythological." [*Ice rhymes part of King Sun's song, to prove it.*] We took the beat, turned it around, played a bass line over it, and I used pretty much the same cadence that Sun had. I turned it in to the Warners people and they loved it. Dennis Hopper and them was looking for gang-based records, so I was perfect for it. We knocked out the song over the weekend. I mean, c'mon, ain't nobody can write a record about gangs if they haven't been in a gang. The Ice-T style is to put myself in whatever person's place I'm writing a song about. I did that with [his group Body Count's controversial 1992 song] "Cop Killer" and got myself in some trouble [*laughs loudly*].

Afrika Islam: I think that song took us about three hours to record, and I put it together with a Roland 303 [drum machine/keyboard] and an 808 [drum machine]. We did the song on the spot because we understood the film. By the time we did "Colors" I had seen the 'hood, and the Crips and Bloods. I was living in Hollywood but we'd go to parties in the 'hood and I'd be like: "Yo, these motherfuckers are *dangerous.*" It was different than the South Bronx kind of dangerous. I don't know if we saw the whole movie, but I know we saw at least a clip of it. I definitely understood what Ice meant when he said: "I am a nightmare walking." That's where the Moog sound and the big, bumpin' bass came in.

DRAMA

Ice-T: That's the same bass machine on there [the 303] we used to use for a lot of shit back then, like with "Colors" and [*Rhyme Pays's*] "Squeeze the Trigger." I don't see how anyone can think that I'm glorifying hustling in that song, 'cause the guy's dying in the electric chair [*laughs*]. It's a crime record, but at the same time it's supposed to be an educational record. Like I said on *OG:* "That invincible shit don't work." I didn't really care that I was misunderstood in my lyrics, really. And by the time I got to the *OG* album I was done explainin'.

Afrika Islam: For that one, I took a 303 and put it into the SP-1200 and played it from there. That was a new thing, because the 303 was usually only heard in techno music. But the sound was definitely pure drama, that's the best way I can explain it. The 303 sound was so shrieky, it was so different for hip-hop.

THE SYNDICATE *Featuring Donald D and Hen-Gee*

Afrika Islam: Donald D started with me. When I started DJing in the mid-seventies, he was one of my first MCs. He was on my "Zulu Beats" [radio] show too [on WHBI in New York, starting in 1982]. Hen-Gee was on that track too. He's Evil's brother. With that Rhyme Syndicate album [*Comin' Through*], that was my first step into really working with a big-time record company [Warner Bros.]. It was a learning experience for me, and a challenge to work with all those different MCs, to try and get the best out of them.

Ice-T: The Syndicate kind of became a gang of cats in L.A. who wasn't down with the N.W.A. scene. I would collect tapes from people and it just started to become an organization. Guys like Def Jef, Everlast, and [DJ] Muggs was around when he was in 7A3. I was the kind of guy who was like: "Yo, if I get my shit off, I'm gonna help you guys." And that's how the Rhyme Syndicate album [*Comin' Through*] came out. When I got my power at Warner Bros. after the first album, I did that. That Syndicate album did decent, it sold a couple hundred thousand. I was able to get an Everlast and a Donald D album out of it. All the guys who were on that track were actually originally from New York, but it wasn't planned that way, of course. It might seem ironic [New York–bred rappers repping L.A.] but that's just who was in the studio at that time.

RADIO SUCKERS

Ice-T: Yeah, with Chuck D on the hook! The first time I saw Public Enemy I didn't actually meet Chuck. I saw them at the L.A. Sports Arena on some tour. I saw Griff and all these mo'fuckas with guns and I was like, "Oh, this shit is *dope*." I knew of them also through Glen Friedman, since he took pictures for both of us. Me and PE clicked on intensity, we clicked on battle scars, and we also understood each other's position. Chuck was a Nationalist position. He was trying to get all black people to understand the problems of the world. I was a 'hood politician. I wanted people to understand what was going on in the city. He rapped about the president, I rapped about the police. My politics never reached past city limits. I rapped in a smaller room. I was rapping about the guy who says he's gonna kill you tomorrow. That song was basically just saying, "Fuck radio," and I still say it to this day. Fuck 'em! Basically I was able to sell platinum records without ever being on the radio. I would never go to radio and kiss their ass, because if I do, the next day that person is fired and I have to go back and kiss somebody else's ass. If you're playing my records, I'll come in and kiss your ass. One time I asked somebody at a station why I never got play and they told me, "Well, Ice, it's because you're too *real*." Some radio station in Texas. They'll listen to another rapper say they'll shoot somebody, and I guess it seems corny. But with the tone of my voice I guess it sounded too real? So if I made myself corny, they would play my records? I've never gotten radio play and they can all eat a bowl of dicks. You'll never find an Ice-T clean album. N.W.A. did entire clean albums, but I thought that was selling out. C'mon, they can bleep that shit. N.W.A. made more money because of it, but I had my integrity.

I'M YOUR PUSHER

Ice-T: That was the first single and the first video we ever did for one of my albums. We didn't have one for the first album. That song is one of the first rap records to ever have a singing hook on it. Pimpin' Rex sang the chorus of that song. He was one of my buddies, a real live pimp [*laughs*]. The video for that song was just following the lyrics, basically. A drug kid walks up and wants some dope, then I'm on the corner handing out CDs like we're doing drug deals. I dissed LL [Cool J] on that track. You see, LL at that time was on his "I'm the greatest rapper in the world" thing. Me being from L.A., I was trying to rep our entire city alone, so I had to step to him. It was no personal shit with him or anything. I was just shooting at the number-one cat at the time. I didn't have any fear of LL, and I thought I could beat him rapping anyways. Eventually it would have gotten worse. He dissed me in a record called "To the Break of Dawn," I think he called me a little rat raccoon or some shit [*laughs*].

Afrika Islam: That was the first video and yeah, that guy Pimpin' Rex was a real pimp. He was one of the dancers who came up with Ice in the early eighties. His group of dancers was called the Majestics and they were some of the most incredible dancers I've seen in my whole life. Rex would come over to the studio with like twenty girls, but he'd be like, "Don't touch them, I haven't cleaned them up yet." With Ice dissing LL, it was simple. LL said he was bad, and Ice didn't agree with that. It wasn't any of my business because I wasn't a rapper, and I was representing the Bronx and the Zulus, not LL. Eventually we had to stop them from fighting, so we all sat down at a table. I remember it was me, Flavor Flav, Red Alert, Mike Tyson, and Bambaataa, and we were like, "You guys gotta stop this." LL was battling Kool Moe Dee and Dee and Ice were friends. Having Mike Tyson there made sense, because he was down with hip-hop and the Zulus and I've always considered rappers like boxers anyways.

Ice-T: That song [the acronym stood for "Let's get butt naked and fuck"] was kind of another LL [Cool J] thing. We were making fun of the fact that these niggas was making love records. Because we come from the school of if your girl likes the record then it's no good. This is some real male, locker-room rapping. I came up with the concept and [Audio Two's] "Top Billin' " was a big record at the time, so Afrika was like, "We need to do a beat something like that." So we did that beat and I used a similar rhyme flow. That's Evil E talking behind my words on there. That song is always a crowd pleaser when we perform it. It's definitely in the "La Di Da Di" [by Doug E. Fresh & Slick Rick] tradition.

Afrika Islam: That was a dope beat! I don't remember exactly how I made it, but I know I did it with two 909 drum machines, linked together, playing different beats. I think that was a song where the beat came first and Ice put lyrics to it.

HIGH ROLLERS

Ice-T: That was the second single and video. We were all up at this house in the video, just hustlin', high rollin', with guns, girls in bathing suits, and all that. Videos for us were funny back then because we had to use all our own props. There were no car rentals and all that. Nowadays you see a guy in a video and all that shit isn't even his. But we had to bring out the shit ourselves. As I said in one of my rhymes, "The guns in my promo shots ain't props." When we was shooting the "High Rollers" video there was so much heat and so much shit on the set that the crew was getting nervous. We had coke on the set and they was freaking out. It was the real deal back then—it was fun.

Afrika Islam: The video for that song was definitely kinda wild, but that's what the song was about. Some of his friends in that life got killed and some went to jail. I didn't have friends like that. On the production side, I just tried to match the mood, and I think it was successful. I heard the lyrics first and I went digging for something that would match them musically. It was definitely a theatrical song, so the video worked on that angle too.

SOUL ON ICE

Ice-T: That was my tribute to [author] Iceberg Slim. I took my name from him, back when I started out. I started reading him in high school. My buddy Michael Carter, who was a young player, gave me the books and that shit was just fascinating. I was fucking around with gangs at the time but that shit made me wanna be a pimp. It totally introduced me to a fly lifestyle. I started quoting [Slim] in high school, a fourteen-year-old kid quoting forty-year-old man shit. I read a lot of his books before I ever heard his tape [Iceberg Slim's spoken-word/jazz album *Reflections,* from 1976], and also the *Hustler's Convention* album [by Lightnin' Rod, aka Jalal Nuriddin of the Last Poets]. I met Iceberg Slim [who died in 1992] on the phone once, through Fab Five Freddy. And I met his daughter in person.

MARLEY MARL

In Control Volume 1

(Cold Chillin'/Warner Bros., 1988)

L

ong before the Wu-Tang Clan began to spread their tentacles; when P. Diddy was still using the name on his birth certificate; and while the heads of the Cash Money and Roc-A-Fella families were likely trying to get a date to the seventh-grade dance, Marley Marl (born Marlon Williams) and the Juice Crew ruled hip-hop. They were the first rap dynasty, with a distinct ruler and amazingly talented field generals. In the late eighties there was no one making music like producer and DJ Marley Marl. And 1988 was the year it all broke out.

To cap off a year that saw debut smashes by Big Daddy Kane, MC Shan, Biz Markie, and Roxanne Shanté (Lolita Gooden), Marley Marl's *In Control Volume 1* dropped. It was important not only because it contained dope tracks by Juice Crew members young and old. It was also a record that pointed to the producer as much more than a behind-the-scenes puppet master. "It was definitely an important thing to have a producer thought of as an artist, especially back then," Marley says today. "Up to that point, the vocalist or MC was the person that an album was about. Positioning me like that on the album was something different for the whole game. I had never even thought of doing my own album, but with *In Control* I was one of the first producers to actually step up as an artist."

The labels involved, Cold Chillin' and their parent company, Warner Bros., were gung-ho about *In Control* as well. Marley says: "Warner and Cold Chillin' were definitely into the album because I was building seed for them, since they had me as a producer. When we hit them with the idea of me as an artist, Benny Medina at Warners was all over it."

The album itself, rather than a fully planned effort that took years to conceive, was brought about by a fruitful problem: Marley still had great tracks from Juice Crew members that didn't fit on their albums. He recalls: "At that point, we had made a lot of records, and I had a lot of heat in the crib that hadn't even made it on an album, for different artists. Because so much of that stuff was already done, it didn't take long at all to put together."

A close perusal of the artist listings on the platter shows that Marley was more concerned with bringing up newcomers who hadn't hit hard yet, like Tragedy (Percy Chapman), Craig G (Craig Curry), and the newly signed

Master Ace (Duval Clear). Marley confirms this: "Kane and G Rap had gold chains by '88. I was trying to bring the young cats up. At that point I was mostly concerned with Craig and Tragedy. That's why they had solo records on there. Ace, too. Everybody else was already stars, so I wasn't worried as much about them."

Named after his long-running "Marley Marl in Control" radio show on WBLS in New York, the platter did exactly what Marley intended. And aside from introducing the world to the next wave of Juice Crew talent (sadly, none of the three he was pushing ever had the blockbuster success of his predecessors), the album spawned one of the greatest posse cuts in hip-hop history: "The Symphony," featuring Ace, Craig G, Kool G Rap (Nathaniel Wilson), and Big Daddy Kane (Antonio Hardy). It was the only track done exclusively for *In Control.*

The album's cover was a true classic of the late-eighties era as well, with Marley poised in the cockpit of a private jet and a crew group photo on the back. "That cover shot was my ex-wife's idea," Marley laughs. "I told the people at the label about it and the next thing I know we're at an airport, in front of a private jet, with a pilot suit for me. That suit was just a prop, of course. And the gold chains I was wearing were a prop, too. I never owned any big gold chains like that, believe it or not. They were probably Kool G's or Kane's."

"It was good for me that *In Control* came out after everybody else's album in 1988, no doubt," Marley says. "My album was much more anticipated because of the success of all the other Juice Crew hits." As for sales, Marley claims that he never paid too much attention, which would be a first for a producer with points. "I'm not sure if that album went gold," he muses, "but the first week it was out it probably sold about fifty thousand. That was a nice buzz record, definitely." He adds: "That was my approach to that whole era. I wasn't even doing it for the money. I was really loving just doing it. It just so happened that I made money, so I wasn't arguing with that. What I didn't know is how much history we was making.

"I like to revisit my older stuff, like that album, sometimes. It puts me in that state of mind again. I go through those tracks and they give me a sense of how they played a part in forming the hip-hop and R&B that's around today. Like 'We Write the Songs' and 'The Symphony.' They still sound phenomenal to me."

He ends our chat by dropping a news flash that will make Juice Crew fiends froth: "I've got an album called *Juice Crew Unreleased Gems* that I want to put out. I have a Tragedy song on that motherfucker called 'Son of the Block' that I made the same week that I produced 'Make the Music with Your Mouth, Biz' for Biz, 'Eric B. Is President' [for Eric B. & Rakim], and also [MC Shan and Marley's] 'The Bridge.' So you can go figure what that must sound like. Back then I would have a sound of the week. Whatever drum sound was in the sampler, that's what I went with, for whoever I was producing."

TRACKS

DROPPIN' SCIENCE *Featuring Craig G*

Wooooooooooo [makes high-pitched exclamation when song title is mentioned]! That version on the album was the original one. The one that a lot of people know is the single version, which had a different beat to it [using Lou Donaldson's version of "Who's Making Love"]. I think that remix, the single version, is one of my favorite beats of all time, and it was only on the single. It never came out on any album. Craig didn't even like it at first, either—he liked the first version. That track and "The Symphony" were the singles from the album. Craig was only seventeen or eighteen when that came out. He was too young to even sign to Cold Chillin', like Tragedy. Craig had a lot of mic technique and a lot of presence even at a young age. He got that from watchin' us out in the park.

WE WRITE THE SONGS *Featuring Heavy D. and Biz Markie*

Aww, yeah! I loved working with Biz, his spontaneity. He was so quick, you had to record him all the time or you'd miss something. A lot of the time when he was around I'd have a 120-minute DAT recording, rolling just in case. I think Biz must have come up with the idea for that track since he sang the hook. And Heavy D. (Dwight Myers) and I go way back. I helped produce "Mr. Big Stuff" for him and I did some stuff on his first two albums. Heavy D. was a big, fun guy. He brought some fun to the game, most definitely.

THE REBEL *Featuring Percy/Tragedy*

Tragedy recorded his two tracks for *In Control* way before I even thought about doing the album. They were just demos. And when the album came out in 1988 he was only fifteen or sixteen and in jail, still just a kid. So we set up a fund for him so that he came out to some money. He got out the week we did the video for "The Symphony." The first time I worked with him was on the Super Kids' "The Tragedy" single [Nia Records, 1986]. That was him and Hot Day Dante. He was only twelve or thirteen when that record came out, and in jail already.

KEEP YOUR EYE ON THE PRIZE *Featuring Master Ace and Action*

Everybody always said Ace and Action, but Master Ace had two DJs—the other one was Steady Pace. Ace was from Brooklyn, but he got hooked up with me because he won a rap contest at United Skates of America in Queens. The grand prize was to go into the studio with Marley Marl. I liked his style, so I kept him with me after the demo. That was Steady Pace cutting up at the end of that, not me.

THE SYMPHONY *Featuring Master Ace, Craig G, Kool G Rap, and Big Daddy Kane*

That track was the only one made specifically for the *In Control* album. We did the photo shoot for the back cover of the album [with most of the Juice Crew present] at an airport on Long Island somewhere, and went to my studio in Astoria right from there. Everybody was together and was freestylin', and I was like: "Yo! We need to go make a record right now!" Shan (Shawn Moltke) is in that photo shoot, but he didn't come to the studio. He was supposed to meet us later but he never showed up, so he's not on the record. As soon as the record company heard that collaboration, we all knew right away that it was the lead single for the album. We knew it would be huge. I don't know if I could choose who has the illest verse on there [*laughs*]. Maybe mine was [*laughs loudly*]! Kool G Rap actually rapped from where his verse started to the end of the whole song. I have that version somewhere. I had to cut his part off, when Kane's verse comes in.

DUCK ALERT *Featuring Craig G*

That's definitely my favorite song on the album. Definitely don't forget about "Duck Alert"! That was a promo for my radio show and it was directed at Red Alert and Chuck Chillout, both of them. They were both on Kiss FM, the opposing station, and hip-hop was all about dissing. We used to call Chuck "Duck Illout." Craig G only did one verse on the original radio promo of that, and after we decided to use it on the album, he went in and we added a couple extra verses. To be honest, I never saw Red Alert as competition on the radio, but it was just the thing to do, to make a dis track. Red and I both work for Power 105 in New York now [in 2003] and we chuckle about how much radio history we made back then. And how we didn't even know how much history we were making.

FREEDOM *Featuring MC Shan*

That was just a different mix of a track on Shan's album from earlier that year ["Give Me My Freedom"]. Shan and I were going to go on stage with Nas for the Hot 97 Summer Jam this year [in 2003] to perform "The Bridge" in the middle of Nas's show, and then do a quick battle with KRS-One. But it fell through. That would have been something!

WACK ITT *Featuring Roxanne Shanté*

That song was on Shanté's album—I just took a different version of it for mine. I had the track done and she just got on the mic and started dissing. All you had to do was give her an idea and she'd run with it—she never even wrote her lyrics down. That song was kind of like a joke, more like a skit. I don't think she cared that much about Salt 'N Pepa or J.J. Fad either way.

MC LYTE
Lyte as a Rock

(First Priority/Atlantic, 1988)

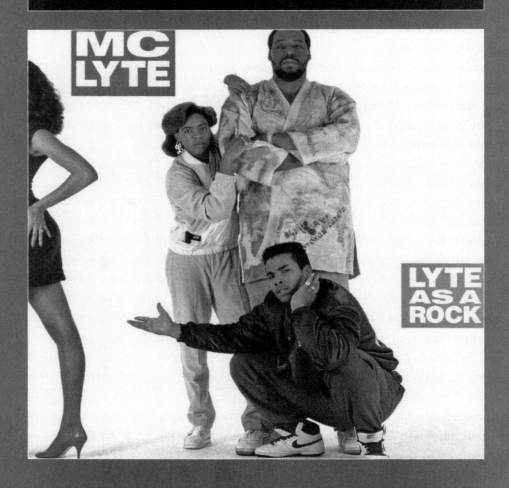

Hearing the classic "I Cram To Understand U" when it hit on First Priority Records in 1986, any listener would have been shocked to learn that the track's author was a mere sixteen years old at the time. But it was true: East Flatbush, Brooklyn's MC Lyte (Lana Moorer) had just roped in her learner's permit when she sagely opined about the woes of both crack and fickle male love. "I was originally just called Lyte," she says today. "But when I got the record back it had MC Lyte on it. Lyte is some positive wordplay. Truth is the light. The light shall lead you out of dark passages. Light was one of the many forces created by God. That kind of thing."

Some people didn't even know what sex the MC who rhymed the lyrics was. "When 'Cram' came out, no one had seen a picture of me, and they all thought I sounded like a little boy," Lyte says. But Lyte was all woman, and a very strong one at that, which she proved on wax and on stage.

On the subject of her earliest years, she says, "I was actually born in Queens, by accident. My mom was out visiting my grandfather and I decided it was time to arrive." Born in Far Rockaway, she soon returned to Brooklyn, where she spent the seventies and eighties. And while every kid in Brooklyn was eating and breathing hip-hop by the mid-eighties, Lyte showed more talent and more ambition than most. "In junior high I used to bang on the lunchroom tables and rap," she says. "And in 1984 I had a couple of songs written already and went to [DJ] Clark Kent's house and did a song in the basement called 'I Cram to Understand You.' " This was the beginning of her recording career, although the song in question wasn't to appear for two more years and in a different form. "The final version of it was with Audio Two's production," she adds. "Clark didn't produce the original song, he just played an instrumental of someone else's record, and I just rhymed the lyrics over that."

The First Priority label on which Lyte had her debut wasn't a random connection. In fact it was a family affair, owned by former club promoter and entrepreneur Nat Robinson, who also happened to be Lyte's stepfather. Producer and rapper Milk D (Kirk Robinson) of the Audio Two was Nat's son and Lyte's half-brother. "Nat formed the label for Milk and Giz [who comprised the Audio Two] and he came to me and said, 'Do you want to give it a go?' " she explains. "And I said, 'Sure!' Me, Milk, Giz, the Alliance,

MC Peaches, and UBL kind of just created our own little world. The First Priority Family."

"Milk lived in Bed-Stuy and I lived in the Nineties [streets in Brooklyn]," she says. "Even though we weren't in the same house, we hung out a lot and grew into the music together." As such, Milk's production wasn't just a great musical match—it was brotherly love. The "Cram" track itself, which followed directly after the Audio Two's smash single "Top Billin'," was a loose, funky storytelling rhyme that was impossible to resist.

Success came quickly for Lyte and the Audio Two, and soon they were standing shoulder to shoulder with the rap stars of the day. "I did a lot of clubbing when I was young," Lyte recalls. "It was okay then to be young and be at the Latin Quarter or Union Square. There were big high school crowds there. I saw Salt 'N Pepa and Boogie Down Productions perform at Union Square, and Public Enemy and Jazzy Jeff and the Fresh Prince at Latin Quarter. Then in 1986 I was performing at Latin Quarter too, after 'I Cram' came out. It was wild."

Lyte and the funky and off-kilter Audio Two were both signed to Atlantic in 1987 through the auspices of First Priority, and both dropped their debut full-lengths in 1988. Believe it or not, it wasn't as easy as it should have been to get Atlantic on board with Robinson's female star in waiting. "Atlantic didn't actually even want to sign me," recalls Lyte. "But my dad said, 'If you want the Audio Two, you have to sign Lyte.'" It was nepotism at its best, but Nat wasn't trying to force bad goods on Atlantic to pad the deal. Actually it was quite the opposite, as future record sales would show.

After the signing in 1987, Lyte and the First Priority family got right to work. "I had 'Cram' and 'Take It Lyte' done already, and a bunch of rhymes, and they had a bunch of beats," she recalls. "So it was basically just fitting the right lyrics to the right production. It only took a couple of months to get everything done. By the time Atlantic actually signed me, they were behind it and ready to roll." With extra work by Stetsasonic's Prince Paul, EPMD's DJ Scratch, and the Alliance (King of Chill, K-Swift, and DJ Skill) filling out the production roster, a classic was born, released in early 1988.

With males surrounding her and in her corner, Lyte wasn't exactly all alone in the rap biz, but then, as now, it wasn't the easiest road on the less-represented side of the gender divide. "I think it was a big deal then, and I think it's still a big deal for a female MC to be accepted and liked," she says.

"Every woman who has been able to stay in the game has come from a certain camp. Men who come out and make it put their stamp of approval on these women, like Eve from Ruff Ryders, Foxy from the Firm. You don't have to have it, but it's definitely a selling point."

Regardless of her gender, Lyte's style was undeniably fresh. With a husky tone, a strong will and flow, and a maturity and intelligence far beyond her teenage status, *Lyte as a Rock* was a quick-selling new entry in the hip-hop sweepstakes. In addition to "I Cram to Understand U," it yielded singles like "Lyte as a Rock," the brutal and dope Antoinette/Hurby Luv Bug attack "10% Dis," and Lyte's own personal favorite, "Paper Thin."

For those who always wondered about who was on the cover of the album, Lyte explains, "That was me, my DJ, K-Rock, and my bodyguard Big Foot. It would have made sense to have Big Foot as my full-time bodyguard since he was so big, but he was really just my road manager. The cover concept was that K-Rock was being enticed by the woman on the side of the picture. Basically we wanted to give him something to do during the shot. He was the loverboy of the First Priority family anyways, so it made sense. And me, I'm all about the business.

"People loved that album because it was something different," Lyte says. "I wouldn't change anything about that first album. It came out exactly as it was intended to be. It's my baby. You know, the first one. I've matured intensely in comparison to the content on that record, of course, but my peers in the biz still love that record. In some ways it was ahead of its time. When the record came out there was a lull in female MCs and in innovative hip-hop in general. So that's why I think it was such a breath of fresh air to people. The timing couldn't have been more perfect. 'I Cram' had done its run and people wanted to know more about who I was."

TRACKS

LYTE VS. VANNA WHYTE

That was a concept that King of Chill came up with. He had this great beat
and decided on that scenario. So I was like, "Okay, cool." But that's probably
one that I would have left off in hindsight. That was a combination of my DJ,
K-Rock, and DJ Scratch doing the DJ stuff. They worked on that one together.
That was the only time I ever worked with Scratch. All that equipment I'm
talking about on the song, stuff to win, was Chill's dream equipment. I didn't
know any of that stuff. But he definitely had a longing for all of those items.

LYTE AS A ROCK

The original version of that song was by Audio Two, but the album version
and the one the video was done to was a remix that King of Chill did, which
had a house vibe to it. The original was a little more on the basic hip-hop
vibe. The video for that was fun, but I remember it was really grueling: It
was like six a.m. to six a.m. The premise was me going through a time warp
and fitting into any era that I was in. That was the second video we did.
"Paper Thin" was the first one.

I AM WOMAN

Yes, "I am woman, hear me roar . . ." I think Helen Reddy did the original
version, right? Once again that was King of Chill's concept. He felt it was a
powerful statement and I agreed. He made up the track and together we
started formulating the lyrics. I was seventeen when we recorded that.

I had wanted to do something with [Kool and the Gang's] "Hollywood Swinging," so I adapted it and sang it. I don't remember if I made up the chorus like that and gave it to Prince Paul [who produced it] or if he gave me the beat and I made the chorus after. I worked that song out with Paul in the studio and then I did some shows with Stetsasonic after that.

10% DIS

The Audio Two had spoken with Hurby Luv Bug about getting a female act and doing an answer to "Top Billin' " called "Stop Illin'." Hurby kept putting it off, and then next thing we knew we were in the car and heard the song "I Got an Attitude" [by Antoinette, produced by Hurby] using the same kicks and snares [as "Top Billin' "]—and she flipped Milk's lyrics also. They [Milk and Giz] didn't want to dis a female MC so they said, "You have to do it." We went into INS [Studios] two days later and did it. It was pretty easy—we just sat there and thought of the worst things we could possibly say about somebody [*laughs*]. It's titled that because that's only ten percent of what I could have said. I didn't even know Antoinette. It was strictly a war on wax. She tried to dis me back but the hype on me was so big that no one cared if she had a rebuttal to it. I think she was from Queens. We actually had a battle once at the World. I won. Even then, it was understood completely that it was just business.

PAPER THIN

That blends in samples from Al Green. My mom used to play lots of Al Green when I was growing up. What I'm saying on that track hits close—it's *me*! It was how I felt. I'm not gonna use you for your money, I'm too strong and independent for that. That's my favorite track on that album.

That was my alias. King of Chill used "Superstition" [by Stevie Wonder] on it. I love that song. It reminds me of the young MC Lyte. I think they actually sped my voice up on that one. Chill did all the drum programming.

I CRAM TO UNDERSTAND U

I still get people to this day who come up on the street and ask me about Sam, but he was a totally fictitious character. None of that stuff happened to me. I mixed in elements of reality, but in 1981 I was eleven years old and wasn't going anywhere near Empire Boulevard [a skating rink in Brooklyn]. I didn't go there until I was fourteen. It was a roller rink—every Sunday it *was* hip-hop. Kurtis Blow and New Edition performed there, but mostly it was just roller-skating and great music. Milk heard that rhyme before he made that beat up, so he knew how he was going to do it. I did it a cappella to show him what it was all about.

KICKIN' 4 BROOKLYN

I love that song because it's for Brooklyn, and the beat is just so original to me. Milk had a sense of making a track sound exactly like you wanted it to sound. That song was a rhyme I had written a while back, even the hook. We called our home Planet Brooklyn. Me and my producer, King of Chill, decided that it made it sound like such a remote piece of land. At the time my whole life was Brooklyn.

DON'T CRY BIG GIRLS

We got sued for that, royally [*laughs*]! Back in those days you didn't get sample clearances. It was Frankie Valli or the Beach Boys or someone like that. [*Author's note: "Big Girls Don't Cry" was done by Frankie Valli and the Four Seasons.*] It came down to whether we'd pull it off the shelves or give the people what they were asking for, and we did the latter. I think Milk came up with the sample first, and I thought it was a cool idea and wrote the lyrics.

MOBB DEEP

The Infamous . . .

(Loud, 1995)

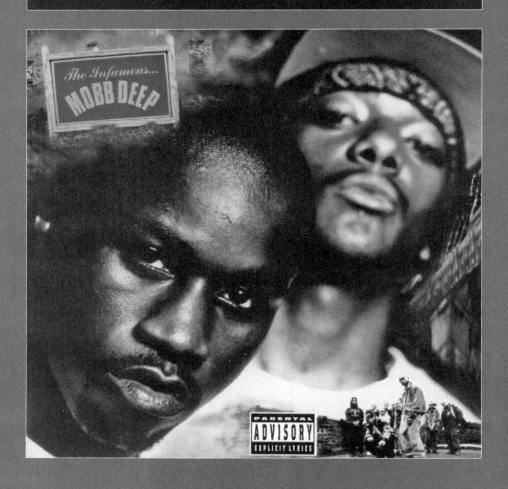

Mobb Deep, the influential producer-MC duo of Havoc (Kejuan Muchita) and Prodigy (Albert Johnson), came to represent the "Queensbridge sound" to the fullest in the mid-nineties. The sound was all about ill tales of cold-blooded illegal life, told with ice-veined calmness over menacing, minimal late-night thuds. Mobb Deep's *The Infamous . . .* album wasn't their first, but it was their calling card, a modern murder-mystery novel set on the mean streets of urban New York, star date 1995.

Havoc and Prodigy first bonded as friends and musical kindred spirits at Manhattan's High School of Art & Design. Havoc commuted from the Queensbridge Houses housing projects where he was raised. Prodigy was from Hempstead, Long Island, although, as longtime group associate Matt Life (Matteo Capoluongo) says: "Prodigy practically lived in Queensbridge when I knew him. Havoc was living in the QB, and those guys were always together, so P was Queensbridge as far as anyone was concerned."

"Not everyone knows, but Prodigy actually comes from a very gifted musical and artistic family," continues Life. "His grandfather was Buddy Johnson, a well-known jazz musician, and his uncle was a musician too. His aunt ran one of the most important dance companies in Queens. So it was definitely in his blood. His family has been in the entertainment business for generations."

After initially calling themselves Poetical Profits, they soon settled on the more appropriate Mobb Deep and began working on demos. One of those demos made its way to Matt Life (then known as Matty C), who wrote the much-jocked Unsigned Hype column in *The Source* magazine. He remembers: "I first met Mobb Deep through Andre Kyles, who went by Omega Supreme and was Organized Konfusion's first DJ. He worked at [Russell Simmons's] Rush Management. He walked Mobb Deep into *The Source* one day, with this kid Schlomo and a whole crew, and they played their tape for me. It was some really amazing, really raw shit, which was kind of ill because they were so young. This is in 1992 and I think they were like fourteen or fifteen years old. I remember one track on that demo called 'Shorty Scores' that had some lines that really grabbed me." The group was featured in *The Source*'s Unsigned Hype column shortly after that meeting.

Matt's cheerleading for the group didn't end there. He explains: "Bonz Malone, who was also at *The Source,* had met [Island Records founder] Chris Blackwell and landed a job doing A&R for 4th & Bway [an Island subsidiary]. So Bonz knew all about the group from me and signed them. I remember that Puffy was also interested in them at the time."

Mobb Deep's first album was the lesser known and, as the group admits, not fully realized *Juvenile Hell,* released on 4th & Bway/Island in 1993. The first part of the album's title was definitely accurate—they were only in their midteens when it hit. Prodigy says, regarding *Juvenile Hell,* "That album was aight, but we wasn't doing our own shit at the time. To us that album don't even count in the books. We was just thirsty little kids, tryin' to get a deal."

Even though the experience wasn't a great one, the duo did get their feet wet on the production side, producing four album tracks (plus a couple of skits) themselves and learning from legends-to-be who helped on production, like Large Professor and DJ Premier. Additional production was done by Keith Spencer, Dale Hogan, Paul Shabazz, and Kerwin "Sleek" Young.

Prodigy explains: "We definitely wanted other producers back then when we started. We was trying to get niggas like Pete Rock and we was fuckin' with Preemo [DJ Premier]. But after a while, we was like: 'Fuck it, let's do our own shit.' No one was jockin' the work we was doing, but we knew we was just gonna *make* it happen." Havoc says: "We started producing because other producers was giving us shit that we didn't like, or they was just charging too much. I didn't know nothing about making music, but I learned by watching other dudes."

Lyrically the duo sounded solid on *Juvenile Hell,* especially considering their age, with a penitentiary-steel attitude already in place on songs like "Locked in Spofford" and "Hold Down the Fort." Listening now, you can hear how they became the Mobb Deep of *The Infamous* just two years later. Steve Rifkind, owner of Loud Records, Mobb Deep's future home, recalls, "I remember I heard the 'Hit It from the Back' record [a single] from that first album back then, when I was still in L.A. I thought they were talented kids, but they were really young back then, like fifteen or sixteen. So I didn't honestly pay too much attention."

"I think that Mobb Deep were ahead of their time when that first album hit," says Matt Life. "Those producers they had on there were no joke. Kerwin Young was down with the [Public Enemy–related] Bomb Squad, Large Professor was the *man* back then, and [DJ] Premier even did a song for them. On the production front, Havoc and Prodigy both learned a lot by working with those guys, even if the album didn't sell that well."

4th & Bway dropped the group after the album didn't take off. Prodigy says: "They dropped us because we only sold like twenty thousand copies or something like that. They was like: 'Nah, we ain't fuckin' with these niggas.' " So with a handful of production skills, hundreds of street tales in their heads, and an impressive amount of confidence, their second battle began.

Luckily, their booster Matt Life was again in a position to help Hav and Prodigy after their 4th & Bway experience. In 1994 he was just about to start doing A&R (while concurrently writing for *The Source*—he would soon ease into the record world full-time) for Rifkind's Loud Records, who had hit big with the Wu-Tang Clan in late 1993. Prodigy remembers: "Matt was like: 'Okay, let's try this again.' And Loud was definitely behind us. They needed something else to push."

"When it all fell through at Island [4th & Bway], Havoc came to see me at *The Source,*" Life remembers. "He had one new song that they had put together at his crib, called 'Patty Shop.' That song actually never came out, although we tried to do it for the first album. It just never sounded as good as it had on the demo. But when I heard that song, after having just heard the advance of [Nas's upcoming debut] *Illmatic,* I knew that Queensbridge was about to explode, and these motherfuckers were going to walk right in behind the momentum that Nas was starting."

Life continues: "I gave a tape of 'Patty Shop' to Stretch Armstrong [a popular WKCR DJ who also did A&R for labels in the mid-nineties] and he played it on WKCR. He was helping Steve Rifkind with A&R at the time, so he made Steve aware of Mobb Deep. I told Steve about Mobb Deep, too, but I think Stretch told him first. When I did start working for Loud, I brought Mobb Deep in there for a meeting. They got signed, and that was my first job, to do A&R for *The Infamous.*"

Rifkind has a different recollection of how he first heard about the group: "A kid by the name of Soup Henderson [who is thanked on the album] brought them to my attention, because he was friendly with their manager. Aside from the music, when they walked into the office I knew that they were stars, immediately. Considering all the people that were telling me this group was the next thing, there was no way I wasn't going to sign them." Havoc recalls: "With Loud, we was just happy to be signed to another label, so we didn't even give a fuck. We hadn't even heard of Loud back then. We were just glad to be somewhere."

Work started on *The Infamous,* and the duo couldn't have been more focused and driven. "All we cared about was makin' some gangsta shit that *we* liked," says Prodigy. "If we was gonna like it then the world was gonna like it."

The newly hired Matt Life and his friend Schott Free—one of Loud's longer-tenured (at two years) New York office employees—were in charge of logistics for the sessions that followed. Life recalls: "The whole vibe during that time in the studio, for me, was like a dream come true. I had been covering hip-hop for five years as a journalist and now I was a part of putting together an album like that. I was also learning every step of the way. To be honest, so were Mobb Deep. It was pretty new to all of us." The album sessions were completed at two locations in Manhattan, Platinum Sound and Battery Studios.

"*The Infamous* is definitely our real debut, as far as I'm concerned," says Prodigy. "We were doing our own production and settling into it. That first album was more like our demo. When we were making *The Infamous* we really wasn't paying much attention to how it really sounded. But when you look back on it now, it's like: 'Damn!' "

"We definitely weren't in control back then," says Havoc, referring to *Juvenile Hell.* "I don't feel like that album was like a demo, though. It was special for me because it was my first shit. And I definitely learned how to take matters into my own hands after that, instead of having other people produce our shit."

Loud was fully supportive of the group being self-contained. Rifkind explains, "I never really interfered, and I never had any problems with Mobb Deep, ever. I knew I had a good team with those guys and with Schott and Matt. Schott and Matt were in the studio every day with them, and they'd call me every day with updates. The news was always good."

Life says: "I always loved Havoc and P because they were willing to take that step forward and self-produce. Actual *groups* were getting rare at that time. As a fan, that was always the highest form of hip-hop to me, to have someone in the group produce that group's tracks. And when it came to the actual recording, their thing was always to go in there [to the studio] and just wing it. They had rhymes prepared and they had beats, but they would just show up with everything they had and figure it out from there. Havoc had an [Akai] MPC-60 [sampler] at home, so he'd do a lot of prep before he actually got to the studio. The thing about those guys that people don't realize is that they taught each other their own strengths over the years. Prodigy credits Havoc with teaching him how to rhyme, even though people always thought that P was a better MC. And Havoc told me that Prodigy taught him a lot about making beats."

Life continues: "On *The Infamous,* Havoc was definitely more in control [than Prodigy] when it came to production. Havoc and I used to do a lot of [record] digging—we'd go to record conventions and listen to shit together. Even so, Prodigy would still bring in shit to use for beats even though his main thing was focusing on lyrics. I would say that Havoc was less focused on lyrics on that album, since he was *so* focused on production."

The album was self-produced—credited to "Mobb Deep"—with three tracks done by another important ally, Q-Tip of A Tribe Called Quest (credited as the Abstract). Q-Tip might have seemed like a provocative match considering the non-thug image of A Tribe Called Quest. But keep in mind that Q had stepped onto a very high freelance production plateau in 1994 with "One Love" on Nas's *Illmatic.* Havoc remembers: "I admired Q-Tip's production a lot, so I was like: 'I want that sound.' It wasn't even a Queens thing (Q-Tip was from the borough's Hollis–St. Albans section) either—that was just a coincidence."

Matt Life says: "Tip was very involved in *The Infamous* from early on, probably more than people know. Tip was just a fan of theirs and I knew him from way back, so he was really helpful, giving them advice about different engineers and studios. Then he came in later in the sessions and said he'd help mix a couple records. And *then* he ended up picking a couple of records [that Mobb Deep had already finished] to redo. Except for 'Drink away the Pain,' the songs that Tip produced were already a full song before he got to them. He liked the lyrics on those [original] songs, but he redid the beats. It was the same song title, same hook, same rhymes, just new beats."

The group also enlisted another Queens neighbor for *The Infamous:*

Nas, who had blown up in 1994 with *Illmatic*. Prodigy says it was good to have him in the mix, but they didn't do it because of his popularity: "The success of Nas and *Illmatic* didn't affect us. He was in his own world, and our worlds never really mixed that much. But if more people paid attention to us because of him, then we didn't have a problem with that." Matt Life agrees: "I think that Nas was such a god on the mic that he just gave anybody from Queensbridge a little extra confidence, a bit more swagger. And Mobb Deep were part of that, even though they always stood on their own two feet as artists."

The Infamous was released on April 25, 1995, and it wasn't an instant smash. The album did go gold, though, and proved itself to be one of the most influential albums of the nineties. Rifkind recalls: "We didn't have a huge first week—we might have done sixty thousand. But we stayed at that level for four weeks in a row, and people were amazed that we were doing numbers like that. It was simple: We were just letting the record sell itself, slowly, with the buzz that Mobb Deep had created. It was all part of the movement that Wu-Tang had started and Nas had continued. Mobb Deep were next. It went gold at the time and is close to platinum now, which is pretty amazing considering that this was a group without any radio play outside of New York. That record was a very big success for Loud."

Lyrically chilling and sonically unequalled to this day, the album's power flows from its unaffected honesty. Looking back, Havoc says of *The Infamous:* "I love that album. How raw it was, how grimy it was. I didn't try and make it sound grimy, but that's just the way I felt living in the 'hood. We might have sounded older on that album, but we was still only eighteen or nineteen. Living the life we led matures you [*laughs*]."

Havoc adds: "Every now and then I listen to *The Infamous* and say, 'Damn!' I wouldn't change nothing about that album. And my last comment on that one is: 'Thank God for that album.' "

"*The Infamous* definitely set the trend for us," Prodigy says. "I have a lot of great memories from back then. In the end, back then and today, as long as the street loves us, that's all the fuck we care about."

TRACKS

Prodigy: That track [spoken only, no music] was just somethin' I was feelin' when we was goin' through the struggle. Everybody took those words like we was mad at somebody, and different people thought we was talkin' about them.

EYE FOR AN EYE (YOUR BEEF IS MINES) *Featuring Nas and Raekwon*

Prodigy: We made that track right there, when Nas and Raekwon was in the studio. We did everything like that—as we went along. We called them and when they arrived, Hav made the beat in like two seconds. We knew Raekwon because he was on Loud, so we'd see each other every day at the Loud office. If niggas is taking care of they business, then they're going to be at their label's office, so there we were.

Matt Life: Nas had so much talent, but he never brought the real energy of Queensbridge. Mobb Deep were the ones who brought that energy to tracks, and also when they were out in public. They used to roll pretty deep out there with all their boys, probably ten guys most of the time. And while we're talking about energy, Raekwon is by far the most animated dude on that track. He was amazing on there, and just hanging around the studio he had everybody cracking up.

Steve Rifkind: That's one of my favorite records of all time. Not just my favorite of Mobb Deep records, either. *Anyone's* records!

GIVE UP THE GOODS (JUST STEP) *Produced by Q-Tip, featuring Big Noyd*

Havoc: Q-Tip definitely bent his style a little bit to get with what we was doing. Like with "Drink away the Pain," you see him trying to get gangsta with it. Big Noyd goes way back with us—he was on our first record too. He's like an unofficial member of Mobb Deep. He lived on the same block as me. His moms hung out with my moms.

TEMPERATURE'S RISING *Produced by Q-Tip*

Havoc: That was about a situation my brother was in, and we made a song around it. [The song's lyrics are a conversation directed at someone on the run from police after a shooting.]

Prodigy: We met Q-Tip because we used to go up to Def Jam back in the days, to try and get on, before we was signed to Island [4th & Bway]. And a little altercation happened at Def Jam and somebody got shot, and we became a little famous over there. That's when we met Q-Tip. He was there networking too. Tip was there when the shooting happened. That's why Def Jam has security there to this day. People say that song was more "pop" than other stuff, but that shit pisses me off. To us it's just music, and all music comes from R&B. So it's only natural to have some singing on a song.

Matt Life: The guys changed a lot of their original lyrics on that one when Q-Tip redid the music. That one definitely went through a big transformation from the original to the final album version.

TRIFE LIFE

Prodigy: That song is about some interborough battles. We was definitely going all over the place back then, because we met people from all boroughs at our high school.

RIGHT BACK AT YOU *Featuring Ghostface Killer, Raekwon, and Big Noyd*

Matt Life: Schott [Free] got co-production on there because he brought that Les McCann record ["Benjamin"] in. Schott was an MC, and he used to rhyme off that track back in the day. I think Schott and I were such a great combo [as A&R for the album] because he would focus on the rhymes with those guys, and I would focus on the music.

DRINK AWAY THE PAIN (SITUATIONS) *Produced by and featuring Q-Tip*

Havoc: Hell yeah, we was drinkin' a lot at the time. It wasn't gettin' in the way of anything for us, but we know niggas who drink a lot, so we wanted to make a song about it. You can either drink to have fun or to escape. Prodigy came up with the title for that one.

Matt Life: That was the only song that they did with Q-Tip where they started from scratch.

SHOOK ONES, PT. II

Prodigy: Both parts of "Shook Ones" ["Pt. I" and "Pt. II," which is included on the album] were two of the first tracks we ever did on production, when we had just started making beats for the second album. No one would ever be able to find that loop [used for "Pt. II"] and do it over, 'cause it's not a loop. We took a record and chopped it up and did somethin' to it.

Havoc: "Shook Ones, Pt. I" was actually our first single, before the album was out. It got some play on college radio, but people never really heard it too much. It was aight, but I said to myself, "We need somethin' that's going to be more up-tempo, something that can bang in the clubs." Then I went back in and did "Shook Ones, Pt. II." "Pt. II" was the second single from the album, and it also came out before the album hit. It definitely blew up. I mean, that's why I'm talking to you right now.

Matt Life: That's the centerpiece song of the album, hands down. I don't think that anyone could deny that. I remember when the album came out, I wrote the promotional sticker, and it said that "Shook Ones, Pt. II" was an *anthem*. People didn't really call hip-hop songs anthems back then, but I really believed that it was. I remember that they had already done "Shook Ones" [the first version], but they went back in the studio and redid it right away with different drums [also different samples, and many new lyrics]. I think that they called it "Pt. II" instead of giving it a whole new title because it could come out faster if it was considered a remix [rather than marketing a new single]. As soon at "Pt. II" came out, the first version was obsolete. [Popular New York DJ Funkmaster] Flex fronted on that record for *months,* but we kept at it and eventually people came around. Even the big-name DJs didn't get that song at first. Some of the promos for that had both versions on it, so I guess people could decide which they liked better, although I can't imagine anyone taking "Pt. I."

Steve Rifkind: At the time when "Pt. II" came out in 1994, I had just found out that my girlfriend was pregnant with our first child. She was telling me on the phone that she was pregnant, and I was wrapped up in that and then I got call-waiting. It was Havoc, telling me to put on [the TV show] *Video Music Box,* because "Shook Ones, Pt. II" was on. Once I turned it on, I was so mesmerized that I told my girlfriend that I had to call her back. I remember that like it was yesterday. Later that same day, I was in a car going to the airport for the "How Can I Be Down" conference, and Bobbito [Garcia, an industry insider also known for WKCR's highly influential "Stretch and Bobbito" radio show] was in the car with us. We had a Loud sampler and it had that track ["Pt. II"] on there, and he just lost his mind when that came on. I just started putting pieces of the puzzle together, that something was going on with this record organically. It was impossible to deny.

PARTY OVER *Featuring Big Noyd*

Havoc: That was the last track we made for the album, definitely. We was feelin' good, we had done it, and we just wanted to get the album out so the world could hear it.

Prodigy: That's probably my favorite track on the album.

Matt Life: I was co-producer on that one because I had given those guys several drum samples on the album, including that one. I was a drummer, so that was my thing. Some A&Rs would slip their names onto tracks that they didn't have anything to do with, but I never did that. If I'm ever listed on a track, then I did some work on it. At the point we did that song, "Shook Ones, Pt. II" was already doing well as a single, so there was pressure to get that album done and *out*.

M.O.P.

Firing Squad

(Relativity, 1996)

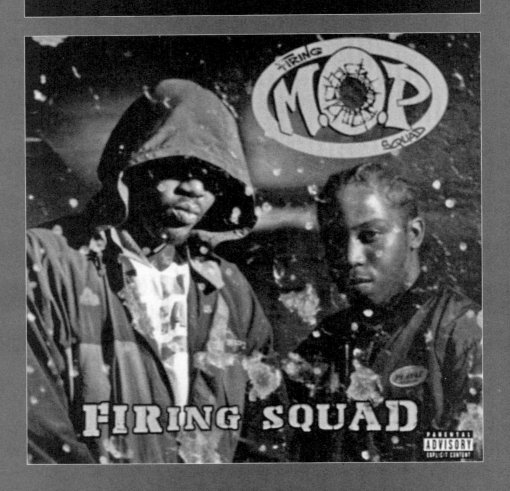

When M.O.P. talks, people listen. Because Billy Danzenie (Erik Murry, aka Billy Danze) and Lil' Fame (Jamal Grinnage) don't actually talk, they *yell*. Billy lays it down as simply as he can: "We do yell a lot, but we're never mad. We're just frustrated at the way shit goes on, in hip-hop and in our world. This is just how we deal with it."

M.O.P. stands for Mash Out Posse, and they have always proudly and aggressively represented Brownsville, Brooklyn. The neighborhood crew of the same name was together in the late eighties, but Billy and Fame didn't start using M.O.P. for their musical pursuits until 1992. Billy says: "We were formed as a rap group using that name in '92, but we had Mash Out Posse for years before that from hanging out in the streets."

Billy remembers his earlier years on the mic, going back to his preteens: "I started rapping way back—like, I still remember learning off my sister's Sugar Hill records. At one time I was even more of a conscious rapper, when I was still young, because it was a little strange for a young dude to be rapping so tough. As I worked my way up through school I was a little more stylish, too. I had a calm style back then." He used different names before he settled on Billy Danzenie: Baby D, Cool E, GMC. "Different names for different styles," he says. "But I brought something different every time I wrote a rhyme, and songs came really easy to me. Once I got an idea in my head, I just couldn't shake it." He says he has been using his current gruff, aggressive rhyme style since 1989.

Billy and Lil' Fame knew each other since they were in elementary school, and Fame was even nice on the wheels of steel early on. Billy remembers: "Fame was really good at DJing back in the day, and he eventually grew into being an MC." The two would work on rhymes while they were out hustling. Their street activities even landed Billy in the big house in the early nineties. He says of his stint on lockdown, "I wasn't really writing any shit in prison. The only song I wrote in there was [M.O.P.'s debut single] 'How About Some Hardcore?' Just the first verse."

Lil' Fame got his start in hip-hop in the mid-eighties. "I'm nice on the turntables!" he yells. "I love DJing more than rhyming, even still to this day. I really started rhyming just to keep up with Billy. And I never did clubs or parties or any of that shit, I just DJed on my own. But motherfuckers around the way knew I was nice." His DJ name, before he started using Lil' Fame on the mic, was Slap.

Fame's older brother, Big Mal (Malik), was also influential in his hip-hop development and pushed Fame to rhyme. "He even gave me Fame as my rhyming name," Fame says. "Mal didn't DJ, although he thought he could. He stole somebody's DJ equipment back in the day. He went right from our roof to the next building's roof, then downstairs and stole the guy's shit. And when Mal would be in school I'd sneak into his room and use his shit, like when I was in third grade. He'd get mad, but he didn't know how to really use that shit anyways."

Before M.O.P.'s first single came to fruition, Fame was the first of the duo to get his name out there, appearing—as Lil' Fame—on four tracks of the 1992 compilation *The Hill That's Real* (4th & Bway). The album featured production by Silver D and Broke Ass Mo, and isn't something Fame looks back on fondly. He says: "I hated the beats and that compilation was trash. So after that, I told Laze [friend, manager, and sometime producer Laze "E" Laze, sometimes spelled Laz-E-Laz] that we had to get some beats from D/R Period, because he was always talented. So that's how 'How About Some Hardcore' came about. That was originally going to be my song, but I put Billy on it."

With part of Billy's verse already written from behind bars, "How About Some Hardcore" became M.O.P.'s entrée to bigger things and helped them get signed to Select Records, a label that had great success in the eighties (UTFO, Kid 'N Play). The single, produced by D/R Period (who is listed on the single as Darryl Dee, his DJ name) and co-produced by Laze, was released in 1993 and did well with hardcore hip-hop fans, setting rugged rhymes against jazzy horns.

After the success of the single, their debut album, *To the Death,* appeared on Select by mid-1994. Although flashes of the in-your-face M.O.P. attack were there, the album on the whole lacked the intensity that the group would be known for, partially because of the languid tempos and a usually mismatched jazz vibe. With production on all but one track by their Brownsville neighbor D/R Period, who lived right around the corner from the MCs, they hadn't yet found their musical niche.

Fame says: "I remember recording that album with D/R. I had my Olde

English and my weed and we'd walk right around the corner to his spot. But we couldn't smoke in his place because his moms was a church lady. A lot of times we'd come up with ideas for songs on the way over there, while we was walking. It only took about a month to record the whole album."

Neither MC has any major complaints about *To the Death*. Billy says: "That album was our first shot, and we were happy to be a part of the industry and to be signed by a label. We had a lot of things to say back then, and we said them." Fame concurs: "Yeah, that album felt like a success. My moms [who passed away in 1996] got to see me do a video, so that was special."

Among many other New Yorkers, there was one M.O.P. fan in particular who would come to play a major role in the group's future success: Gang Starr's DJ Premier.

"I remember the first time I heard those guys," Premier says. "It was when they had their single 'How About Some Hardcore?' out. I used to see ads for it in *The Source* all the time. It was a small ad with a knife on it, but it stuck out. I was intrigued. Then Kid Capri played it on WBLS, so I heard it from that, and that record just took me way out. I was just wowed by it. Then when I saw the video on *Video Music Box,* I knew what they looked like. What they were doing was long overdue. It was like heavy metal, it was so hard! I was workin' at WBLS and I was allowed to bring guests on the show, so I really wanted to see M.O.P. in person. Billy came in with a Crooklyn hat pulled so far down that you couldn't see his eyes, and he was lookin' at me all tough, like he wanted to beat my ass."

"He always teases me about the first time we met because I had my hat pulled down and my face all screwed up, all antisocial," says Billy.

"Back then Billy wasn't talking as much," Premier continues. "He was fresh out of jail and he was wild. I mean, he's an '87 stick-up kid, for real. And Fame had that gold-toothed smile. But they came on the show and played me the whole *To the Death* album. Around that time I also saw them live. Onstage they was all in black, just like an army. The energy was so intense that I knew I wanted to be down with these dudes. At the time we [Gang Starr] were shooting a video for the song 'Code of the Streets,' and M.O.P. is actually in it. If you look close you can see them working on cars in the chop shop."

Billy remembers: "Preemo liked our stuff and he was supposed to remix 'How About Some Hardcore' for us, because that single was pretty big. But when we started that remix, the beat turned into 'Downtown Swinga' [a B-side on the group's second single, 'Rugged Neva Smoove'—'Downtown Swinga' never appeared on an album]. On that single, Premier also did his 'Rugged Neva Smoove' remix. That was the first time we worked with him." Premier gives his own recollection of their first collaboration: "I was supposed to remix 'Rugged Neva Smoove' and I did two versions of it. The 'raw' version was called the 'Downtown Swinga' mix, and I did a second remix that was a laid-back version. So they did a whole new song [lyrics] to the raw version and we ended up doing two songs for the price of one."

Billy says of the group's relationship with Premier, "Working with him was really important to us, because it let us know that we could go outside of our family and still get respect. Sometimes we feel like we're in a world by ourselves, like nobody understands us. But Premier understands us, and it was beautiful. We embraced him and he embraced us. Every time we work with him, it's like going over to your cousin's crib." Fame says: "Premier's the type of dude who would fuck with us [i.e., be friends with us] whether we were known or not. He's got a good heart. He hangs out with our homies who don't even rap, and he looks out for those niggas. And I always loved Premier's shit, from back when the earliest Gang Starr shit was out in the eighties."

In 1994 and 1995, M.O.P. played more shows and continued working on their sound, doing everything they could to get their music out. But by the time the album had run out its promotional cycle, it was most definitely time to step up to the next level in many ways. Billy explains: "I think the first album was pretty decent. We liked it and it got some love. But—and no disrespect to [label owner] Fred Munao—those guys at Select didn't have what we needed. So we had to move on. It was a necessary parting. So for a lot of reasons, you could definitely say that *Firing Squad* was the first album in M.O.P.'s modern era."

In addition to needing another record label, the extended M.O.P. crew was in transition as well. "From 1994 to 1996 there were internal problems within the M.O.P. family," Billy explains. "Our friend Bu-Bang was murdered during that time, and we were going through a lot of personal shit as well. Family is very important to us, because without it you're nothing. So we had a lot on our minds." Fame also experienced tough times during this period, losing his brother in 1994 and then, in 1996, his mother. He says: "I was sixteen years old and it was only me—I was the last one left because my father had died in '86. I was living in a fucked-up house in Brownsville after my mom passed, with no heat, no hot water, no bathroom, no nothing. It was hell. The only good thing was that my son was born, two months after my moms had passed."

On a less tragic but still serious note, adding to M.O.P.'s turmoil was the fact that they were attracting unwanted attention from club owners throughout New York. Billy explains: "They used to ban us from clubs back then because there was always some madness at an M.O.P. show—but a lot of those fights wasn't even us. It got so bad at one point that they wouldn't even allow DJs to play our music in clubs."

Their label problems were solved by the on-the-rise Relativity label (home to Common and the Beatnuts) expressing interest, and Select agreeing to let them go. Billy says: "It wasn't that bad, the transition from Select to Relativity. Fred understood that he couldn't market and promote our product properly. It was definitely no hard feelings, and in the end he made money on top of it."

With a new label on hand, there was still one piece of the puzzle to deal with: a producer. Their friend D/R Period had become very in demand at the time, which created problems. According to Billy, his busy schedule explains why he is conspicuously absent from *Firing Squad*. Fame tells a different story when it comes to D/R's absence: "With *Firing Squad,* I think Laze and D/R fell out. I think that was the deal. Either way, we were always dealing with Preemo before *Firing Squad,* and he was right there to step in. D/R came back later. He's always first because he *is* M.O.P., like Swizz Beats and Ruff Ryders. He was there from the beginning, so he will always be family."

For whatever reason D/R left the fold, their biggest fan, DJ Premier, was available and more than happy to jump on board. Preemo remembers: "At that time they were having a problem with D/R and were ready to start the new album, so I was like: 'Yo, I'll contribute whatever you need.' I wasn't trying to take D/R's spot because he set the precedent with them. And they got back together with him after that anyways."

"D/R still does lots of tracks with us to this day [including producing their smash hit 'Ante Up' in 2000]," says Billy. "D is family, he lived right around the corner from the block that we grew up on, and we've known him from so far back. He's a member of M.O.P., and it's a foundation that we built with him."

Preemo stepped up in a big way on the album, contributing six strong tracks alongside work from Big Jaz and Laze. Mostly recorded at Premier's home base, D&D Studios in Manhattan, Billy says that *Firing Squad* took only about two months to record. "That record came together really quick," says Premier. "Their work ethic at that time was very strong and they worked really fast." Billy recalls, "It wasn't a hard record to make because we was comfortable with the people around us. All our people were there."

You'd never know it from his powerful vocal presence on the album, but Lil' Fame claims that there's very little he actually can look back and visualize about the album's recording. He says: "Honestly, I really don't remember a lot of that stuff around *Firing Squad*. I'd go to the studio and whatever, but I was going through so much during that time. It was all a big blur to me."

Proving how comfortable their recording environment was, the group's bedrooms were also transferred to D&D on occasion. "We actually had sleeping bags, and we would sleep in the studio a lot of times," recalls Billy. "We just wanted to be there—it's what we do. For those couple months it was our home and we treated it that way." Premier adds: "Billy would get drunk and go in the back and we'd forget he was even there [*laughs*]." Fame remembers: "I loved going to D&D. That was a cool spot. I remember picking out beats and writing rhymes and laying shit down, and before we knew it, the album was done. We'd go in there at six p.m. and leave at seven or eight in the morning, with our eyes burning."

Interestingly, M.O.P. were so intimidating and intense that even a world-class producer like Premier was worried about the beats he was giving the group. Preemo says: "I really didn't think that certain tracks I was doing for them were appropriate. I was trying to outdo myself. That's how much I wanted to make an impression, because I really believed in them and in what they were saying. They were really trying to fix the wackness in the hip-hop game back then. They ended up liking everything I gave them, but I wasn't always sure that it was up to par."

Premier continues: "There were things that I was able to do with M.O.P. that I couldn't do with Gang Starr because they can flow more intensely, and in different ways than Guru can. So with *Firing Squad* it was a chance to work with some dudes who just wanted to *shout*. Even on the slow songs, they're gonna shout on them! So I wanted to test my ability with that type of style. Next to Run-DMC and N.W.A. they were the next loudmouths. And they're believable, because they *really* are the way that they rap."

Billy explains what the M.O.P. approach and aesthetic is all about, then and now: "Even today, we're still educating people about how it is in our world, for people who don't know what it's like in Brownsville or any other ghetto. We don't cater to radio and we're still a little bit frustrated about shit. We've changed, too. I mean, we were children when we first started. And with *Firing Squad* we were both coming out of childhood into manhood. That's the only album of ours where you got both young M.O.P. and then our progression. That's really the only difference, because every time we do it, it's the same."

Firing Squad, which hit shelves in the fall of 1996, was a triumph musically and lyrically. The group embraces its old and new lives at once, rolling through the "ghetto warfare" of Premier's "New Jack City" to the slower, soulful "Dead & Gone."

"We will be M.O.P. until it's all over," says Billy. "Nothing's ever going to change that. We don't make music to make money, we make music just to make dope shit. Because in my opinion, you ain't getting it from nobody else."

TRACKS

DJ Premier: I think that was the second track that we laid down for the record. I loved working with Teflon—he was an amazing talent. At that time he had just come home on work release from Attica [Correctional Facility]. He's always been a big spark plug. He's very hyper, very hungry, and he's down to work no matter what it takes. At that time, DuPont actually made us cease from using that name. He was spittin' rhymes all the time, and he was gonna be the next thing to come up out of the M.O.P. camp. So they put him on the *Firing Squad* album. I made the beat but I didn't think it was right for the song, at least not until they actually laid it down. But when I heard the combination of the three of them, I knew it was definitely a keeper. I can remember a funny night where it was me, Teflon, and Biggie [Notorious B.I.G.] hanging out at a club in Jersey at a show, back when [Biggie's hit] 'Juicy' was poppin'. Fame and Billy was there too, and after the show Fame was yelling at Biggie because he had said that M.O.P. were from [the] Prospect [section of Brooklyn]. Fame was yelling at Biggie in his car: 'I'm from St. Marks, nigga, and you *know* that!' "

Fame: Teflon is my nigga—he helped keep me together after all the bullshit I had been through back then. Tef would make me want to rhyme more seriously because he was more of a serious lyricist.

Billy: That's my favorite track on the album. That was Teflon's first introduction to the rap world. We had been standing in hallways and rapping for years, but we never had a chance to do it professionally with him until then. That was deep to us. We all grew up together—me, Fame, and Teflon.

Fame: That's my favorite track on the album [*recites his first lines of the song a cappella*]. I like the "Bring it back!" part. That song is dope, that's when hip-hop was the shit, back in 1994 and 1995. Those were the days!

STICK TO YA GUNZ *Featuring Kool G Rap*

Billy: That's such a memorable track for me. We had always wanted to work with Kool G Rap, but that was the first time that we had ever had a chance to. When he came up to the studio, I met him at the elevator, and was like: "G, I am *so* glad that you're here!" We both loved Kool G's shit so much and he was such a huge influence on us, you don't even know [*laughs*]! I have to be honest and say that I was slightly intimidated. But I was so happy that he was there that he made me shine and made me pull out my potential. I didn't want to let him down. I mean, it's Kool G Rap, he just makes you want to get down!

Fame: I had never met Kool G before that track, although I had spoken with him on the phone a couple times. G Rap was always my favorite nigga. I was like a "Baby G Rap" in high school. And he was exactly as great as I thought he would be when we did that track with him.

ANTICIPATION

Billy: We produced that one, with Laze [E Laze]. Fame is so good with music, since he used to be a DJ, so he can make a song out of anything. The first track Fame did was the intro to *To the Death*. Even to this day people don't really know that we produce. The only track I ever produced by myself was the joint that we put on the *Bad Boys 2* soundtrack.

Fame: I produced that. When it says "Produced by M.O.P.," then that means I did it. I kind of got that from Mobb Deep [where group member Havoc does most of the production, even though it is listed as Mobb Deep]. I did that beat right on the spot. I can always make beats real quick. It's much easier to just do what you feel, right there, than to sit down and think about it too much.

BORN 2 KILL

Billy: Big Jaz [aka Jaz-O, known as the producer and mentor who gave Jay-Z his start] produced that one. His beats were always incredible and we loved working with him.

BROWNSVILLE

Fame: I was born and bred in Brownsville, that's my heart. That's the only thing I know, and I'm still there today. My mom was from Trinidad but my pops was from Brownsville, so it goes way back with me.

DJ Premier: That was the first song that I actually did for the album. I remember that Billy was distracted by all the extra sounds on there, and he just wanted the drumroll when he laid his vocals down. So I took them out, he laid the vocal, and I put them back later on. Fame laid his vocals down over the original, no problem. They just distracted Billy for some reason.

Billy: Brownsville is just our home—we're both from there since we were so young. And I've known Fame since second grade. When my mother had me, she was living on Fulton Street, about four blocks away from St. Marks, where we grew up at. And we gradually moved down the hill.

WORLD FAMOUS

Billy: That was a single, and we did a video for that one. Scarface used that same music for [his 2002 single] "On My Block," and that was dope. I love Scarface, and I can't believe we never did a track with him. On our *Marxmen* album we did a cover of [the Geto Boys'] "Mind Playing Tricks on Me."

Fame: That one was pretty much Billy's idea. We actually stole that beat from Big Jaz. He was originally rappin' on that shit himself, but I heard that beat and I wanted it. He's from Marcy [in Brooklyn], which is right next to Brownsville.

DOWNTOWN SWINGA ('96)

Billy: That was the second one of those "Downtown Swinga" tracks that we did, out of three so far. Premier did all of them.

DJ Premier: The first one of the "Downtown Swinga" series [on *To the Death*] was so dope that they said, "We want to do another one." And it just turned into a series on every album after that. Except on [M.O.P.'s 2000 album] *Warriorz.* With *Warriorz,* it was the last day on that one and we had to master the album right then. So I was like: "Let's just pull an all-nighter." I made the track and they both laid one verse each and then fell asleep, and I couldn't wake Billy up. He was unconscious! They had been celebrating because it was the last day and he just passed out, drunk. And that's the only reason that a version didn't appear on that album.

Fame: Billy had to set that one off, because he set the first one off so well. He goes first on every one of those.

ILLSIDE OF TOWN

Billy: That's Laze rapping on there—we produced that track with him. He grew up on the Hill with us [in Brownsville]. We go way back.

Fame: Yeah, Laze is on there. I produced that one. Laze came up with a lot of hooks and choruses when he produced. He's more emotional with that kind of shit.

Billy: I really love that song—that one had so much meaning to us. We had lost so much, and we really did feel like it was all or nothing at that point.

Fame: I *hate* that song! I was like crying on that shit! Like I was the only one who ever felt pain [*sounds very ashamed of himself, and upset*]. That was like a cry for help from me, I sound like a fuckin' punk. It's like: "Grow up, nigga, toughen up." I laugh at myself on that track now. I can just hear my [late] brother giving me shit about my punk ass on there!

DEAD & GONE

Fame: That's when I had my son. I was talking to my son on a song called "Dead & Gone"! That's fucking stupid. Nowadays I would *never* put my son together with the word *dead*. Laze did that track. Me and Billy didn't have anything to do with it.

Billy: On that track I was talking to my man Bu-Bang, who was gone. Bu passed away right before we was finishing up the album, one day before his daughter's one-year birthday. We had always vowed to be together. And I was also trying to get across to my son that I would always be there for him. Me and Fame had both had children around that time. Our kids are the reason that we're here. The song was about how I missed my homey and how I was living for my son. That was just a real crazy time for us. We wanted to enjoy life while we're still around. Battle was on there—they were a group out of Chicago. Laze [who co-produced the song with M.O.P.] hooked up with them some kind of way. The guy being the preacher on there was my boy Easy D from Jersey City.

ONYX
Bacdafucup
(RAL/Columbia, 1993)

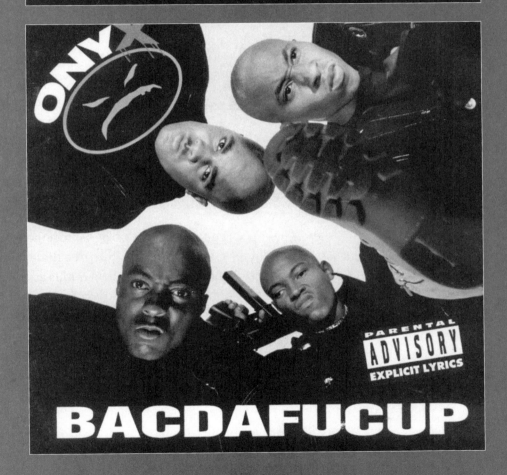

When you think of Onyx, one of the most bombastic and groundbreaking NYC crews of the nineties, two things are hard to imagine. First is the image of group members with hair, considering their steadfast bald-headedness. Second is this image from the late eighties, related by Sticky Fingaz (Kirk Jones): "Me and Fredro DJed my mom's baby shower, for my little brother." The four-man crew Onyx was always full of surprises, and they stomped through many adventures in the early nineties, eventually scoring double platinum with their 1993 debut, *Bacdafucup.*

Group leader Fredro Starr (Fred Scruggs) was born and raised in Brooklyn, but "I moved to Queens when I was thirteen, and that's when hip-hop started for me. LL Cool J made me want to become an MC. He had the girls and the cars. So I started rhyming on Rockaway Boulevard in Queens when I was fourteen or fifteen. The first time I picked up a mic in front of a crowd was at a place called Baisley Park. It was a spot where people in Queens went to do their thing. But every time they had a jam at the place, there was a shoot-out. I didn't give a fuck—every week I'd go there to rhyme. I didn't care if there were bullets flying or not, I knew that was what I wanted to do with my life."

Fredro met the original Onyx trio, which included Sonee Seeza (then known as Suave, now known as Sonsee) and Big DS at John Adams High School in the Ozone Park–Woodhaven section of Queens. Other classmates included Mr. Cheeks and Freaky Tah from the Lost Boyz. Sonee had DJ equipment and some skills, although he rhymed more than DJed. Big DS, who died from cancer in 2003, was a close friend of Fredro's. "He was always my boy," Fredro says. "He had the attitude, but he wasn't a great rapper. We looked past that and put him in the group."

Sticky Fingaz wasn't in the group at the time because he was merely a snot-nosed shorty, three years younger than his cousin Fredro (their mothers are sisters). But Stick was most definitely around and had started honing his style in the late eighties. "Fredro is my older cousin," Stick says. "I was in Brooklyn and he was in Queens, so I'd spend some weekends out there."

Stick also recalls his first sparks from the hip-hop fire: "I wanted to be a DJ back then because I wanted to control the music. I was making pause tapes off the radio back then, in the late eighties. I told my moms that I wanted turntables for Christmas when I was twelve or thirteen, and she bought me some corny-ass ones. You know, the ones with the straight arm. I had those and a mixer and I had all the records of the time. Sparky D, UTFO, Run-DMC. So I tried to be a DJ." This is the time when the two rocked the baby shower in question. But DJing wasn't how Onyx members were meant to be heard.

During his formative years, the mic called out to Stick and he attacked it. He recalls: "I was DJing a bit, but I would always also be writing rhymes. I went to bad schools, and I'd be rhyming in the cafeteria, outside on the street, battling everybody." In the late eighties he moved to Queens to live with Fredro, who says: "Stick was having problems with his moms, so he basically moved to Queens to live with me. I had my own apartment and he was living there with me when he was like fourteen."

An ironic twist, considering their later trademark baldhead style, was the fact that both Fredro and Sticky were accomplished, in-demand barbers working at the Nu Tribe barbershop on Jamaica Avenue in Queens. "We were working there in the late eighties and early nineties," says Sticky. "We were still working there when the album came out. We still had to make money until it took off." Both claim to be skilled with scissors and shears, but Fredro might win in the bragging rights game: "I started cutting hair there at Nu Tribe when I was about fifteen. I was like the best barber in New York. I was cutting Kool G Rap's hair, Kid 'N Play, Rakim, every drug dealer in Queens. I was making a thousand dollars on a Saturday back then—I had fifteen heads all in line waiting for me. I was an artist, doing all kinds of designs in people's hair." Being there also gave them a chance to rock their own tonsorial experiments. Stick says: "Being in a barbershop with all those tools, I had about every hairstyle you could name, out of curiosity, creativeness, or just boredom."

Haircutting wasn't Fredro's main goal, though. Wax called after they hooked up with manager Jeff Harris, and Onyx as a trio was first heard in 1990 on their debut single, "Ah, and We Do It Like This" (Profile). The single came and went with little fanfare (and rightfully so). But it wasn't the Onyx that the world knows today, and at the time lead rapper Fredro was even rapping with a southern accent. Fredro says: "I went down south every summer to visit my grandmother and I kind of picked up a southern accent from my time down there. So when I got back to New York I was rhyming like I was from the south, country style. Niggas are doing it now, but I was with it like fifteen years ago. We put out a single on Profile but the label just didn't understand the material. It was a whole different style. Smoother, and with the country thing. It was about partying, girls in the club, having fun with it."

At the time of the first single, Sticky wasn't in the group and had no intentions of being in the group. He says: "Onyx was three people back then, and I was just a solo rapper. I was working on songs with a producer, but I wasn't even shopping them or anything. I was just doing it because I was nice on the mic. Fredro and Onyx had that song out [on Profile] and it was kinda hot, but I was doing my own thing. I wasn't even trying to be a rap star back then, honestly. I was just living my life. I would cut school to go to the barbershop, because if I wasn't there, I'd lose money."

Two things changed Onyx's course back in 1990 and 1991. First was the low sales of their first single. Second, and more important, the trio's producer and Fredro's close friend B-Wiz was killed. (Manager Jeff Harris is credited with producing the first single; there is no mention of B-Wiz on it.) Fredro remembers: "B-Wiz was my producer when I was fifteen and sixteen, even. When all the other kids was getting turntables, he had an SP-12 [sampler]. He was one of the first niggas in the 'hood with a beat machine." After the single was out, Fredro says that B went down south to deal drugs, against Fredro's urgings, and was killed. "Our beat nigga was dead," he says. "After B-Wiz got killed, people were getting locked up in the 'hood, so we started rhyming about different things."

At the time the group also added a new, less hirsute angle to the package. Fredro remembers: "When B-Wiz got killed, one day I just went into the barbershop and cut all my hair off. I wanted to start clean. Then Stick and them did it and we had an image going. I didn't plan it, but it was a cool style for us."

The trio of Fredro, DS, and Suave continued to work on demos, with manager Harris shopping the group to labels. By the end of 1991 they had more than two dozen songs in the can when fate brought Sticky into the picture. Fredro remembers: "Sonee and DS got stranded out of town, up in Connecticut, but we had paid for time and had to go into the studio that day. So Sticky came in instead of them and we did 'Stik 'N' Muve,' which

Onyx (left to right: Sticky Fingaz, Big DS, Sonee Seeza, Fredro Starr) in Los Angeles, 1993.
PHOTO: B+ (FOR WWW.MOCHILLA.COM).

is basically about two niggas from Queens gettin' up in the morning, puttin' on their clothes, and stickin' everybody up. Just another day to get paid, you know? That's when he really got the name Sticky Fingaz, on that record right there."

Fredro, who was in Southside/Jamaica, Queens at the time, continues: "We did about thirty demos [but only one with Stick], and then I met Jam Master Jay at Jones Beach and played him the demos. Jay really liked 'Stik 'N' Muve.' The attitude, the sound, the direction. He said, 'Give me twelve songs like that one.' So that's when the album came to life. That changed our whole direction. Because at that time we were like a cross between De La Soul and a more hardcore group. Right in the middle. Jay was always the hardcore dude in Run-DMC, so it made sense that he'd want something more street."

From that point on Onyx was a quartet, and with the legendary Jay and his new JMJ imprint (through Def Jam/Rush Associated Labels) behind them, it was full steam ahead, whether or not DS and Suave wanted another member in the group. Fredro explains: "I was the leader of the group, so it was my way or there would be a problem. So Stick was in the group. Those guys didn't really mind that much on the MC side—they were more concerned about the money split. And DS knew that Sticky would take all his light." Stick says that Big DS ended up leaving the group as they were recording their second album. "He didn't feel like he was getting enough light, so he wanted to do his own thing."

Demo work continued under Jay's tutelage. And the group had brought a skilled new producer into their camp: Chyskillz (Chylow Parker), who produced or co-produced a majority of *Bacdafucup*. "We met Chyskillz on Jamaica Avenue one day," remembers Fredro. "We was buying weed at the weed spot and Chy was chasing my truck down the street, yelling, 'I got beats!' His stuff back then was jazzy, on some Tribe Called Quest shit, but it was hot. I knew he could put beats together right away. We brought him into our zone and made him do some grimy shit."

"We had one hundred percent input with the music with Chyskillz and Jay," Stick says of the group's dynamic. "We would sit down with Chy and make the beats with him. He was nice on the beats, but he was into that jazz shit, and a lot of them were kinda soft. We had to make sure he didn't make shit sound too happy."

Stick adds: "I think that we were creating the sound we wanted as we went along. All the songs on that first album were brand-new as we were in the studio, not old stuff from our demos [except for 'Stik 'N' Muve']. It wasn't planned out or anything. We knew at that point that we was street, that we was hardcore, and that we had the screaming style. We was just wild. So we were against all that soft shit. At that time Digable Planets were out, they were trying to be eclectic. But we were on some street shit, not that other funny bullshit. With jazzy type of samples they could be happy or they could be evil. We took the harder shit."

At first the group was given only a single deal to test the waters. And their first single as a four-man team, "Throw Ya Gunz," was most certainly a sure shot, combining Chy's rolling, jazz-inflected sensibilities with the grit and hardness of Jamaica Avenue. Sticky says: "That single was so incredible—radio was eating it up. So they [Def Jam/RAL] turned it into an EP deal, and then into an LP deal. All of that stuff happened pretty quickly." Fredro, who was twenty or twenty-one when the album came out, points out that Sticky wasn't even "street legal" at the time, being only seventeen. "His moms had to sign the contract," Fredro laughs.

Within the course of a couple months, an album's worth of songs were embarked upon at various studios (including Power Play, Soundtrack, and Apollo), continuing the group's new, and more natural, grimy image. Sticky talks of their intensity in these proceedings: "We wasn't just like: 'Hey, let's go make an album.' I mean, we used to go out and *battle* motherfuckers and disassemble them. We'd be in line at a club like Red Zone [in Queens], waiting to get in, and we'd just rip people up. That's what we specialized in: having the best punch lines, being louder than everyone, and having very high energy. Basically, just more personality."

Jam Master Jay was a strong presence in the studio and guided the group through the album's recording process, adding production work to many tracks. But even so, he mostly let Onyx and Chyskillz do their thing. Sticky says of the late, great JMJ: "Jay was very hands-on, one hundred percent. He was always there in the studio with us. We learned everything from him. He was our mentor."

In the end, the early 1993 album, which Fredro says took "most of 1992" to record, was a slam dunk because the group brought more energy (or, at least, decibels) to hip-hop than just about any group in the music's history. The sound was an extension of the group's bombastic live shows, which could be a bit messy at times but could never be characterized as laid-back. Fredro says: "Jam Master Jay definitely showed us how to perform in front of a big crowd. Back then, when we came out, hip-hop was missing a lot of energy. We brought that grimy Queens sound to the game while [L.A.'s Dr.] Dre was doing his laid-back thing. We just came out of nowhere."

Stick remembers: "We blew up lots of stuff onstage at shows. Speakers, mics, everything. Sound guys used to put Saran Wrap on the stage speakers because they knew we'd be throwing water all over the place. Every show was pandemonium back then, and a lot of groups didn't want to go on after us. They'd complain about it. And I wouldn't have wanted to go on after us either!" Fredro adds: "At our first show, I was yelling at the audience and acting kind of ill. Jay and Ice-T were there. And Jay was like: 'Yo, what the fuck are you *doing*? Don't do that. You want the crowd to be *with* you.' So instead of saying, 'Fuck y'all' to the audience, I'd just say, 'Fuck everybody else!' "

The live-performance aspect of the group also showed up in their catchy call-and-response choruses, which showed up on smash hits like "Throw Ya Gunz" and "Slam." "We all worked on those choruses," Sticky says, "because when you do shows, you have to have crowd participation." Fredro adds: "We were definitely influenced by Naughty by Nature with that kind of stuff, because 'O.P.P.' and 'Hip Hop Hooray' were such big stadium records. That's where we got our choruses from, being inspired by those records." And were they as amped-up offstage as they were onstage? Stick says: "Well, you of course have to turn it up a little bit when you're performing live, but we was always like that to a certain extent. I was probably the wildest."

Fredro drops a very interesting fact about the group's mind state when recording *Bacdafucup:* "While we were recording the album, niggas was on LSD the whole time, straight up. We was dropping papers, taking meth tabs, during that whole album. That's just the creative side of making music. We were like Jimi Hendrix. And that's partially what kept our energy going at that high level. We had that battery pack. LSD was our secret weapon. It kept us creative."

In the end the group, inspired by psychedelic drugs, stadium choruses, and, most important, the grimy streets of Queens's outer edges, made a classic record that put high energy back into New York hip-hop. It also brought a new rock angle to the equation, introducing slam dancing—previously seen only at punk rock shows—to the hip-hop world through their "Slam" video and subsequent live performances. The album went double platinum and paved the way for high-energy gangsta rap throughout the next decade.

TRACKS

Sticky: Chy and Jay played the music on that, because motherfuckers would want like ten G's to sample shit. So we was like: "Fuck that, just play the shit over and we'll change it a little." That happened a few times. Chy wasn't like a keyboard player that could play in a band, but he could figure shit out. He could play by ear.

THROW YA GUNZ

Fredro: That single came out in November of '92. I remember because we had a show at the Muse and somebody got shot and killed up there. That was our first real show. We were signed for that single first. Personally, I don't think that [Def Jam/RAL] were sure about us. They weren't sure they wanted to invest in a group that they didn't know about. They trusted Jay, but we had to prove ourselves to Def Jam. With that beat on "Throw Ya Gunz," I knew it was going to be a serious record. I knew it would be big, a hip-hop anthem, because that's what we made it for. We planned it out. It was for the streets, it was energetic, and it was grimy. That single went gold, so Def Jam was very happy about that.

Sticky: With choruses, like on that song, we definitely all worked on those. Because when you do shows, you want a lot of crowd participation.

Fredro: That's one of my favorite tracks on the record. I love the energy on that record, and definitely the beat. I always loved doing that one at our shows [*he repeats chorus*].

ATAK OF DA BAL-HEDZ

Sticky: We started the bald thing right before we came out as Onyx, the four of us. Kool Tee produced that. He was Jay's boy. He did "Da Nex Niguz," too. We didn't just work with him because Jay told us to. I mean, he had hot beats.

DA MAD FACE INVASION

Fredro: With our mad-face logo, I made that up. I made a mad face, something very simple. Naughty [by Nature] had a hot logo, even though back then most people weren't really fuckin' with logos. That whole thing was new. We knew we should make something marketable, something we could make clothes with, shit for stickers. I mean, we had mad faces, so that logo just worked for us.

Sticky: Me and Fredro came up with the logo for the group. Fredro was looking at my face, 'cause I was like the troubled youth. I never smiled, I was always mad at the world. I was just an angry black youth and . . . just dangerous. Fredro looked at my face and drew a sad face. And I went to art school for two years, so I fixed the eyes and the mouth and turned it from a *sad* face to a *mad* face. And that was it.

NIGGA BRIDGES

Fredro: It might say it on the album, but Jeff Harris didn't produce that track. Hell no. All that guy did was run his mouth—he was like Don King.

He was with us for our first single in 1990, and after the first album we went our separate ways.

Sticky: I don't know why Jeff Harris got production credit on that song. One of Jeff's producers might have made the beat, but Jeff didn't produce it. Jeff helped us out in the early years. He was the one who called me in to do "Stik 'N' Muve," so without him maybe I wouldn't have even been in Onyx.

Fredro: With influences on that one, it would have to go back to Naughty by Nature again. "O.P.P." was such a huge thing and I went to their show and people were loving that song. So I wanted to make a record even bigger than that one, for stadiums. Chyskillz had the beat and we were in the studio for maybe five days just listening to it. Then I had that old record "Champ" [by the Mohawks, a classic old-school break that is the basis for the chorus] and the chorus just developed from there. We knew it would be big because it was all planned. We wanted to bring slam dancing to rap. Believe it or not, Nirvana was a big influence on us. Red Hot Chili Peppers too. When we was writing the album, [Nirvana's] "Smells Like Teen Spirit" would come on all the fuckin' time [on MTV] and they had slam dancing in that video. So that kind of triggered that. Run-DMC did the rock thing before, but nobody brought slam dancing until us. We took it to another level. That single went platinum, so I guess it worked. We did a remix of that with [the metal/punk band] Biohazard. It was Lyor Cohen's [from Def Jam] thing to do a white version. He basically said, "This is going to make you rich." So I was like, "Let's do it." We wasn't worried about our credibility, so we had no problem with reaching more people. The Biohazard guys were cool and we sold 250,000 copies of just the remix version, on top of all the other sales—so everyone was happy.

Sticky: We had "Throw Ya Gunz" killin' the radio and the streets, but it was mostly just mix shows. We needed something that would go aboveground. Something that was still hard and stuck to our guns, though. I think me,

Fredro, and Sonee probably came up with that chorus simultaneously. That song was less violent and less graphic than "Throw Ya Gunz," so that it could get played in more places. And it was very high energy. It was made for live shows. The slam dancing just started in our shows—people would just wild out. With that Biohazard remix, Lyor from Def Jam made us do it. We didn't really want to. I mean, we was street dudes, we wasn't thinking about no rock shit. Lyor said: "White people are loving the song and they're crossing over to you." Jay was for it and we really didn't care, so we did it. But "Slam" was already huge before we even did that shit. That was just icing on the cake. It reached some more people than the original, I'm sure. It was a trip because eighty percent of our audience back then was white. We was like: "Holy shit!" And the white dudes was crazier than our black fans. They didn't give a shit about anything.

STIK 'N' MUVE

Sticky: That's the first song I recorded, when Fredro called me in that day. It was the first thing we did as the new Onyx, I guess. We had to change the beat when we recorded it for the album because we couldn't get clearance. I'm mad at that, because the original beat was fuckin' incredible. With the new one they had to play it over and it didn't sound as ill as the sample we had in the first place. But it still sounded cool. When it got time to sign the contract, Jay was like, "Wait a minute, where's the guy with the deep voice?" Because Onyx was only three guys—I wasn't really even in the group. But Jay said he didn't want Onyx if I wasn't in it. So that's how I got in. I was just helping them out at that point. I was a soloist with my own little vision. But I was like: "Okay, fuck it, I'm in the group, let's do it." Once I was in, my solo idea went out the window. And as for the subject matter on that track, I don't want to incriminate myself, but I probably had the most stick-up-kid history in the group. We were doing what we had to do. I mean, we wasn't Scarface and shit. Obviously we were still good guys, because it wasn't no full-time shit. I mean, I worked at a barbershop.

Sticky: We got arrested because of bootleggers back in those days. We was down on Canal Street [in Manhattan], driving. I can't remember if we was just driving or whether we set out on a mission to fuck up the bootleggers. Probably the second option. We went to one of the bootleggers' tables and flipped it over and broke all their shit. One time Fredro was flipping a table and stepping on shit and an African dude came out of nowhere, about to snuff Fredro. But I seen him coming and I grabbed him around the neck and threw him up against the wall. Then one of the African dude's homeboys grabbed a chair and threw it through the window of the van we was in. The police came and arrested all of us. We dropped the charges against each other, because we was all black and we didn't want to be in jail. But the ill shit is that the police gave the guy back all of his CDs, the ones that weren't broken! So after that day I felt like it was hopeless to fight the bootlegger system. Ten years later, 50 Cent capitalized off the same bootlegging [mix CD] situation, so there you go.

Fredro: Nowadays bootlegging is cool, but not back then. That day on Canal Street we just basically flipped out. There was Chinese niggas coming at us with bats, we were kicking niggas in the face. Chinese and African dudes were attacking us together. It was fucked up.

Fredro: That was a single later in the year. It was our third single on the album.

Fredro: That was another one of my favorite tracks. It was something different for the album, and Kool Tee produced that one, so it had a different sound. At the shows, all the bitches loved that one. We actually did a video for that song, directed by my man Brett Ratner. It was his first video! Now he's doing big *Rush Hour* movies with Chris Tucker for fifty million. That song was the B-side to "Slam."

PETE ROCK & CL SMOOTH

Mecca and the Soul Brother

(Elektra, 1992)

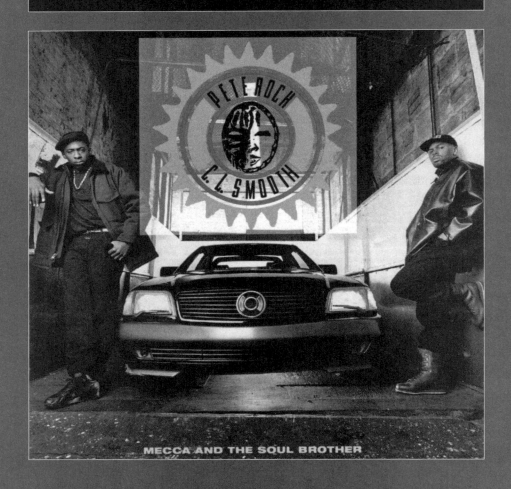

O nly a few people have ever changed the way that records are made. Pete Rock is one of them," states veteran hip-hop A&R man and producer Dante Ross. "People like Pete change the sound palette for the whole world. He had a true signature sound, and that's so hard to get."

"*Mecca and the Soul Brother* is one of my great accomplishments," beams Pete Rock, on the phone from Greene Street Studios in New York, where his classic debut had its genesis. "When hip-hop was changed around, it started with that album."

Pete's is a hefty boast, but he's got a strong argument. When the album hit stores in 1992, rap music was most definitely looking for the next big thing. Rock had experienced Nirvana to reinvent itself. And hip-hop had exhausted the James Brown sample vault and was starting to stagnate as it grew. But hip-hop got a new jolt of East Coast energy from Pete Rock & CL Smooth that year to counterbalance Dr. Dre's G-funk revolution out in L.A. Transitioning from the late eighties to an era when deeper soul and jazz chunks were the prime fodder for crate-digging producers, the Mt. Vernon, New York–based pair of Pete (Peter Phillips) and CL Smooth (Corey Penn) were the perfect soul brothers to lead the charge.

The audio maestro of the group, Pete Rock was born in the Bronx and moved to nearby Mt. Vernon (about three miles away) when he was eight years old. His first influences were the deepest of the old-school pioneers, like Grandmixer D.ST and Grandmaster Flash. He recalls: "I saw Prince Whipper Whip with Grandwizard Theodore and the Fantastic Five and the Cold Crush Brothers at the Harlem World when I was about fifteen [in the mid-eighties]. All those old-school cats, the DJs from 1978 and 1979, were big for me."

Closer to home, he had a crew member who showed him the ropes first-hand: DJ Cheeba M. And Pete's crew was no joke, considering that his cousin was Heavy D., a man who had already made hip-hop waves by the late eighties. "Cheeba M's real name is Floyd," says Pete of his DJ mentor. "He showed me how to scratch, how to cut on time. I was the youngest in our crew of like seven or eight dudes, the Classy Rock Crew. Heavy D. was in it back when he was known as MC Star, with a guy named Bob Two, this guy Gary, and Easy Lee. This was all in Mt. Vernon."

CL took a more circuitous route to get to where he would connect with his future musical partner. "I was born and grew up in New Rochelle and was around in Queens," says CL. "My grandparents and aunts and uncles were big influences on me. Everyone's around the same age, since my grandparents were young, because I had a teenage mom. It was all very tight-knit and it was a truly rich atmosphere.

"There were always instruments playing in my house," CL continues. "Jazz, soul, all kinds. I always had a love for music and a big imagination and I never really needed a lot of friends to play with. So being an MC was a natural thing for me to get into. I equate writing rhymes to drawing, in the way you need to be detailed. The more detailed something is, the more real it is to those who hear it."

Aside from his days in New Rochelle (which is two towns from Mt. Vernon), CL also spent time in his early years—he says from ages eight to fifteen—in Queens. He remembers: "Even when I was young, there was always a seriousness in my approach, and it was always just about meshing with the people around me. When I was in Queens, there was no mesh. Queens made me understand the hustle, the street life. It turned me out and took away my innocence."

Eventually he landed in the place some call "Money Earnin'." He moved to Mt. Vernon in his midteens, at the same time he caught the music bug and started rhyming. "There's only one high school in Mt. Vernon, and me and Pete were introduced through mutual friends," recalls CL. "When you're a known person doing what you do, it's not too hard for you to find each other like that. We just found that the love of the music was the same in both of us. It was definitely deeper than two average teenagers talking about music and aspiring to be rap stars. There was a rich cultural history there, and knowledge of older music and where it came from. It kind of gave me an edge to go from Queens to a suburban town like Mt. Vernon, even though Mt. Vernon still had the mentality of a place like Harlem."

CL was known as Corey Love early on, but was using CL Smooth by the time he had met Pete. "I heard him rhyme in high school and he definitely impressed me," says Pete. "So we started to put some stuff together in the Basement."

The Basement was Pete's infamous music lab where all preproduction for songs was done. It was indeed subterranean, but it wasn't actually in Pete's house. CL remembers: "The Basement started from just hanging out in Pete's room, but the music-making got bigger, from pause-tapes to working with actual equipment. You can't have people creating in your room with your bunk bed, so he took it a couple doors down to his friend Damien's house. That's where the Basement was created. We called Damien D.O., and he was Heavy D.'s right-hand man at the time."

Pete built up his DJ reputation throughout high school, and by graduation day in 1988 he was ready for the big time. His first major opportunity was on Marley Marl's "In Control" radio show on WBLS. Pete remembers: "That's the thing that really opened the doors for me. I was fresh out of high school when I started with him. I met him through Heavy D. Marley needed a DJ to work with him because his DJ, Kevvy Kev, was in a car accident. So I jumped in, and at that point I was on the radio in New York with Marley every Friday and Saturday night." Dante Ross recalls: "Pete started playing his own demos on the air. Word got around quickly."

"Being close to Marley made me take all my work a step higher—it brought me to that next level," Pete explains. "He brought sampling to the world's attention with the tracks he did, and so many cats followed what he did. I wanted to know, 'Damn, how can *I* make beats like that but also have my own swing and my own aura to them?' And after a while of doing beats on my own, I made my own identity. But I learned a lot from Marley, and from listening to guys like Larry Smith and Howie Tee, and Teddy Riley on the R&B side.

"I really started to step things up as a producer in '89, after Heavy D.'s first album [*Big Tyme,* on MCA]," says Pete. "I was travelin' with him to different producers, people like Howie Tee and Marley Marl, and learning from that. I was going to the sessions and seeing the greatness that was being made. I was putting beats together in my head and me and Eddie F [Heavy D.'s manager, who would also go on to manage Pete and CL] would mess with recording equipment."

Even today, Pete still uses the piece of equipment that he started out with back in the eighties: the E-mu SP-1200 sampler. "That's definitely my favorite piece of equipment," he says. "I have an MPC-3000 [sampler], but I never put out any beats on it. I have to keep all my old equipment, it's antique! I've got four or five SPs at home."

Dante Ross recalls: "Pete was just tremendous on the SP-1200, and in the Basement he had a twelve-track-to-cassette [recording/mixing] board, and the mixes he did with that sounded just like album mixes that were done in a professional studio. What's also crazy about Pete is that he's not a trained musician, but nothing he does or samples is ever out of key. Q-Tip has that same ear for pitch. It's just something you have or you don't, naturally."

Pete toured nationally and internationally with Heavy D. and co-produced several songs on *Big Tyme.* The first appearance of Pete Rock *with* CL Smooth as a duo was on a remix of Johnny Gill's "Rub You the Right Way" single in 1990. CL says: "That was the first time that we worked together, professionally. It came from Eddie F, because we were his protégés."

"Heavy D. really helped us immensely," says CL. "He let us know what style was about, what sophistication was about, and he showed us what level your live show had to be on. He had an aura of invincibility, and everybody loved and respected him. He showed me, personally, that you have to be a gentleman, and you have to have a strong character to succeed. It was always important to be articulate and serious about your craft and how you approached it."

CL comments on his own personal inspiration: "I was an old soul, acting beyond my years at age eighteen, because I hung out with my grandfather a lot and fed off his style. My grandfather, Graham Williams or Doc [name-checked as 'Papa Doc' on the duo's hit 'They Reminisce over You'], was very supportive of my music. The rest of my family wasn't very impressed, but Doc knew I should keep going. If I hadn't succeeded, the rest of my family would have been like: 'I told you so.' "

CL continues: "With my grandfather it was like putting his soul in my body. It was like me saying: 'You can't do this on the mic, but I can.' Everything about me was from him. The way I talked, the approach, the words I used. My family always looked at my grandfather's house as the underprivileged house, the gutter-rat house. Me and Doc were the black sheep of the family, the alcoholic and the underachieving street kid. But we proved them wrong, and now they can't do anything but praise it."

Pete had a familial influence as well. "My pops had *everything* in his record collection. He had classical, jazz, reggae, soul, funk. When I started building my collection, it was built off of what he had. He would have two or three copies of some records, so I'd just take me one of those. Out of everything, he had more reggae, then jazz and soul. Once I started digging with guys like Large Professor, Q-Tip, Lord Finesse, Mr. Walt, and Evil Dee, my crates definitely grew fast."

Dante Ross, a producer and record collector himself, went to the Basement on several occasions and remarks, "When I looked at Pete's record collection I was so mad! Not only did he have every record I had, but he also had every record that I *wanted.* It was amazing." After heading out on wax-hunting missions with Pete, Ross also remembers, "Pete has more stamina for record shopping than anyone you'll ever meet. He was in [legendary funk retail outlet] Groove Merchant in San Francisco for three days straight one time when we were out there. He listened to every 45 in that whole store, probably about five thousand of them."

Considering Pete's huge exposure as part of Marley Marl's "In Control" show, the fact that people in the industry were starting to hear his production finesse through his Heavy D.–related work, and that Pete and CL were managed by growing industry powerhouse Eddie F's Untouchables Entertainment, getting a production deal for the duo wasn't a chore. Their deep reserve of music didn't hurt either. Pete says: "We had like thirty or forty songs done when we got signed."

Pete Rock & CL Smooth in Los Angeles, 1994.
PHOTO: B+ (FOR WWW.MOCHILLA.COM).

After talking to different labels, they were landed by Elektra Records, with Raoul Roach and Dante Ross tapped to oversee and develop the group's work for the label. Ross recalls: "Eddie F knew what he had and what he was doing when he was shopping them. I remember how much Raoul Roach loved Heavy D. and Eddie F. He told me that Eddie had a new group he was shopping and it was Pete Rock, so I was like: 'Hell yeah!' But Raoul was having problems at the label at the time, and he didn't want to sign them on his own. He said: 'I'm only gonna do it if you do it with me.' "

Ross continues: "After Raoul signed them, Elektra fired him before Pete and CL even started recording. So I was more than happy to take over. Because with Pete Rock, there was almost nothing to do on the A&R front. He knew exactly what he was doing, and that was the easiest record that I was ever involved with. Pete and CL were completely unproblematic and Pete was really nice—very quiet and respectful. CL was great, too—he was really funny."

Work began on the EP that would become *All Souled Out,* which hit in 1991. CL says of their debut on wax as headliners: "With *All Souled Out* we were definitely still learning back then. I was even still getting comfortable with hearing myself on record."

The EP made the splash they had hoped for, and in 1991 Pete was quickly becoming the go-to man for remixes, working on tracks for artists like House of Pain, Public Enemy, Run-DMC, and DAS EFX. Pete recalls: "I was the new young guy doing a lot of music at the time, and people thought it was different. CL was someone they hadn't heard before, too, and people were feeling it." CL adds: "The record label definitely liked the response they got for that EP, and it was a success from their standpoint. And although I didn't have time to analyze any of that shit back then, I was just happy at that time to be doing something so positive. I decided that I wasn't going to go to college like the rest of my family. I was out to see the world and write my own ticket."

Dante Ross recalls: "We set up the album with that EP [*All Souled Out*], and I think the first song we put out to radio was 'Go with the Flow' and the B-side was 'The Creator.' That was the wrong A-side, but people found 'The Creator,' and once they did, I saw what that track was doing in the clubs. That song was everywhere, and people loved Pete's rhyming on there. When 'The Creator' hit and the [Pete-produced Public Enemy] 'Shut Em Down' remix hit, I knew that I had a star on my hands."

Even though the duo had built up a vault of more than three dozen songs—using only five on *All Souled Out*—they brought out precious few remaining ones when they began their album sessions. Pete says: "Of those first forty joints we had done initially, very few of them got used. I still like those unused ones to this day, and some of those are even lost, but I'm looking for them."

Preproduction for *Mecca and the Soul Brother* was done at the Basement, and once Pete and CL got to the studio they were as focused as can be. CL says: "After a while, everybody around us just left us alone, because they knew how we worked." Dante Ross backs up this assertion: "Making that album was like: I go to the studio; Pete Rock's playing something incredible; we smoke a little weed; I get some food and come back; I tell Pete that it sounds great; I get a DAT of the track and we're all good. It was painless."

"The record might sound complex to people, but it's really not," reasons CL. "Even the song titles that I chose were meant to be simple. It was really just one, two, three to us after the learning curve of the first EP, because we did so much preparation in the Basement. We always went into the studio knowing what we were going to do. We knew how important the studio was. It was the final analysis, what separated the men from the boys.

"Pete was like a mad scientist when he was doing tracks," CL continues. "And if you weren't up in the same zone with the same intensity, then he was on your ass. But that was great, because you knew that it would be the best music possible. A lot of my [vocal] stuff was done in five minutes with one take, and sometimes we'd finish three or four songs in one day, and we always mixed the tracks the same day that we made them. It was all about building a rhythm."

The album's liner notes list co-production on all songs by CL, despite the fact that Pete was one of the finest producers of that era. "When you go through old records to decide what will be used for different tracks, it's a mutual collaboration," says CL. "My voice is on our records and that's an instrument too. We all decided things together as to what went in and what stayed out. It was very even with the musical input, in a way, because Pete had to know what I liked in order for me to rhyme on it to my fullest potential. He couldn't just say: 'Here's what I like, do something with it.' So we'd go over thousands of beats and old songs to figure it out."

Pete adds: "We would both come up with ideas as we went along—him visually and me musically." And Dante Ross says: "CL was definitely a huge part of that album as a whole. His vocals were another great instrument in the mix." Ross says that the group's advance was around $250,000, not including recording costs, and that the album sold "just under gold, four hundred thousand and some change."

Mecca took about six months to complete, and once it was done, the title was an obvious one to those in their inner circle. Pete explains: "The album title came from our man Adofo Muhammad. He came up with Mecca as a name for CL, and the Soul Brother was me. So we just put them together."

CL says: "As I look back on that album, it was all about how original we were. It was about mine and Pete's personalities as old souls. We did something simple, but we made it very original. The streets co-signed what we were doing, so it was respected. And while all these groups had huge entourages and dancers and bands, it was just me and Pete up there onstage. People were trippin' about how *regular* it all was."

"That record is almost flawless to me," says Ross. "Musically, it just flows so well, and CL was the icing on the cake. The music was always allowed to shine. His sound was so warm and soulful. A lot of *Mecca and the Soul Brother* just sounds to me like a nice day in the sun."

TRACKS

RETURN OF THE MECCA

CL Smooth: That was like a pilgrimage, returning with something new and vibrant. That's what that energy was about, returning to the roots of where we came from. I was always spiritual, because there always has to be a certain amount of love involved in anything you do.

FOR PETE'S SAKE

Pete Rock: Grand Puba [of Brand Nubian and Masters of Ceremony] wrote that verse for me. He was always like: "I want you to rhyme, I want to hear how *you* sound." He liked the way I sounded, 'cause he heard me when I used to play around, just buggin' out. I would rap sporadically, but I wasn't into rapping as much as I was into the music. I never took it as serious.

Dante Ross: I think that Puba wrote that stuff for Pete for dinner and a bunch of beer! Pete wasn't really a rapper, but he rapped on "The Creator" and he has a cool voice, so he always just wanted to get on tracks.

GHETTOS OF THE MIND

CL Smooth: That was to let people know how conscious you could be, even though you were in a place where there is no consciousness [i.e., the ghetto]. It was telling people to beware about judging a book by its cover. Just because you're in a certain place doesn't mean you're oppressed. Maybe we had a choice to be there, and maybe we can leave at any time.

But don't think that the ghetto has me oppressed. Everything is a mental thing, and if you're letting the ghetto run you, then it *is* a ghetto of the mind.

LOTS OF LOVIN'

Pete Rock: That was done with Nevelle Hodge [who also co-produced] on the keyboard. He was a keyboard player and producer cat from Mt. Vernon. He did a lot of stuff on the R&B tip and was doing stuff with [our manager] Eddie F [and Heavy D.]. That was my concept, and he would bring his keyboard to my house and play over different beats that I had made.

CL Smooth: On that one I was paying homage to the birth of my son, and about how being a father had affected my life. That song was about being a man about certain things and a child about other things. I was in the midst of growing up. My son was probably a few months old when we did that, and he was even in the video.

ACT LIKE YOU KNOW *Co-produced by Large Professor*

CL Smooth: Calling Large Professor an outside producer doesn't really count, because he's just another guy on the level of Pete Rock, in the same zone. There's not much difference between the two, really. It was like: "Who's gonna get to this loop first?" It's like two crackheads fighting for a rock [*laughs*].

STRAIGHTEN IT OUT

CL Smooth: That was one of the songs that I wrote right there in the studio, on a rare day that I didn't come in there prepared. We weren't ready but we just wanted to go in there and do *something*. No pressure—we just sat there and made that one. On the song, I was talking about sampling, and I was basically reacting to how everything was such a procedure when you had to clear stuff. You were paying homage to these artists and they just wanted everything from you. They didn't seem to care about how their music affected anyone else, they just wanted money. So it was just something that needed to be straightened out. It seemed like a valid statement, considering the title of the song. Older artists thought that us younger cats were ripping them off, but it wasn't like that. It was a tribute.

Pete Rock: We used to clear a lot of our stuff and all the samples on *Mecca* were cleared, just not right when the album was done. I never got sued for anything. That incident with Biz Markie [Gilbert O'Sullivan's sampling lawsuit against Biz in 1991] was such a big court issue. That was crazy. Getting sued just for making hip-hop music. We did a video for that song too. I definitely liked all the videos we did for songs on that album.

ANGER IN THE NATION

Pete Rock: I always thought I could have done better with that beat, but I'm my own worst critic. CL liked it because it fit with what he was saying. It was something militant that he wanted to do. I liked what he said on it.

CL Smooth: Adofo Muhammad [credited for lyrics, with CL] is my cousin, but we're really more like brothers. He's a professor now—he has his doctorate. He knows so much about different cultures and different societies. We got together and I told him that I wanted to make something real conscious, and be deliberate about it. Adofo showed me how to approach it and what I should say. We talked about it for hours and I did the song. I didn't know that Pete didn't like the music to that song. I definitely didn't have any problem with it.

THEY REMINISCE OVER YOU (T.R.O.Y.)

CL Smooth: I wrote that song without music—that was the only one like that at the time. I told Pete that I had a deep song that was about how I grew up and what it all meant to me, and I pointed out a reference beat for him. He took a day and came back with that music. I did the lyrics over it and it fit like a glove. The song didn't have a title when I first wrote it. I wanted to name it "Troy" but I wanted it to mean even more, so I took his name and carved out an additional meaning with the letters. T-Roy [Troy Dixon, who was part of the Heavy D. and the Boyz crew] had passed a year or two before I wrote that song. The success of that song was more than I could have ever imagined. It moved so many people, the way it depicted a family with a magnifying glass like that. How this kid grew up, where this kid came from, and how he ended up being who he was. My family really respected that song. It totally took my family by storm and that's when my family really started showing me respect with the career that I had chosen. They even started to want to go to my shows at that point.

Pete Rock: Everybody was buggin' when that came out. It was big right away, and that was the first single off the album, with "The Creator" remix ["Slide to the Side" remix] on the B-side. T-Roy was a good friend and he was only twenty-six or twenty-seven when he died. He was playin' around and fell off a twenty-foot ledge. So we dedicated it to him. That was the track that definitely blew our shit up. I definitely did a lot of filtering with bass lines, like you hear on that song. Prince Paul was doing it a lot back then too. He was another cat that was kind of ill with the sampling. Stretching stuff, changing the tone of the sample, just to make things sound a little different. I love that kind of stuff.

Dante Ross: The album came out and I of course picked a song that doesn't have a hook as the first single [*laughs*]! Trouble T-Roy had died, and Eddie F wanted that to be featured and I had no problems going with it. And that single took off—it was an instant hit. That song definitely overshadowed everything else on the album. It was even on Z100 in New York, which is a pop station. A childhood friend of mine, Marcus Raboy, did that video, even though he hadn't done very much up to that point. It was an amazing video, really influential. I think that song was so well-loved because it's just so emotional. It's really hard to be emotional in hip-hop. The only emotions are usually anger or angst. But what CL came up with was very soulful. Even to this day there aren't many records like that. There's so much honesty and emotion. And no one had ever used horns like Pete did on there.

Pete Rock: The freestyle at the beginning of that is my brother Grap, and that's me beatboxing. He was probably sixteen or seventeen at the time. He does underground stuff now. I just gave him some beats recently. I have two brothers, Grap and my older brother, Ruddy.

THE BASEMENT *Featuring Heavy D., Rob-0, Grap, and Dida*

Pete Rock: Rob and Dida were just cats that used to get on my albums back in the day. Rob was in a group called INI and he branched off from there.

CL Smooth: Back then, we'd be down there in the Basement for hours, putting together great music and having artists come through and pay homage to the movement. And it wasn't just us—it was a movement of young kids like Rob-O, Grap, and Dida really being original with their swagger and their look.

SKINZ *Featuring Grand Puba*

Pete Rock: That was the last track we did, and it's Puba's only rhyme on the album. I wrote my own rhyme on that track. "Skinz" was really when I started writing my own shit to put out on wax. Puba had written three album rhymes for me up until what I did on "Soul Brother #1," and he wrote my rhyme on "The Creator" also. I always knew him, from way back. We were all from the same area—New Rochelle and Mt. Vernon.

THE PHARCYDE

Bizarre Ride II the Pharcyde

(Delicious Vinyl, 1992)

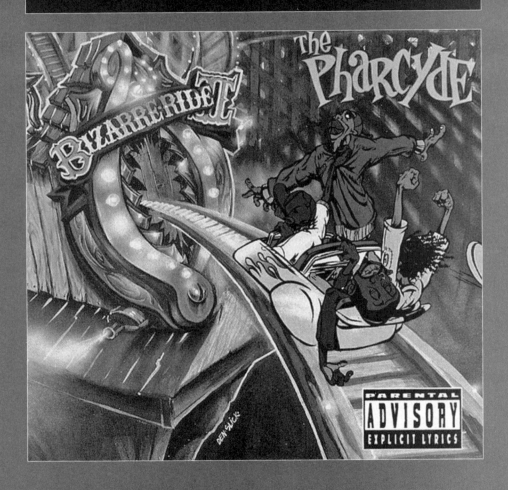

When people think back on early-nineties Los Angeles hip-hop, the image of gangsta rap stands almost singularly strong. But somehow, through this gat-clouded atmosphere, the Pharcyde—Tre "Slimkid" Hardson, Romye "Bootie Brown" Robinson, Derrick "Fatlip" Stewart, Imani Wilcox, and producer John "J-Swift" Martinez—was not only born but flourished. Their style was funky, freaky, fun in a time when most L.A. raps were about harsh realities. They rocked Lollapalooza and toured with Korn. Tre says: "There was black music, but we weren't really considered in that area. We were just considered some goofy guys."

Three out of four MCs in the group—Tre, Bootie, and Imani—were well-known dancers in the Los Angeles club scene in the late eighties and came together from that angle. Tre recalls: "In 1989, I was at El Camino College [in Torrance], hangin' out and dancin' in the courtyard with friends. A friend of mine introduced me to Imani. We used to go to this club called Zapp in Anaheim every Wednesday and Saturday, and that's where we met Romye, and his friend Robert Vincent. Imani and Romye actually knew each other already, so I was like the new guy in the crew."

"Dancing came first," says Imani. "I made records because it was fun and because I didn't have to pay to make them. J-Swift loved our voices and so he made sure he worked with us. But before we all came together, as rappers and singers we all just kind of sounded like whatever was popular at the time. KRS-One, Guy, Teddy Riley. I myself loved Michael Jackson and New Edition. And that's why when you listen to the Pharcyde it's not just like a boring typical group. It's more musical."

After Robert Vincent left the clique around 1990, Tre, Romye, and Imani were a trio, and dancing was still at the forefront of their aspirations as entertainers. Tre and Imani were in a group called the Play Brothers with two other members, but they didn't last long due to, as Tre says, "a lack of focus." Imani recalls: "Me and Tre were first in a group called As Is, before the Play Brothers. I was a rapper and dancer and he was a rapper and singer and dancer, and there were two other guys. Me and Bootie used to dance together and he used to be a backup dancer for Fatlip. So we were all kind of connected together."

The rapping wouldn't start to come to the forefront until they began hanging out with a man named Reggie Andrews. Reggie's influence on these talented but unfocused young men was huge. He ran a makeshift after-school program in South Central Los Angeles called, simply, the SCU (South Central Unit), which specialized in helping boys and girls from L.A.'s most disadvantaged 'hoods explore and refine their artistic talents. Andrews himself taught at Locke High School (in South Central at San Pedro and 111th Street) and he was a respected R&B musician and music producer who had his own band, Karma, and also worked with the Dazz Band and Rick James. The five-man unit that would give birth to the Pharcyde's first album was crystalized here, with rapper Fatlip and teenage prodigy producer J-Swift.

Tre, Imani, and Bootie were actually brought to SCU through J-Swift, whom Tre had met through a mutual friend in 1989. Tre recalls: "I first met J through a friend who was dating his sister. We went over to J's house and he was all about the [Roland] 808 kick. Before we met J-Swift and started going to SCU, our rap thing was definitely something very different. SCU was part of Reggie's house—he had a duplex and there was a dance area and two recording studios in one part of it. Not only did Reggie feed us all the time, he let us use his practice and recording facilities, and he helped us learn how to write and structure music. He just cared about the music, and he made us care too."

The final link of the Pharcyde chain was Fatlip. Tre says: "Fatlip came to SCU a little later in the game than the rest of us. I even remember the first day he was there, there was some crazy scene where Reggie had to hide him and his girl in a closet. He was in this group called the Jammers, and his name was Jammer D before he was with us. He was a solo artist in SCU. Me and Fatlip would always argue a lot and get into fistfights. He was like my brother, my sibling."

Imani explains the SCU story from his side: "Reggie funded SCU because he had some money tucked away from when he produced 'Let It Whip' for the Dazz Band. The SCU was basically a high school thing, but we were all way out of high school at that point. We were like nineteen or twenty. Locke High School, where Reggie teaches, is in one of the toughest sections of L.A., where people don't have a lot of hope. And when Reggie let us perform at Locke talent shows, that's when the group really started."

Pharcyde (left to right: Imani, Bootie Brown, Slimkid Tre, Fatlip) at Pharcyde Manor, Los Angeles, 1993.
PHOTO: B+ (FOR WWW.MOCHILLA.COM).

Brown adds: "Reggie was also getting money from Herb Alpert from A&M Records. It was basically an after-school program for kids who Reggie thought had a little extra talent that needed to be expanded. And J-Swift was one of those kids, a protégé of Reggie's. P.E.A.C.E. from Freestyle Fellowship went to Locke too. Reggie had so many records, we'd just go and get crates of records in the back of Reggie's garage and we'd bring them to the studio. It was me, Fatlip, and J-Swift's brother Pedro. Pedro's the one who first sat me down and showed me how to use equipment and loop stuff up."

J-Swift was a young and prodigious musical talent back in the late eighties and early nineties, and he was Andrews's star pupil, a gifted pianist who was the son of a jazz musician. Bootie Brown recalls: "I remember that Swift was about sixteen when we first met him. He was doing a lot of R&B and disco stuff, kind of like the Cover Girls. He wasn't sampling or messing with hip-hop." Imani adds: "Yeah, he was doing Spanglish stuff, like [Mellow Man Ace's hit] 'Mentirosa.' And New Jack Swing spin-off kind of stuff."

After working with J-Swift and coalescing as an MC quartet, the Phar-cyde got their first demo done by 1991. It contained three songs: "Passin' Me By," "Ya Mama," and "Officer." Imani says: "After we did that demo, we had no idea if it would go over with people or not. But [their new manager] Paul Stewart said: 'Do what you're doin', and put it on tape.' So we brought him those three songs and he was like: 'I can get you signed anywhere with this demo.' That was good news, because we seriously had no idea if it was good or bad."

Stewart—who also worked with House of Pain, De La Soul, and Cypress Hill at the time as a promoter and manager—had no problem attracting record-label suitors. Tre remembers: "There were lots of labels back then offering us lots of money, but there was a fear that we'd get signed and shelved. So we wanted to go with the label who was going to give us the most creative control. That was Delicious Vinyl."

Delicious Vinyl was definitely a great match for the group. Founded and run by DJs Mike Ross and Matt Dike, the label was small enough to be hands-on with its artists (both Dike and Ross were producers as well), but also powerful enough to have clocked multiplatinum sales in 1989 with Tone Lōc's *Lōc'ed After Dark* and Young MC's *Stone Cold Rhymin'.*

Mike Ross recalls his first encounter with the quintet: "I remember that Lamar Algee and Paul Stewart both brought me that first Pharcyde demo—they might have even both brought it to me together. Lamar was doing promo for the label at the time, and Paul had worked for me previously. I listened to the first two tracks, 'Officer' and 'Ya Mama,' and really liked them. Then 'Passing Me By' came on, and once Tre said: 'I guess a twinkle in her eye is just a twinkle in her eye,' I was sold. I had never heard a group like them before, and I wanted to sign them on the spot."

Aside from the artist-friendly atmosphere at Delicious Vinyl, the group leaned toward the label because of the British funk group the Brand New Heavies, who were very popular among MCs and producers. The group's U.S. debut, *Brand New Heavies,* was released on the label in 1990, and one year later they were working on their soon-to-be breakthrough album, *Heavy Rhyme Experience: Vol. 1.* The album was significant because it paired their throwback funk jams with some of the best rappers of the day, like Grand Puba, Black Sheep, Kool G Rap, and more. Tre says: "We *loved* the Brand New Heavies! Them being on the label definitely made us want to be on there."

Ross also recalls how the *Heavy Rhyme Experience* helped his cause: "When they came into the office the first time, I told them that I knew exactly what to do with them, that I was going to be behind them one hundred percent, every step of the way. I also told them about the Brand New Heavies record that I was working on, and mentioned that I could put them on there even though it was almost finished. The MCs on that record were pretty heavy at the time. It was definitely great company to be in for your debut appearance." They signed in the summer of 1991.

J-Swift was the group's producer from their earliest formation. Mike Ross recalls: "I remember that when they came into the office for that first time, J-Swift was with them and he was the one who did all the talking. J was always the guy calling the shots, and I even think he was in the group at first, like they were five members, instead of four and a producer."

Aside from their lives in the studio, one of the big parts of the Pharcyde puzzle in 1991 and 1992 was a house at West Twenty-fourth Street and South Budlong Avenue, on the edge of South Central, where all four rappers lived. It was dubbed the Pharcyde Manor. Tre remembers: "Before we had the Manor, we were all sleeping on Paul Stewart's floor. But the Manor was a spot where we lived and did all our rehearsing and preproduction when we weren't at SCU. Our Delicious Vinyl money paid the rent, and it was definitely a good place for us to grow our ideas."

Imani, of course, remembers the Manor, recalling, "We definitely felt that all of us being together was important, because that's how we all came together in the first place, being at SCU every day. And at SCU there was actually more of an R&B thing going on there, so we were kind of the outcasts. The Manor was our place, for us and no one else. We were smokin', listening to records, learning the [recording and sampling] machines, dancing, rapping. It was like Animal House, just for hip-hop. We didn't have no locks on the door and mo'fuckas would come through whenever they wanted. The Manor is the place where our lives transformed from being dancers to being MCs."

The Manor was also a place where Pharcyde group members would truly act like brothers, frequently coming to blows with one another to resolve arguments. (These fights were frequent in the recording studio as well.) Imani remembers: "Hell yes, we used to fight. Not me and Brown, but Fatlip and Tre and J-Swift, those guys would brawl, they'd take it outside.

It wasn't like: 'I hate you!' but it was more like: 'Fuck you! That drum machine doesn't sound right!' I guess we were like brothers, but it was just friends who were very emotional about what they believed in." Brown adds: "There were just strong feelings about what we believe in, so you'd fight for it. Like: 'You're gonna hear my side even if I have to put my fist in your eye.' I remember when Jay Dee [aka J. Dilla, who passed away in 2006] started working with us [after *Bizarre Ride*], he was shocked. He was like: 'You guys fight *all* the time, I just don't understand.' "

Live performances were always important to the group, and they used their hyperactive stage antics to attract a loyal fan base from coast to coast. Tre says: "At some point we knew that we had to get out there and hustle for a fan base, because it wasn't going to just fall in our laps. We wanted to show the world what we were all about. We never tried to be something that we weren't, which was kind of tough sometimes, because we weren't a typical hip-hop group. But as we learned when we were on Lollapalooza [in 1994] or when we opened for Korn back in the *Labcabincalifornia* days [1995–1996], you have to show yourself to any crowd you're given."

Before work on the Pharcyde album commenced, there was the important cameo on the Brand New Heavies album to deal with. Mike Ross recalls: "The day that they signed the contract with us, we went right to Paramount Studios, and that's where we did the song 'Soul Flower' for the *Heavy Rhyme Experience* album. The guys were working hard on their rhymes, and J was always adamant that the group have as much weed as possible at all times [*laughs*]. I would guess that there was a full ounce of weed smoked at that first session. It was ridiculous. But it was all good to me. I was so excited after that first day. I was like: 'I've got four of the funniest fuckin' MCs anywhere, and they're all in the same group together.' "

Ross continues: "After finishing 'Soul Flower,' we didn't wait too long to start on the Pharcyde album, maybe a couple days later. And we were there at Hollywood Sound at least every other day until we finished the record. The first thing we did once we got there was get some of the demo tracks, which I think were on four-track, and get them transferred to twenty-four-track. Then we just kept churning out more tracks. They had four or five songs ready to go, and we just had to get another six or seven going, with skits on top of that, of course." Tre says that the actual recording time for *Bizarre Ride II* was nine months, "like a pregnancy." Ross guesses that it was closer to six or seven months.

Ross, who was there in the studio with the group daily, says, "J-Swift was definitely the main creative force on the music side of that album, although I will say that the [other] guys contributed too. They picked out some of the records to use [for samples]. There were always tons of ideas flying around. But J did all of the programming. I think towards the end of the sessions for the album the group wanted full production credit alongside J, and I probably told them that they should take co-production. That seemed like the fair thing to do."

Tre explains the fine print on the album, with the group getting co-production on all album songs and J-Swift listed as producer: "Basically, everybody put in the same amount of time on that album. Beatmaking is beatmaking and producing is a different thing. You don't have to write the song or make the beat to be a producer. A producer just makes sure that everything sounds like an actual record. It's like taking shifts when you're driving long distance, and we were all there in that car for that album!" For various reasons including personality conflicts, the group didn't work with J-Swift after *Bizarre Ride,* switching things up by working with Jay Dee on 1995's *Labcabincalifornia.*

Tre remembers, "There was one song that we recorded that I really wish had gone on the album. It was called 'My Man.' It was funny and daffy and just amazing. It didn't make it on because we weren't finished with it, but we had to turn in the record. It never got finished, although I'm sure J-Swift has it somewhere. Ross says: "Yeah, I remember 'My Man.' The beat actually ended up later on a Jazzyfatnastees record [Mercedes Martinez of the vocal duo is J-Swift's sister]. I wanted it on the Pharcyde album, but at that point the sessions were just slowing down and the creative energy was running out. J-Swift and Tre were fighting, and Fatlip had some beef about something, so I just figured that it was best to just finish the album up before they all killed each other."

"We had probably five other songs that we wanted to put on there," says Brown. "It wasn't a complete project. They rushed the album out, so we didn't get to do our complete album the way we wanted."

Bizarre Ride II the Pharcyde, which hit in September of 1992 and was certified gold by the RIAA in 1996, combines a jazz sampling aesthetic that much of the hip-hop world of the mid-nineties would be using more frequently. Most important, though, the album had a sense of fun that matched its intelligence. Besides glib fare like "Ya Mama," "Oh Shit," and "Pack the Pipe," the group's biggest hit, "Passing Me By," while rapped through smirks, was heartbreakingly serious, and cuts like "On the DL" and "Otha Fish" weren't just pure foolin' either.

As for the album title, Tre explains, "It was just supposed to be us explaining what our bizarre ride was to us. It's a journey, and that's why there's a rollercoaster on the cover. We all had so many influences, and when you put us all together, it was just a great mesh."

Tre points to being accepted on the East Coast as a major turning point for the group at the time. "Getting over in New York was really big to us back then. We had to get over our New York fear, and after we did a show there at the Muse and got a nice response, we knew that we could be accepted anywhere. Because New York is just *real.* They're very honest with you."

Imani recounts: "We could never figure out why we never sounded like other records out there, because I think back then we wanted something to compare it to. But then at some point after the record hit, we realized that *that* was our twist. People loved us because we sound like *us.* Once we embraced that, we realized that we actually did like ourselves better. We never tried to be hard or like other people, and that was definitely what set us apart."

Tre says: "I just recently listened to that album again, and I laughed my ass off! For some reason I never really got why people thought that album was so funny at the time. But that shit is *so* fuckin' funny! We were so busy having fun and acting crazy that we didn't realize that we had put it onto the album like that. The whole album is an experience—it's like taking a trip."

"That album was never a success as far as money or record sales," says Imani. "But it was huge in the hearts of our fans. They felt it so much, and that's something that will always mean a lot to us." Brown says: "Our record is still only at gold status, I think. But Delicious Vinyl did everything they could. They just weren't used to spending money on records, and sometimes that's just what it takes."

Mike Ross beams: "Those guys made it cool to not have to front. They just saw things from a different perspective, even though they grew up in the 'hood like the gangsta rappers out there. The Pharcyde were trying to dodge the bullets, not shoot them. In a way, I think they were speaking for a silent majority of normal kids who were creative and talented, but didn't live the gangsta life and didn't have any desire to act like they did. That album to me was about those guys just experiencing things on a very real level. And it was funny, too.

"The record always seems to me like L.A.'s version of [De La Soul's] *3 Feet High and Rising.* It's just a classic record, no question about it. And I think it still has relevance today for a lot of people."

TRACKS

OH SHIT

Imani: That's my favorite song to perform live, because I can get loose and cuss [*laughs*]. That one's even more fun than "Ya Mama."

Tre: That was definitely our most requested song when we did shows. Like: "Yeah, do the one with all the curse words!"

IT'S JIGABOO TIME (SKIT)

Imani: The name of the group was actually going to be the Jigaboos at one point, but people were like: "That's like calling yourself the Niggers or something, no way!" We just felt like no matter what, when you're up there on stage you're definitely being exploited, and you're definitely lining someone else's pockets.

Bootie: Yeah, I remember we were going to call ourselves True Jigaboo, and everyone thought that was insane.

Tre: We always thought that it was really tough to escape that. Whenever you have to be something other than yourself to gain something else, it's "Jigaboo Time." You either pay the bills or starve. Basically, we just called anything we didn't want to do "Jigaboo Time."

Mike Ross: We didn't really have a budget for a fourth single, but we all loved that song, so I let the band do the video they wanted to make for that song. They had a lot of creative freedom on that one, in some ways because I felt bad about what happened with the "Otha Fish" video [see entry for "Otha Fish"]. We put it out on twelve-inch and it had the song "Return of the B-Boy" on the flip.

Imani: That's definitely my favorite video we did, because all of us did exactly what we wanted. It might not be our best video, but it's my favorite, and that was the last one we did for that album. A video for "Jigaboo Time" was connected to it. When I see that video I say, "That's the Pharcyde." It makes perfect sense to me.

Tre: That was like a slogan for what we were in. It was like a marriage, and we were even living together at the Manor. That was a lot of J-Swift playing on there, his own original music. He was a really talented pianist. I don't know if there are even any samples on there. We had keyboards set up at the Manor, but not drums. I think we actually recorded that song at SCU, then later we redid it at Hollywood Sound. I remember when Fatlip went in to do his part, he was slobberin', spittin', like a real maniac.

I'M THAT TYPE OF NIGGA *Featuring Buckwheat*

Bootie: Buckwheat was from New York, so he was the guy we could ask when we were fantasizing about there. He helped us learn about New York hip-hop, and we showed him what Cali was all about.

Tre: That's a really funny song, especially Buckwheat's verse [*laughs*]. That was a lot of fun to do live. Buckwheat was like our little brother—he came up through SCU too. He was in this group called Da Wascalz. They were like sixteen and fourteen at the time, a couple of kids who just ditched school all the time. They did a full album which was really dope, but it never came out.

Tre: That was different than the original one we did with the [Brand New] Heavies [on the *Heavy Rhyme Experience* album]. Well, the drums are different, a more clubby thing. Everything else is the same, pretty much. My verse is the same but Romye's [Brown's] is different. I like that one better anyways.

Bootie: I remember the first night in the studio we tried to record the song, but we was all too excited and faded. We had to come back the next day and try and do it right. And I did change my verse up on the album version of that, the remix. Basically, after we recorded the song, that set off a lot more production with it. J-Swift and Fatlip did a remix of it that never got released, because it had like forty or fifty samples on it!

Mike Ross: Once we had finished the *Heavy Rhyme Experience* version of that, the first song we did when we actually started recording the Pharcyde's album was that remix, the one we used for the album. I remember the remix that Fatlip and J did ["2 Tha 3 Mix"]. It had every sample under the sun on it, and it was pretty amazing. We actually put it out on a promo-only twelve-inch that we did. We could never put that out commercially because we would have never been able to clear all the samples.

OFFICER

Imani: With that track, we wanted to take a light approach to a serious topic. We definitely used to get pulled over by the cops a lot because they thought we were hippies and shit. But we had gun charges, I mean, we're from L.A. and you just get into shit. No one could ever figure us out, really. Tre is Mr. Peaceful, but he's the one with the gun charges. We'd be rolling around with guns under the seat and shit [*laughs*]. I think the Flavor Flav impression on there is J-Swift doing that. And Fatlip did the Chuck D. We loved Public Enemy. I think that Chuck D is actually the only person I've ever asked for an autograph.

Tre: That track was really funny. There was a time when I didn't like it and I didn't get why people liked it. And we never really did that one live for some reason. That was on our original demo, and ended up pretty much the same. We added some skit parts inside of there, the part about the girl, the part with: "Don't you live with your homeboys?" That Chuck D–Flava Flav thing at the beginning was great—it was a really good way to start it off. All that stuff in the lyrics is real shit. The cops are just dicks out here.

YA MAMA

Imani: We got dissed for that song by hardcore rappers. But, I mean, we dissed ourselves on that song, so who cares? Nobody is ever as hard as they say they are, so we just had fun with shit. We smoke weed, we fuck chicks, and we don't give a shit about what you think about us, so take that! I remember there being a debate about that one being our first single, definitely. No one had ever done a single like that before. Some people thought it was funny, some people thought it was wack. But ultimately it opened up a lot of doors for us because a lot of people talked about it.

Tre: We had to come out funny. We respect the originators of the conscious rap stuff, but there were so many other people coming out then with contrived shit. So we went the opposite way. My favorite things on that track were what we *didn't* use. If we said shit like, "Ya mama smell like two skunks fucking in an onion patch," it wouldn't have worked too well on the radio [*laughs*]. Our whole thing was just raggin' on each other for hours and hours.

Mike Ross: That came out as a single around June of 1992, a couple months before the album came out. I felt that it would be a great first single, to introduce people to the group's fun and irreverent side. People took notice and it laid their foundation—it got us going in the right direction. It was definitely a change of pace for people because [Dr. Dre's] *The Chronic* was out, or just about to come out, and the gangsta thing was getting so huge in L.A. So "Ya Mama" stood out because the Pharcyde were more like an anti-gangsta group.

Tre: The classic! Romye and J-Swift found the loops for that one and put them both together. Right when we heard the vibration, the loop, we knew it was a hit. We'd just have the music behind the chorus running, looped, for hours and days. This was back when we was still sleepin' at SCU, when we was working on the demo. It came together piece by piece. First the music, then Fatlip's chorus, then the lyrics. That's definitely the song people know us for most to this day. All that shit on there that we was talking about was real, all those stories. Somebody [Aphrodite] did a drum-and-bass version of that a while back, and I really liked that. We're looking for that dude, though, and trying to get a check [*laughs*].

Imani: Okay, let's break that one down! J-Swift didn't want to put those two loops together. Romye [Brown] found the loops and put them together, and J said: "You can't put those together, that doesn't sound right." We weren't producers and we didn't have any technical skills for recording—we was just doing what we felt. Romye and Tre had their verses for that song for a long time. And as I recall, the video turned out differently than we had wanted it to turn out. The director had all these ideas about different things to do, and effects to use, and we were all collaborating on ideas. Then we took it to Delicious Vinyl and they started crossing out shit. That costs too much, this costs too much. So the only effect we could keep was the up-side-down effect. But it's all good, the video is still dope.

Mike Ross: I remember going up to MTV in the spring of 1993, because that single came out in February and it was really bubbling by March. MTV had a really tight playlist when it came to hip-hop in regular rotation slots, not counting play on a show like *Yo! MTV Raps.* The record was doing well enough so that it was being considered for regular rotation, and I met with Rick Krim at MTV and he said, "We're going to make a commitment to push a new hip-hop group this spring and summer, and it's between you guys and Onyx." Onyx had "Slam" out at the time, and I guess there was a meeting at MTV and we lost to Onyx. We still got MTV play, but not regular rotation. If we got that MTV slot, I can only imagine how big that song would have gotten.

Tre: That song went through a lot of changes. The album version was actually a remix. The original was by my friend V-Love. It was dope and I liked it, but when L.A. Jay [John Barnes] made another beat to it, I knew that was it. Out of nowhere one day, in an hour's time, I went from doing those vocals totally straightforward to all those different things I did. I was by myself just acting silly, and the next thing you know it sounded like that. The lyrics on there are about one particular relationship I had, my one greatest love of all time, and she crushed the shit out of me. So I just took that and thought of every relationship I had ever had before that, and put it into one song.

Mike Ross: That was the third single for the album. Kevin Kerslake was a big video director at the time—he was doing Nirvana videos, and he did that one. And that song was basically just Tre spitting this amazing hip-hop poem. He's the only one who's really on there. It was a weird video, because Tre's the only one on the vocal, but the other guys were supposed to be in it. Having that as a single alienated Fatlip tremendously, so he refused to be in the video. That was a pretty low moment in the group's history—it definitely created problems. Then, after spending like eighty-five thousand dollars on the video, MTV didn't play it that much, so that kind of messed up the momentum we had gained with "Passing Me By."

QUINTON'S ON HIS WAY (SKIT)

Imani: Quinton was the big homey. We met him when he got out of jail, and he was just down with us. He didn't go on some "kill somebody" shit, it was just like traffic warrants or whatever. He was just a funny guy and he had the bud and he came around. We had a lot of great characters around us, and they were all part of the record in their own way. On the second record [*Labcabincalifornia*] it was just us, and there weren't as many people around, so the energy was different.

Mike Ross: In a lot of ways, I think that song sums up *Bizarre Ride* really well. The vibe of the song is great. Each guy is telling his own story, so it's very personal. If you listen to the lyrics on there really closely, I definitely think that you get a perfect summation about what that first record is all about.

Imani: Well, yeah, I was smoking a lot of weed back then, that's a gimme. At the Manor it was really just smoking. Stress smoking. We didn't have no chronic at the time—there were some mushrooms here and there.

Tre: That was Quinton's anthem! I wasn't smoking too much [weed] at that time, because I had a very, very bad trip that fucked with me for a while. That's why my verse is the way it is, about the bad trip I had. I thought I had like four hands! After a while 'shrooms came into play, and that shit was just the most fun ever.

RETURN OF THE B-BOY

Tre: We were trying to re-create old-school style on that one. I didn't do too well at it [*laughs*]. But everyone else did. We never did that song live. For some reason it just didn't fit.

Imani: We never performed it because no one could ever remember the words [*laughs*]. It was just a good song to listen to, not to perform. We didn't put it so far back on the album because we didn't like it, we did it because that was the exit of the roller coaster. Time to go!

POOR RIGHTEOUS TEACHERS

Holy Intellect

(Profile, 1990)

A righteous life is a work in progress," says Poor Righteous Teachers frontman Wise Intelligent. "The greatest war is always the one between you and you. Your spirit and your flesh, every day." Wise admits that even the righteous aren't perfect. Musically, though, PRT was pretty damn close.

As the new decade turned in 1990, this three-man group, bolstered by producer Tony D, made huge strides in expanding the "conscious rap" wave being propagated by comrades like Brand Nubian and the X-Clan. Their name said it all, and their debut was one of the most intelligent and provocative albums of the decade.

Although the world didn't give it much respect and it hadn't proven itself in the hip-hop world of the late eighties, Trenton, New Jersey, and its surrounding towns were most certainly hip-hop hot spots. For proof, look no further than the late-eighties underground power of lyricist YZ (aka YZ.G-Rock), who was from nearby Highstown. And—more important—Trenton's Poor Righteous Teachers: vocalist Wise Intelligent (Timothy Grimes), with comrades Culture Freedom and DJ Father Shaheed.

At the center of Trenton's hip-hop activity at the time was producer Anthony "Tony D" Depula—a mustachioed Italian American who would propel some of the most innovative pro-black hip-hoppers in New York and New Jersey to national prominence. Still very active as a producer today, Tony recalls the local eighties scene. "Trenton is like a mini version of Brooklyn," he says, speaking of the town's grittiness and roughshod image. "I mean, back then in the late eighties, Trenton was the only place that ever dissed Rakim. They booed him off the stage at the War Memorial [auditorium]. I was there, backstage, and I couldn't believe it. This was probably '86, after the first [Rakim] single was out."

Tony was born in Trenton and his home (and studio) in the late eighties was in the neighboring town of Ewing. Starting out as an all-around DJ, he eventually focused in on hip-hop. "I got into hip-hop as a DJ. After high school I was playing everywhere. I'd be on bills with Ready Red [of the first incarnation of Houston's Geto Boys]—he was from Trenton and was really influential in town. Johny C from the Geto Boys was from Trenton too."

Tony started out producing and working with rapper Gino G around

1986, including productions like Partners in Rhyme (Grand Poobah Tony D & Cool Gino G's "It's My Day" single, from 1987 on Body Rock) and the Live N Effect Posse. By 1989, Tony had his first real hit with YZ's "Thinking of a Master Plan," which came out first on the local Diversity label (owned by YZ and Tim Baylor) and was picked up by Aaron Fuch's Tuff City Records a year later. Soon enough, Tony was known as the man to see if you were an MC from Trenton.

Wise Intelligent, who was born in New Brunswick, New Jersey, but moved to Trenton at an early age, says, "The scene in Trenton was incredible. There were guys like DJ Truth and Duke Productions throwing block parties all the time. DJ Juice, Father Shaheed. Guys around the way were much bigger influences to me because they were touchable, unlike the radio MCs like Sugarhill Gang or Run-DMC. We'd hit shows at the Capital Skate Rink, people like LL Cool J, Roxanne Shanté. And the bigger shows, like Fresh Fest, would come to the War Memorial."

Wise continues: "I grew up in the early and mid-eighties, and everyone was being drawn into hip-hop. At the same time, crack was growing in the community. You had degradation there, but hip-hop was so positive. Unfortunately at the time, hip-hop wasn't making you no money [laughs]. So a lot of hip-hoppers were involved in selling either crack or marijuana. I was selling joints at thirteen, I was like on a savings plan with weed [laughs]. At the same time, we were all break-dancing, doing graffiti, and rappin'."

Aside from the low-level drug game that Wise and his crew were working, the hip-hop world was where all their free time was spent. "We were just so in love with it," he says. "It was the first music genre that was youth-specific, and especially black youth–specific. It was the way we spoke, the way we dressed, just in recorded form." Wise dove headfirst into hip-hop with eventual groupmate Culture Freedom, whom he had known since the two were very young. Wise recalls, "Me and Culture would make home tapes when we was ten or eleven years old, with a mic and one speaker and a tape deck. Culture was a DJ and producer way back—he had drum machines and turntables."

Eventually the two friends starting getting more serious about hip-hop. They made demos and did smaller local shows. "I was rhyming with another MC named Godfather, and GF was in a lot of chaos—he had a lot of problems with the law. Culture didn't really get along with GF, so me and

Culture broke out. I was MCing and he was making beats and DJing." From there, Poor Righteous Teachers was formed in Trenton's Donnelly Homes housing projects, where both Wise and Culture lived. Their first DJ was named Devine, but his tenure in the group was short-lived. Wise says: "If you get the cassette of the first single, Devine's on there. At the time we had two DJs, Culture and Devine." For reasons unspecified by Wise, Devine was phased out after the first single.

Many of Wise's lyrics discussed themes that flowed from his affiliation with the Islamic-based faith called the Nation of Gods and Earths (or Five Percent Nation), which had been part of his life since he was fourteen or fifteen. It was a message about uplifting men and women of African descent and fighting against oppression, whether it was skin-color-based or stemming from religious intolerance. But PRT wasn't necessarily a mouthpiece for the Gods and Earths, as Wise explains: "Our message was always something that supercedes any identification with the Nation of Gods and Earths. Our message is universal."

After the group was solidified, they began working with producer Tony D, whom they had met through mutual friends in Donnelly. But it wasn't an easy connection. Tony relates, "One of my boys from the Donnelly Homes in Trenton, Rocksteady, said: 'You gotta check out this kid Wise Intelligent, he's amazing.' So we went looking for him and he was like a ghost. Then one day I got a page and the person said that Wise was waiting for me. I drove up and there's this skinny kid just sitting there. He wouldn't rhyme when I asked him to show me what he had. So I was like: 'Okay, fuck it, I'll rhyme.' And I started rhyming and he must have gotten pissed off, because then he started and I was blown away. He definitely had it, that was obvious from the start."

Tony continues: "Wise was definitely defensive when we started working together, maybe because I worked with YZ and Wise was beefing with YZ. But Wise was also hungry as hell, and he knew that I knew how to put out records. Those guys would come to my crib and record, and my place was in Ewing, which was pretty far from Trenton if you didn't have a car. Sometimes they would walk home even after I offered to drive them back. They wanted to listen to the songs we had just recorded, all the way home."

The first single they completed was recorded in 1988 and consisted of three tracks: "Time to Say Peace," "Butt Naked Booty Bless," and "Word Is

Bond." The first two songs made it onto *Holy Intellect* without retouching, while "Word Is Bond" never did. With all three songs produced by Tony D, it was originally slated to come out on YZ and Tim Baylor's Diversity label. But things didn't turn out well with the deal. Wise remembers: "We had the music on a quarter-inch reel, all mixed, and we were going to put it out on Diversity Records. They wanted to hold our record for a year before putting it out, and we was like: 'We can't wait a year, we're poor kids from the projects.' They didn't want to give us our reels back, so we went to their house, with twenty or thirty kids from the projects, on their porch. After the screen door got ripped off the front door, Tim stuck his hand out of the door and handed us the reel."

Wise continues: "Eric 'I.Q.' Gray from Donnelly, who lived in the same building as Culture, had North Side Records with his partner James Lee. And we put out the record with him, with some money from heads around our way. We knew Eric but had never dealt with him on a business level before." Diversity never tried to get their reels back, apparently. "If they would have called the police, I think they knew that it would have just gotten worse," reasons Wise. "They lived a couple blocks down from the projects, so that would have been a day-to-day problem for them and their family."

The single was released in mid-1989 on North Side Records and it was a success, at least on the airplay front. Most important, it got much love on DJ Red Alert's hugely popular Kiss FM radio show in New York. Saleswise the single never got much of a chance, at least not on the North Side issue. According to Tony D, the single had a run of one thousand copies total on vinyl and cassette. And, as Wise recalls, "We never re-pressed it because Profile signed us up after the first couple spins on Red Alert's show."

In the fall of 1989, Profile Records took the North Side version of the single and printed it up, dropping the a cappella version of "Time to Say Peace," which was only ever released on the North Side single, and adding an extended remix of it instead. As Tony recalls: "Cory Robbins [owner of Profile] asked Red Alert about 'that song that has "Peace" in it,' and he called us and offered us a deal."

The deal with Profile was originally for a single, with album options at the label's discretion. After "Time to Say Peace" did well in the marketplace, Profile was ready for an album. Little did they know, but PRT hadn't

Poor Righteous Teachers (left to right: Wise Intelligent, Culture Freedom, Father Shaheed)
on the roof of Profile Records, Hollywood, 1991.
PHOTO: B+ (FOR WWW.MOCHILLA.COM).

been waiting for them to ask. Wise says: "Once they really listened to the single and saw how it was doing on the radio, they asked us how soon we could have an album done. We said: 'It's already done!' We had the whole thing on cassette, ready for them to check out."

Tony remembers: "After we did 'Time to Say Peace' we all just felt that the studio was the best place for us to be, so we just kept going." They did preproduction at Tony's home studio and finished tracks at Epsilon Studios in Trenton, almost always with engineer Tom Zepp.

Tony says that the group's advance to make the album was fifteen thousand dollars, a meager amount even for an indie label at the time. But, as Tony says, PRT wanted to be on wax and didn't feel like waiting. Tony recalls: "With Profile, Wise really wanted to just sign that contract. I was the one who was holding it up for a while. I knew that the money was really low, and the lawyer was saying it was a terrible deal, but they really wanted the money because they didn't have any. The only benefit was that if the album sold, there was hardly anything to recoup." According to Tony, Poor Righteous Teachers were signed directly to Profile, and Tony's Two Tone Productions was hired as the group's producer.

With the success of "Time to Say Peace" and new management in place, the shows started coming in. But it wasn't long before the PRT posse became somewhat infamous on the live circuit. Wise recalls: "The thing that stood out about our shows back then was that we *always* got in fights. With all the heads we had with us, sometimes twenty-five or thirty people, it was bound to happen that someone was going to step on someone's toes. And promoters were like: 'We want to book you, but please leave your crew at home.' When we started traveling by plane rather than shows that were closer to Trenton, things got a bit less crazy."

Wise looks back on those days now and chuckles about it, considering their self-given "righteous" tag and their obvious attraction to trouble. "For some reason the press never caught onto that contradiction, but we didn't care," he says. "We wasn't that politically correct. I mean, if you cross me, I'll punch you in your face [*laughs*]." He also explains that once the group became popular, they left their drug-selling days behind them: "We made some serious transitions in our lives back when we got our message out. We evolved and elevated for the better. Dealing drugs is immoral, but we evolved out of that. I mean, we weren't selling when we were Poor Righteous Teachers. The main message that we were trying to get across was to show that you could be righteous and poor. Because it's so easy for a poor man to do what is immoral—because he lacks the means to support his heart's desire. We wanted to show poor youth that you can accomplish and achieve without the negativity, without jeopardizing life, limb, or freedom."

After work had begun on the album, the PRT lineup was finalized with the inclusion of DJ Father Shaheed. "Shaheed came in after we had recorded about five songs, just as we was signing to Profile," Wise recalls. "He was DJing and producing for a lot of the top MCs in Trenton at the time. He was a couple years older than me and Culture, and he was just destroying other DJs at the time." Tony says: "Shaheed added just what was needed to the group. He was a great DJ and he was righteous, so he fit the bill. And up until then I was doing all the scratching, so I was glad to have him on board for that."

One important thing to point out regarding the PRT group dynamic is the contribution of Culture Freedom to their sound, which is harder for fans to assess since he's isn't frequently heard on the group's recordings. "Culture was the guy who was puttin' it all together," Wise says. "Song titles, choruses, even some beats. He would choose a lot of the tracks that we'd end up using. He composed and arranged a lot of the songs." Tony says: "Culture had a lot of input in the way that some of the songs ended up, but on the vocal side he just really did ad-libs and sang on some things. I'm pretty sure that Wise wrote any lyrics that Culture said, as far as I know. I never heard him speak out about having a problem as the number-two guy in the group."

Tony D was listed as producer on the album and he brought most, if not all, of the music for the group to write lyrics to. "The final versions of songs were pretty close to what I would present to them at first," Tony remembers. "I didn't have much to do with choruses and hooks, so after Wise and Culture did those, we'd finish it all up."

Wise says: "Without a doubt we did as much production on that album as Tony did. Hip-hop has this thing where if you're a beatmaker, you're all of a sudden a producer, which is totally different than the rest of the music industry. A producer is the person who brings it all together. Loops, chorus, samples, bridges—me and Culture did those on every song. Tony would loop beats and let us hear them, and we would choose them and take the beat and go back to the projects. Then we'd come up with the whole concept for the song. So it's not like we were just rapping on it, we were involved the whole way."

Lauding the lyrical content of *Holy Intellect,* Tony says, "It was teaching people and it was doing it by not teaching too much. Just enough. And it's a little-known fact, but most of the vocals on that album that Wise did were first takes. He was amazingly good about nailing stuff the first time."

Holy Intellect sold well upon its release and had a significant impact in 1990, standing alongside cultural freedom fighters like X-Clan, Public Enemy, and Brand Nubian. The group also had to weather a high-profile lawsuit by the group War after the PRT song "Rock Dis Funky Joint" (which sampled War's "Slipping into Darkness") blew up nationally.

Tony D says that sales of the album were more than four hundred thousand during that time and estimates it has gone gold by now, although he claims that Profile and Arista (which owns Profile) haven't given them accurate accountings of sales in years. "It was definitely a hit," says Wise Intelligent. "It was one of those records that when you did a show, everyone coming to the venue was blasting your music in their car, and they were singing along with the lyrics when you were onstage."

"*Holy Intellect* is definitely my favorite Poor Righteous Teachers album," says Tony D. "It was new, it was different, and it was *us*. As far as being groundbreaking, that album is way up there on my résumé. It was my first national exposure. I mean, after 'Rock Dis Funky Joint' came out, I was getting calls just to mix people's songs."

"At that time, we gave hip-hop the ability to convey a serious message and in an entertaining way," says Wise. "We showed youth that intelligence was fresh. You could read books and study and still be 'hood at the same time. One week we'd be at Celebrity Hall in Washington, D.C., with guns crackin' everywhere, and the next week we'd be at M.I.T. in Boston, doing a talk. We straddled the spectrum."

TRACKS

CAN I START THIS? *Featuring Tony D*

Wise: Tony D's on that one, on the mic. I always thought his rhymes were wack! We let him on because we were all just having fun. That was the last song we recorded for the album, and for whatever reason Profile thought that would be good to put first. Honestly, we didn't really care.

Tony D: I definitely had to force my way onto the mic on that song. I mean, Wise didn't want me rhyming nowhere [*laughs*]! That's why he said: "Rock some of that rubbish you been writin' [*laughs*]."

ROCK DIS FUNKY JOINT

Tony: For some reason Wise just always sounded good on those offbeat loops, so I started throwing more of them at him, and that one was a perfect example. I first knew it was blowing up when it was number one in Philly. They had a countdown every night on Power 99 that everyone listened to, and that song was number one for like six straight weeks, over "The Humpty Dance" and all kinds of other shit. You'd ride around and every car was blasting it.

Wise: The style of that song, my style on there, came out on the first take. Tony played the original [War's "Slippin' into Darkness"] and when it came on, I just started rhyming to it like that. I already had the rhyme, I just put it onto that groove. And all the starts and stops and bringing the music in and out, everybody contributed to that. That was definitely the biggest song on the record, by far. War [the group] sued us on that one, and that was the beginning of PRT's education in the music industry. We put it out but Profile didn't clear it. We [PRT] got penalized, but we didn't feel that we should have taken the responsibility for clearance. PRT were signed as the group, but we felt that it was Two Tone's [Tony D's production company] responsibility because they was the producers. All we did was write the rhymes and choruses to it. We had to pay fifty percent of the cost and Tony and Profile paid the rest. War threatened to pull the record off the shelves, but they never did. It was just bad because we needed every dollar we could get and the situation was unfair. So we regressed to our old bag of tricks [*laughs*] and . . . a couple heads got punched around a little bit. It got a little violent—things got a little testy between PRT and Tony.

Tony: One of the jobs of the producer at that time was to hand in a list of all the samples on any given album. So when I handed in the samples, Profile [presumably] cleared all the ones that they thought were recognizable, or that people would really hear. They cleared most of the stuff I gave them, but not that War sample, and it ended up being the single. Once it blew up, War came knocking, of course. It was definitely Profile's fault, but Wise and them wanted me to pay for it. I was like: "Wait a minute, this is the song that blew you guys up." And those guys jumped me one night. Wise didn't really partake, but Culture and Shaheed, the bigger guys, snuck up on me and started punching on me. It took about a year for us to work together again after that. And then I had this stigma, like I'm the [white] devil trying to rob PRT. It was pretty upsetting.

HOLY INTELLECT

Wise: I don't know if Tony was going for a hip-house thing on that song. I didn't really feel that tempo, at least at first. But that ended up being one of my favorite tracks on there.

Tony: As I recall, Profile wanted to put that song out as the first single from the album, which I thought was ass-backwards. It was faster, made for the clubs. "Holy Intellect" was another War sample, and they got us for that one too. But not as bad as "Rock Dis Funky Joint." Wise actually rhymed pretty fast, but he'd usually pick slow beats to rhyme over. After like eight songs that were all under 95 beats per minute, I was like: "Let's step one up to 110 or something!" I knew he could deal with it, and it wasn't his strongest style, but it worked. The remix of that song [on the single, the "Tryandblendit Remix"] is one of the most slept-on things that PRT ever did.

SHAKIYLA

Wise: The lyrics for that one were really old. That was the first song I ever wrote, when I was like fourteen or fifteen. I never had music to the song when I wrote it at first—it was just lyrics. I was trying to find a girl I could sing it to, and maybe if I did she'd give me some butt [*laughs*]. Shakiyla wasn't any girl in particular. That song was just about a good, wholesome, monogamous relationship. That's Culture [Freedom] singing on the chorus. Sometimes he would just turn into Billy Ocean [*laughs*]. His singing wasn't so hot [*laughs*], but our whole thing was: don't go for perfection, do it with your feeling. I still love that track. We brought in the loop to Tony for that one.

Tony: That was a Zapp sample. Wise just liked that beat, so he took that one for his love song. He had that rhyme for a long time and that music was perfect for it. Everyone had a song like that on their record back then, so it made sense. It wasn't cheesy like [LL Cool J's] "I Need Love." I actually thought it was kind of funky.

TIME TO SAY PEACE

Wise: That was our first single, on North Side Productions, before we signed it up with Profile. We brought vinyl in to Tony D for that song, and he looped it, because he had an SP-1200 [sampler]. We weren't that technically inclined [*laughs*]! He looped the beats, we rhymed, and then we left his house. After that he called us and had the tracks for "Butt Naked Booty Bless" and "Word Is Bond."

Tony: When I first started working with PRT, we went into the studio and did "Word Is Bond." And the next time we went into the studio, Wise was rhyming totally different [*laughs*]. That's when he did "Time to Say Peace," and there was no turning back at that point. I don't know if that single sold huge numbers, but it did well enough for Profile to want to continue working with us.

STYLE DROPPED/LESSONS TAUGHT

Tony: There's a remix of that one that never got released, but it's phenomenal.

Wise: There's a Malcolm X speech on there that we sampled, and that was Father Shaheed's thing. He had all those kinds of speeches on vinyl. Our philosophy was always that our lessons were going to be taught regardless of what people thought. If you have a problem with us, then prove your cause, talk to us about it. We weren't trying to make friends, that wasn't really our goal.

SPEAKING UPON A BLACKMAN

Wise: I always thought that track deserved more attention. I'd have to say that it's my favorite track on the album. That one was ridiculous—the beat was kind of sinister. Eric "I.Q." [Gray] produced that one. He was really new on the SP-1200, but it really came off [*laughs*].

Tony: I liked the stuff that I.Q. did. The samples were good. I knew that he didn't know how to loop things up properly, but I didn't get in the way.

SO MANY TEACHERS

Wise: Tony D brought in that loop. Every one of our tracks was supposed to teach in some way. We always felt that hip-hop could be leveraged in a positive way to motivate people towards positive lifestyles. It was a powerful tool and it often went untapped, and still is today. It wasn't a competition [with other MCs]—I wasn't trying to be their teachers or anything. I did have some problems with Christians, though, and talk about it on that track. My problems with Christians were always that they didn't study their own doctrine. Once in Ohio we had Christian parents calling into a radio station we were being interviewed on and saying, "Those rappers are wrong, they can't say they're God, that's devil worship." And my whole thing is just this: don't know just what you know. Try and know what *I* know, too, so we can understand each other.

Tony: There's some anti-Christian stuff on there, and I used to get questions all the time back then about being an Italian Catholic and working with all these righteous groups [like YZ and PRT]. I was like: "Man, it's just music to me." I was never offended. I was always looking for vocal samples like I used on there [sped-up R&B, which is more popular today]. I was one of the originators of that R&B thing, starting with YZ's "Thinking of a Master Plan." Those two songs were the first two that ever used vocals in the sampled loop itself.

WORD FROM THE WISE

Tony: That song [which I.Q. also produced] was really dope. Me and Diamond D used to talk about that sample all day and I was like: "I didn't do that one, Diamond." But he's convinced that I did it. It was sparse as far as production, but great.

Wise: I mention on there how people called me a racist, but racism is much more structural and institutional than it is personal and individual. How can you tell an oppressed youth that he's racist when he's just speaking out on the injustice that he's dealing with every day? It's very important to know who the victim is and who the victimizer is. It's frustrating to be put in the same box as they do Hitler, or a white, wealthy, slave-trading landowner.

Wise: That song isn't really about booty, of course. But where we come from, if something was "butt-naked," it meant it was stripped-down and raw. The naked truth. In our 'hood, heads used to smoke PCP and what we called "boat," which was marijuana laced with embalming fluid. When they'd smoke it, the most common reaction would be to take off all your clothes and run down the street. So they started calling it "butt naked," or "love boat." Police had to keep extra blankets in their cruisers to cover people up. So I guess that's the vibe on that one. Crazy and funky.

POOR RIGHTEOUS TEACHERS

Tony: I think "Rock Dis Funky Joint" is the *best* song on the album, but "Poor Righteous Teachers" is my favorite. It has this backwards Quincy Jones sample on it, I think on the drums. I love that loop. It was filtered before filtering was really even done. Large Professor was the first to put filtering on record, although he won't admit it. He did it on [Main Source's] "Fakin' the Funk." I did it back then, not with any effects but just through the mixing board. We bounced the sample to two tracks—one with the bass and one with the highs. Each one of those tracks had different effects on it. I didn't know that it would work, but me and the engineer fucked with it and it did end up working. Wise uses some of his older, Rakim-style lyrical style and lyrics on there. He must have just had them, and it was towards the end of the album and he wanted to use them somewhere.

PUBLIC ENEMY

It Takes a Nation of Millions to Hold Us Back

(Def Jam, 1988)

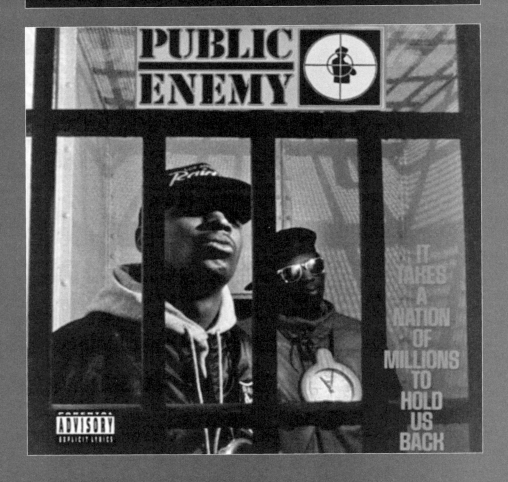

Mine and Hank's goal, originally, was to destroy music," says Public Enemy's Chuck D (Carlton Ridenhour) about how he and "antimusician" Hank Shocklee approached hip-hop. Provocative words, but in reality what Public Enemy destroyed was the hip-hop status quo, changing everything that came after them. Public Enemy hit the rap scene of the mid-eighties like a black nationalist Noah's ark, preserving the essence of artists like Run-DMC, Melle Mel, and Schoolly D and leaving the rest in their wake. Repercussions and shock waves were felt not only in hip-hop but all music, making people reconsider the power of music and lyrics in a way that arguably hadn't been done since Bob Dylan brought real issues to real music more than two decades earlier.

The extended Public Enemy family that the world came to know—William "Flavor Flav" Drayton, DJ Norman "Terminator X" Rogers, Richard "Professor Griff" Griffin, musical patriarch Hank Shocklee (born Boxley), Hank's brother Keith Shocklee, producer-musician Eric "Vietnam" Sadler, and conceptual and musical overseer Bill Stephney—came together in Hempstead and Roosevelt, Long Island, long before Public Enemy began their musical assault on wax. Shocklee started his Spectrum City mobile DJ crew in 1975, with brother Keith helping by 1978 or so. "Hank was always a legend in Roosevelt, and he always had Spectrum City," says Chuck.

Chuck joined the crew in 1979 after enrolling at Garden City's Adelphi University (he studied graphic design, graduating in 1984). "I rapped back in 1978 and '79, and I was vicious," Chuck brags. "I had a Satchel Paige story by the time I got to records. I had the strongest voice of anybody around me and that was key, because most sound systems were cheap. You had to be able to cut across a cheap system. Guys like DJ Hollywood and Melle Mel had no problems with something like that. Back at that time Hank heard me on the mic and I spanked everyone else, so he figured I would be the final component to what he had going. Me and Flavor was blessed with having voices on two different ends of the spectrum, and they could both cut through any live situation very easily. Flavor has bass in his treble and I have treble in my bass."

In 1982 the Spectrum City crew made it to Adelphi's radio station, WBAU, encouraged and guided by program director Bill Stephney. Flavor

Flav also had a show on the station. "Flav was the greatest of all time on the air," Chuck laughs. "He was just the same as he was on our records. Sometimes he would play like six tracks of his own stuff a night. He was the Uncle Floyd of hip-hop radio! Flav's early ad-libs would come from him mimicking this guy who lived around his way named Youngster or something like that. It was a weird thing, but I think the better he mimicked that guy, the more he found an identity for himself."

The ninety-minute "Super Spectrum City Mix Show" was a popular attraction on the station, and Hank and Chuck quickly embraced the power of radio. The two made preshow tapes at their homebase/clubhouse/studio: 510 South Franklin Street in Hempstead. The studio, in use by Spectrum City since 1981, became an important breeding ground for local Strong Island rap talent. "We would host ten or twenty local rap groups from the area," Chuck recalls. "We'd record 'em up at our spot and put 'em out on the radio."

At 510 South Franklin they also met an important future component to the PE sound: Eric "Vietnam" Sadler, a local musician who had a studio in the same building. Vietnam soon became part of the Spectrum City mix. "We called him Vietnam because he'd always wear these old army jackets and these shades that made him look like he was a paratrooper," laughs Chuck. "He had a studio downstairs at 510, and we went down there and asked him to come up and start making music. He was a good guy and he worked well in our mix.

"Initially, Spectrum City never put out anything on wax," Chuck notes. "We just made tapes and put 'em straight on the radio. People always thought we had stuff on wax, but we only made songs to promote the radio station. I would do a song every once in a while to fill the void of not having enough records for our airtime. We was only interested in being radio jocks back then—we even tried to get a syndicated radio deal back in the day. Records just didn't hold much interest for us. I had interviewed so many people with nightmare stories about the record business that I just wasn't interested in being involved with that."

Hank and Chuck grew ever better at recording, eventually acquiescing to record a single (as Spectrum City) on the Vanguard label in 1984 called "Lies." "We recorded the song 'Check Out the Radio' with the extra time we had on the session," Chuck recalls of the other song on the single. "It was a *severe* B-side [*laughs*] and was damn near fallin' off the record. The only reason we did that cut was to have more people know us as DJs and radio jocks. But that whole [recording] situation wasn't good, and it kept me from recording for a while." Even so, he says, " 'Check Out the Radio' was a very influential cut for artists like Run-DMC and the Beastie Boys, who listened to the radio station religiously. It was a slower track, and it definitely influenced DMC and Run to write 'Slow and Low' for the Beastie Boys."

Despite the single, in the end it was a 1984 radio-only cut, "Public Enemy #1," that gave Spectrum City its eventual new name and its future record label as well. Def Jam co-founder Rick Rubin pursued Chuck for two years after he heard it on WBAU. "I put that song together on two tape decks and a Roland 8000 drum machine," Chuck says. "I pause-buttoned it together, did a vocal, and overdubbed it on another tape deck. Flavor just happened to be in the other room, so that's how he got on it. 'Blow Your Head' [by the JBs, the main sample on the track] was a favorite of mine, but you could never find anyone who could DJ it and put it together quick enough, so that's why I had to use the tape decks."

Chuck and Hank left WBAU in 1986. (Stephney had bailed two years previous.) "Hank and I left to run a club full-time and, at Bill's insistence, to move into recording," he explains. And move they did. After Rick Rubin's championing of the group, a deal was eventually signed and the group was making a record for his quickly growing Def Jam empire, which he ran with partner Russell Simmons.

Public Enemy's 1987 debut, *Yo! Bum Rush the Show,* was one of the more powerful albums of the era, comprising intense battle rhymes like "Miuzi Weighs a Ton" and "Public Enemy #1" and pointed social-political fare seen on the anticrack manifesto "Megablast" and the talkin'-loud, saying-nothing update "Rightstarter (Message to a Black Man)." Most of the album's preproduction work was done at 510 South Franklin. "Everything on that album was prerecorded, and then we would enhance upon it at regular studios like INS in New York," Chuck recalls. "We knew exactly what we was gonna do before we even went into the real studios. We wanted to execute quickly because we didn't want to pay somebody else's bills."

Musically, the album was complicated and dark, with highly musical 808 drum programs, righteous funk samples, and funky live wah-wah guitar (by Vernon Reid and co-producer Bill Stephney). And, of course, there was Chuck's booming voice, which grabbed you by the lapels and spit knowledge at you. In the background, edgy court jester Flavor Flav did the honors, getting his own solo shot on "Too Much Posse." It pushed forward, but it also stood on the shoulders of giants.

"The first album was something presented off the heels of *Raising Hell* [by Run-DMC], which I would call my favorite record of all time," Chuck says. "We came at things differently than other people back then. The fact that I rapped about a car [on "You're Gonna Get Yours"] on the first album was different than most rappers. I was older and had a different point of view. I was twenty-six years old in 1986, so of course I wouldn't rap about no high school shit. I was rapping from a grown man's viewpoint."

Despite the greatness of the album, PE didn't enjoy its growing popularity for long. "On the day that *Yo! Bum Rush the Show* was released [in the spring of 1987], we was already in the trenches recording *Nation of Millions*," Chuck states. Hank and Eric didn't tour with Public Enemy—they stayed behind to work on cuts in the lab, so that the vocalists could hit the ground running whenever they returned.

"The first record should have come out October of '86," says Chuck. "When it actually came out it was past the timely point. [CBS labelmate Bruce] Springsteen pushed back the Beastie Boys, which pushed back our shit. *Yo!* was outdated to us. By the time it came out, Eric B. & Rakim and BDP had come out and changed the terrain of how you can rap. Our records were all recorded at the same time as theirs, but those guys came out first, so they were thought of as more innovative. Either way, they changed the phrasing of rap, which allowed you to be able to rhyme on a faster tempo, a faster groove."

The Bomb Squad, as PE's production team was now calling itself, had an intense work ethic, and they knew all too well that they were on to something big. The duties shared by the trio of Shocklee, Sadler, and Chuck himself (credited in the album's liners as Carl Ryder, a pseudonym dating back to sports reporting he did at WBAU) had become much clearer as they began their epic sophomore album, *It Takes a Nation of Millions to Hold Us Back.* "Eric was the musician, Hank was the antimusician," Chuck explains. "Eric did a lot of the [drum] programming, [Hank's brother] Keith was the guy who would bring in the feel. And me, I would scour for vocal samples all over the Earth. I would name a song, tag it, and get the vocal samples. The friction between Hank and Eric worked very well. Hank would put a twist on Eric's musicianship and Eric's musicianship would put a twist on Hank.

"Hank would come up with the final mix because he was the sound master," emphasizes Chuck. "I wouldn't even fuck with the mix. Hank is the Phil Spector of hip-hop. He was way ahead of his time, because he dared to challenge the odds in sound. Once hip-hop became corporate, they took the daredevil out of the artistry. But being a daredevil was what Hank brought to the table."

Crucial cuts "Rebel Without a Pause," "Bring the Noise," and "Don't Believe the Hype" were recorded at various times between tours in '87, but the bulk of the record was laid down during eight intense weeks in early 1988 for a modest fifty-two thousand dollars. (Chuck says that *Yo! Bum Rush the Show* cost seventeen thousand.) "From January to the end of February, we just *rapped,*" Chuck recalls. Originally using the working title *Countdown to Armageddon,* the group decided to call it *It Takes a Nation of Millions to Hold Us Back* in the end, which was a line from *Yo! Bum Rush the Show*'s "Raise the Roof."

"We made [*Nation of Millions*] like it was just for cassettes," Chuck says. "We wanted to have an album that was equal on the first side and the second side. We didn't want to have any room at the end of a side. There would be no dead time. We worked really hard to equal those sides, through the interludes and also the timing of different songs. Because of the interludes, the album was also the first rap record that didn't go cut to cut— it had stuff in between songs to make it all stick together, like glue."

Some of the interstitial material was live crowd noise from a show in London, recorded on November 3, 1987. "We used that live stuff for two reasons," Chuck explains. "First, to build on our importance overseas, since we were having lots of success over in Europe and no rap group had ever done that. But we also wanted to show people in America that we had it goin' on, with 'em or without 'em [*laughs*]."

A little-known fact: The album's two sides were originally the other way around, the album starting with the song "Show Em Whatcha Got" and going into "She Watch Channel Zero?!" (which is side two, the "Black Side"). Shocklee decided to flip them at the last second, just before mastering. "Of course the change worked!" Chuck laughs.

Bolstered by *Yo! Bum Rush the Show*'s acclaim, no small part of which came from overseas, Chuck, Shocklee, and Sadler knew that the work they were doing for *Nation of Millions* was going to be big. "*Nation* was just pure confidence," Chuck boasts. "We were like, '*Nobody's* doing this shit here.' We wanted to build on the concept of faster tempos. We wanted to take a lot of shit over 107, 109 beats per minute. We knew our music would be faster paced than anything out there. We knew that we could handle the speed and do it strong. Nobody out there could perform live on our level. That record was so intense that these young cats couldn't even keep up with us. We were all jocks and into martial arts, so we could go for an hour in a frenzy. It was like Mike Tyson at his peak. Because the material was so strong and because we could kill on the stage, we knew for a fact that the album would be a big hit. We made our records to tour, and we toured to make our records."

From the provocative cover by photographer Glen E. Friedman—shot at the city jail at Thirty-second Street—to every last one of the dozens of samples buried in the mix, the legend of *It Takes a Nation of Millions to Hold Us Back* is one of the most storied in hip-hop. The album still stands to this day as, in this writer's opinion, the best and most influential rap platter ever made.

"Sometimes on the outside looking in I say, 'Damn, did I really have anything to do with that record?' " Chuck muses. But he most certainly did, and hip-hop is better because of it. "*Nation of Millions* made [N.W.A.'s] *Straight Outta Compton* possible later that year," says Chuck. "The first two copies that I had of *Nation* actually went to Dr. Dre and Eazy-E. We were in Vegas and they were on tour with us, and I had just got the vinyl in. That's what this is all about. Because Run-DMC and LL Cool J gave me energy. And if our energy happened to be transferred to N.W.A., then that's what this whole thing is for. Schoolly D influenced me on the first album as much as Run-DMC and I found out later that Ice Cube was influenced by how I broke shit down. Schoolly told me that he was influenced by Melle Mel. And that's just how the cycle goes."

TRACKS

That came out first on the *Less Than Zero* soundtrack, before our album. We recorded that in late September of 1987, after we did "Don't Believe the Hype." The original name of that song was "Countdown to Armageddon." I got the music to it while I was on the Def Jam tour with LL and I tried to tackle it all summer long in '87. I wrote three different verses for it and it just didn't pan out for me. I just could not nail it. Then Hank came at me with the suggestion that I attack the song with three different verse styles. We were doing a show in Atlanta and Harry Allen came down, and he had a mix of it from Hank. I listened to it on headphones and got so mad at it that I threw it across the room and damn near out the window. I was like, "We fucking failed!" I came back from tour in September to record that at Sabella Studios here in Long Island and I still could not nail it. All of us plus Terminator were there at the time. Eric and Hank did all the drum programs. I brought in the top stuff, those samples. We were seventy-five percent of the way through it and I hit a creative wall, but then I pulled through in the end. At five thirty in the morning Terminator came over to scratch, and we all thought what he did was kinda wack until we took the bass out during the mix. I love that scratch to this day, now! We learned that you can pull the bass out during the mix and there can still be some great topping. We went overseas the second week in November and me and Griff told Terminator to put the track on, because we had an acetate. We did it and the crowd went berzerk. So it was meant to be. Flavor's comments on there, and on all tracks, were always ad-libbed. I don't think he ever wrote anything down. We would guide him on which ad-lib to use, but that was about it.

When I was coming off a tour in '87 I was given some crazy terrain by Hank and Eric, like "Bring the Noise" and "Don't Believe the Hype." "Hype" came up before the tour and we recorded it right after "Rebel Without a Pause," although it didn't come out until '88, as the first single off of *Nation of Millions*. We recorded that in September of '87. It didn't have a video. We said, "Why the fuck should we? We ain't gonna see it nowhere." A video was actually put together over in London because of our massive following over there. We refused to do one in the U.S. because there was no guaranteed national exposure. When *Yo! MTV Raps* came about, PE did the pilot show, in the summer of '88. That was the green light to say that our second single should have a video. We actually originally were going to use "Don't Believe the Hype" for the *Less Than Zero* soundtrack, but we wanted the jam to be turbulent, not funky. "Don't Believe" was more regular than something like "Bring the Noise," so we just put it in the can and forgot about it. It got the eventual nod of approval because Hank went to this spot on the Lower East Side and heard DMC play the shit in his car, and it renewed his interest. The comments about writers were pointed at guys like John Leland [from *Spin* and the *Voice*] who just didn't get it. When I say, "It's a sequel," we meant that it was the sequel to "Rebel Without a Pause." That song was a really big hit in Atlanta first, thanks to Ray Boyd at B103. I got him tickets for our show and the next week it was added. To this day "Don't Believe" is played as one of the classics in the ATL.

COLD LAMPIN' WITH FLAVOR

Initially we wanted to bring Flavor through into the recording contract, and Rick [Rubin] and Russell [Simmons] pretty much detested the idea. They were like, "You gotta sign a vocalist, and what the fuck does he do?" And me and Hank said, "Well, we can't really explain what he does, but he brings flavor to the situation. You'll see." I said I wouldn't sign with Def Jam unless they signed Flavor. We knew he was an integral part. We were big fans of James Brown and Bobby Byrd, and that was the kind of stage relationship it was, in a weird way. "Cold Lampin' " was bringing more Flavor flavor to the equation. On the third album he really came forward because "911" was our first single.

TERMINATOR X TO THE EDGE OF PANIC

The music to that is "Rebel Without a Pause" backwards [*laughs*]. We was rockin' that freestyle out, around '87. We had the track backwards, and we wanted Terminator's name to shine more. We put some Farrakhan speeches on it and we had something out of nothing. It was one of those things that was put together at the last minute. Griff gave me that album with the Farrakhan quote at the end. It was the Minister from the 1980 Jack the Rapper convention, telling black radio that they had a responsibility to inform the people.

LOUDER THAN A BOMB

With that Kool and the Gang "Who's Gonna Take the Weight" sample, we just found the sound that fit the ideal. I don't remember who brought that one into the mix. Spectrum City [the studio at 510 South Franklin] was just two rooms full of records. That song was simply about the fact that the FBI was tapping my phone. My phone would go dead between one and two o'clock every night, even when I got the phone people to fix it. I was saying, "I'm not keeping any secrets because everything I'm saying, I'm saying it on record." It was one of our favorite records, but we never performed it in concert. We designed our show around peaks and valleys. That song would start on any other team, but not on this bench.

CAUGHT, CAN WE GET A WITNESS?

That record was dead and damn near out the window. It was a good topic, talkin' about samplin' beats, but we couldn't build upon that groove until the last minute. The topic made it come through in the end, we put some Bar-Kays on it. We got sued religiously a lot after the fact, but not at that time [when we made the song]. The song itself was just challenging the situation that other artists were in when they had that happen to them.

SHE WATCH CHANNEL ZERO?!

That's a Slayer loop there ["Angel of Death"]. We already had that record. We had Rick Rubin's blessing [Rubin produced Slayer] but he didn't spend any time in the studio with us, except some of the mixes on the rock songs that we'd bring him in on. We were the group that Rick gave total confidence and total blessing to do our thing. People said that it was an anti-female song, but my answer to that is that you're not looking at the self-criticism in other songs on the album. We attacked everything. I didn't think it was misogynist. I said, "Hey, fuck those soap operas." And I say it to this day. Jerry Springer and all of that. I'd say the same to a guy if he's just sittin' in front of the football game with a beer, talking shit. I mean, you couldn't say, "He/She Watch Channel Zero." You make a song and you make a statement.

NIGHT OF THE LIVING BASEHEADS

That's a Khalid Muhammad speech at the beginning. A lot of those speeches came from Griff and the S1Ws, and I would figure out where they would fit. Most of them were off of tapes. "Baseheads" was the second single off the album and the first video that we made, which we did by committee. We knew we had to make it as cutting-edge as our music because we were coming out late in the [video-making] game. We filmed it outside of the Audubon Ballroom [where Malcolm X was murdered] and other locations. I think we did that video for about forty thousand dollars. It got played like crazy, because *Yo! MTV Raps* had come out, which forced BET to come out with their own show, *Rap City*. For the track itself I wanted to write a song about how much crack was affecting us. It was all the way around us, 360 degrees.

Back when I was seven years old I saw my uncle come to my grandmother's house to get his draft papers for Vietnam. Of course as a kid you're trying to see what's going on. I saw their faces drop. I thought about the whole draft policy—it just stuck with me. I was like, "If I have to go to jail for not fighting in a war, then breaking out is righteous."

REBEL WITHOUT A PAUSE

By the time we actually came out with *Yo! Bum Rush the Show,* Hank and I began putting together "Rebel Without a Pause." It came out first on the B-side of "You're Gonna Get Yours" [from *Yo!*]. Hank and I came up with the track and then I locked myself in the house for two days, trying to nail it. There was so much aggression in it because we were trying to prove a point—that we knew what the fuck we were doing. Hank got a partial writing credit on the lyrics, it was a Lennon/McCartney thing. It took about two weeks to get that right. I did it the first day and wasn't happy with it and I went home mad. Then I came back three or four days later and nailed it. I can't recall ever nailing anything on the first take, at least not anything that I was satisfied with. I remember when me and [Ice] Cube and [Big Daddy] Kane were recording "Burn Hollywood Burn" [which came out on the next album, *Fear of a Black Planet*] and I was amazed how they could actually nail a cut in one or two takes. But they had different vocal delivery styles. I could never rely on just sittin' back, relaxing, and letting the studio make me sound good.

PROPHETS OF RAGE

That was a late-addition cut. I was going through a whole bunch of old tapes that happened to be sitting in the studio, something that Eric and Hank had concocted. I was sittin' in traffic and I was so impressed by it that I actually wrote to it right there. To this day I still love it—it's one of my favorites. That was a big live song, especially with Griff. When he left the group we stopped doing it, and when he rejoined a couple of years later we brought it back into the set. You have to be really physically fit to handle that song [*laughs*]. It's breakneck speed. The title came from an article I saw in *Life* magazine that had that caption about Malcolm X. It said, "What ever happened to the prophets of rage?" I like to make the title to a song first because it helps me write the rest of the song. I operate from the title on down. That track was done later in the recording process. I think, vocally, I stretched the limits on that one. I was just never satisfied with my takes. I was known as the Hundred-Take Man [*laughs*].

PARTY FOR YOUR RIGHT TO FIGHT

With flipping the Beasties like that it was like, "Together we're on Def Jam, but we're not them" [*laughs*]. It wasn't a dis, it was just saying we were the opposite of what you think the Beastie Boys are. The Black Panthers were the party we were talking about, of course. The track itself was so quirky that it definitely fit inside the concept of the album, and we knew that we had enough muscle bangers on the album that we could afford to do something that was totally left-field. It became a performance cut because of the difference. It was a contrast that set a stronger record up.

REDMAN

Whut? Thee Album

(RAL/Columbia, 1992)

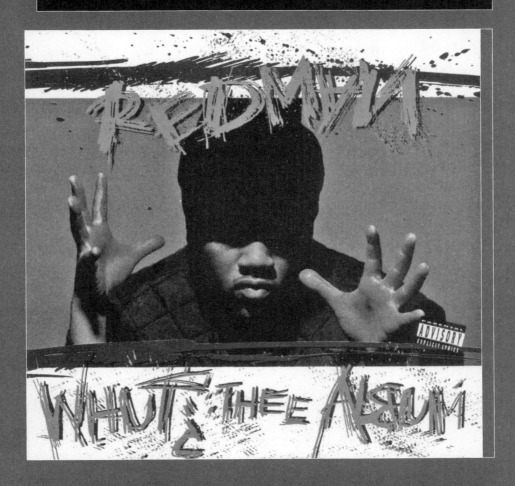

You already know Redman (Reggie Noble) as a hilarious MC, but he wasn't always the man on the mic. The Newark, New Jersey–raised hip-hop joker was on the turntables first. "I started DJing when I was eleven and twelve years old," he says, "and I did the 'hood things like everybody else. I sold drugs and was out in the street. But I always stayed with the music. When I was younger, I used to DJ at clubs around Newark, and I ran with a couple of local hip-hop crews."

He says of his Newark environment: "The scene there was just like New York. Anything that New York got early, we got early. All those guys from the city had to come to Jersey to play to prove themselves. Newark is wild now, but it was even wilder back then in the eighties when I was coming up."

Throughout his teens he continued to hustle and DJ. For three years he also attended Montclair State University, just outside of Newark, where he DJed parties. But once two Long Island artists, EPMD and Biz Markie, flooded the airwaves in the late eighties, things changed for Redman. He recalls: "I started MCing when I was sixteen and was more serious about it when I was around eighteen. I always had kind of wanted to MC but I really started into it when I heard EPMD and Biz. I knew that I had it in me to do it. When I heard EPMD, I knew that I had that same energy inside me. Everybody else at the time was more technical, but Erick and Parrish were more 'slow flow' and natural."

Luckily, Redman had a chance to meet his idols, EPMD, in Newark shortly after he had started woodshedding his MC skills. It was 1991 and the duo was just starting to expand its empire by developing and producing other acts—like K-Solo and DAS EFX—under the EPMD/Hitsquad umbrella. Redman recalls: "I met those guys at an underground club in Newark called Sensations. MC Lyte was supposed to be there performing that night, but she had to cancel and EPMD took her place. I wasn't even supposed to go that night, but I went anyways."

He continues: "Earlier in the night we met EPMD in the back of the club, me and my boys. I was there at the club DJing for my boy DoItAll from Lords of the Underground [who were also from Newark]. There were a couple of guys there, freestyling for EPMD, and I was being quiet. But those guys told Erick that I could rap, too, so he asked me to freestyle and I started spittin'. He liked it so much that they put me onstage that night with them, and after that Erick was just a phone call away."

The newly minted MC was quickly brought into the EPMD family and went out on the road with them as a roadie and even occasional opening act. He says: "I was still DJing that whole time after I met EPMD. I didn't just start being an MC and leave my roots behind. At that time I even went on the road as K-Solo's DJ. I did that for a couple of years, until my first album came out. DJing helped me a lot in the rap game, so I'm glad that I had those techniques. The first time I ever really performed was when I went out on the road with EPMD and K-Solo. I was carrying bags for them and EPMD would put me onstage with DJ Scratch and I just used to rip it."

After Redman's quick rise to the top of the EPMD next-up list, by late 1991 it was time to find the Newark rapper a record deal. As he notes: "After EPMD had signed K-Solo and DAS EFX [their albums came out in 1990 and spring of 1992, respectively] they pretty much had mo'fuckas where they wanted them, so it wasn't hard to get me a deal." One of the obvious choices was hip-hop powerhouse Def Jam, and a deal was struck.

On the production side, Redman was obviously new to the game, so he wasn't on the job alone. His mentor was Erick Sermon. As Redman explains: "It was always Erick more than Parrish with my record. Parrish was more involved with DAS EFX and K-Solo. I was E's first real artist. And I picked up shit real quick." Recording was done mostly at EPMD engineer Charlie Marotta's North Shore Soundworks studio in Long Island, along with a couple other spots in the LI vicinity. "I went out there to Long Island and stayed out there," he says.

Although Erick was overseeing Redman's production work on the album (and getting co-production credit on most tracks), Redman says that he was mostly left on his own—and not by his own choosing. Red remembers: "For that whole album I was under a lot of pressure to learn, and learn quickly. E [Erick] showed me a couple of [recording] moves, then threw me in the studio and just left me there! I had to learn and do it myself, so that's just what I did. Erick was always there if I really needed him, so it wasn't *that* bad. But he basically had his own shit to deal with and he figured I was okay on my own."

Aside from production techniques, Redman had also come a long way with his rhyme style since he first got on board with EPMD. He says: "I had to work at MCing back then, definitely, and I obviously learned a lot from Erick and Parrish. They had the knowledge and they passed it on. But that whole time I just wanted to DJ, man. That was everything to me. I found out that DJing and MCing are the same, in a way, because in the end your main goal is to make the crowd move."

He also shouts out another influence on his style who helped him personally: "I also want to big-up Biz Markie, because he used to take me on the road to battle motherfuckas back then, to make money. Back when I was first getting down with EPMD, Biz took me to a park in Queens and I did a freestyle there that everybody in New York heard about. Biz definitely helped me out in a big way back then by showing me how to do it like that."

After a couple months in the lab, Redman had obviously learned quite well on the job, since *Whut? Thee Album* popped out fully formed. And he did it all almost without any guest artists, an unheard-of situation in today's hip-hop world. He says: "There's very few guest spots because I never believed in having guests on an album just to help sell it. Any guest that's gonna be on my shit has got to be family. It's never a casual thing, never something that someone at a label just thought up."

And as for his "on my own" status when recording the album, he says today: "When I first started doing the album I used to be mad at E for leaving me in the studio. I was like: 'What the fuck am I doing here?' I had an album to hit the world with, and it was just up to me. But I'm glad he did it, because I learned everything that I needed to do. I'm not mad at him for that shit no more." He adds about his learning experiences: "Everything was great back then. Definitely the touring, but it was all just a new experience for me, learning in the studio as well. It was all brand-new and it was fun."

Never one to be timid even when he was a new artist, Redman was definitely confident once *Whut?* was finished. He recalls: "Once I finished the album I knew it was the shit. I learned about putting in drama and stopping the music for effect from EPMD and Ice Cube, and I was following them with that. And I learned how to mold an album and how to put it together from listening to N.W.A."

The album, which came out in the fall of 1992, went gold. It announced Redman's unique, charismatic rap and production style to the world—and confirmed EPMD's star-making touch. Redman says: "That album went gold quickly—it was big back then! It was big as hell! Once I finished the album, I knew that I was ready. I knew I had a classic."

TRACKS

TIME 4 SUM AKSION

That was the second single on the album, after "Blow Your Mind," but the second one was much bigger. The video for that track was wild, man. We actually had guns in that video. We was wildin' back then. That was when hardcore videos really started taking off, and the networks didn't know how to handle it. I was getting electrocuted in an electric chair too.

DA FUNK

There's a lot of P-Funk on there, because that was my shit. The P-Funk influence may have started fading from some East Coast records back then, but I've always been on the funk shit, so that's the way I had to come. Using P-Funk at that time, with people like Dre on the West, wasn't really a West Coast sound, it was a West Coast *feel* to an East Coast sound. I built my album around guys like EPMD and N.W.A., and they both had the funk. East or West, it didn't matter to me.

SO RUFF

That's the only cut on the album where I didn't do my own scratches. DJ Scratch [from EPMD] did the cuts on that track. All the rest was me. There were a lot of stories on that track, because people like Slick Rick were very influential to me. He was so nice with the lyrical play. I learned the personality of rap from Slick Rick and KRS-One, too. Storytelling style was definitely a pain in the ass for me, though. Even trying to think of these

"Sooperman Lovers" [like EPMD's "Jane" series, there is a "Sooperman Lover" on every Redman album] now is a pain in the fuckin' ass. I definitely had to work harder when it came to storytelling stuff.

RATED "R"

I was a big horror movie fan, as you know from that song, so being in the *Seed of Chucky* movie [in 2004] was great. I'm definitely glad to be part of the Chucky thing.

WATCH YO NUGGETS

That was Erick on there with me, and that track was a lot of fun. It was heavy.

BLOW YOUR MIND

That was the first single I put out. It did well—definitely started people hearing my sound. The part with the Korean translation ["Super fly human being/Let me freak it in Korean . . ."] was done by Sophia Chang—she used to work at Jive Records a long time ago. She's Korean and I asked her write that part for me. I told her to talk about weed and women [*laughs*]. You know, the shit that I do. And she did.

HARDCORE

Parrish [Smith, from EPMD] co-produced that one, the only one on the album he helped on. P was more on the business side of shit. He helped the process of getting tours together, shit like that, more than the musical side. That was Erick. With groups, P was more involved [musically] with DAS EFX and K-Solo. I was Erick's first artist in the Hit Squad thing.

REDMAN MEETS REGGIE NOBLE

Reggie Noble is my name, and that side of me was more business, more in tune with what was going on with the album itself. Redman was the name being sold—Redman was wilding out, doing what he wanted to do.

I'M A BAD

That's actually my favorite track on the album. The beat on there was so fuckin' rough! I always loved that one.

HOW TO ROLL A BLUNT

That was Pete Rock on that one. [Pete co-produced, listed on the inside album credits but not on the back album cover.] I used to go over to Pete Rock's house all the time and do beats with him. Pete was out there, man, he was hot. He's still hot, even today. That was some of his earliest stuff. That song was definitely one of my favorites too. Everybody was on my dick for that song, for showing people how to roll a blunt, and in a song.

A DAY OF SOOPERMAN LOVER

I was the first guy to use that song [Johnny Guitar Watson's "Superman Lover"]. I had to be. That's my shit from way back. So I just used that and did my own version of a song.

THE ROOTS

Do You Want More?!!!??!

(Geffen, 1995)

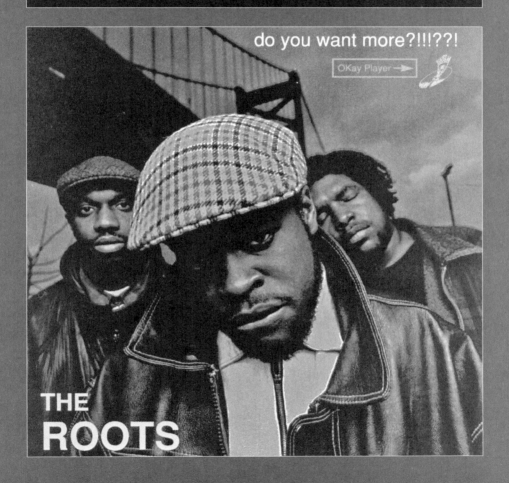

We did a lot of unorthodox things back then," says South Philly's Black Thought. "But," he adds, "the Roots is an unorthodox group." Truer words were never spoken in the rap world.

The Roots weren't the first group to use live instruments onstage in hip-hop, nor were they the first group to use jazz to inform their sound. But it can be argued that the true melding of live hip-hop and jazz didn't come together until this thick but limber unit came on the scene in the early nineties. They shunned sampling, rocked virtuosic live prowess, and always gave listeners more than just loops and tired battle rhymes. They constructed songs, and they slowly built a grassroots following that still flocks to see them more than a decade later.

Although each member of the group stands on his own two unique feet, there is no doubt that the boom-bappedly beating heart of the group is drummer and producer Ahmir "?uestlove" Thompson (listed as B.R.O.T.H.E.R.? in the liner notes to *Do You Want More?!!!??!*). "I was born in Philly, and my parents say that I started in music at about two years old, abusing household appliances and such," he says. "One big thing when I was growing up was that I wasn't allowed to watch much TV. So a lot of my time was spent listening to records. That started my love affair with music."

Ahmir only needed to prick his finger to figure out why he was drawn to music—it was in his blood. His father, Arthur Lee Andrew Thompson, led the fifties doo-wop group Lee Andrews and the Hearts, scoring hits for Chess Records with "Long Lonely Nights" and "Try the Impossible." Going back further in the bloodline, Lee's father, Ahmir's grandfather, was a member of the venerable Dixie Hummingbirds gospel group.

"By the time I came around in the seventies, there was a fifties-music resurgence, so my father would do a lot of revival shows at big places like Madison Square Garden and Radio City Music Hall," recalls Ahmir. "They'd have lots of fifties groups on one big bill, and I would go and watch the shows from backstage. At that time, my father and mother [Jackie] also had a soul group called Congress Alley. They put out a record in 1973 on AVCO. By the late seventies he parlayed Lee Andrews and the Hearts into a nightclub act, which would play in Atlantic City and Vegas."

Ahmir's musical education didn't stop backstage. He says: "By the time I was thirteen, I was actually band-leading the group whenever I wasn't in school. It was a family act at that point with me, my father, mother, and sister. That's where I got my real musical education from. Things like how to pace a show and how to really entertain an audience."

"My father had plans for me," Ahmir explains. "He wanted me to be a young lion [a term used in the eighties to describe young, slick, successful jazz musicians]. His dream for me was to be the ultimate session musician. My mom was very encouraging too, no matter what I was doing in music. But hip-hop was the route I wanted to go in as I got into high school, and at the time that wasn't really seen as an art form, and it definitely wouldn't have sat well with my dad." Ahmir got top-shelf musical and arts schooling from an early age—attending performing-arts-focused schools from first through eighth grade—then finished his high schooling at Philadelphia's High School for the Creative & Performing Arts.

High school classmate and lead Roots MC Black Thought (Tariq Trotter) remembers Ahmir's family situation well. He recalls: "I was over there at Ahmir's place a lot. If I wasn't over there, he was over at my house. His dad was definitely strict, kind of a Joe Jackson type of dad. [Think Jackson 5, not "Steppin' Out."] He was cool, but I was friendlier with his mom and sister. I remember his dad being an imposing dude with a deep voice."

Although Ahmir was being groomed for a Juilliard education (he says he was accepted to the prestigious New York music academy for jazz and classical studies), an event in 1988 changed everything for the young drummer. Ahmir explains: "The second week of May that year changed everything. That was the week that Public Enemy came out with *It Takes a Nation of Millions to Hold Us Back.* I listened to that album so much that I had to quit my job that summer. I would listen to it like 'Name That Tune,' where I would pick out all the stuff they were sampling. I was like: 'I can do this!' even though I had no idea how the Bomb Squad [PE's production team] was making the music. I think I assumed that they did it with pause-tapes or something."

There was just one roadblock to Ahmir's new hip-hop career goal: the musical plan that his father had for him. He says: "I wanted to make hip-hop, but how could I tell that to my father, who was saving thousands of dollars for me to go to Juilliard?" The answer was to continue jazzing it up and keep the hip-hop on the down low. He was able to do this for several years to come.

Tariq was born and raised in South Philly and started taking hip-hop seriously at a young age. He remembers: "At the time when I became interested in hip-hop, I also became a vocalist, around 1981 or '82. I didn't just listen—it was always very serious for me." He first came into contact with Ahmir at Philly's High School for the Creative & Performing Arts. Tariq says: "I was studying visual arts in high school. At that point I didn't know exactly what I wanted to do, but I was good enough in art to get me into a school where you needed to audition. And at that time, when I first met Ahmir, I was definitely still forming my rhyme style. I was mostly in the battle-raps zone back then. With me and Ahmir, I think it was definitely a thing of opposites attracting. Our backgrounds were very different, but our musical interests were similar. I always listened to all kinds of music, and jazz too, but Ahmir taught me even more about that world."

One thing Ahmir had done on the hip-hop side, before his Public Enemy awakening, was purchase the battery-powered, portable, and now primitive Casio SK-1 keyboard. Not for the keyboard part, though, as his parents may have figured. It was also a low-budget sampler. He had met Black Thought by then, who was two or three years younger. Ahmir remembers: "When I got that SK-1, that's when the Roots really started. I was the goody-goody kid and Tariq was this thug-ass mo'fucka, getting suspended on the first day of school. Tariq was very, very quick and incredibly sharp as a lyricist. I had never seen anyone rhyme off the top of their head like that. So I'd play [live] drums and sample the beat and then replay it on the SK-1 while he would freestyle over the top. I'd have to play the beats twice as fast and slow it down, though, because the keyboard only had about three seconds of sampling time."

After a couple months of SK-1 work together, the first Roots gig went down on February 14, 1988, at a school Valentine's Day assembly. Ahmir says: "That day, [classmates] Amel Larrieux, Boyz II Men, and the group that would eventually be known as the Roots gave their very first performances. It was me on drums, [future jazz star] Christian McBride on bass, and Tariq rhyming. We did a song called 'P.I.R.,' Partners in Rhyme. We got a thunderous applause. The name of our group at that point was Radioactivity." Even back then, years before their first recordings, the group had never thought of having a DJ.

Across town in Philly's Germantown section, the man who would eventually manage the Roots and form the Okayplayer family umbrella, Richard Nichols, was exploring a different musical path. A funk and soul fanatic and respected avant-garde jazz DJ on Temple University's venerable WRTI (he DJed there until 1990, and Ahmir was a frequent listener), Nichols had started recording and managing young hip-hop talent in Philly in the mid-eighties. He says: "I started being more interested in hip-hop when Run-DMC hit, in '83. I was definitely attracted to what they were doing, on some avant-garde-noise type of level. It was really raw to me. In the mid-eighties, I started messing around recording the kids of people I knew, because they bugged me until I gave in. And after a while, more and more of them just started coming my way."

In the late eighties, Nichols made things a bit more formal (and affordable) by calling his efforts the Urban Music Project and receiving grants to fund his recordings. Nichols explains: "I was getting the grants to teach kids how to make contemporary music, and I was also just trying to get more equipment. I started building up a cadre of talented kids, and it started to become some sort of weird extended family. Eventually these kids wanted someone to shop the demos we were making, so I'd go to New York and pitch stuff to A&R people at labels." Many future Roots performers and associates came through the Urban Music Program, including keyboardist (and now super-producer) Scott Storch, keyboardist Kamal, producer Kelo, MC Dice Raw, and De La Soul affiliate MC Shortie No Mas.

Eventually Nichols ran across a popular local hip-hop radio DJ and promoter named Joseph Simmons, who went by A.J. Shine. Shine did a show called "The Avenue" on Drexel University's WKDU with DJ Cosmic Kev, and it was the best outlet in town for up-and-coming groups to get heard. Nichols and Simmons eventually started a "behind-the-scenes" hip-hop video show on local access, using a high-end video camera that Nichols used for a day gig recording law depositions. At night they would attend hip-hop shows in Philly and do backstage interviews with the stars of the day.

After Ahmir graduated from high school, he took classes at Philly's University of the Arts and jazz courses at the Settlement Music School. He and Tariq continued to perform, using Settlement classmate Josh Abrams on upright bass. Ahmir also kept busy around town. Very busy, in fact, as he relates: "Back then, Tariq suggested that I join as many bands as I could so that we could have even more sample source material (from recording the groups' performances). I joined a jazz group, a rock band, a church group, and a pop type of thing. I also drew Tariq into those groups. The rock band would perform and he would jump up and do a verse. The gospel group would do some teen workshop and Tariq would do that too." Tariq says: "I was definitely comfortable on the mic in all kinds of situations. I never had a steady DJ or anything. Linking up with Ahmir was really my first time being in any kind of group, so it was all I knew."

Despite all their hustling, Tariq and Ahmir struggled to find a niche in Philly. They had dreams of rocking on DJ Cosmic Kev's and A.J. Shine's show, which was, as Ahmir says, "Philly's version of the Stretch & Bobbito show." But it took them a while to get the DJs' attention. Eventually A.J. Shine would warm to the group—after seeing them perform at one of his talent shows—and bring them to Richard Nichols's attention. Shine also played a significant role in the group's early albums. (He was co–executive producer and co-producer of the group's first album, *Organix,* and *Do You Want More.*)

Richard Nichols remembers the first time he met Ahmir. "He was wearing Birkenstocks! It was really weird," laughs Nichols. "They were definitely in a post–*Peoples' Instinctive Travels* [the first Tribe Called Quest album] thing. Tariq was wearing a poncho, and they had a white dude [Abrams] on bass. It was pretty different, that's for sure. I remember that the big thing for A.J. the first time he saw them was that they played [the theme to the cartoon show] *Inspector Gadget.*" He was excited about that."

Around this time, Tariq graduated high school and attended Millersville University, an hour outside of Philly, for just over two years. Tariq says: "I went there as a communications major, for radio and TV. During that time it was still pretty easy to come back home if I needed to, so it wasn't like I was stuck there."

At Millersville, Tariq met rapper Malik B (Malik Abdul Basit-Smart), who was affiliated with the group as they built steam in the coming years. Tariq says: "Malik is one year older than me, and I met him through a family member who said we needed to get together because we both rhymed. When I first met Malik, I didn't envision him in the group at all. But whenever I did hip-hop stuff at school and Ahmir couldn't make it, then the Roots became me and Malik."

Up until 1992, Tariq and Ahmir performed together whenever they could, but it was still a time in flux. Ahmir says: "For a while I had even gotten a job as an insurance salesman. I used that money to pay for some studio time." He says the duo recorded during 1991 and 1992 with group names Radioactivity and Black to the Future, but the songs never made it to wax.

Ahmir continues: "There was a lot of pressure on me in 1992 to really make some shit happen. Clearly I was supposed to be up there on bandstands with Christian [McBride] and Joey [DeFrancesco, another classmate and rising jazz star], but I had bigger plans. Tariq had a lot of pressure, too, because he didn't know whether he should stay in Millersville or pursue this hip-hop thing more seriously."

The summer of 1992 proved to be the turning point. After being in New York and seeing the percussionist Chocolate—the man who was featured in a 1988 Spike Lee–directed Levi's commercial, banging on buckets—performing on the street, they decided to give busking a shot. In July, during Philly's "Greek Picnic Weekend," Ahmir and Tariq gathered buckets and crates and set up on Philly's much-traveled South Street. Ahmir banged, Tariq rhymed. Ahmir recalls: "Our whole test was to see if we could get fifty dollars for our whole crew to go see [the movie] *Children of the Corn*. We made about $116 in the first twenty minutes!"

The next weekend went even better, this time with the addition of bassist Josh Abrams. Now that they had Abrams's car, Ahmir also replaced his buckets with real drums. Ahmir says: "The response that second weekend was astounding! We set up and started and this time we made a hundred dollars during the *first song*. So we played from one P.M. until seven P.M., all over the city. We didn't have a song repertoire back then, so Tariq, who didn't even have a microphone, just freestyled all of it. Half the time I couldn't even hear what he was saying."

After their busking the group got more gigs, mostly house and frat parties, while Tariq and Josh were both still home from college during the summer. Tariq says: "After we made that name for ourselves on South Street, things definitely started getting a bit better—we started getting more shows. We still had a lot of trials and tribulations, but we made it through them."

Ahmir remembers: "The most crucial show we did that year was in September of 1992, before Josh had to leave for Northwestern [University, outside of Chicago] and Tariq went back to Millersville. We finally got to play

The Roots (clockwise from lower left: Hub, Kamal, Ahmir "?uestlove" Thompson, Dice Raw, Black Thought, Rahzel) in Hollywood, 1998. (The dead guy is artist and graphic designer Brent Rollins, not a member of the group.)
PHOTO: B+ (FOR WWW.MOCHILLA.COM).

at a WKDU show that A.J. Shine put on. It was a thug crowd, and we were an interracial group wearing Osh Kosh clothes and throwing peace signs. But once I started playing breaks they knew, they just flipped out. We walked in thinking that we'd get booed or shot and we walked out as winners. A.J. Shine called us the next day and said: 'I just got some settlement money from a car accident, you want to put out a single?' "

In the next month they recorded a total of what Ahmir says was eight tunes. Nothing happened on the vinyl front until 1993, though. Nichols recalls those first sessions: "They came by this studio that I was using at the time, a sixteen-track place with an [Akai] MPC-60 sampler. We knocked out 'Pass the Popcorn' and 'The Anti-Circle' [both would appear on *Organix*] in a weekend and the shit sounded really good. Josh was on bass for those sessions—it was during a school break. And with those first two songs, I remember thinking: 'This shit is really good, but it'll never get on the radio, no chance in hell!' "

Nichols also started booking the group, a step up from their original managers, Krikit and Tin Tin, who were booking them at parties and smaller clubs ("barbeque gigs," Nichols calls them). Nichols says: "Back then I was basically selling them as a jazz act, because it was easier to get them into rock clubs and nontraditional hip-hop venues that way."

Early 1993 presented an interesting new opportunity for the group after Philly-based jazz bassist Jamaaladeen Tacuma (who had produced a hip-hop single of his own—La La the Leader of the Pack's "The Wop," from 1985) saw the Roots perform at Philly's Painted Bride. He recognized

Tariq's friend and classmate Malik B, whom he knew from his mosque. After the show, he met the group and told them about the lucrative European jazz-festival scene, which might be open to them considering their jazz slant. Through Tacuma, the group was booked at that year's prestigious Moers Festival in Germany, which took place in June.

Ahmir says: "Since we had all that advance warning, we wanted to use that gig for everything we could get. We couldn't believe we were getting paid for a gig like that, because we weren't even big in Philly yet. We wanted to use it to get our music out there, and to convince record labels that we were huge in Europe. It was a six-month plan from that point [spring of 1993], and we played everywhere we could in Pennsylvania, New Jersey, and New York to get ready."

In addition to playing everywhere they could, the group also needed something to sell in Germany, so they decided to finish the recordings that they had started in the fall of 1992. These sessions, which were put together in a matter of days, became the Roots' first CD: *Organix* (Remedy Recordings). According to Ahmir, they pressed up one thousand copies on CD—no vinyl or cassette. Some group members still consider it a glorified demo; others consider it their legitimate debut. Either way, it captured the group in all its rough-around-the-edges glory circa early 1993.

There were two big developments as a result of their appearance at the Moers Festival in June 1993. First, Ahmir says, "We sold out of our CDs after we had played our first four songs over there. We did three encores. They loved us!" And second, the Roots put Malik in the group permanently, as a thank-you for helping them get the gig through Tacuma. "It's not like we didn't know that Malik was nice on the mic before," says Ahmir. "It's just that we already had an MC in the group. But it was good to have him there, to give Tariq some relief when he needed it up there."

Ahmir compares and contrasts the two MCs: "Malik was always dope as a rhymer. He was abstract and he was the best of both worlds: a thug and a backpacker all at the same time. Tariq's strength in rhyming is his clarity and his logic. Malik's strength is being cryptic and abstract. I mean, I still don't know why cattle were in the steeple! (referencing Malik's rhyme on the Roots' 1993 single, "Distortion to Static").

The last piece of the puzzle was the group's new bassist, Leonard "Hub" Hubbard, who had been with them in Germany. Josh Abrams wasn't able to make the Moers trip, and it had become clear that he wasn't going to be able to trade school for a potential rap career. A longtime friend of manager Richard Nichols, Hub was classically trained but also very, very funky. In other words, he was a perfect match for the wide-ranging Roots crew. Richard Nichols says: "By the time the German festival happened, they had made the transition to Hub. I had known him since around 1979, and he even had his own version of the Urban Music Program in South Philly, so he also brought other guys into the crew."

Ahmir recalls: "When we got back from Germany, we felt like we had an important window of opportunity to make things happen—we knew that was our time to get signed. So we got a lawyer who spent July through October trying to get us a record deal, using *Organix* as our demo and all the European press we got to entice people." The group went to New York for several showcases, playing for A&R executives, and had several offers on the table by the fall of 1993.

"When we first got back from Europe, no one was really jumping on the Roots," recalls Nichols. "But eventually Kenyatta Bell at Mercury was first up to bat. He offered $75,000, which eventually got bumped up to $150,000. That was definitely respectable money at the time. Then Epic and East West made offers. In the end, Wendy Goldstein at Geffen was the one who offered the most. After Arrested Development got big, I think her boss told her: 'Find a band who play their own instruments and don't talk about guns.' They offered $350,000, which was huge at the time, and Mercury and everyone else just couldn't mess with that. That money was for the recording budget, and they got a small advance outside of that, maybe $50,000. In the end, I think we spent about $450,000 making *Do You Want More*."

The group was signed by Geffen Records in late 1993. "I only knew them as a rock label, from Nirvana and Guns N' Roses, so at first we laughed at the idea that they'd want to sign us," says Ahmir. "But we found out that rock money is real money, and we reaped the benefits of some great years that company had in the early nineties. Wendy was starting an urban division at Geffen and she had to have us, so she spared no expense."

One other good thing about getting signed was that Ahmir could finally tell his family about the Roots. Amazingly, he had kept the group a secret from his family during the group's first several years, since he knew that his father wouldn't approve. "I was successful enough in keeping the Roots from my father, and I didn't even tell him until one week before our signing celebration gig in Philly in late '93," says Ahmir. "He didn't even know that we had done *Organix.* I just didn't want to tell him about the hip-hop stuff until it was a sure thing. He wouldn't let us play hip-hop in the house because of the profanity, that kind of thing. I told my older sister about the group in 1992. As for the hip-hop thing and my father, my shield was always taking the college classes that I did. That kept him distracted."

And so, with a fat advance in hand, the group walked into 1994 with a plan and a new boost of confidence. Ahmir recalls: "Our main plan in early 1994 was to *survive.* We knew what our strengths were, and we knew that we had to develop a live show that was so goddamn sharp that it would literally embarrass the label if they ever thought of dropping us."

The group began songs for *Do You Want More* soon after their advance check cleared. "We started recording a week after we had our final signing dinner with Wendy Goldstein, in late November [1993]," recalls Ahmir. "Basically we got a record deal and then we realized: 'Wait, we don't got no songs!' [*Laughs.*] At first we even debated whether we should just rerecord *Organix,* but we decided against it. On the first official recording day we had a cram session, and in that first forty-eight-hour period nearly created the blueprint for the whole record."

The Grand Negaz (credited as producers for *Do You Want More*) were Ahmir, Richard Nichols, A.J. Shine, Kelo, Tariq, Scott Storch, and Hub. "The top three are always Rich, myself, and Tariq, although production is pretty equally divided among all of us," explains Ahmir. "We got the name from this episode of [*Star Trek*] *Deep Space Nine,* and when we named it that we didn't really think about how every time we went to a bank that was on all our checks, and we'd always have to say that name to the clerks. Later on, we changed it to Grand Wizzards.

"When it comes to specific production duties, my area of expertise was always in how we built and sequenced the albums," says Ahmir. "Kelo's job was basically to fatten up the sound we introduced on *Organix.* He knew how to do stuff like putting hand claps over your snare sound, that kind of shit. He was an integral part of the Grand Negaz production team. And Tariq holds a lot of power, because he can't write to something if he doesn't feel the beat—so he can veto anything."

Richard Nichols points out, "We were at a disadvantage sonically because we didn't sample. When old drums were recorded, they had tons of compression on them, so when you sample them without other instruments [as most hip-hop producers did], they sound amazingly *loud.* Also, with our approach to the records, *Organix* was based on songs that they had been perfecting live over time. *Do You Want More* were all songs that we wrote in the studio. It was a totally different thing."

Ahmir relates a funny story, and a bit of hip-hop trivia: "We actually made half the songs on *Do You Want More* on Bell Biv DeVoe's equipment. Our producer Kelo was the in-house engineer for BBD after the *Poison* album came out [in 1990], and once the follow-up came out and flopped, they were like: 'Okay, all this equipment we bought you to produce us, we need it back.' He was in L.A., living at Ronnie DeVoe's crib, and when Ronnie went out on some errand, Kelo basically packed up the whole studio and took a plane to Philly. We flew him in and paid all that cargo weight. There were thirteen huge Anvil cases with all that shit, and it cost about thirteen thousand dollars! That first week, when we were working on 'Distortion to Static,' Ronnie DeVoe was calling every day, like: 'Where the fuck is our equipment?' [*Laughs.*]"

"With *Do You Want More,* it was all very much a learning experience," recalls Tariq. "It was our first major record, our first time working in real studios with mixing and mastering engineers. I was learning what to do and what not to do, and we were figuring out how to manipulate the live instrumentation and overall sound."

Ahmir remembers: "Basically, round one of the recording all ended up on the [import-only] EP *From the Ground Up* [Talkin' Loud/Geffen, 1994]. [DJ and label owner] Gilles Peterson had convinced Wendy Goldstein that Talkin' Loud should put out an EP in Europe before the Geffen album came out. We called it 'The Paul Revere Record.' It was a warning for people about what was to come. It came out in May of 1994 because we were planning on doing more European festivals in June that year."

Most of *Do You Want More* was finished by the spring of 1994, with an initial release date set for late June. But April 8, 1994, presented a new wrinkle in the group's plan to ride the Geffen rock wave to major-label success. Ahmir recalls: "We now call it 'Cobain Day'—the day that [Nirvana's] Kurt Cobain died. That was a crazy day, because he was Geffen's cash cow, and now he wasn't there. Nirvana had already made [labelmates] Guns N'

Roses obsolete, so Nirvana were the ones Geffen was relying on back then. We knew we had to get our album done as quickly as possible after that, before the shit really hit the fan, so we shot our album cover that same night, and went into the studio and finished up 'The Lesson,' 'The Unlocking,' 'Lazy Afternoon,' and '? vs. Rahzel' in the next couple days."

Tariq definitely remembers "Cobain Day": "I don't think it was a do-or-die type of thing, but his death definitely visibly shook most of, if not all of, the employees we knew at Geffen. That definitely worried us as artists who had just signed to the label."

But that wasn't the most dramatic thing that the Roots did in the spring of 1994. After finishing the album, shooting the album cover, and freaking out about their future at Geffen, Ahmir explains: "Four days later we were on our way to Europe, and we wouldn't be back for a long time. We pulled a Jimi Hendrix!" Their first single, "Distortion to Static," had been released, but the group wouldn't be around long enough to hear it on the radio.

Richard Nichols says: "The point was always going to be that we were going to break this shit overseas first, and European Festival season was coming up. Once we realized that Geffen wasn't going to give us the tour support we wanted in the U.S., it made sense to go to London. The record had gotten pushed back to a fall release, and we saw no reason to stay in the U.S. when all that money was waiting for us over there. Me, Tariq, and Ahmir got flown over to do a *Straight No Chaser* [the UK music magazine] event, and we had a little bit of money from a remix we were going to do for [the group] Galliano, so we flew Malik and Hub over. Scott [Storch] had left the group at that point, so we didn't have a keyboard player."

Nichols managed to get Geffen to give the group a fifteen-thousand-dollar royalty advance, and, Nichols says, "We took that money and paid up front for an apartment in London for six months. It was in Queens Crescent. Honestly, at that point we weren't sure when we was gonna return to the U.S. We were fine with just staying as a European band. Since Geffen was shorting us on tour support there at home, we were like: 'We'll come to the States if Geffen wants, but they have to pay for it.' It was our way of giving the finger to the record label. We did a lot of gigs in Europe, but it wasn't making us a lot of money. We ate a lot of cereal while we were there."

"We played everywhere, wherever we could," says Ahmir. "The South Street days [in Philly] had prepared us for all those situations: how to deal with hecklers, quiet crowds, small crowds. Going to London was definitely strategic, because at the time, after [Dr. Dre's] *The Chronic,* I was convinced that we wouldn't be able to bring people around to our brand of hip-hop."

"It was game theory," says Tariq. "That's just what needed to be done at that point in time, in order to be able to travel to and from the shows that we were getting. We couldn't afford to fly back and forth internationally from the U.S., so London made the most sense. We were working with artists associated with the Talkin' Loud label and all kinds of other musicians there. In fact, those are some of my fondest memories of my whole life."

Tariq adds: "We became the go-to people in London for hip-hop, and there was more to be made and done there than if we were just one of the hundreds of artists in the U.S. It was that simple. It made our sound tighter and gave us our legs, stagewise. It also gave us a tighter personal bond for the long run, even though there were times when we were at each other's throats."

The group had one strong ally in London when they arrived: Gilles Peterson. Peterson was a big fan of the group since the *Organix* days, and Ahmir says he liked the CD-only release so much that he pressed up a vinyl acetate of the album to play when he DJed in clubs. Peterson founded the Talkin' Loud label and was definitely influential in Mercury's initial pursuit of the group, since Talkin' Loud was allied with Mercury in Europe. Once the Roots hit London, Peterson helped them get session work with artists like saxophonist Steve Williamson, vocalist Omar, and acid-jazz group Galliano—and was most certainly their biggest fan on that side of the pond.

In the fall of 1994, Wendy Goldstein convinced the group to finally come home and start promoting the *Do You Want More* album. "Even after we got back to the U.S., our whole plan was for Geffen to keep flying us back and forth," says Nichols. "We had a buzz in London back then, but still couldn't make enough to stay. And it was the same when we got back to the U.S., although at least in Philly you could crash on your mom's couch [*laughs*]."

After an indisputably strange journey to get there, *Do You Want More* was somewhat anticlimactically released in early 1995, and the group did as much touring as it could in the first part of the year. Astute fans undoubtedly took notice of the unique numbering system on the new album's tracks, which started at number 18 [there are seventeen tracks on *Organix*].

The idea came from an unlikely source, as Ahmir relates: "That's an idea that I actually stole from Billy Idol. His second album starts like that, so I used it as a way to announce to people who were paying attention that this wasn't our first album. That was the best way I could think of to do it, and we still use it today."

Ahmir says that sales of *Do You Want More* were around two hundred thousand in 1995, and the album finally hit gold status in early 2006, more than a decade later. Nichols says: "It was definitely a pretty wild time back then for the Roots. When we did that record, we figured that we'd be competitive with A Tribe Called Quest, I guess. Eventually things just kept getting better, and the guys stopped living with their parents and our show guarantees kept going up. And overall, that album was the last of the innocent Roots albums, when they were just being artsy. It was probably what can also be considered the last 'post–Daisy Age' record. Although I have to say, when I look back on *Do You Want More* now, that record sounds pretty fresh to me. We'll never have a vibe like that again on a record."

Tariq says: "I always know what I think of an album long before it's mastered, and *Do You Want More* always felt like a decent introduction to the world for us. *Do You Want More* was our first real group recording effort. Once I started meeting other artists that I respected and getting their opinions, all the stuff coming back to me was good. People dug what we were doing, and that's all you can ask for. We got a lot of good press too. Far more than I ever imagined that we would, honestly."

Ahmir says: "I was disappointed after the response to *Do You Want More,* because we didn't become huge. But that's exactly why we're still around today. If there was ever a tortoise-and-the-hare group in hip-hop, it is most definitely the Roots. If we had actually blown up on that album, then I really don't think that we would have lasted this long together. It humbled us and it made us try harder and appreciate doing our live shows. There are only a handful of mo'fuckas left from the class of '94 who are still active and making important music today."

"I didn't feel like we had failed at all after that record," adds Tariq, counterbalancing Ahmir's view. "I thought it was a great introduction for us. It was the attention-grabber that garnered the respect of our peers, not only in hip-hop, but with all kinds of musicians. It set the bar and the precedent for the quality of our performances and all our recordings that followed."

TRACKS

INTRO/THERE'S SOMETHING GOIN' ON
Recorded live at Painted Bride, March 1993

Ahmir: Basically I just took the music to "The Unlocking" [the album's final song] and made an intro out of it. We had to go to DC the next day for a show and Tariq wanted to go home, so he left the studio. Malik stayed and we were all in a rush. You can hear him saying: "Cue me in!" after we had already pressed record. So I took Malik's first take and all that singing and stuff is me. I wanted Tariq to do it, but he wasn't there. So I called him on the phone and told him to say: "There's something going on . . ." He was home packing at that point.

Tariq: I don't remember leaving that session. I'm not sure that that was the case. In some cases, you have to take a certain percentage off whatever Ahmir says about stuff like that. He's a drama king [*laughs*]. With the phone thing, we'd always do different shit like that, with a phone or walkie-talkie. It was just a sound that we liked.

PROCEED

Tariq: All the lyrics on there were written down, not freestyled. But when I wrote the stuff down, it was also always the first thing that came into my head. So I guess it was half and half. And when I say: "Representing Philly on the twenty-eighth of June" on there, that was the original [1994] release date of the album, when we were recording that song. It got pushed back a lot later than that, eventually. I think that's a really classic

Roots song. People really love that one. It did really well as a single, but the video killed it. The video was just wack!

Ahmir: "Proceed" was our second single. Before we got our album deal, Hub had a friend who was a gospel singer and they were heading out on a tour of the Midwest. I think his name was Ben Lewis. So we went out with them, as part of his band. In Minnesota and Kansas, that area. There was intro music we had, before the reverend would come out, and that eventually became the verse music for "Proceed." Ninety percent of the songs on *Do You Want More* came from us starting out with other songs and then going to other places, just like that. We were recording "Distortion to Static" and Hub and I were joking around about the gospel tour, so we played that groove. Malik liked it and wanted to use it for a song, so we stopped working on "Distortion to Static" and started working on "Proceed."

DISTORTION TO STATIC

Ahmir: That was another early song we started, and it was our first single off the album—and our first video off the album. It came out in the summer of 1994 and had been on *From the Ground Up* before that in Europe. There's an interlude on Gang Starr's *No More Mr. Nice Guy* album, in the middle, I forget the name of it, but there's some laughter in there somewhere. We'd always mimic that laugh, so that led to that chorus, and the song came out of that. Lyrically it was one of the first songs that Tariq and Malik lyrics written together, when they were in college. I remember that I got the vocals to that song FedExed to me when I was mastering the song at Battery Studios in New York with Bob Power [their mixing engineer], and they were all new! They were totally different than what we had previously recorded, and I was really angry about that shit. That was a really big conflict, because it changed the whole climate of the song. It had had all this jazzy inflection before, and now they had destroyed that for a harder approach. They did the new version the night before in Philly. At first I thought that maybe they had sent the wrong reel or something. I was asking the assistant engineer to check the dates. I just thought that the new shit Tariq had done had us coming off like Black Moon. That song has another mix which came out on the single, called "Bob's Mix" [by Bob Power]. He was a real perfectionist when it came to mixing. The Bob Power one was done first, but A.J. [Shine] wanted us to mess with the Fender Rhodes sound—he wanted a faster tremolo [effect] on it to make it sound more scary. We always had the tremolo very dry, and it didn't sound very interesting. With one press of a button, he turned that song into a much more strange affair. Bob's mix wasn't psychedelic enough—it was too normal for A.J. And he was right! When that single came out, Rich and Tariq and Malik went on a promo tour with Black Sheep in North Carolina. They were in some club and the DJ threw that song on and it was like the parting of the Red Sea on the dance floor. It just cleared! We didn't even know that the song wasn't danceable, that's how naïve we were. I guess there was one girl who insisted on trying to dance to it, and they thought she was going to throw her back out [*laughs*]. She just gave up during the third verse and walked off. And we were like: "Fuck! We failed!"

MELLOW MY MAN *Featuring Steve Coleman, Josh Roseman, and Graham Haynes*

Tariq: Steve Coleman was very helpful in setting an industry standard for us, and giving us a lay of the land in the business. He brought us to the realization that it doesn't matter what happened to you earlier in the day or earlier that week—if you agree to do a show or a session, then you do it at your top ability or you won't get your money. That dude was really frugal and really tough as a bandleader. We'd go from Philly to Austria to perform with him and if we were late for the bus, he'd dock our pay. He'd dock us for all kinds of shit, and we'd come home with like $1.75 in our pocket. Musically, Steve's shit was crazy-metered, very progressive stuff. If all you listened to was hip-hop and R&B, then you'd really have to adjust. Working with Steve and Greg Osby and those guys made it much easier for me to catch the beat with any other weird meters that I'd come across in the future, no doubt.

Ahmir: Yeah, that's not a very calm song, really, is it? [*Laughs.*] We didn't make it like that on purpose, though. By week number three of the sessions, we were having some tension in the studio. I think Tariq was feeling like he wasn't contributing enough to the music, like he was at the mercy of whatever we created. So that was one of three songs that were his brainchild. His method was to basically go up to Hub and hum the bass line he wanted, and then we'd spice it up. That was one of the only songs that we recorded at my old stomping grounds, Studio 4. I used to intern there. [*Author's note: The album liners say that the song was only mixed, not recorded, at Studio 4.*]

Tariq: When I had bass lines like that, I just kept it in my head until I could hum it to someone. If it wasn't going to stay with me for whatever that period of time was, then it wasn't worth keeping anyways.

DATSKAT *Featuring Steve Coleman, Josh Roseman, and Graham Haynes*

Tariq: I was definitely working my vocals like a horn solo on there. I just thought of it one day when we were staying with Cassandra Wilson at her place in Harlem. Malik and I stayed there for a week before we were going overseas with Steve Coleman one time, because Steve wouldn't put us up in a hotel. Cassandra was a friend of his and she let us stay there. I was a fan of hers and she inspired us with the energy at her place, and that's where we wrote that song.

Ahmir: With the music there, I was trying to create the "Easiest Way to Fall" [by Freda Payne] break, which hip-hop people know as JVC Force's "Strong Island." I still wish we could have made it sound dirtier, though.

LAZY AFTERNOON

Tariq: Yeah, I came up with that bass line, too. Rahzel was initially brought in for that one, and it led to "The Lesson," as I recall.

Ahmir: That was another one of Tariq's concoctions. There were two versions of that song and at the last minute we decided to roll with the "Groundhog Day" verse, where Tariq did the same verse, having the same experience three days in a row. Originally it had a verse for me and a verse for Malik on there, but we didn't like them enough to keep.

? VS. RAHZEL

Ahmir: Malik and Tariq met Rahzel [the human beatbox specialist, from New York] at a Lyricist Lounge night in New York, where they all just freestyled for hours. Rahzel was in the studio and learned all the noises and bass lines that he was going to do for "Lazy Afternoon." I hadn't been there earlier in the day, because I went to see Fishbone at Temple's "Spring Fling." But later on I was there sitting at the drum set, because I'd have to play the beats that we wanted Rahzel to re-create [by beatboxing]. Rahzel didn't really know the breaks that I was playing necessarily, but if you tell him what to do, he'll execute it. That song was recorded in between breaks of "Lazy Afternoon"—we just kept the DAT running, like we usually did. The funny thing was that Rah still didn't know what my name was at that point, because we had just met each other. You can hear him call me "Roots." My drums weren't even mic'ed on that song—all that sound is from his mic.

DO YOU WANT MORE?!!!??! *Featuring Steve Coleman, Josh Roseman, Graham Haynes, and Rufus Harley*

Ahmir: That was the third of Tariq's bass lines that he gave Hub to play. It was the first song that we worked on during the second day of recording. Tariq just wrote one long-ass verse on it, and it was cool, but it was missing something. A week later I was watching Arsenio Hall and there was a thing that I guess was a version of [David Letterman's] "Stupid Human Tricks." And I saw this dude with long-ass dreadlocks, wearing a kilt and playing the bagpipes. I told Rich about it and he knew it must be [jazz bagpipe virtuoso] Rufus Harley, and that actually really depressed him to hear that he was doing something like that, since Rich was such a jazz fiend. Even crazier was that Rufus was from Philly. We had no idea. So we were in Sigma

Sound and we just looked him up in the White Pages and called him. He didn't believe that we'd actually pay him, so he wanted the cash up front, and he got his fifteen hundred dollars when he walked in the door. Because the bagpipes are just in one particular key, we had to devise a way to slow the song down so that he could play along with it and solo over it. He knocked it out with fifteen minutes to spare and left to go pick up his son at school. We never saw him again after that.

ESSAYWHUMAN?!!!??! *Featuring Steve Coleman, recorded live at Trocadero, December 1993*

Tariq: The show we recorded that song at was great! It was our party to celebrate getting our record deal with Geffen. We hired Jeru the Damaja, Rahzel, and maybe Onyx too. And Ruff House [Records] wanted the Fugees on there, because they were new at the time and they didn't know what to do with them. On a track like that one, it was different every time we performed it. I just went with whatever I felt like saying. It would be a challenge for me to sing some shit that they couldn't replay, and I always tried. It's like that old song "Dueling Banjos."

Ahmir: That show we recorded that at was at the Trocadero in Philly, after we had gotten signed to Geffen, to celebrate. It was the result of a three-year buildup of local acclaim. It was all about how Josh Abrams [who isn't on the track] and I learned to trade fours with a saxophone player in our classes. We just applied it to hip-hop. That night was significant because just that week I had ended my internship at Ruff House Records, and I did a favor for one of my bosses, because he had helped us do the "Pass the Popcorn" [from *Organix*] video, which cost seven hundred dollars. The favor was to let a new Ruff House group open the show with a fifteen-minute set. It was this girl I recognized from [the soap opera] "As the World Turns," because my mom watched it, and a whole bunch of the most gangly-looking Jamaicans I had ever seen. Although we later found out they were Haitian. That was the Fugees, in their Philly debut. To be honest with you, I don't think the Fugees realized their full potential until they saw a couple Roots shows [*laughs*].

Ahmir: We ran out of two-inch tape when we were recording that, which is why the song ends after Tariq says, "I'm on a mission." There was a third verse that just never got recorded. I think Cassandra Wilson brought that track to life, and we wanted her on there because that one had the easiest melody for her to work with.

Tariq: Yeah, I remember running out of tape on that one. I don't remember what the verse that got cut off was, but it didn't bother me. We labored over the *sound* of songs, but shit like that, we never sweated over that.

YOU AIN'T FLY

Tariq: Ahmir [who rhymes on one verse of the song] was pretty funny on the mic—it was comic relief. That song was just a narrative about different females. I know it was a stretch, but we even thought that one might turn into a club song.

Ahmir: I listened to the [original] verses on that song and I realized that there was something missing. There was no direct narrative. And I felt that the original verses those guys did were dangerously creeping into misogynist territory. I didn't rhyme back in the day, although people wanted me to, since they said I had a unique voice. But we already had incredible MCs in our midst, so why should I? Malik came up with his verse first, and I saw where it was going. Both of them had two verses each on the song, and only one each made it. The ones that got left behind were just too harsh, and I didn't see the point. Being the critical nerd that I was, I knew that the number-one trick to impress liberal [*Village Voice* yearly music poll] Pazz & Jop type critics was to always let the woman get the best of you on a hip-hop song. So I had to sacrifice myself on my verse, which only took me about fifteen minutes to write. I was the sole loser and that was fine, because that shit was the truth anyways!

Ahmir: We knew that that song was going to be a hit with everyone. Even Biggie loved that song. He sung it to us when he first met us. [*Ahmir does spot-on imitation of Notorious B.I.G. singing "Silent Treatment."*] That was the greatest validation ever! That was the first song that we worked on for the album. With that one, we were just kind of mocking Jodeci and R&B songs in general. Somehow that song just came out of it. With Cassandra on there, that was like our first real celebrity moment. All the girls we dated, they all came into the studio to see Cassandra. I wasn't even listening to Cassandra's stuff much back then, but I knew how great she was. She knocked out her parts on there in about an hour. That song was pretty long [6:53], but most of our songs back then were pretty long. I was already thinking about our box set! Tariq's mix is my favorite one. It was an homage to [Camden, New Jersey's unsung hip-hop heroes] the Krown Rulers. We also got sued for that remix, which was a rare thing for the Roots. We did an interpolation of Bill Summers's stuff on the Headhunters. He thought we sampled it, but we hadn't, so it was an interpolation, not a sample clearance. He still thinks we did to this day! I guess I'm partially flattered and partially insulted by that.

Tariq: We never worried about doing a slower song like that. Certain songs are just undeniable. I was writing the lyrics to that as they were working on the music. Back then if they put down music, I could have my vocals ready five minutes later. I didn't write my verse on there about anyone in particular.

THE LESSON PART 1 *Featuring Rahzel and Dice Raw*

Ahmir: That's my favorite song on the album, because it's so simple. The showing-off thing can sometimes really ring very minstrel for me. We did that right at the end of recording, on Cobain Day. Rich pointed out that we didn't have any songs that really heavily featured Rahzel's forte: beatboxing. The revelation of that song was discovering that the fifteen-year-old nuisance kid named Dice Raw was ill on the mic. He was in the crew through Kelo and Rich, and he was always hanging around, but I never paid much attention to him. Kelo convinced me to let him on, and Dice walked in and did that in one take, with only one punch-in.

Tariq: That was one of my favorites on the album, if not my favorite. I didn't always know that Dice Raw was that nice, but I had learned it by the time he got on that track. The day I met him, I heard him rap and thought he was dope. He was young, but there was no question about his skill. Rahzel was on there, and he brought more than just a percussion thing to the Roots. He brought an element that made us more than mortal, especially onstage. He brought out the competitive edge in us.

THE UNLOCKING *Featuring Ursula Rucker*

Ahmir: Two weeks before Cobain Day, we had gotten in touch with our friend Ntozake Shange, poet extraordinaire and teacher. She agreed to be on the track that would close our album, and we went to her house and we all talked in great detail about what she would do. It was very important for us to dispel the image that I think most people have of hip-hop, which is that it's antiwoman. The day she was supposed to record we showed up at her house when she said she'd be there and she wasn't there. We waited thirty minutes, kept calling, buzzed her doorbell. Then eventually a guy answered the phone and said she had just left for Barbados! We were just dumbfounded. Honestly we haven't seen her since, to this day. But it just so happened that Ursula Rucker, who was an up-and-coming poet in Philly, worked around the corner from the studio at the Painted Bride [performing arts space]. If there was ever a person who I have come across who was ready for their close-up, it was Ursula on that day. She did that poem in one take and all our jaws absolutely dropped. The funniest shit was at the very end where she says: "What's my name?" After that, in the studio, I was saying, "I wish we had something else there, for an even bigger exclamation point." At that point, out of the blue, Tariq reaches into his pocket and pulls out a Glock. And I was like: "What the *fuck* are you doing? Is that real? Where did you get that?" So he walks up to the mic and told the engineer to hit record, and we thought he was going to let off a round in the studio.

But he just cocked it, and that's the last sound you hear. In mastering, I insisted that Tom Coyne turn that sound way up. That whole situation shows just how opposite Tariq and I were. I don't think I had ever even seen a gun up close like that before.

Tariq: Yeah, that was my gun on there. During the recording of that album, back in those days, there were a lot of guns around. Everyone always had one on them or out on the table. Malik and I and the company we kept had them. Maybe Ahmir just never caught it. He never had a gun—he just wasn't street like that.

RUN-DMC
Raising Hell

(Profile, 1986)

If there was one hip-hop group on top of the world at the end of 1985 it was most certainly Run-DMC, who had been on an unstoppable tear since their debut single, "Sucker MCs," in 1983. But even with gold and platinum albums under their belts (1984's *Run-DMC* and 1985's *King of Rock,* both on Profile), the group still had much more to accomplish. Darryl McDaniels, aka DMC, says today, "1986 was when Run-DMC really *became* Run-DMC. That's when we really gelled."

Raising Hell was only the cherry on the top of some of the best years a hip-hop artist or group has ever experienced. The group (also featuring Joseph "Run" Simmons and Jason "Jam Master Jay" Mizell) grew from modest beginnings in Hollis, Queens, with one main goal: to be iller than the old-school legends they worshipped. "Our whole thing was to be like the Cold Crush Brothers," says DMC. "To have the best show, the best rhymes, and the best DJ, with more beats than anybody. Cold Crush were our idols, and all we wanted to do was be better than them. In 1983 Cold Crush were on their way down because they wasn't making powerful records.

"On [1986's] 'My Adidas' we said that we took the beat from the street and put it on TV," he continues. "And that's exactly what we did. We didn't really think it was pioneering, we just did what rappers before us was doing on tapes. When a lot of the old guys, like Kool Moe Dee, Treacherous Three, and Grandmaster Flash, got in the studio, they never put their greatness on records. Me and Run and Jay would listen to tapes in our basement and we'd say, 'They didn't do that shit last night in the Bronx! What the hell is this 'Birthday Rap' shit and 'What's your zodiac sign?' So we said that we weren't going to be fake. We ain't gonna wear no costumes. We're gonna keep it real."

Believe it or not, even though they had huge sales and loads of critical success with their first two albums, the group knew that they hadn't even begun to spread their wings artistically. "Everything before *Raising Hell* was written when we was in the shower, on the way to the studio, or even at the studio," DMC explains. "A lot of the rhymes on the first two albums was just stuff we had in our rhyme books from way back, and Russell [Simmons, the group's manager and Run's brother] let us put it on record. But we didn't want to make no more corny, bullshit records. With a lot of [tracks] on the first two [albums], you like them, and you can recite them because you've listened to the album a lot. But they weren't *dope*.

"We wanted to do an album where every track on there is our best," he continues. "At the time we didn't think that [certain] tracks on the first two albums were necessarily filler, but after *Raising Hell* we looked back and saw them that way. We knew both albums could have been doper, especially after what we did in 1986. When we were making *Raising Hell* there were records we looked back at on the first two albums and said, 'We should never have made that one.' " With their change in attitude also came a change in format and songwriting. "Back then it was like: 'You rhyme, I rhyme, then Jay, you scratch,' " DMC says. "But *Raising Hell* was Run-DMC working simultaneously. That's why the album came out so def."

So after worldwide tours in 1984 and 1985, the group was finally ready to record their masterpiece, which they had sketched out on the Fresh Fest 2 U.S. tour in 1985, which also followed their film debut in 1985's *Krush Groove*. "We wrote that whole album [*Raising Hell*] on the road, that's why it was so dope," DMC says. "We would write a song every night after a great performance, so we had a lot of energy and momentum going."

There were some important changes within the Run-DMC camp at the time. For one, the group was starting to grow apart from producer Larry Smith, who had worked with the trio for their first two albums. DMC says that there wasn't any bad blood. "It was actually more [his choice]," he recalls. "He wanted to do a lot of musical stuff, more complex things, but we wanted to keep it raw. He wanted to do Whodini type of stuff [Smith was producing Whodini and Run-DMC concurrently in 1984 and 1985]. What he had for us we didn't need anymore. It wasn't that we didn't want it, it's just that we had our shit down pat because it was us three on the road every night. It was like, 'We got dope shit and we're gonna use *our* shit this time, not yours.' I don't think Larry was pissed. We just all wanted to do something different."

Returning home to Queens in late 1985 after their extensive touring, they soon put themselves on lockdown at Chung King studios in Manhattan for three months. In place of producer Smith, a cocky new maverick was brought in: Rick Rubin. "Rick came in because he had the rock thing, and we wanted to take rock to the left," says D. "We went to Rick's dorm room at NYU and he had like every rock record in the world. Plus he could play stuff on guitar. So we said, 'We need this guy, Russell.' Rick was that sound we wanted at that time."

Even though Rubin's and Russell's names were on the production marquee, DMC says that the two non-group members oversaw and added to the music on *Raising Hell* more than create it. "Rick and Russell got production credit, but we [the group members] really did everything," he states. "They just put their names up there so they could look big. Rick was very hands-on, no doubt about it, but we were in charge. Rick would give us ideas and we'd just run with it. Russell would sit back and say, 'Go left! Go right! Go up! Go down!' He directed everything."

After slaying audiences with the material on the road every night for months on end, the Run-DMC that walked into Chung King had the eye of the tiger. "Our main goal with *Raising Hell* was to have the best tape [*he emphasizes this format, rather than* album, *likely to hark back to the old days*] of anyone else's being sold," he says. "People used

Run-DMC (left to right: DMC, Jam Master Jay, Run) in Hollywood, 1994.
PHOTO: B+ (FOR WWW.MOCHILLA.COM).

to buy a lot of Cold Crush tapes, so we wanted to have the fullest tape rolling around. And since we were huge at that point, we had the chance to put it on an album for everyone to hear.

"We did that album in like three months," DMC recalls. "It was so quick because every rhyme was written on the road and had been practiced and polished. We knew what we wanted to do. Rick was all music and instruments. Jay was music and DJing. And me and Run was lyrics. Run and I would tell them to change this thing and that with the music from time to time, because we was the ones rapping over it. We definitely had a game plan.

"Some songs were on the radio before the label even had a chance to figure out what they was gonna do with them," he adds. "Songs like 'My Adidas,' 'Peter Piper,' and 'Hit It Run.' We took them right to the radio stations as soon as they were recorded. Red Alert, Chuck Chillout, and Mr. Magic. And they ate 'em up! Then, after we finished the album [in early 1986], we did a show at the Apollo for two nights. And instead of playing old shit, we did the whole *Raising Hell* album. People went *crazy,* and they hadn't even heard the songs before. That's when we knew the album was dope. It was the proof we needed."

There were, of course, numerous highlights on *Raising Hell.* But none was more impressive than their first worldwide smash, "Walk This Way," a cover of the Aerosmith rock perennial with group members Steven Tyler and Joe Perry on board. That was exactly what Rubin's new rock angle brought to the table, and it's a big reason why the album ended up selling, as DMC says, "Around six million, something like that. That's what they told us. Worldwide maybe like ten or eleven million copies." (The RIAA's website lists the album as triple platinum in the U.S. as of 1987.)

Although "Walk This Way" was the second single, it was the album's first video and most certainly a main reason why the single took off like it did. Why was there no video for the first single, "My Adidas"? "We was on the road too much—we didn't have time to do a video for it," says DMC.

The group also continued to expand upon its duties as role models, especially with the song "Proud to Be Black," the album's parting shot. "We knew that there was power in this music," DMC says. "We could teach, we could innovate, we could inspire and motivate. We made it cool to put messages in lyrics. [*He rhymes the first verse of "Sucker MCs."*] Nobody ever bragged about going to college! Especially in the 'hood. But we knew we could make education cool—we knew we could make a difference.

"It's definitely our best album," he says. "Everything about it was perfect to me. That album was everything that hip-hop was and wanted to be. It brought hip-hop to life, for every generation, every race, creed, and color. No one could hate it. It stands as the only album we really *made,* and it made us the legends that we are today. That's because it was a visual record. We did it live onstage every night, before we even went into the studio. Everything now and then was and is too one-sided. It wasn't broad enough. But that changed with *Raising Hell.* It was a record that everybody just *got.*"

And in tribute to Jam Master Jay, the main musical force in the group and a sorely missed hip-hop legend, DMC remembers, "He was the first DJ to DJ for the rap cause. We didn't use no band, we didn't use no tape play-back, we never had a DAT. Jay DJed vinyl, live. Without Jay there's no Run-DMC, and that's why we disbanded. We can't make records anymore, because Jay was the backbone of the group. He was every DJ then, today, and in the future. Hip-hop brings joy, happiness, enlightens people, and makes them think. Jay did all those things as a DJ, an artist, and as a person. There will never be another."

TRACKS

PETER PIPER

That was our collective favorite record on the album, because it was a rap/DJ record. Jay cut that all up live in the studio. We had been rhyming over that loop [Bob James's "Take Me to the Mardi Gras"] since before rap records was even made. We always used to just freestyle over those beats, but for the album song we wrote those lyrics down, while we was on the road.

IT'S TRICKY

That was a routine like [the] Cold Crush [Brothers] used to do, how they'd use a melody from another record and put their names and words in there. That was just based on [*he sings Toni Basil's hit "Mickey"*]. So I just changed the chorus around and we just talked about how this rap business can be tricky to a brother. It was our idea but Rick [Rubin] had a lot of musical input on that one. He and Jay both. With that video, we didn't know who Penn and Teller [the magicians, who were featured in the video] was. I have a line about my dad in there. When we'd go on the road my parents became celebrities in our neighborhood. They couldn't go to the market without getting recognized. They enjoyed it—they were famous too.

MY ADIDAS

That was the first single, with "Peter Piper." We were sponsored by Adidas, and that was definitely a big deal. But more to other people than to us. We was just intent on bustin' ass. We wore Adidas and then everyone started wearing Adidas, but we didn't want people to dress like us. We just wanted people to like our beats and rhymes. We got the sponsorship deal in 1985, the night we had everyone hold their Adidas up at Madison Square Garden. Someone at Adidas heard about us and sent a rep out to one of our shows to spy. And he saw how big it was.

WALK THIS WAY

One day me and Jay was in the studio and we was sampling Aerosmith and Rick said, "Yo, do you know who that is?" and we was like, "No, but we like this beat." We used to always rap over that beat in the 'hood. We didn't know the group name or anything. So Rick gave us the 411, the whole history of the band. We had our own rhymes over the beat, but Rick said, "No, do *their* lyrics." Jay was the person that knew that "Walk This Way" was going to be a hit. Me and Run had our doubts—we thought it was taking the rock 'n' roll shit a little far. Because me and Run didn't want to use their lyrics, we thought that they was hillbilly gibberish. We was so pissed, but Jay was a visionary—he saw it. After Jay gave us a kick in the head we went in and laid down the [Aerosmith] vocals. If you listen to their version and our version, a lot of it isn't the same, because we couldn't understand what they was saying. We just went by what it sounded like. We never got to do our own original lyrics because they knew that if we had, then we wouldn't have learned the Aerosmith lyrics.

When Steven Tyler came into the studio, Jay was cutting up [Aerosmith's original version of] "Walk This Way" and he said, "Here's what we used to do with your record." And Steve said, "Yo, when are you gonna hear *me*?" And Jay looked up and said, "We never get to hear you. After this guitar riff, it's back to the beginning." And Steve thought that was so amusing. Those guys were real cool. That record was a rebirth [for Aerosmith] and a birth, because as a result you have Kid Rock, Limp Bizkit, Korn, all of those bands today. But that wasn't even our first rock-rap record. "Rock Box," on the first album, was the best one we did. We always used to rock over rock beats in the street. We wanted to be hard, and rock was hard. Other groups didn't use as much rock because they didn't know *how*. A lot of them still don't get it right.

After we did the video to "Walk This Way" we was like, "That's a wrap, we don't gotta make no more videos." That one let us know that we was more than just rappers, we were rock stars. So we didn't want to keep making videos because it might spoil the greatness of that one. Any ones after that one was just because we wanted to make one to go with a record. We were never able to do a better one. "Walk This Way" was serious and historical and everything else was comedy and fun. Some nights out on tour we'd have to play "Walk This Way" first because there were nothing but white people out there who had only heard that song. Then they'd buy the album and the next time we came to town they'd be yelling for "My Adidas."

IS IT LIVE

The go-go flavor on there was because of Davy D [David Reeves, aka Davy DMX]. You remember Davy D, right? He was involved in production on that one. He had a lot of beats, and just as many records as [Afrika] Bambaataa. He's not listed on the [*Raising Hell*] album, but he was there. He did a lot more on [Run-DMC's 1988 album] *Tougher Than Leather*. We loved go-go and we did shows in D.C. all the time. People get into a go-go trance, it's like voodoo down there.

PERFECTION

That was our drum record. This kid Styxx played drums on that—he was Run's neighbor's son. He was maybe thirteen at the time and he was dope. We wanted to make a song like [Doug E. Fresh and Slick Rick's] "La Di Da Di," but we didn't want to bite. So instead of Run doing the beatbox like Doug E. Fresh, we got a drummer. A lot of people still love that record.

HIT IT RUN

That's Run on beatbox, like we did onstage every night. We started doing that song live around 1985, just the same way as it came out on the album. That's probably my favorite track on the album, because I'm poppin' *sooo* much shit on there! And I love Run doing the beatbox [*laughs*]! That record just has a lot of energy—it's like our battle anthem, our park jam.

RAISING HELL

That one definitely has a Beastie Boys influence on there. Because of Rick [who produced the Beastie Boys' album *Licensed to Ill*], and also because the Beasties took stuff from us and we took stuff from them. We learned that punk rock is just as hip-hop as Afrika Bambaataa is. And you can be silly and still be dope. Rick played guitar on there, and he was definitely getting his rocks off, especially towards the end [*laughs*].

YOU BE ILLIN'

Run thought of that one—he wanted to do a record like Prince, that type of funk and R&B. But we had to put some humor on it so people wouldn't say, "What the hell are they doin', trying to be Prince?" We met Prince a lot of times, but we never performed with him.

DUMB GIRL

That was what people in the South was doing, with the deep bass [*imitates deep bass thump*]. Back then there was a lot of dumb girls runnin' around, so we paid our ode to the dumb girls. We wanted to be humorous and not too preachy.

SON OF BYFORD

That was just a beatbox routine we would do live onstage. It started as a freestyle, but we did it all the time and we all wanted to put it on the album. That's my dad's name, Byford. The song was always that short [as it appears on the album]. People would go crazy when we did that shit.

That song was influenced by Public Enemy, because we would hang around them all the time. They didn't have records out yet but we'd go to their radio station, WBAU in Long Island. Chuck was like a father—he would educate us. So we said, "Let's make a record that Chuck might make." We all went to college and that record was more about education than a black thing, really. We wanted to educate kids. Nineteen eighty-six was a perfect year for a song like that, for the transition. Because back then in the 'hood it was either be a basketball player or a drug dealer. The world is bigger than just going to the party and having fun.

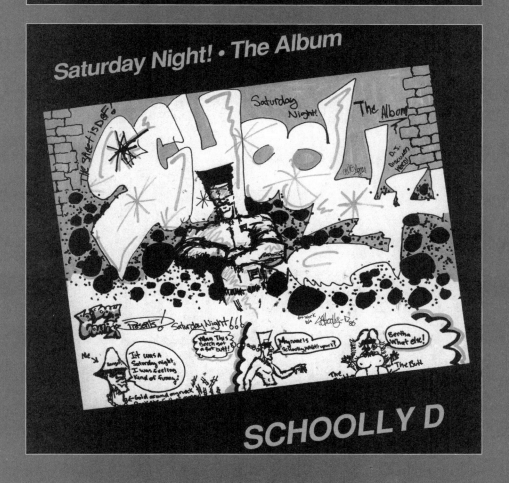

I knew I was going to do this when I was nine or ten years old. I knew I wasn't going to be the weatherman or working in some office. I was either going to be some crazy painter or a musician," says Jesse B. Weaver Jr., aka Schoolly D. Schoolly actually ended up doing both of his prophesized vocations, in a way. A musician, for sure, and a crazy painter as well—of street tales. Straight outta Philly, he invented gangsta rap, and his charisma and approach were immeasurably influential in the rap world.

"I first started thinking I was gonna be a DJ—I used to spin records all the time," he remembers. "But there was like twenty DJs in the crew and like ten rappers. So I went with rapping." The crew in question was the Park Side Killers, aka the 5-2 Crew (named after their part of West Philly, Parkside Avenue and Fifty-second Street), consisting of Royal Ron, Pimp Pretty, Disco Len, Mixmaster Mark, and T-Ski Flash. "I was the last cat to be let in," Schoolly adds.

Immortalized in the songs "P.S.K. What Does It Mean?" and "Parkside 5-2," they were his musical family. Royal Ron was younger than Schoolly, but was a father to his style. He taught Jesse how to become Schoolly D. "Ron made me work hard at rapping," Schoolly recalls. "He put a lot of thought into his words, a lot of complex stuff. And when everyone was trying to be Melle Mel or Kurtis Blow, he told me to just be myself. He was also the first guy I knew with a [Roland] 909 [drum machine], and he let me borrow it." Aside from his lyrics, Schoolly's use of the 909 was his calling card, and with his potent mix of subwoofer-shredding beats and lyrical mischief, Mr. D messed up rap music forever.

Schoolly was born in the City of Brotherly Love, high-schooled in Atlanta, and then landed back in West Philly. In 1984 he began his assault on the rap industry at the age of nineteen with his first two self-released singles, "Gangster Boogie/Maniac" and "C.I.A./Cold Blooded Blitz" (both on his Schoolly D Records label). The combined four songs were an odd mix. "Maniac" was straight electro, with processed space-mutant vocals on the chorus and high-pitched keyboards. "C.I.A.," on the other hand, stood for "Crime in Action," an uplifting tribute to the artistic efforts of local graffiti writers. " 'C.I.A' was me trying to be positive," Schoolly chuckles. "A week after I put that out I was laughin' at myself. It sounded like every record I *didn't* want to do. It was so forced."

After his singles that year, he sought advice from Philly rap radio goddess Lady B in a meeting that cemented his desire to go for self. Schoolly remembers, "I took 'Gangster Boogie' [a prototypical gangsta rap track] to her and she said: 'Are you crazy? Go back and do something else, like Grandmaster Flash. You'll never get signed talking about guns and drugs. Not until you do something positive.' So I said: 'Fuck that shit, I'll just keep putting records out myself.' " Schoolly's course was set—no more positive messages and no more asking for people's permission to do anything in the rap game.

Schoolly's first DJ was a guy named DLB, featured on the first two singles and then never heard from again (at least not on a Schoolly track). The reason? "He was a chicken!" Schoolly laughs. "In the studio he could do anything, but when it came time to perform onstage he always had cold feet. That muthafucka said he had tennis elbow and couldn't perform. And he don't even play tennis!" The problem of DLB's absence was solved quickly enough. DJ Code Money, just out of high school in 1984 and a family friend (Schoolly's older brother served in Vietnam with Code's father), "just walked up to me and said that he wanted to DJ." And, like many other things in Schoolly's musical life, that was that. Code was a skilled DJ and an innovative one for the time. DJs were making names for themselves back in '85, but they were still mostly relegated to flashing out between verses only. Schoolly points out, "Code was one of the first DJs to scratch through a whole fuckin' record, not just on the chorus."

Schoolly's true musical calling card, the song that people remember him for even to this day, came in 1985 with the single "P.S.K. What Does It Mean?" with "Gucci Time" on the flip. Both songs were cooked up in a classical recording studio, with the aid of a massive reverb chamber. "In 1985 there were *no* rap studios, not in Philly at least," he says. "So we had to go to a real studio, with this guy we called Jeff Cheesesteak [engineer Jeff Chestek]. We recorded 'P.S.K.,' 'Gucci Time,' and 'Freestyle Rappin' ' there. And the craziest shit was that they had a real reverb, not just a processing effect. It was these big fucking plates—they took up a whole room. It takes like three or four people just to move them around.

"Even years later I've tried to get that sound again, but I can't," Schoolly laments. "People ask me how the fuck I got that sound [as heard on the

Schoolly D (at left, with his hype-man Cheese)
in Philadelphia, 1995.

booming "P.S.K.," for example] and I still can't duplicate it. One other thing with the recording back in those days is that we was *hiiiiigh*. It was like—*puff puff*—more reverb! More reverb [*laughs*]! We stayed at that studio working and smoking all night, until like six in the morning, and when I woke up at one or two the next day I played it and was like, 'What the fuck is this?' But I played it for the crew and they went ballistic. It was instant. Those songs went everywhere in like six months."

Both cuts were combinations of booming drum programs and Schoolly's dusted, arrogant style, detailing—in decidedly un-PC fashion, and laced with profanity—the alleged tales of his Park Side Killers crew and Schoolly's own actions in his quest to take out all biters. The rap world had never heard anything quite like it, and fans took notice, snatching up copies anywhere they could. The demand was so large, in fact, that nationwide bootlegging was a major distribution avenue for Schoolly, albeit an unpaid one. "Those bootleggers made me big because when it came down to it, I didn't have the money to get the records out there," he explains. "The person who helped me figure that shit out was Luke [Luther Campbell of 2 Live Crew and Luke Skyywalker Records]. He took me all over Miami and showed me all the different bootlegged versions of my own records. It was crazy."

Schoolly even jokes that, in his opinion, the infamous Vincenzo the Godfather of Vinyl (legendary in the annals of Philly old-school mythology) "made 'P.S.K.' go gold because he bootlegged it so much." Success came quick, partially because of Schoolly's learn-on-the-fly business savvy (aided by eventual Ruff House Records head honcho Chris Schwartz) and also because he continued to pave new ground in the rap world—gangsta ground, which would soon be emulated and expanded upon by Ice-T and N.W.A. out west. Schoolly claims that the "P.S.K./Gucci Time" single "definitely went over five hundred thousand" in sales. But since many of those weren't accounted for, he'll never be sure. Either way, he made paper and a name for himself on the national scene.

By 1986 he was in the studio recording his debut LP, *Saturday Night! The Album,* originally released on Schoolly D and rereleased with extra tracks as part of a "disheartening" multialbum deal with Jive. "I signed with them partially to pay a lot of bills that we had, because distributors weren't paying me for the records I was selling," he says. "Jive didn't understand that I was an *artist,* not an entertainer. You can tell an entertainer what to do, but you can't do that to an artist. It insults them."

The artist part of Schoolly's work was no joke, especially regarding his productions, which favored the heavy kick of the Roland TR-909 drum machine. "My brother was a drummer, so I used to study him," Schoolly explains. "By 1985 I had mastered the 909. I'd stay up until five in the morning, just trying to get better at it. I was like drum-machine crazy. The [Roland TR-] 727 had the best cowbell and percussion sounds, the [Roland TR-] 505 had the best hi-hats. At first I didn't want to use the SP-12 [E-mu's then newly unveiled sampling drum machine, which could sample drums from records or other external sources, instead of relying on pre-programmed sounds], but when I saw that I could link up all my machines and use that, I went even more crazy."

His production methods might have been powerful and influential, but they weren't necessarily complicated. "I'd do the drums first," he explains. "Then we just sat there and smoked and drank until we got silly enough and drunk enough. At that point, the first thing that hit my mind—that was the song. We kept the tape rolling and we'd just do it over and over again and by the end of the night I'd have the song down on tape."

After getting barred from the classical studio they used for the "P.S.K." single, they landed at a more rap-friendly recording haven: INS Studios in New York. "The only way I knew how to record back then was like old James Brown style, all in the room at the same time," Schoolly explains. "If you listen real close to 'P.S.K.' and 'Gucci Time' you can hear me hittin' the buttons [on the drum machine], rappin' at the same time, with Code cuttin'. But the cats at INS were like, 'You don't have to do that, you know.' "

Schoolly's first real introduction to the world at large (thanks to legitimate distribution), 1987's Jive version of *Saturday Night! The Album* was a major event in rap's teenage years. It was drenched in his unique vocalese and flippant and frequently hilarious lyrical content (he admits to letting the music take over certain tracks because he "didn't have anything more to say"), DJ Code Money's influential scratches, and, perhaps most important, Schoolly's crisp conga-and-timbale-drenched drum programs. The album was well received by rap fans around the world and was almost immeasurably influential.

Schoolly says that one Jive decision had an adverse effect on his next album, the still warmly received and definitely dope *Smoke Some Kill* from 1988. "The extra tracks they added to the second [Jive] version of *Saturday Night* [including 'Parkside 5-2,' 'Housing the Joint,' and 'Get N' Paid'] were actually supposed to be for *Smoke Some Kill*," he explains. "It was a total scam to reissue *Saturday Night* like they did, with those tracks, because it had already sold hundreds of thousands of copies. If those tracks would have come out on *Smoke Some Kill* like they were supposed to, it would have been an even better record."

In the end, *Saturday Night! The Album* was everything that Schoolly D was all about: funk, loose rhymes, and attitude. It was the embodiment of his own personal philosophy, which he sums up as: "Stick to your guns, because you're either gonna catch up to the world or the world's gonna catch up to you. If you're a true artist, just stick to your guns. I'm glad I did, because I love my freedom."

TRACKS

P.S.K. WHAT DOES IT MEAN? *Originally released as a single in 1985*

"P.S.K." sold a hundred thousand copies in New York before they even knew I was from Philly. People were trying to figure out where I was from, because no one from Philly had made that impact before. It's really very simple, that drumbeat. I came up with it sittin' at the dinner table at my mom's, with my 909 and my headphones on. And she's like, "We're trying to eat dinner, so take that shit and get the fuck away from the goddamn table!" And I was like, "But Ma, I'm trying to create a masterpiece!" "Master yo ass!" she said. I used to always listen how they'd put together hi-hats in all the James Brown songs, and I just listened and listened and listened. It's similar to "Gucci Time," but "Gucci Time" was more about the hi-hats. Code did all the scratches on "P.S.K." With that track we was fucked up. We was high. It was the first big thing we did in a big studio, and it kind of made us nervous. When we recorded that, the engineer, Jeff Cheesesteak, was all nervous, too, with eight black guys showing up. He was worried about motherfuckers stealing shit, which they did. I didn't know, but all my homies was upstairs cleanin' out all kinds of microphones. I made them bring the mics back, though. At about five or six in the morning, after so many takes, I was like, "Yeah, that's *right*." It made the speakers do this kind of sucking motion and that's when I knew it was right. The engineer, Jeff, was like, "What the fuck are you doing to my speakers?"

GUCCI TIME *Originally released on the "P.S.K." single, 1985*

We recorded that one the same night as "P.S.K." DLB [Schoolly's original DJ] did the scratches for it. People used to bite my shit a lot, because we used to make mixtapes and sell them around town. We would sit in the room and just make tapes and copy them—we had like eight tape decks running at the same time. I used some nursery rhyme shit with those lyrics, like P-Funk did on [their song] "Let's Take It to the Stage." I took a lot of my writing style from George Clinton and Richard Pryor. Pryor could be real mean, but he knew you couldn't get your point across unless you make muthafuckas laugh a bit. I was influenced by those two more than any rappers.

HOUSING THE JOINT

Me and Spoonie Gee was going through a little somethin' back then. He made a record about me ["The Godfather"] saying I stole his style. So that was a response to that. Later on we did shows together and it was cool. I only performed that song live once, and that was because Chuck D was on the bill and he liked it so much. I got the idea for that song out in California when I saw Sly Stone on some talk show and they played [Sly's song] "Thank You (Fallentinme Be Mice Elf Agin)" when he came out. I got home, got that Sly record, booked some studio time, made the track, did the rap, and recorded it all in one day. For some reason I just never felt comfortable doing that one live.

WE GET ILL

That was a Bootsy [Collins]–inspired track. If you listen you can hear Bootsy's shit all over that track. It was going to be an instrumental originally. But everybody at the time was saying "We get ill," so I went back and did vocals over it.

DO IT, DO IT

That started in Code's basement, before we were going to record "Saturday Night." We rarely did anything at Code's house, but he started just going back and forth with that Funkadelic ["You'll Like It Too"] break and I started rapping over it. He put the tape machine on record and we taped it. That was the first time we worked with Joe ["the Butcher" Nicolo]. We did it on three tracks, with one each for the drum program, Code cutting, and me rapping. Joe looked at us like, "Aren't you going to put anything else on there?" since we had twenty-four tracks to use. And we said, "Nope, that's it." That was his introduction to hip-hop. The "big bad wolf" stuff on there came from an old nursery rhyme record and Code cut that up. It was his message for all other DJs.

DEDICATION TO ALL B-BOYS

That's something I always really wanted to do, and it was inspired by the Commodores. I was doing the drum program and Code started singing [the Commodores song] "Young Girls Are My Weakness," and it was just magic. That early shit was all just magic. There are a lot of [DJ] cuts at the end because people always wanted to hear as much as possible. I recorded records the way I heard records. Isaac Hayes always made long records, and you never got tired of it. Also, [when you performed] live, people wanted to hear the long break at the end. Just like in rock and funk groups, everybody who was part of the band got to do their thing. And Code was part of the band.

GET N' PAID

That was about shit we was going through at the time. You show up at these shows and everybody got a goddamn excuse. The promoter would say, "Yo, School, I'll be back. My grandmom's sick, but you just go on and by the time you're off, I'll be back and I'll pay you." Then after we're done it's like, "Where's Jo Jo?" "Oh, Jo Jo left with two bitches right about when you went onstage." So we was like, "Gimme my money before I go on, or I ain't rappin'."

DIS GROOVE IS BAD

That's when I first started fuckin' around with the 808, with the heavy, sub-low kick drum. Code came up with that concept. I was also messing around with the SP-12. I was sampling the 909 and the 808. I worked on that track for two days, then played it for Code and he started scratching over it. That was the first track that I used the 808 and the SP-12 on. I was sampling all those 808s off of old Mantronix records before that. With that backwards tape stuff at the end, that was Joe [Nicolo] and his tricks. He wanted to be part of things, so that's how he did it.

PARKSIDE 5-2

5-2 is for Fifty-second Street. I had already done the drum program for that and we just sat in the studio smokin' and drinkin', like usual. I said: "Parkside!" and then Pimp Pretty said: "5, 5 . . . 2," just like that. I talk about lots of my growing-up stuff in there. Royal Ron taught me how to rap and always helped me keep my shit straight. Disco Len was the first DJ in the neighborhood, and the guy who always had money. He was basically the guy who kept me from doing anything illegal. That song had a lot of lyrics on it, for me. Sometimes with a song I'm just like, "You know, I ain't got no more to say." It's just that simple. Sometimes the music just speaks so strong that you don't need as many lyrics. Some songs are about what I got to say and the music is secondary. Some tracks, the music is in the front, on purpose.

B-BOY RHYME AND RIDDLE

That's me and a live drummer at the same time. Joe [Nicolo] brought him in and wanted to experiment with it. Code just let the organ thing keep going. Right there it was just magic. I came up with the lyrics, ran in real quick, did the vocals, came back, and Joe's just lookin at me like I'm fuckin' crazy. The drummer was some cat from some group like Experimental Project or Product. He had burnt his eyelids off or something. On purpose. I like weird guys like that.

SATURDAY NIGHT

That track was actually an accident. It was a fuck-up! We got to the studio to record that track and Code forgot the AC [power] cord for the 909 after I had let him borrow it. I wasn't going home to get that shit, and they had a drum machine there [at the studio], so I programmed the beat into it. But by accident I hit some button and it made the kick and snare go to timbale sounds. I was like, "Whoa! What the fuck is this shit?" But I just kept looping it. And we just put it on tape right there. I can't even remember the name of the drum machine, and I've never seen it again. The original 909 program I did was the exact same, just without the timbales. A lot of that shit on that track actually happened. My mom didn't have a gun, but it *felt* like she had a gun. She did catch me plenty of fuckin' times trying to sneak somebody in the crib, and she fucked up my room and kicked some ass. It's truth, just a bit exaggerated.

IT'S KRACK

I just wanted to make a statement, that's why I put in those keyboards. I wasn't just a rap producer, I was a *music* producer. So I did that instrumental to show off my other talents. That's me playing keyboards, and Code named the song. Back in the day people was like, "Ahh, that shit is *crack*." Meaning it was hype like crack.

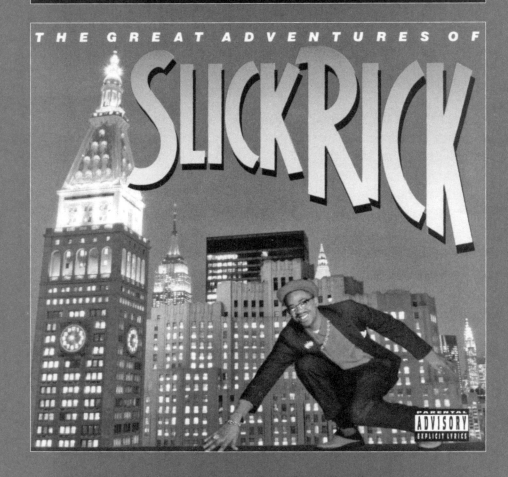

No one will ever forget the almighty Slick Rick, in part because of the four nonsensical words that started his illustrious MC career: "La Di Da Di." Released as the B-side of Doug E. Fresh and the Get Fresh Crew's 1985 smash hit "The Show" (on Reality/Danya), the famed vocal has endured even longer than its flip. Sampled by dozens of producers, covered by lyrical ascendant Snoop Dogg, cut up by DJs ad infinitum, and memorized by most Americans old and/or schooled enough to remember the hip-hop explosion of the eighties, it endures as Rick's defining rhyme, and is still part of his stage show.

The British-born and Bronx-raised Rick [Walters aka Ricky D] had storytelling skills from a very young age. "When I was growing up in the Bronx, everyone was into rapping," he remembers. "In junior high it was the big thing. We all used to bang on the desk and say raps and such. I guess I must have stood out. And once you stand out at something, you're probably going to end up pursuing it." Although many of his friends (including fellow storytelling master Dana Dane, with whom he went to high school, graduating in 1983) reveled in flowing off the top of the dome, Rick always preferred the lyric book. "I was never the type to say freestyle raps," he explains. "I usually tell a story, and to do that well I've always had to work things out beforehand."

Rick met Doug E. Fresh in 1984, when Doug was a judge at an MC contest he was entered in. "He liked my style and he started carrying me around with him," Rick says. "We used to do early versions of 'La Di Da Di' during his shows, with him doing beatbox and me rapping. Stuff like we was doing back then had never been heard before. Two guys with no instruments, just microphone and mouth. The crowd liked that song a lot, so we decided to make a record of it. To everybody's surprise, it did really well." As for his fans still loving that cut today even after all the other classics that Rick has churned out, he says, "Sure, I'm glad that the public still likes 'La Di Da Di.' I'm shocked that they do, honestly. I could understand more if they liked 'Children's Story' or 'Mona Lisa,' because 'La Di Da Di' is kinda slow. But if it makes the public happy, I'll do it all day long."

With his onstage and on-record rhyme skills, which specialized in evocative and frequently bawdy stories, Rick became a major attraction as part of Doug's high-energy stage show in 1985 and 1986. And in a move that disappointed Doug E. Fresh fans, Rick left at the apex of his popularity to pursue a solo career. There have been different stories of Rick's leaving, many of which focus on the paltry royalties he is rumored to have received from his part in "La Di Da Di." "I wasn't mad," Rick says. "I was a guest on Doug's ship—I wasn't an artist that was signed. The Get Fresh Crew was around before I was. I was a guest appearance. After the success of 'La Di Da Di' I figured it might be better to branch off and let Doug take control of his ship again, instead of us disputing over how to break up the pie. I was feeling like I should have gotten at least thirty-five to forty percent for royalties, but I can't really knock him. It was his ship. And I was still doing okay. Hell, it was better than working as a mail clerk."

After setting out on his own, it wasn't hard to find record-company suitors. He was signed to Def Jam in 1986 for an album—not a difficult task since he was being managed by Russell Simmons at the time. Nevertheless, Rick fell prey to some record-label delays. "There were conflicts with different producers and the label saying how they envisioned me, and me not agreeing with what they thought was hot," says Rick. "We had our little conflicts, so that stretched shit out a little longer. In the end, the label held some things up. Russell and Lyor [Cohen, at Def Jam] had their visions, I had mine."

The album recording itself started in 1987, even though the album didn't hit until late 1988. "It was hard for me to make a whole album," Rick says. "I was just a kid on the street who said one popular rap and that was it. Now it became a situation where you had to make twelve songs and it's all on you. It was a new experience and I didn't want it to sound wack. Plus you had to deal with a record label and their opinions and politics and all that. Most people were still just making singles back then, and I had never even envisioned making an album, so it was pretty crazy."

But after an almost two-year absence from the hip-hop spotlight, Rick returned with the monumental album *The Great Adventures of Slick Rick*. Impressively self-produced by Rick, with help on six tracks from Hank Shocklee and Eric Sadler (two-thirds of Public Enemy's legendary Bomb Squad) and on one from Run-DMC's Jam Master Jay, it's a wild ride through Rick's psyche, veering from highfalutinly moral to hilariously bawdy, with everything in between. Just a look at the song listing and you will quickly remember how important the album was: "Children's Story," "Mona Lisa," "Hey Young World," "The Ruler's Back," "Teenage Love."

Its greatness was shown to the world in time, but it didn't happen overnight. "The hype built slowly," Rick recalls. "When 'La Di Da Di' and 'The Show' was out, I was way up there—I was very popular and known. But there was a gap between then and the time when 'Children's Story' [the album's first single] came out. I had to regain that momentum and that hype again. During that time I wasn't performing at all. I was so used to performing with Doug, and I was like: 'How am I gonna do 'La Di Da Di' in a show without him?' "

Rick also had to build his confidence back up a bit after being out of the limelight. "When the album came out I just figured it was another rap album, like everybody else's," he says. "I knew I liked a lot of the songs and they made me dance, but that was about it. I think when you're younger what you want to do is just hear your record on the radio. That's just a great feeling. So that's all I really wanted. You're not thinking about how big it's gonna be, saleswise or any other way. My main thing was just that I didn't want to rhyme on no wack beats. I wanted to rhyme on stuff that was fun and that was hype. And I think I accomplished that."

Just as "La Di Da Di" had begun Slick Rick's career, *Great Adventures* cemented his place in hip-hop history. Rick's words, thoughts, lyrical execution, and smooth, British-tinged flow were—and still are—absolutely unique. "I think *Great Adventures* made its mark because my personality came through and the album had direction, to some degree," he says today. "It was almost like a diary: 'When I was nineteen, this is what happened and this is what I learned from it.' It's all just writing down life experiences as you go on. I just put them in rap form.

"Any time you've got something that isn't too preachy and has a positive point of view, it's going to last longer than if you're just having fun and doing straight party rhymes," Rick says, looking back on his classic. "People definitely remember that time in their life today, back in 1988. They remember hearing those songs for the first time back then, and I'm glad those were good times for them."

TRACKS

TREAT HER LIKE A PROSTITUTE

Jam Master Jay actually did the music for that. [*Author's note: Credit on the album says Rick produced this song. Rick may be confusing this with "The Ruler's Back," which actually does credit Jam Master Jay.*] It was something that me and Doug used to do, with [him on] the beatbox. We used to do it live and people used to just *snap.* The punch lines would always liven up a party. That was the only older song I did for the album. All the rest of them on there was new. That was like real-life experiences, and then making them humorous to a certain degree. I just figured that that was how it goes. It was more my outlook on life at the time. I wasn't trying to be disrespectful to no *good* women.

THE RULER'S BACK

"Teenage Love" was the first song that we did for release as a single, but "The Ruler's Back" was actually out before it. I put it out there to [DJ] Red Alert on a cassette. It started to get so much play that the label got mad at me [*laughs*]. We had a version of the track that was a little more bouncy, but we didn't get to drop that one. With the keyboard playing on there and other songs, it was definitely nothing too complex. Just a one-finger thing. I would just envision bringing in a whole orchestra, but do it one track at a time. Stuff like that is done in layers.

We got a little more creative with that one, with the sound effects. We tried to make it a visual picture, especially with the ending. The "Knock 'em out the box, Rick," was like the climax, the big party part. We did the overlapping vocals because we wanted to keep the effect that was on [Doug E. Fresh's] "The Show." I saw that scene in real life, so I just put it on paper and added a little fiction to make it more interesting. I didn't see the people get shot, but I saw the people go to jail and ruin their whole life.

THE MOMENT I FEARED

That was my track—I produced it. I don't know how they [Hank Shocklee and Eric Sadler] got credit for that. But that's another thing. It was a story of me envisioning myself—you know how when you're young you envision yourself being with the drug dealer's girl. And you just imagine yourself falling into a story like that.

LET'S GET CRAZY

I didn't really like that one. That was just filler. I didn't even write all of that shit. It was like somebody wrote it and I just fixed the raps so they didn't sound so crazy or whatever.

INDIAN GIRL (AN ADULT STORY)

That was a story that had a funny ending. We were just having fun. I didn't work on that one for *too* long. When that song and "Treat Her Like a Prostitute" came out, you had people saying they were bad and vulgar and all that. At the time I was writing them I wasn't thinking of being disrespectful to any religion or to women in general. I was just a young guy who was having fun. I figured "Indian Girl" would be humorous to other people just like it was to me when my friends were sitting around telling stories.

TEENAGE LOVE

The version I myself had done for that song was a more dancey type of track— you could definitely dance to it more than listen to it. But they envisioned doing it the way it came out. [*Author's note: By "they" he probably means Def Jam's Russell Simmons and Lyor Cohen and producers Shocklee and Sadler.*] That song was just expressions of what I went through in high school. You know, getting my heart broken and all that type of stuff. The rap wasn't written to follow the [LL Cool J] "I Need Love" trend, but the music was done for that type of feel. I think it was a good idea to make it more of a ballad. It would have been something to see how that song would have turned out [if they had released the original version]. But it's too late now. It would have had to come out at the exact same time, to see which one the public would have responded to more.

MONA LISA

That was a dance track, to dance and have fun. We put a little "Walk on By" [by Dionne Warwick; Rick sings his own version in the song] at the end. If that kind of thing sounds good with a nice dance track, then there's nothing wrong with that! It just fit in there somehow.

HEY YOUNG WORLD

I wanted to put down a positive message with a reggae twist. It was a statement from my point of view. Seeing people going the wrong route and trying to explain to them that it's not the route to go. I wasn't trying to be too preachy.

TEACHER, TEACHER

That was another filler track. I wasn't really feeling that one. That was there just to make the album reach twelve [songs]. It was empty, it had no soul to it. I didn't put no effort into that song.

That was supposed to be a little more aggressive. Talkin' shit. Braggadocious. I liked it to some degree. That was the one that Eric Sadler made that I thought wasn't so bad. Bringing in Sadler and Shocklee was the label's thing—they decided they would make it a hot album. It was pretty smooth working with them, overall. I liked "Lick the Balls," but the rest of the stuff they did I wasn't feeling as much.

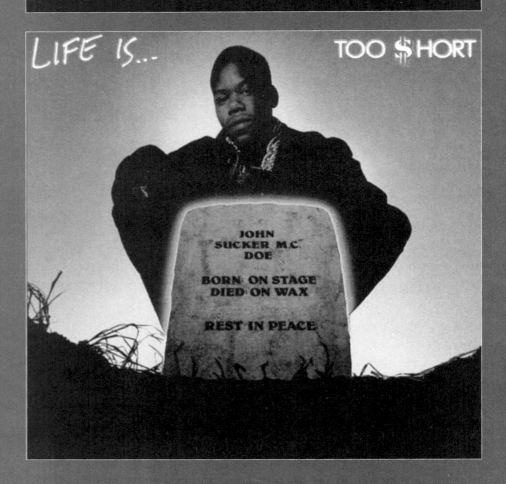

TOO $HORT

Life Is . . . Too $hort

(Dangerous/Jive, 1989)

Oakland rap legend Too $hort may be a pimp, but he's always been a relatively low-key one. "From day one, I told everyone around me that I didn't want to be famous," he says today. "In Oakland everybody knew the voice and the name, but in my early years nobody had a face to put with it." Anonymity may have been easier in his preplatinum days—he released four albums before 1989's classic *Life Is . . . Too $hort* and has released more than a dozen since—but he soon had to give up his dream of living the nonfamous life.

Born in Los Angeles in 1966, Todd Shaw moved to East Oakland in 1979 to live with his mother, and shortly thereafter began his dream of being a rapper. He was influenced by the music, of course, but pimps he saw in his neighborhood had just as much sway. $hort's first experience in the rap world was with his friend Freddy B. In the early eighties they made their first tape, a tribute to a local pimp named Hot Lips whom they knew from around the way. He paid them twenty dollars for it and they were off, making many more homemade tapes on a regular basis with names like "Game 1" and "Game 2." These sold well locally.

While his tape-selling days were going strong, $hort noticed other local artists who put their music out on vinyl with professional-looking packaging. "I had always figured that you had to be on a label from New York to have a real record out back then [in the early and mid-eighties]," $hort recalls. "But before MC Hammer started doing his thing in the Bay, there was a guy named Motorcycle Mike who put out a record called 'Super Rat' on a label called Hodisk. [*Author's Note: The artist was Super Rat and the song was "Motorcycle Mike," released in 1981 on Hodisk.*] The label was owned by a drug kingpin named Mickey Moe. The song was on the radio—it was good. The rat was talking shit, basically. And there was another record by a guy named Steve Walker that was real inspirational to me. His record was called 'Tally Ho' and he pressed his own record up and took it to the store himself. He was from Oakland too."

$hort and Freddy's partnership putting out local tapes was going along at a steady clip, regularly selling thousands of copies of each release around the Bay. But they hit a big snag in 1983: Freddy got locked up. "We were one hundred percent a group, and there was no possibility of us going solo up to that point," $hort explains. "But Freddy went to prison, not jail. It wasn't just county jail for a few months. He was gone for a while. By the time he got out he wanted to do something, but then he went right back to jail." $hort didn't want to stop the momentum that they had started, so he reluctantly embarked on a solo career. According to $hort, Freddy himself did the same thing years later, releasing solo albums once he was out of the big house for extended periods of time.

$hort's solo career began on the 75 Girls label, owned by local entrepreneur, manager, and producer Dean Hodges. (Some sources say $hort's first solo release was in 1983, but he himself says his solo debut came out in 1985.) He made three records—more like long EPs than full albums, since the most tracks on any album was seven cuts—for 75 Girls from 1985 through 1987: *Don't Stop Rappin'*; *Raw, Uncut & X-Rated*; and *Players*. Each release sold more and more copies, mostly on cassette and almost exclusively in Northern California. "Those were as popular as you can be in that area," he says. "It was the hottest shit around there, but it was only local." The tracks themselves were basic, with replayed funk riffs swiped from popular seventies and eighties tunes. They were also far from brief. "Playboy Short," from *Don't Stop Rappin'*, was more than nine minutes long. "Don't Stop Rappin'" wasn't just the title of his first album, it was also his songwriting motto.

$hort admits to making very little money in his 75 Girls career, but on the plus side he didn't have any contractual entanglements. "Believe it or not, we never had any paperwork with that label," $hort says. "It was just like: 'Make an album, here's some money.' At first I had wanted a contract, but in hindsight it was the best thing that ever coulda happened to me. When I started my own company there was no conflict, no paperwork to resolve." $hort says that the label actually dropped him, instead of the other way around.

As always, Todd bounced back, as he had when Freddy hit the slammer. $hort started his own label and production company in 1987 with his manager Randy Austin: Dangerous Music. The first release, that same year, was *Born to Mack,* which featured the hit "Freaky Tales," the song for which $hort may be best known to this day.

Around this time, $hort started working with musician Al Eaton out of Eaton's spare bedroom in El Cerrito, dubbed One Little Indian Music.

$hort continued to use live playing, even though sampling was dominating hip-hop production at the time. "I always kept two or three guys in the studio with me who knew how to work drum machines, knew how to play keyboards," $hort explains. "A lot of those songs were me—the drums, the beat. But I never like to do it all myself. I always like to have a bit of extra expertise with me in the studio. Back then we were just fascinated by the procedure of recording a whole album. I didn't even know you could stop and punch your vocals in. Every rap I did before *Life Is . . . Too $hort* was one take. I think a lot of rappers were doing that in the mid-eighties. I still do it today, a lot of times."

Too $hort in Atlanta, 1996.
PHOTO: B+ (FOR WWW.MOCHILLA.COM).

Aside from being a prolific vocalist, $hort also was a savvy rap recycler: "I've made every one of my albums in thirty days or less," he states. "From 1980 to 1985 I had released hundreds and hundreds of tapes with Freddy B. So between 1988 and 1996 I was rapping the same rhymes that I rapped before 1985. All the same words! I was writin' new stuff too, but I was also rewritin' most of the old stuff. I recycled every rhyme I ever wrote that was on those underground tapes. That's why I was puttin' out albums so fast—I already had all the raps! I was doing an album every nine to eleven months."

Born to Mack sold fifty thousand copies in the Bay area alone in 1987. Jive Records president Barry Wise got wind of $hort's raunchy and grassroots record-selling rep and signed him to the label in February of 1988, rereleasing *Born to Mack* nationwide and selling another two hundred thousand without any promotion. "No advertising, no single, no video, no radio," $hort says. "Not even a poster. They just put that shit on the shelf and they sold two hundred thousand, with the extra sales mostly in the south and Midwest. That was my first real introduction to America." $hort claims that the album is far past gold by now.

Always a hands-on kind of guy, $hort sidestepped major-label politics altogether. "I never even knew that they [Jive] *could* be saying something if they wanted to," he says. "I was under the impression that it was the artist that was in control. I basically would make the album, we'd mix it, and we'd send Jive the complete product, all sequenced. They'd master it at Sterling Sound and then manufacture it. That's all they'd ever have to do with me. I never really even knew any of the staff members at Jive. I would basically just talk to Barry and that was it."

As 1988 went on, it was clear that $hort was on a roll. And this time around, with a major label behind him, things looked better than ever. Recorded in less than thirty days at Al Eaton's, *Life Is . . . Too $hort,* released in January of 1989, was another huge step forward. "That album just felt good from the start," $hort says, adding, "The only difference between *Born to Mack* and *Life Is . . . Too $hort* was that there was going to be an official single and it was going to be played on the radio. It was the first time I ever got a poster, too. I always like to think that that's where the real Too $hort career started."

After selling three hundred thousand copies in three months with no promotion, Jive got behind it and released the title track as a single. "The only reason I remember that it was three hundred thousand copies at the time was because that was their whole ad campaign: 'Three hundred thousand copies in three months.' RCA (Jive's parent company) had Elvis, *Dirty Dancing* [the soundtrack], and country-and-western shit, and here's this rap guy that nobody ever heard of selling three hundred thousand. They was like: 'Damn, what happens if we actually promote this shit?' "

A 1989 tour with N.W.A. bolstered his national rep and cemented his left coast immortality. "That tour was the biggest thing that ever happened to me in my life. We were playing ten-thousand- and fifteen-thousand-seat arenas every night and I had never even toured before," $hort says. "N.W.A. became commercial about the same time as me. When I put out 'Freaky Tales' they had 'Boyz-N-the Hood,' and when I dropped *Life Is . . .* they dropped *Straight Outta Compton.* I was just on some pimp/player shit, though, you know? I wasn't trying to throw the controversy up in your face like they were. While we were on that tour sales of my album went from three hundred thousand to eight hundred thousand."

And a bizarre rumor pushed the album into rap history: "There were always a lot of stories about me back during 1988 and 1989. 'He's got light skin and long hair,' all kinds of rumors," he says. "There was even a fake Too $hort going around as me. Some little dude named Anthony. To this day Too $hort is bigger than I am. Oakland always had the rumor around that I was a crackhead. But after the N.W.A. tour somebody started the rumor that Too $hort got shot at a crack house. It started in Oakland and went everywhere. The biggest place that the crack house rumor hit was in Texas, where they were having memorial services for me and shit, and moments of silence on the radio. It was serious. But I wasn't mad at all. I was lovin' every minute of it. I've always been with whatever goes down."

He was also loving the fact that the rumors of his demise had driven up demand even more—as listeners sought to find out what this late (and, of course, falsely accused) crackhead was all about. "Those rumors made the album go even more crazy with sales," $hort grins. "It went from eight hundred thousand to 1.3 million and eventually went double platinum. To this day it's my only double-platinum record.

"*Life Is* . . . is definitely my favorite album. It's the purest work I've ever done," he reminisces. "That's what you get when it's for free. There's nothin' on the line, you don't have to follow up on a platinum album, and you've never been on tour. Just, 'What can you do?' I was a broke mo'fucker when I made it, and it came from the heart."

TRACKS

LIFE IS . . . TOO SHORT

When we finished the album there was no doubt that "Life Is . . . Too Short" was the hottest track on there, so that was the first single, my first official single through Jive. The song definitely took off at radio. Then after selling three hundred thousand copies with no promotion, Jive said, "You gotta shoot a video." For the video we didn't have a treatment or anything, we just turned on the cameras, pulled out the Cadillac, and drove around Oakland and did shit. We showed up on a Saturday night at the Sideshow, where everybody brings out their fancy ghetto cars and guys are burnin' rubber and shootin' dice and whatever.

RHYMES

That was definitely Run-DMC influenced. Like where they'd just have a drum machine and you grab a record with horns and the DJ just scratches [*imitates sound of a DJ scratching a horn stab*]. My DJ was from New York— DJ Universe. He always kept breakin' out these records that had East Coast drums. And we liked that shit. I might sound more New York–style with my rhymes on that because Universe was in the studio, messin' with different stuff.

I AIN'T TRIPPIN'

That was the second single off the album—it's like a down-south anthem to this day. It did well, we shot a video, it got a lot of video play. But it didn't get as much radio play. I still to this day listen to a beat and have a different rap style for every beat, a different tone of voice. It's the musician in me. I took music lessons all my life and marched in a band and all that shit. So the musician in me said, "Don't rap the same way every time. Listen to the track and tune your voice to the track." That track was pretty laid back, and it took me a long time to come up with that style I used on there. I don't think I rapped like that ever again on record. It was a one-time style.

NOBODY DOES IT BETTER

There were a lot of positive things said on that song, which went along with the rest of the album plan. Side A was supposed to be me, Todd Shaw, and side B was supposed to be Too $hort. That was just the difference in me. I was always a good, positive guy. But I was always a smart guy too, and I always saw that people wanted the dirty stuff. So I gave it to them as dirty as I could because it was like a joke to me. I'm famous for being a dirty rapper, but the biggest records I ever made, like "Life Is . . . Too Short," "The Ghetto," and "Gettin' It" were positive songs. I could have made all positive songs if I wanted, but I knew that people wanted dirty stuff. Nobody seems to know that fact. Nobody ever dwells on that. I made one clean side and one dirty side for that album. I wasn't trying to clean anything up to make a video or anything. I was like, "This one is clean, this one is dirty."

DON'T FIGHT THE FEELIN'

That was kind of a posse track, with Rappin 4-Tay and my girls N'Tyce and Barbie on there. Those two were some little homegirls of mine, they were in high school back then and they're both doing good right now. That is definitely one of the most classic Too $hort records ever. To this day teenage kids are discovering that record for the first time and loving it. And old hip-hop heads have that record memorized in their minds for life.

CUSSWORDS

That's my favorite track on the album because it just comes on and I'm rappin', and it goes off and I'm rappin'. It's no hook, no nothin'. That was how I came up. Everyone wanted hooks but I was like: "Fuck a hook, I just rap!" On there I was trying to say the most explicit, extreme things I could say. I'm like, "How far can you take it?" Well, dammit, the president's wife gave me head. It was a big thing for the president [President Clinton] to get a blow job himself, and that was the late nineties. I was ahead of my time.

CITY OF DOPE

That song to me was painting a picture of where we lived, like, "This is us." It was like a Friday night on the first of the month, with people selling dope, crackheads out on the street. That was my version of [Grandmaster Flash and Melle Mel's] "The Message." I did the drum program on that and Al Eaton is playing guitar.

ALIAS CRAZY RAK

That's a DJ track. I think I met DJ Universe through Chris Wayne, who was very important because he owned an 808 drum machine. That's like saying, "I got a million dollars in the bank." Chris was from San Francisco and Crazy Rak was too. Universe's name was Enrique but his homies called him Rak. That track was just his thang, from what he grew up on. So I gave him a song. That was a one-time thing. I heard that he got burnt up in a motel or something. I had no DJ when I went out on the road with N.W.A.—I went off of a best-I-could-find super hi-fi reel-to-reel. Put the quarter-inch reel on that shit and it was like CD quality. Just push play and I do a show. Records don't sound as good, plus they can skip.

That's the whole Al Eaton flavor there. He wanted to redo that Cameo song for that. I loved that. But when Al started acting like an asshole, I immediately went out and got me another guitar player, Shorty B. Hammer came out and he was so phony, and I came back in the studio after Hammer had sold like fifteen or twenty million and Al was like, "You gotta do what Hammer does. Hammer makes records for white people. You need to do that, because white people are gonna make you rich. Pop music is *it*." Al said he wouldn't play on an album that used the word *nigger,* either. He just went the fuck off. Al boycotted before we made *Shorty the Pimp* and that's when I started working with Ant Banks and Shorty B.

A TRIBE CALLED QUEST

The Low End Theory

(Jive, 1991)

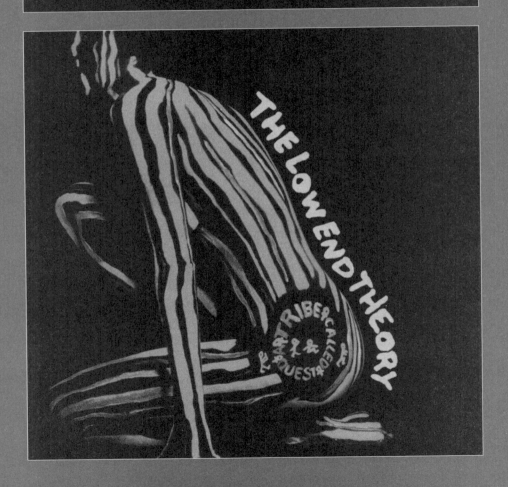

I just remember hearing music constantly. It was all around us." Q-Tip from A Tribe Called Quest isn't talking about being anywhere near a turntable or a recording studio. He's further back than that, reminiscing about his childhood in Jamaica, Queens. Linden Boulevard in the early eighties. He continues: "Me and Phife [Tribe's other talented MC] heard [the Sugar Hill Gang's] 'Rapper's Delight' when it came out, but once Run-DMC started doing it, we knew we wanted to do *that*."

The world can be thankful that they decided to do *that,* because Q-Tip, Phife Dawg, and DJ Ali Shaheed Muhammad, like their idols Run-DMC, blazed a new path in hip-hop in the late eighties and early nineties. Every time they hit the studio they added a serious, studious, jazz edge to their supremely innovative productions.

"I was born in Queens," says Tip, who was born Jonathan Davis but has since changed his legal name to Kamaal Fareed. "My mother almost gave birth to me in Harlem, because that's where I started kicking. But they got her to Queens in time." Growing up, both Tip and Phife had musical families. Tip remembers: "There was a lot of blues and gospel in my house when I was young, and my dad was a big jazzhead." His older sister was also influential, because in the mid-eighties she began dating a member of hip-hop's Zulu Nation and became exposed to the deepest roots of true-school hip-hop.

Tip also recalls, "My neighborhood had all these bands who would play all around. [Drummer] Omar Hakim had a band; [drummer] Billy Cobham, too. They'd play at Roy Wilkins Park and at the Village Door [club], around our way." Probably as a result of this, the producer-to-be was the definition of a musical sponge. He recalls: "I was drawn to all kinds of music as a kid. Al Green, Stevie Wonder, Joni Mitchell. I listened to rock radio stations too, so I heard lots of Led Zeppelin and Pink Floyd."

"I've known Phife since I was like three years old," says Tip of his childhood neighborhood friend and future rhyme partner. "Phife is the one who got me into rhymin' in the first place. He was the one who pushed me into MCing. I was always into books, so I guess that's why I fell into rhyming so easily."

The Queens-born Phife [Malik Taylor] had an arts-heavy upbringing by Trinidadian parents: His mother wrote poetry and his father was a big music fan. Calypso and reggae filled his childhood home, and Phife picked up patois and extra island slang since his father played soccer and socialized with many Jamaicans. Phife says of his childhood pursuits: "Around my neighborhood, if you didn't play basketball, rap, or DJ, you were an outcast."

Phife went to a couple different high schools, including Pine Forge Academy for his freshman year (a Seventh-Day Adventist school sixty miles outside of Philadelphia), then Springfield Gardens High School in Queens. He and Tip stayed in touch during high school but didn't hang out as much as they had through junior high because of school circumstances. After getting back from his year in Pennsylvania, Phife met up with the man who would be the fourth, and least easily defined, member of A Tribe Called Quest—Jarobi. Phife says: "Jarobi was originally from the Bronx and he moved to Queens when he was like twelve. He was a year younger than us. He used to beatbox and I would MC. We'd battle cats out in the park." Although Jarobi would never have a vocal presence in the group, he was an important behind-the-scenes force, especially on the group's first album.

As his mid-teens approached, Tip faced a major turning point as an artist at the musical and geographical melting pot that was lower Manhattan's Murry Bergtraum High School for Business Careers—home to future hip-hop luminaries like X-Clan's Brother J, the Jungle Brothers, and his future Tribe-mate Ali Shaheed Muhammad. Tip explains: "Going to Murry Bergtraum was a big influence on me, in one way just because it let me get out of Queens. And there was just so much crazy stuff going on there. The first person I met there was Brother J—he was just there rhyming in the lunchroom. It was just a fly-ass school." Tip graduated in 1988 with a specialization in computer science.

Aside from his contact with Ali Shaheed, Q-Tip's association with two other Bergtraum students, Mike G and Afrika Baby Bam of the Jungle Brothers, was what really started his career. The group was signed to Idlers/Warlock Records in 1987 and released their *Straight out the Jungle* album on the label in 1988. Tip wrote and performed on their songs "Black Is Black" and "The Promo," a nonalbum cut. It was his first time in a recording studio and he soaked up the experience. "I also helped mix the song 'Straight out the Jungle,'" Tip adds. "And those guys used some beats that I had found. I was on that album a good amount."

"I never really looked at hip-hop as a career," Tip says. "I guess that I kind of knew, though, because I didn't really apply to any colleges. I went to City College for a couple of weeks and dropped out. Hip-hop was always a dream, but being around the Jungle Brothers and seeing them do it—that made it more of a reality to me."

Going back to the pre–Jungle Brothers days, during freshman year Tip had also hooked up with Bed-Stuy, Brooklyn resident DJ Ali Shaheed Muhammad, and the two quickly started working on music together. Tip says: "I met Ali through Afrika [of the Jungle Brothers], and I would go to his [Ali's] place in Bed-Stuy to work on demos. Me and Ali did the demo for 'Bonita Applebum' [which appeared on Tribe's first album, in 1989] around sophomore year in high school."

Regarding his rhyme partner during their high school years, Tip says, "Me and Phife went to grade school together, but in high school we didn't see each other much, because he went to a school [outside] Philadelphia and then in Queens. But I was always in touch with him, and was telling him that he had to come by our school and meet these people, because things were popping off there."

As previously mentioned, the final part of the Tribe picture was Jarobi. He rarely rhymed with the group and didn't officially produce, but he was an important part of the crew nonetheless. Tip says: "After freshman year in high school, Phife was rhyming with this kid around the way in Queens, and Jarobi was that guy's beatboxer. We'd all hang out, so I met Jarobi when we was like fourteen." Phife says of Jarobi: "He was down with us when we started, but he was always into the culinary arts. He toured with us a lot on the first album but eventually he chose his other career instead of running with us in the music thing. But he's around—he still works with me today."

By their junior year in high school, things were starting to come together for what would become A Tribe Called Quest. Tip and Ali originally called themselves Tribe, but Afrika from the Jungle Brothers suggested their expanded moniker. By 1987 the four-man crew was working on music together more regularly, and had even added a drummer named Sha-Boogie to the mix. Tip says: "Originally there were five of us [including Jarobi]. Eventually Sha dropped out of the group." He continues: "We rented a rehearsal space in Manhattan, Giant Studios, and we'd practice there for a couple hours on Saturdays. It was actually kind of pathetic, now that I actually think about it [laughs]. My sister was dating [producer] Skeff Anselm and he was in the Zulu Nation and knew Jazzy Jay, so Jay came down one time to check us out. He basically said: 'Um, keep working on it' [*laughs*]."

And work on it they did. Throughout their tenure at Murry Bergtraum, Tip and Ali continued to hone their four-track skills in Bed-Stuy. "I would do beats, and Ali would put cuts on them. By senior year [1988] I was also doing shows with the Jungle Brothers, after their album came out." Tip also continued to work on his vocal style, with Phife by his side whenever they could find time to link up. Q-Tip remembers: "Phife was always the battle rapper—he would take what was happenin' on the street and rhyme about it. And he was a great freestyler as well. My shit was always more cerebral, and the combo always worked really well. We'd always make up routines that would emulate Run-DMC."

Aside from the Jungle Brothers connection, Tip's musical development progressed even more after meeting Amityville, Long Island's De La Soul. The JBs, De La, and Tribe would form the nucleus of what would be called the Native Tongues movement, which would catch the hip-hop world's ear after De La's monumental 1989 album *3 Feet High and Rising*. Tribe would be the third of the crew to release an album, and they rode the Native Tongues wave to national recognition. Tip says: "We did a show with De La Soul in Roy Wilkins Park on July 4, in 1988. The Jungle Brothers had just met De La up in Boston at a show a couple days before, and we all just clicked. I started hanging out with De La all the time after that."

Phife remembers: "When Tip and the Jungle Brothers met up with De La it just seemed like they had known each other for years. We were just kids back then, and it was just a family affair, not like a marketing thing. It's like in elementary school, on the weekends you have a sleepover. But the sleepover with Native Tongues was in a recording studio instead. People would just roll by other people's sessions and we'd be in there all night, eating Chinese food and working. We had fun being around each other, and that was really the main thing."

Tip was at many of the recording sessions for *3 Feet High* (he was featured on several songs including the single "Buddy," and says he co-produced the song "Description") at Manhattan's Calliope Studios, and this experience proved to be the final schooling he needed to shine on his own. He remembers: "I'd be in there, mesmerized by all the equipment. I'd even stay after their sessions were over and mess around, figuring stuff out."

Being at a real studio like Calliope (the Jungle Brothers recorded at cozier TTO Studios in Coney Island) was the chance that Tip was waiting for. He says: "At the time, in 1988 and 1989, my original productions were all on pause tapes, when I wasn't messing with Ali's four-track. So I'd just show up at Calliope with a bag of tapes, trying to figure out how to make them come alive." With the help of engineer Shane Faber, Tip started learning equipment like E-mu's SP-1200 and Akai's S-950 samplers. He adds: "[Queens-based producer] Large Professor also showed me a lot of production stuff at the time, and I expanded on what he taught me."

Tip remembers: "After the De La album came out and all the hype it got, a lot of people wanted to hear our demo. Red Alert was managing us at the time and he shopped a demo we had with four or five songs on it. Geffen, Def Jam, Atlantic, and Jive all wanted to sign us. We went with Jive because they just seemed more interested."

A Tribe Called Quest's first album, *People's Instinctive Travels and the Paths of Rhythm,* came out in 1989 on Jive and was a critical success, eventually going gold on the strength of singles like "Bonita Applebum" and "Can I Kick It?" "That album was just a lot of fun," says Tip. "I had all these ideas in my head and I was just letting them out. It wasn't too cerebral—it was about emotions and colors. The label was happy, it sold well, and we had a buzz out there."

Tip details the production duties on the first album, which he says were the same for the first several Tribe releases: "I would do all of the music, basically, and the other guys would be the sounding board, and we'd improve tracks from their suggestions." He notes that Ali Shaheed produced "Push It Along" from *People's Instinctive Travels.* Phife says: "I was being ignorant on that first album, that's why I was only on a couple of tracks. I was hardly around, not like I should have been."

"I wouldn't say that Phife was being ignorant," Tip replies. "He was just running around, doing his thing, being nineteen years old. I was in the studio every day, but it wouldn't bother me if he wasn't there. He was my man and I was going to hold him down. We all helped stitch that album together."

"Everybody had their hand in the production, one way or another," explains Phife. "Tip had the massive record collection, and he used to dig for records all the time. We'd go on tour and right before sound check, Tip would be driving around looking for records. Ali did a lot of the programming and played any live stuff that needed to be played. And Tip did everything else. There were times that I might write a paragraph or two for Tip, or he might write sixteen bars for me. It was really a group thing, and we didn't have any kind of basic format. I do beats now, but back then I left that to Tip and Ali. I just enjoyed their production so much that it wouldn't make any sense for me to mess up something that was good."

The group continued to feed off the artistic energy of the Native Tongues camp, which grew to include Queen Latifah, Monie Love, and Black Sheep. By 1990 it was time to think about their second full-length. Tribe had grown even more as artists and people, and their sound was sure to reflect this. Phife remembers: "Once we got ready to do *The Low End Theory,* we knew that it was do or die. I felt that way, at least. The first album was critically acclaimed, but we knew everything had to be correct to really make it hit like we wanted. Management, record label, distribution, everything." On the management side, they went with industry up-and-comer (and then Jungle Brothers road manager) Chris Lighty, who had been at Rush Management and was just starting his Violator Management company.

Tip says of his 1990 pre–*Low End* mindset: "I felt like there were even more possibilities with the second album, with all that I had learned and how I wanted things to be, sonically. I just went to another level when I was getting ready to do *Low End Theory.* I wouldn't say it was 'do or die.' It was more like: 'Okay, now watch what we can do.' " He continues: "I was definitely on another level at that point. I felt it and I knew it. I was chopping beats differently than other people were back then. The [second] album was like a project. A show. And everybody was invited to watch. The first album was about color, and *Low End Theory* was more about technique."

Phife admits: "On the first album I would have rather hung out with my boys on the street and got my hustle on rather than gone into the studio. I wasn't even on the contract for the first album—I was even thinking that me and Jarobi might have our own group, and so we were more like backups for Tip and Ali. But Tip and Ali really wanted me to come through and do my thing, and towards the end of the first album I saw how the fans really liked us. The difference between the two albums is that on *Low End Theory* I was focused, and that just made it that much better."

Working at Battery Studios in Manhattan with engineer, technical advisor, and all-around recording guru Bob Power (Tip points to Power as a significant behind-the-scenes influence on the group's sound), Tip and Phife recall the album taking six to eight months to record, versus the three months it had taken for their first. And despite Jive Records having offices in the same building as Battery, the label never got any sneak peaks. Tip says: "We would never let the record label hear what we were doing. We didn't need anybody giving us their critique on our music. And like I said [on "Check the Rhime"], record company people are *shady* [*laughs*]."

Phife also remembers their self-sufficiency: "Jive would try to come downstairs and see what was goin' on, but we'd always be real discreet. They wouldn't hear anything until we wanted them to hear it, and that did make them mad sometimes. But in the end they were happy, because they knew what we had, and they knew it was hot." Tip adds: "Jive was really big on letting us just be who we were, and that was pretty important, looking back. You can't find that today."

The album, true to its title, featured bass lines front and center, but had many reasons for being called *The Low End Theory*. Tip explains: "At the time, there were some things that were happening in hip-hop, sonically, that I wanted to expand on, especially with the *bottom*. For example, I loved Public Enemy, but I felt that sometimes their mixes didn't have enough dynamics to them. All their sounds were on the same floor: bass, drums, guitars. I wanted to stack things on different levels. Like with Pink Floyd, I loved that group, and their music and mixes were all about dynamics. So I would always explain how dynamic I wanted things to be by telling Bob [Power]: 'I want this to be more at the *bottom,* at the *low end.*' I guess it was from a lack of articulation, but it got the job done. And that's where the title came from."

In addition to Q-Tip's next-level production and groundbreaking flow and lyrics on *The Low End Theory,* the entire group stepped up. Tip says: "Phife was so amazing, so crazy on that album. He was the fire starter and he always brought that edge. Back then and still today, when I make a beat I always envision how Phife is going to sound on it. His tone over my beats is always such a great contrast." According to Tip, Ali Shaheed didn't produce any full tracks per se, but "he did the cuts and had suggestions about how tracks could be improved. He was a much-needed sounding board for everything I was doing, because he understood everything from a DJ perspective."

Phife laughs when recalling Q-Tip's infamous perfectionism (which Tip himself admits): "Tip being such a perfectionist is good and bad. Because sometimes when a track's blazing hot, he might not feel it and might overdo it. Ali and myself or Chris [Lighty] would be like, 'It's hot, leave it alone!' "

Another part of the album's sonic impact was the sequencing and Tip's philosophy about "blending" songs together. He says: "With the sequencing, I definitely wanted everything to blend together. De La had all those skits and I wanted things on our album to end cold and go right into the next song, *bam.* No space between songs."

Interestingly, Q-Tip claims that he didn't like to make videos for Tribe songs, despite the fact that some of the offerings on *Low End Theory* are among hip-hop's finest of all time (notably "Scenario" and "Check the Rhime"). He says: "I don't like videos, even to this day. I think that they take away the mystery of a song. It makes the relationship between the public and the artist a passive one. Our videos were okay, but I like to leave the imagination in there."

Regarding the album cover, which is one of the most distinctive of the era, Tip recalls, "I wanted [the cover model] to be Naomi Campbell, naked, with all the red, black and green paint all over her, with a Tribe logo on her ass. I guess that was kind of cocky [*laughs*]. We couldn't get her, of course. I don't think that the label even tried. But we got another model to do the same thing. We wanted a shot where we were all walking in Times Square with her, but that was a bit much, too. And I wanted a white background for the shot, but they flipped it and made it black. I liked how it came out, though. Basically I was just trying to go for the new Ohio Players type of shit.

"After the responses came back and they were all very positive, it really did feel like we had arrived as a group," says Q-Tip of the album, which hit gold in 1992 and platinum three years later. "A lot of our albums have been ahead of their time, including our first and third records. But I think that *Low End Theory* was one of the most on-time records we ever did. At that time, it really broke us out of the Native Tongues stereotype, and it made people take us very, very seriously, especially after they had heard a song like [the humorous 1989 single] 'I Left My Wallet in El Segundo.' Most of all I'm just glad that people consider it a classic *musical* album."

"*Low End* kicked the door down and knocked it off its hinges," adds Phife. "In this game, timing is everything, and the timing of *Low End Theory* was perfect."

TRACKS

Q-Tip: I took the original bass line, which was in ¾ time, and I put a beat onto the last measure to make it ¼. I made the drums underneath smack, so it had that big sound. And I put a reverse [Roland TR-] 808 [drum machine] behind it, right before the beat actually kicks in. I loved that Last Poets sample on there, too.

Q-Tip: In some of my lyrics on there, I was talking about the trend of R&B artists at the time taking on hip-hop personas—to get more of an edge, I guess. It always seemed to me that that was done out of commerce more than out of genuine interest. It was just the thing to do. It started happening the other way around later on, with hip-hop artists having R&B guests on their songs, around 1995 or 1996. That whole Bad Boy [Records] era. Back then it always bugged me.

Phife: I wrote that before the first album was done, actually, but I had never used those rhymes. The only reason I got "Butter" [as a solo track] was because I argued about it. That was my opportunity right there. I said if [Q-Tip's] going to do five solo tracks then I should do that many too. But that wouldn't be much of a group album if there were ten solo tracks. I wanted some burn, too. I wouldn't have minded having one more solo shot on that record, but I can't complain too much, because that album was hot.

Q-Tip: I'd always ask Phife if he wanted to be on any songs and he'd say yes or no. "Butter" was the one song that we argued about, because I wanted to be on it. He had to fight for that one. That's probably my favorite overall track on the whole album, honestly. I gave in to Phife on our argument because there was some girl in there yelling at me to let him do a solo, so I was like: "All right!" Some of his rhymes on there were older—I remembered them when he started kicking them in the studio.

VERSES FROM THE ABSTRACT

Phife: That's got to be Tip's best solo work, other than [*Midnight Marauders'*] "Sucka Nigga." That's just a killer. Ron Carter, the jazz bassist, is on there, playing live. He was a really cool guy.

Q-Tip: About getting Ron Carter on there, Sophia Chang worked at Jive and had worked at Atlantic before that. When she was at Atlantic she did a record with Ron, and when she told me that I was like: "I'd love to get Ron on a track!" I was surprised I hadn't thought of it before, honestly. He was a great guy—we had a really good conversation. He was definitely interested in what we were doing with hip-hop or I don't think that he would have done the track for us. I don't think that's one of my own favorite verses on the album. I guess that it is one of my less abstract rhymes, despite the name of the song. Vinia Mojica is singing on there. I met her back in 1987 or 1988, walking down the street in New York. I was like: "*Who* are you?" Aside from being beautiful, she wound up being a great singer.

RAP PROMOTER

Phife: That's one of my favorite tracks. It's just about getting jerked [ripped off by promoters] at shows. Most of the things we were talking about on *Low End Theory* were learning experiences from the first album, and "Rap

Promoter" was definitely about that. Promoters will try and get away with murder if you let 'em. It's the American way, unfortunately.

Q-Tip: There are so many stories about that song. We did a whole other song with Leaders of the New School for the album, but it never made it on there. I met those guys around the time of our first album because Chuck D was fucking around with them. He put them together and named them and all that. I was eighteen or nineteen at that time and Busta was like sixteen. We did two versions of the "album version" [of "Scenario"] with that same music. The one that made it to the album was the first version we did. Then we made a second one, later, with [their manager] Chris Lighty, Pos [from De La Soul], and one of the guys from Black Sheep. Jarobi was even on a third version we did [*laughs*]! We didn't know which one to use. We wanted to get everybody on there, but it was still obvious which one was the best, and we went with that one for the final album version. On the remix [which appears on the single], an MC named Kid Hood is the first guy rhyming on there. He was a guy that I met through a mutual friend. I loved Kid Hood's rhyme, it was on some pre-Redman shit. He could have been right up in that lane in the future, but two days after we recorded him, he got murdered. I think I like the remix better than the album version. And yeah, that video was fun, sure.

Phife: That was one of the first tracks, and also the last track we did. The original version of that actually had Pos from De La, Dres and Long from Black Sheep on it as well, and even Chris Lighty, our manager. There was like nine or ten people on it and we was just buggin' out. It was way too long. No one was really wack on it, though—it was dope. I guarantee you that Pos has it somewhere. He saves everything. I don't think I ever told anybody this, but I wanted to go first because a lot of DJs cut the record [short, before it's over] and whoever is second to last might not get heard [*laughs*]. So I was like: "Fuck that, I'm going first! Niggas is gonna hear me!" [*Laughs.*] And I killed it. I think everybody killed on that album version. And none of the guys from the original version cared that they didn't make it on that final version. I would say that that song is one of the best posse cuts ever, with [Marley Marl and Juice Crew's] "The Symphony" and [EPMD with Redman and K-Solo's] "Headbanger."

THE INFAMOUS DATE RAPE

Phife: Q-Tip came up with the title for that. It was just something that was happenin' a lot at the time [celebrities getting accused of rape]. It never happened to us personally, no no no. If she says no, then aight, beat it.

CHECK THE RHIME

Q-Tip: That song took a minute to develop. And I don't really know why we spelled *rhyme* like we did [*laughs*]. I just liked fucking up words, doing lowercase and uppercase where they didn't belong. I also take full responsibility for making up the word *vivrant* [*laughs*]. When I first did that song I had just discovered how to chop beats up in certain ways. The beat was Grover Washington's "Hydra," and EPMD had used it [on the song "Underground" in 1990], but I knew that I could get more out of it by getting the kicks and the snares out—to make the drums more cohesive. That was a really early version of beat-chopping that I used on there. With the video for that song, that cleaners we were on top of [Nu-Clear Drive-In Cleaners, on Linden Boulevard in St. Albans] was just a staple in our neighborhood. I saw that U2 video where they were on top of that building in L.A. and it was all tall and shit, and I was like [*voice gets very deep and sarcastically macho*]: "Fuck that! We're gonna do it on top of a building in the 'hood!" That day we did the video was a lot of fun—it was like the hottest day of the year, and then there was a thunderstorm and the wind was blowing all around. There were tons of people, coming from all over Queens. People were out there hanging out, barbequing, shooting dice.

Phife: Originally we did that song to a different beat. It was hot, too. We didn't title it at first, but as soon as we put the horns on there, we just named it 'Check the Rhime." The original version would have come across dark, almost like a Mobb Deep joint. Those back-and-forth lyrics with Tip and I on there came very naturally. We grew up together, and when we're onstage he knows what I'm gonna do before I do it and vice versa. Ali is like the referee behind the turntables, making sure we're doing it right. Ali gets the vibe the most by being back there, watching both of us. That video was done down the block from my grandmother's house and a block or two from Q-Tip's mother's house.

EVERYTHING IS FAIR

Q-Tip: I was kind of speaking about a specific woman with those lyrics. It was a story I had heard about and seen, with the different images on there. Skeff [Anselm] produced that one as well. He was working with Brand Nubian at the time and he was around in the studio a lot, so I was like: "Yo, throw us a beat!"

JAZZ (WE'VE GOT)

Phife: When I said, "Produced and arranged by the four-man crew" on there, I was talkin' about Skeff Anselm. He's the other dude with the hat in the video for that. He used to be in the studio with us all the time, whether he was doin' a track for us or not.

Q-Tip: I was hanging out with Pete Rock and Large Professor and we were talking about doing a record together. Pete had come up with that beat, but the song we were going to do never materialized. So I asked Pete if he was going to use the track, and if I could maybe trade him something for it. I already had the record he used, but I wanted to get his permission. He was like: "Yeah, go ahead." I don't think I ever traded him back for it, so I guess I still owe him! When it came to hip-hop and jazz, the work we were doing was a unique opportunity to combine both of them, like the way we used Ron Carter on "Verses from the Abstract." Both musics came from the black underclass, and both are very expressive. There were so many similarities, and that made it even better to sample it and rhyme over it. I thought Phife was talking about Jarobi when he mentions the "four-man crew." Although Jarobi wasn't around much on the second album.

SHOW BUSINESS *Featuring Brand Nubian*

Q-Tip: Skeff Anselm produced that. His style was definitely very Strong City [the label that Jazzy Jay owned]—it had that Jazzy Jay skip to it. We got Skeff on the record because, contrary to what people think, I didn't want the album to be all about me. I wanted it to breathe, and for other people to come in. Tribe meant what it said, it was a community. As for Brand Nubian, we had a song called "Georgie Porgie" that we did with them. It was about a kid who grew up in the 'hood and wound up being gay. We played it for the label [Jive] and they felt that it was a little too . . . strong. So we all decided not to put it on the album. Puba got mad and didn't want to do another track, so that's why he's not on there. We used the same beat.

Phife: That was with Brand Nubian. We'd always run into them at clubs like Power House and the Daddy's Night that Puffy used to throw at Red Zone. I don't know who Tip would tell you that he got a lot from as an MC, but for me personally, Grand Puba was my favorite nigga of all time, with KRS and LL. Puba was mad witty and sarcastic, all at the same time, and that's how I always wanted to come across when I rhymed. With the content of the song, we had seen some real fucked-up things in the business, and we just had the idea to spill it on a record. Everybody looks at it as entertainment, but there's seriousness to it.

WHAT?

Q-Tip: That was done kind of midway through the sessions. The label wanted that song as the first single. It was between that and "Check the Rhime." I'm glad that it went the way it did. Things definitely would have been different if "What?" was the first single.

WU-TANG CLAN

Enter the Wu-Tang (36 Chambers)

(Loud/RCA, 1993)

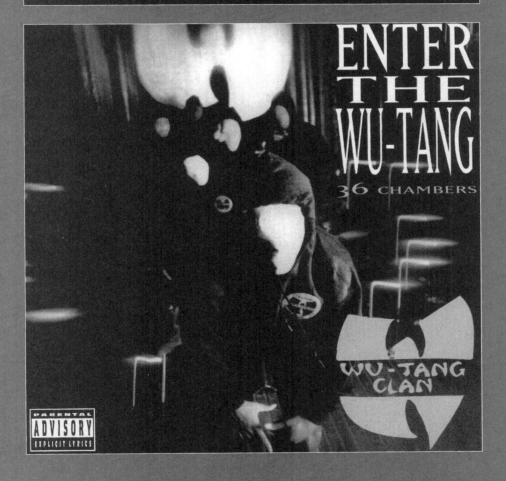

Groups hold their own special and rarefied place in the pantheon of hip-hop. It's hard enough to keep things rolling with just one MC and one DJ. When numbers grow beyond a deuce, things grow exponentially more difficult. There are different visions, egos, and musical likes and dislikes. Keeping this in mind, no group in hip-hop's rich history can compare to the impact, the illness, the innovation, the size, and the longevity of the mighty Wu-Tang Clan.

The mostly Staten Island–based collective boasted nine members in 1992, all of whom could melt a mic at ten paces: the RZA (Robert Diggs, aka Prince Rakeem), the GZA (Gary Grice, aka the Genius), Ol' Dirty Bastard (Russell Jones, aka ODB, who passed away in November 2004), Inspectah Deck (Jason Hunter, aka the Rebel INS), Raekwon (Cory Woods), Ghost Face Killer (Dennis Coles, aka Ghostface, aka Ghostface Killah), Method Man (Clifford Smith), U-God (Lamont Hawkins), and Masta Killa (Elgin Turner). Not only did the group produce one of hip-hop's ultimate classic albums, they also showed amazing business acumen, as group members, under the RZA's watchful eye, lucratively went solo shortly after the *Enter the Wu-Tang* buzz was established.

At the epicenter of the Wu-Tang artistic maelstrom was producer/MC the RZA. He was born in Brooklyn and says he moved more than a dozen times before building a home base in Staten Island's (ahem, Shaolin's) Stapleton section in the latter half of the eighties. "I spent most of my life going from Staten Island to Brooklyn, like most of the other guys in Wu-Tang," he explains. As for his earliest entrées into the world of hip-hop, he recounts: "I started MCing very early, around eight years old, and eventually I started DJing and producing. But MCing was always my first hip-hop love." He adds: "I always wanted to make records, all my life, ever since I heard that there were records to be made in rap, like back in the early eighties. Since the day I heard records on the radio, I wanted to make my own."

GZA, sometimes (and always appropriately) known as the Genius, is the eldest member of the Clan. He also shuttled around New York's five boroughs as a youth. He says: "I was in Staten Island when I started rhyming, at around eleven years old, but I was born in Brooklyn. Staten was more like a secondary home. I went to public school and Junior High there. I've known Raekwon and Deck since elementary school—we all grew up together." He continues: "I always MCed, from a young age. I used to travel a lot, so I would pick up on a lot of different styles and slang, from borough to borough. I have family in every borough, and I've lived all over. Because I was writing all the time and because I picked up so much, I was always pretty far advanced compared to other MCs around me."

Considering his advanced mic prowess, GZA surprisingly admits, "For a certain number of years, I was scared to get on the mic. I had the rhymes, but I would give them to other people to say them. I didn't like the way my voice sounded back then, even though I knew my lyrics were the best around." Thankfully he got over it.

Although the "Shaolin" that Wu-Tang portrayed in their lyrics was far from idyllic, it wasn't always so rugged, as GZA relates: "When we got to Staten in the seventies, our neighborhood there was young and fresh. There wasn't any type of violence or drugs. It was a good place to be. You gotta take a boat to get there. It was kind of exciting." But as the eighties progressed, Staten Island, like urban areas in any state you'd like to name, started to get a bit grimy around the edges.

As they entered their mid- and late teens in the late eighties, GZA, RZA, and Ol' Dirty Bastard—the former two were traveling between Staten and other boroughs while ODB (who, in his earliest rapping days, was known as Unique A-Son and A-Son Unique) always called Brooklyn home—came together as a group, calling themselves All in Together Now. Each member of the trio had his own outlook on All in Together Now's potential and the group's future goals. It was just a tryout for RZA, as he explains: "I just did it to do it back then. It wasn't as big to me. I think it was bigger to GZA. I was just really making songs and seeing what would happen."

GZA recalls: "Back then, with All in Together Now, I was in Bed-Stuy [Brooklyn] and my house would be the meeting place. RZA would come from Staten and Dirty would come from [Brooklyn's] East New York. Generally I spent more time with ODB because we was from the same borough, but all three of us met pretty often. I think I was more into it than the other guys at the time, maybe because I was older. I was seventeen then and ODB was only thirteen or fourteen."

GZA continues: "I used to spend most of the time back then writing the group's routines. Ol' Dirty was more into fashion and looking fly back then. He was one of the best beatboxers around, though. I used to write ODB's beats, write out the sounds on paper and orchestrate them. I'd hold my hands up like a conductor. We definitely had a bugged chemistry. We'd make up routines, battle other crews, that kind of thing. Most of our songs were based on other popular songs, just like Cold Crush Brothers and the Treacherous Three used to do." Around that time they recorded their theme song, "All in Together Now." GZA recalls: "It got around—it was pretty popular, I guess, around 1985 or '86. It was based on some song that girls would sing when they played jump rope, and it was basically about me dissing and degrading a female."

By 1988, both GZA and RZA (then known as the Genius and Prince Rakeem, respectively) were being managed by oft-forgotten but important old-school manager/producer Melquan. After they had worked on about fifteen songs together over the course of a year or two, GZA says: "Before you know it, Cold Chillin' [Records] wanted to sign me." The result was the 1991 full-length *Words from the Genius,* chiefly produced by a young Easy Mo Bee. But the deal wasn't all that GZA was dreaming of. He recalls: "Cold Chillin' didn't promote the record, unfortunately. I felt good to be on that label, because they was the Def Jam of that era. But things just didn't work out for me. I wasn't getting no recognition, so I bounced. It was back to the drawing board."

RZA, as Prince Rakeem, also got signed under Melquan's auspices, but he went to Tommy Boy Records. The result was the self-produced 1991 single "Ooh, I Love You Rakeem" (complete with a corny cartoon picture sleeve). He explains: "It was a single deal, with an album option, but they never picked up the album." He adds, to explain why the deal didn't work out for either end, "At the time [when the single was out] I got arrested and had bail for like ten thousand dollars, and I figured the record company could throw up ten Gs to get me out if they thought I was a good enough artist. But they gave me my contract back. I was going to put out Wu-Tang on Tommy Boy, but I realized I had to just do my own shit. "

Thus in 1992, All in Together Now groupmates RZA and GZA were both on the rebound. Also important at that time was the fact that RZA, after the dissatisfaction of dealing with other beatmakers, had started producing much more of his own music. He explains: "I started doing my own shit because most producers weren't matching rappers for the rhymes they had. They'd just throw a beat at them and expect them to do all the work and match things up. I'd always have to travel around to different producers' houses to make my rhymes and demos and songs. I was an MC first and a producer second, but I just started making beats that I could rhyme to every time. Being an MC first definitely made me become a better hip-hop producer."

While RZA and GZA were battling with their record labels, another future Wu-Tanger was battling his way up through the MC ranks in Staten Island and the Bronx: Inspectah Deck. "I came to Staten Island from the Bronx, from Park Hill," explains Deck. "Me, Raekwon, U-God, Method Man, we was all from the same 'hood. I was in Staten in the eighties through high school, after getting there when I was ten or eleven. But I was always shipped off to other places, like the Lower East Side [in Manhattan] or my grandma's in Brooklyn. GZA and Ol' Dirty used to come through Brooklyn, and RZA was in Stapleton with Ghost [Face Killer]."

Deck continues: "I don't know where my transition was from just loving hip-hop to rhyming on my own, but it was probably around the time I heard [Big Daddy] Kane's 'Raw' or Rakim's 'My Melody.' Those two made me want to rhyme. I was never a serious writer back when I started. In high school I was more like the nigga that would do the beats on the table. U-God was good at beatboxing, and with us and Method Man, we had a serious unit, an entourage. We didn't have a name as a group—everyone was just on their own, establishing their own identity. Back then, in high school, I only rhymed to certain people. I'd be more likely to just snap on people than do a whole rhyme. But eventually [Wu-Tang affiliate] Cappadonna really sat me down and showed me how to put it all down on paper. I owe Cap a lot for that."

As for how Deck, who was also known as the Rebel INS, got his dual stage name, he explains: " 'Deck' was from when I used to write graffiti— that was my graf name. I wrote all over the city, but had to give it up 'cause I got caught too many times. And I used INS as just another way to say Inspectah, because you'd have idiots saying: 'Hey, Inspector Gadget!' or they'd spell it wrong or something. So I just put Rebel INS together. That's my mic persona. You'd never really hear me say Inspectah Deck. That's just what other people call me."

From 1987 through the early nineties, RZA had a swarm of MCs coming through his home studio in Stapleton, and many of these became the Wu-

Tang Clan. "I had done different demos and worked with everyone in the Clan before *36 Chambers,*" RZA recalls. GZA also notes the longstanding connections between the extended family: "Meth and them were doing demos with RZA even when he was with Tommy Boy. And even before I signed with Cold Chillin', me and Dirty used to go out to Staten and battle Meth, U-God, and those dudes. RZA was doing tracks with all them too. So eventually it all just came together." Or, as they had said before: All in To-gether Now.

Deck recalls first meeting the Wu-Tang leader at a Staten Island block party in the late eighties: "RZA was a DJ back then. He and his brothers [one of these brothers was Divine, who eventually headed up Wu-Tang's busi-ness affairs as head of the Wu Music Group] would do block parties and they'd all do routines and shit. They'd spin around and cut with their fuckin' feet, you know? One day I saw RZA doing a block party in a neigh-borhood that is one of the roughest on Staten Island, the kind of place you don't fuck around in, and he was out there all by himself, holding it down. I was out there by myself too, so we just cliqued up, and that's when I kicked my first block party rhyme."

A major turning point in the birth of the multimember Wu-Tang was the result of a subsequent, and cinematic, meeting between RZA, Deck, and U-God. "I was on the block with U-God, standing out there selling crack, and we'd have rhymes on pieces of paper in our hand," remembers Deck. "We'd trade thoughts and work on shit. Then next thing we know we're runnin' from the cops. We came back later and RZA found us and told us to come to his crib. U-God had to make his money, so just me and Meth ended up going. This is when RZA had his own crib, after he was in Stapleton. RZA said: 'You guys do this for fun every day, but are you ready to do this shit for real?' And he put this elaborate vision on the table. I wasn't even able to see it at that point, but I saw it through him, because he was so sure of it. Eventually, me hooking up with RZA and U-God every day is what formed the Wu-Tang Clan, with all the other guys who were making their way in. We didn't have to come together and form a group, we was really al-ready there the whole time."

Deck even recognizes RZA as one who helped to hone his raw skill and make his rhymes more cohesive. "With my writing, I always admired poets like Langston Hughes, and I used to read books to pick up different styles of writing," he recalls. "And RZA always told me to write my shit in *sentences,* so even when you freestyle you sound like you're talking about something. That helped a lot."

Soon enough, RZA had a plan in place to form an MC army out of all the "killa bees" swarming around him. GZA states: "RZA definitely had the idea of Wu-Tang by 1991. I don't know if his vision had nine guys in the group, but he knew what he wanted." RZA recalls: "To me it was definitely a realistic goal to have that many people in a group. I was one hundred percent sure that my plan would work, and that plan was to make the first album and then get all the solo deals right from the start. If you read any of my contracts from back then, they reflect in some ways that I was even maybe betting on myself *too* much. But I fulfilled all that."

RZA says: "My apartment was always the spot to come and rhyme. And everybody around us who was MCing was speaking Wu-Tang slang at that time. When I first made Wu-Tang as a name, before the Wu-Tang Clan group, it was started with maybe Method and U-God. And it became more of a style. If you look at my first single [from 1991], it says 'Wu-Tang Mix' on there. So the name and the idea was out there, even before I used the name RZA and before the whole group came together."

Deck remembers the hive of activity: "I remember RZA's first place in Stapleton, we'd be out on the balcony rhymin' with a banged-up mic, all of us, even [Wu affiliates] Pop Da Brown Hornet and Shyheim. We was out there because his moms wasn't toleratin' all that noise. This is before the Clan was even started. We was there at RZA's every day, man, like the Fat Albert kids, out in the junkyard. And by the time we were recording *Enter the Wu-Tang,* RZA was out of the projects in a new spot. Wherever he was at, we'd come to him, 'cause he had that shit. When he got to Morningstar [Road, RZA's new address], that was the real 'killa bee hive.' We'd hustle by day and at night we were MCs. Then RZA would take everything we did and chef everything together. He was the common denominator—we all just gravitated to him."

In this chefly manner, RZA brought eight MCs [Masta Killa is not on the song] together for a soon-to-be monumental song in 1992: "Protect Ya Neck." It was self-released and self-promoted, and it was a verbal beatdown like New York had never heard before. Dusty, clunky, and spewing MC energy at every turn of its four-minute, fifty-two-second length, it was unstop-

Wu-Tang Clan (left to right: U-God, GZA, ODB, Inspectah Deck, Ghostface Killah, RZA, Method Man [crouching], Cappadonna, Raekwon) in Hollywood, 1997.

PHOTO: ERIC COLEMAN (FOR WWW.MOCHILLA.COM).

pable. Deck remembers: "There was no record label on that one, it just had RZA's phone number on the back. The cassette had the Wu-Tang book on the cover, the Wu-Tang manual. The cassette had 'Method Man' on the other side, and the vinyl originally had 'After the Laughter' on the B-side, not 'Method Man.' [*Author's note: He means the song 'Tearz,' which samples the Wendy Rene song 'After Laughter (Comes Tears).'*] But people were feeling 'Method Man' from the tape, so when we did the 'Protect Ya Neck' video, we reissued the vinyl with 'Method Man' on the B-side. The original vinyl had a sunshine sticker on it, and it had RZA's address on there: 143 Morningstar Road in Staten. [*Author's note: Pre–Loud Records copies of the vinyl and tape I have seen list the address as 234 Morningstar Road.*]" Deck says that the original pressing run for both cassettes and vinyl was five thousand.

GZA recalls: "We didn't have any radio in our corner, really, and we had gotten turned down a lot in the industry. A lot of doors were slammed in our faces. Kid Capri, who was a Cold Chillin' labelmate of mine, played that song on the radio, and [Funkmaster] Flex was brand new then and he played it also. It definitely started from the streets up. After that song we had a buzz and labels were interested." Deck explains: "With the promotion for 'Protect Ya Neck' we all just hit the streets—we had forty dudes in a fifteen-passenger van. We gave the tape away or we'd sell it for two dollars in stores. That shit was moving like hotcakes! It was in Baltimore, D.C., North Carolina, L.A. That's what made Loud really want to fuck with us."

Wu-Tang was courted by several labels and landed on a savvy, forward-thinking, RCA-distributed imprint called Loud Records. Steve Rifkind, founder and president of Loud, remembers why he didn't need much convincing to sign the group up: "A street-team guy of mine brought them to my attention originally. He sent 'Protect Ya Neck' to my Los Angeles office and they sent it to me in New York. Next thing I know, the group—yes, all of them—just showed up at my office. We put on the record and a guy from the mailroom came running into my office and yells: 'That's that *shit!*' and then ran out. To this day I've never seen him again. After that, I knew that Wu-Tang was doing something pretty big. I didn't really care how many copies of 'Protect Ya Neck' they had sold on their own, I was convinced purely by their energy. Loud Records had a movement and so did Wu-Tang."

Rifkind continues: "RZA would come to my office every day at about five or six p.m., back when they still just had the twelve-inch deal for 'Protect Ya Neck.' He'd have a notepad with him, and he'd just go over all his plans. And I'd say yes to about ninety-eight percent of what he asked for. He would be amazed at that, and I'd say: 'RZA, everything you're saying makes perfect sense, why wouldn't I agree?' He came in there like a businessman and there was nothing I ever had to worry about with Wu-Tang. Everything about RZA's vision truly made sense. Wu-Tang, along with [Loud Records labelmates] Mobb Deep, are two of the easiest groups I've ever worked with. Because they're all about *business,* and because they work their asses off."

Touring (and the resulting show income) would become important to Wu-Tang for many reasons, one being the fact that the group didn't get much advance money for the album itself—even shorter cash when it was divided up nine ways. GZA recalls: "Our live shit was crazy. We were doing shows with all of us wearing stockings on our face when we first came out, so no one would know who was who." Deck recalls: "I remember our big

New York show, in 1993 after the album hit. We did a show at a place called Trafalgar Square in Queens. All of New York was there. People don't usually come out to Queens like that. Shit was wild, dudes got sliced up, females got into fights. And that show was the one that blew us up on the East Coast. After New York started pumping Wu, other places started following and we started really spreading after that."

Aside from the amazing music that was being produced in RZA's "hive," the most shocking thing about the making of the record may have been the professionalism shown by all nine hungry, competitive young MCs. "No one was even thinking about solo deals when we were making that album," GZA recalls. "We was all thinking: 'Let's do this bangin' album.'" Noting the different styles of all the members, Raekwon adds, "It was like being in the Superfriends. You don't have the same power as the next nigga, but you're all amazingly strong."

RZA reinforces the memories of camaraderie: "Competition was there, but it was MC competition, not any kind of squabbles between guys. It's like being in Shaolin [the real Shaolin, in China], where the monks all train with each other. One monk may be nice and another monk may be nicer, but if anyone else fucks with them, then that's the end of the story. It was like sharpening metal against metal. We had respect for strength in numbers."

"After 'Protect Ya Neck' we weren't trying to put eight or nine people on every song," explains GZA. "A lot of the album songs only had two guys on them. We just took our time and knew where we fit in. Back then we was just patiently waiting to get on songs. And even though everyone might have looked up to me as being the most lyrical in the Clan, my role was no bigger than anyone else's. We were all just MCs."

"You gotta move with force," Deck says. "RZA told us that we could get a hundred thousand or two hundred thousand each for a solo deal, but together we could make millions. And he was right." GZA says: "We didn't get any money at all from that [first] album. We may have gotten fifty thousand for an advance for the whole thing. But with our solo deals we all got to spread out and make our loot."

With all preproduction at RZA's lair and final work completed at Brooklyn's Firehouse Studios, Wu-Tang's debut, *Enter the Wu-Tang (36 Chambers)*, was released on November 9, 1993. The album helped bring NYC hip-hop back to the forefront of the national scene, away from Dr. Dre's post-*Chronic* left-coast uprising. Boasting multiple singles including the soulful thug anthems "C.R.E.A.M." and "Can It Be All So Simple," it was a never-ending array of verbal styles and kung fu motifs. GZA recalls: "With the kung fu stuff, it's not like we sat down and studied any of that stuff, but we all definitely went along with what RZA was trying to do. I knew all those movies and all the philosophies when it came to kung fu, so it wasn't a big thing."

RZA's tracks were also a revolution of their own, oftentimes pitting muffled, penitentiary-steel beats against mournful piano samples and itchy-fingered bass lines. It was soul on ice, and it was the start of a dynasty. "When I finished that album I thought it was the illest hip-hop record ever made," RZA beams. "I had listened to every hip-hop record already and I had hung around hip-hop stars. But I played that record as much as a person who had bought it, and for a long time, so I knew that it stood out."

Steve Rifkind says: "That album was a slow build, saleswise. Radio and some of the people at BMG (who owned RCA, Loud's distributor) thought the record was too hard, too noncommercial at first. But after Wu-Tang started selling, they turned it around. The album ended up scanning over a million copies, and that's about what we were expecting." The group was both confident and patient about its success. "We knew that nothing ever happens overnight," says GZA. "We were all mature in our own way. But I knew, and we all knew, that somewhere down the line we was going to break through. We weren't going to give up."

Deck recalls: "There was a mystique about the group when 'Protect Ya Neck' and the album was out. I mean, we were wearing stocking caps on the cover! We didn't care if people saw our faces. It wasn't a fashion show, we weren't trying to be the richest dudes. Nobody knew us, but they knew *of* us. They knew the name. And that was powerful.

"The power of *Enter the Wu-Tang* was just the chemistry that we had back then," Deck continues. "It was us coming off the street and just being us. If we came to the studio feeling fucked up, you'd hear that on the track. There were mistakes on there too. You could hear RZA hittin' the buttons and making shit slur. That was on purpose, to show that we weren't robotic. RZA's sound just sparked a whole new wave of production, bigger than I could have imagined. I'm personally still feeling the impact of that album today, the glow of it. It was deep to people because everybody in Wu-Tang represents somebody that you know, or maybe they're just like you yourself. We were universal. We'd go overseas and play for fifty thousand Germans or Irish people, all screaming and saluting Wu-Tang."

Steve Rifkind glowingly states: "That album will go down in history as one of the best albums ever made, hip-hop or otherwise. They proved, more than anything, that you could sell a shitload of records without tons of radio play. It was a grimy record, the opposite of [Dr. Dre's] *The Chronic,* and I would have signed every one of those guys up as a solo artist if I could have. But RCA and BMG just didn't know what the fuck we had, so the Wu-Tang solo artists ended up going all over the place [to different labels]."

"There were five albums that came out after that first album," brags RZA. (Solo albums by Method Man, Ol' Dirty Bastard, GZA, Ghostface Killah, and Raekwon followed within three years of the Wu-Tang debut.) "And they were all from the direct plan we were working on from the beginning. For the first five albums, up through *Wu-Tang Forever* [Loud/RCA, 1997], everything went exactly as planned."

TRACKS

BRING DA RUCKUS

Deck: That song brings me back to some wild nights, man. That might have been some shit that Ol' Dirty started in the studio. That's one of his types of slogans. He'd say shit like: "We're thinking too hard, let's just try to bring it, bring the ruckus!" That's how he used to talk. We all thought about things too much sometimes, including myself. I'm the Inspectah, so that shouldn't be a surprise to anyone.

SHAME ON A NIGGA

GZA: Ol' Dirty has some great stuff on there. He was always so talented. His parents sang real well—they'd sing at parties. He just never had one ounce of shyness in him, unlike me. I wished I was more outward like that sometimes. His style has always been wild and crazy, always unique. He had good lyrics, and sometimes people overlook that. He was good at taking rhymes and flipping them around. He'd sometimes even tell me: "I'll say your rhymes better than you!"

Deck: I remember the first time I met Ol' Dirty. RZA brought him over to his crib, and as soon as Dirty got there, he was like, "Turn that beat on!" He was straight off the street with a 40 in his hand, and he got on the mic and kicked some crazy shit. ODB was the same dude off the mic as he was on the mic. He never held anything back. When we'd be done doing a show, he'd still be doing a show. He'd be in the mall, just performing, singing the theme to *The Love Boat* or something. That's what I miss about him. Wu-

Tang is real serious, we're always in deep concentration, and he's the dude who would show up and fart in the middle of all of it.

CLAN IN DA FRONT

GZA: That's a great track. When I recorded that, Ol' Dirty recorded "Brooklyn Zoo" [the single] at the same time. We all loved that track even though I don't think it's my best work, looking back. I go first on there. The guys would be like: "We can't go after GZA, he's got to close it." I got kind of tired of hearing that shit! And with eight or nine people on a song, if you go last, you're gonna get cut on the video or the mix show. So I told them we gotta switch it up on this track, I'm going first.

WU TANG: 7TH CHAMBER

RZA: I had some lines on that one. I never wished that I had rapped more on that first album, because when Wu-Tang Clan was MCing, I knew I didn't have to MC, to tell you the truth. If they wanted me to rip it, I'd just come and scream on it. I was full of anger back then, I had an anger style.

Deck: That's probably my favorite track on the album, the one that starts with "Good morning, Vietnam!" Because it was war, it was M.A.S.H., the 4077th. And we was a fuckin' platoon. [*Deck raps some of his lines from the song, a cappella*]. And RZA didn't get on the mic as much as he could have on the album, but that was his plan. He said that to us. He didn't want to overdo it and be on there too much. He focused on the other MCs, the next wave. There were thirty-six chambers that we were going to show people, and that was only the seventh. I did the "9th Chamber" on my album [*Uncontrolled Substance,* 1999, Loud], and GZA had the "4th Chamber" [on *Liquid Swords,* 1995, Geffen].

GZA: Oh yeah, that was another one of the bangers. That was a great video, too, an early Hype Williams one. That was a dope reminisce track, that Gladys Knight vibe. I mean, RZA was doing the R&B samples like they have nowadays so long before these guys now. He sped it up a little but it didn't sound like chipmunks [*laughs*]. The vibe was good and the lyrics was nice. It was just a different sound for that time.

PROTECT YA NECK

Deck: RZA must have come up with that title. It was a personal statement from him to the whole industry. Like: "Y'all niggas fronted on me, now you better watch your ass!" On the original recording session for that, I didn't go first [Deck's is the first verse on the final song], I think I went second. Once I heard the final of that one, I knew to never doubt the RZA when it came to this music shit. Because the music that was underneath in the final version wasn't the beat that we originally rhymed to. We rhymed to something totally different, and we were all in a different order. The original beat was tight too, and RZA was just like: "I just need y'all's voices." We wasn't used to doing songs like that. And so we came in the next morning and voilà, there it was, karate chops and all. It was like magic. There just wasn't anything like that beat at the time, especially with the karate chops in there! That dude at the beginning of the song calling into the radio station, he was a real dude calling into a station. It was part of an interview we did, the same one that appears at different points in the album. It was some station in Virginia or Maryland, WPGC, I think. We did a video for that song on our own before Loud came along, and we never did another one after we got signed. It was pretty grimy.

GZA: That track has the most of us on it, eight of us. Masta Killa's not on there. That's where it all started, with that one single. I dis Cold Chillin' on there, but I edited it and cut that rhyme up a lot. If you would have heard the original rhyme, it was much worse—I was really venting. There was all kinds of other shit in there, it was some personal stuff. I always rewrite my rhymes and cut stuff out. I wasn't just lashing out at Cold Chillin', I was telling people how I felt. I came to a label where I was just as lyrically talented as their top artists and they didn't recognize that. They fucked my album up.

RZA: There were a few people around us at the time of that first single that didn't make the group, like Pop Da Brown Hornet and other niggas that also talked Wu-Tang slang. But as far as Wu-Tang Clan, the family of niggas that came together for a common cause, we was bonded by a different bond. And those were the niggas that came for "Protect Ya Neck."

DA MYSTERY OF CHESSBOXIN'

Deck: That was just a crazy idea that RZA had, about us being chess pieces on a board. Everyone was really into chess. I play, but I'm not as obsessed as RZA and GZA. They'll go twenty games straight, but I can't hang like that. GZA had a visual and saw how we could do that song. My man Gee Bee, Gerald Barclay, he put the video together. I guess I was on the black team [*laughs*]. It was just trying to give people something different than cars, chicks, and glitter. Giving people something mental.

WU-TANG CLAN AIN'T NUTHING TA F' WIT

Deck: The illest thing about that song was how RZA took the cartoon Underdog and he chopped [the theme] up and twisted it all around. I watched him do it. There's a moaning noise in there and he slowed it down dramatically, took two pieces, and put them together. To watch him doing that was just incredible. He was using an [Ensoniq] ASR-10 [sampler/keyboard], and he taught me how to use it. Then he fucked with the bass line and got that part of the song going. I was amazed.

RZA: I put that track farther back in the sequence even though it was one of the strongest tracks we did. When you listen to the album for the first time it hits you and entertains you like a movie. So you're already satisfied at a certain point and then you get hit *again*, like an epilogue.

GZA: Lyrically, RZA has more than showed his skills over the years. He doesn't have the best flow, the best delivery, and because of that sometimes people overlook his lyrics. Some people have no lyrics but have a bangin' flow. Anything they say sounds good. But RZA doesn't always sound as good. It wasn't a good-tasting vegetable, but it was still a vegetable.

Steve Rifkind: I knew that the album was really exploding when I was on Melrose in Los Angeles grabbing a bite to eat and I saw this white skateboard kid with hair down to his ass wearing a Wu-Tang hat, with headphones on, singing that song at the top of his lungs. That was a very good sign.

C.R.E.A.M.

Deck: Originally on that song it was me and Raekwon on a different beat, with four verses each. RZA found a new beat, took my best two [verses] and his best two, and put them together with Meth on the chorus. That kind of stuff happened often. A lot of the lyrics and songs were around in different forms, and RZA was the one who had to sit down with all the puzzle pieces. My rhyme on there was about me coming home from jail, trying to put my thoughts down and really take my life seriously. Dudes were telling me that I had talent, so I wanted to stop fucking around. I was handcuffed to the back of a bus, a young nigga up there with grown men. Upstate, not county jail—I was with the big boys. The streets taught me to adapt to all situations, so I became the Inspectah. I learned to close my motherfuckin' mouth and peep what was going on. I learned a whole lot during that era. My rap sheet is long. Two felonies, six misdemeanors. Drugs, burglary, gun possession, all that shit. I rarely talk about that shit in my rhymes, but you can hear me breathing it. So the stuff on that song was just a page out of an encyclopedia of rhymes I had back then. I've still got verses that were supposed to be on there that got cut out. When I'm done rhyming, I'm gonna put out a book of all my lyrics. I saved all that shit, even from back when I was in high school.

RZA: There's a version of that song, the original, called "Lifestyles of the Mega Rich." Deck and Raekwon probably went about four and a half minutes before the hook even came in. It was the same rhymes but longer, and the same exact beat too.

GZA: That was probably the biggest hit on the album. It definitely had the most impact. That's the one that we performed on Arsenio Hall.

Steve Rifkind: That's probably my favorite video from that album. I remember that it was shot on the coldest day of the year.

METHOD MAN

Steve Rifkind: I was in New York during the summer of 1993 and the "Method Man" song came on in a club I was at, and motherfuckers were *running* to the dance floor. They were losing their minds over that song. I called up the Los Angeles office [of Loud] and said: "We've got a monster on our hands."

GZA: [Fly] Ty and [Kool Ass] Lenny at Cold Chillin' heard that song two years before that came out on the Wu-Tang album, and they didn't want it. That track was three or four years old by the time the album came out— we might have just done the vocals over. I remember RZA playing it for them.

RZA: We definitely recorded that a couple years before *36 Chambers,* at my crib back in the day.

TEARZ

RZA: That was an exaggerated story, based on stuff that was happening to me and to everybody at the time. It was therapeutic to put it on a record like that. There was a lot of [bad] things going on when I wrote that rhyme.

RZA: That's maybe my favorite track on the album. It used to fuck me up and shit when I listened to it. It shows MC style, it shows producing style, and there's just so much crazy shit in that song.

X-CLAN

To the East, Blackwards

(4th & Bway, 1990)

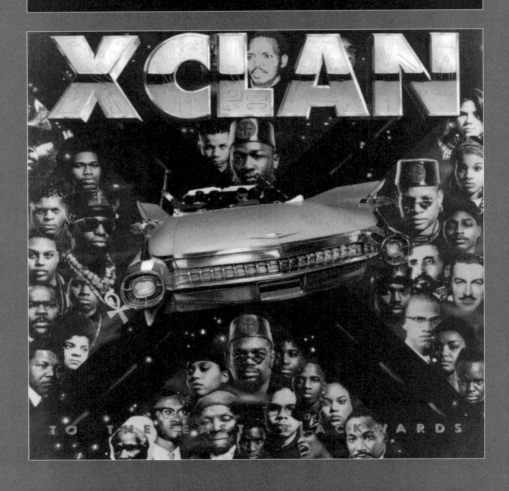

uthor's note: The Professor X interview for this chapter was conducted on August 17, 2004, a year and a half before he passed away. The Brother J interview for this chapter was conducted on March 15, 2006, only two days before Professor X passed.

When a young New Yorker named Robert Lumumba Carson became immersed in the hip-hop world of the mid-eighties to help bring the sound to the masses, his family wasn't happy about it. But it had nothing to do with fears that he was causing trouble with hoodlums or out partying. Lumumba's situation was different because his father was famed Brooklyn-based black nationalist leader Sonny Carson.

"The pro-black side of my world thought I was stumbling from my mission in life," says Lumumba, aka Professor X (who, sadly, died from spinal meningitis on March 17, 2006). "I wasn't being appreciated by them. I was torn between two lives."

But Elder Sonny eventually came to realize the power of hip-hop in spreading black nationalist thought after his son formed X-Clan, who released their funky, intelligent, and powerful debut in 1990. Their Blackwatch organization (with Isis, Unique & Dashan, Queen Mother Rage, and others) came before the X-Clan, and it was more than just a fan club. X explains: "I always watched how music groups became successful and I knew that fan base was very important. My idea was to make our fan-club base into a *movement.*"

Back in the early eighties, Lumumba was dating a woman who had been a radio DJ in Detroit. At her suggestion, he would conduct interviews in New York with R&B and hip-hop stars of the day (Billy Ocean, Luther Vandross, Kurtis Blow) and send them back to the radio station where she had worked. With this, Lumumba became an early ally of Russell Simmons and his growing Rush Productions stable of artists. By 1984 or 1985, Lumumba even road-managed Rush artist Whodini. As Lumumba casually observes, "For my whole career, hip-hop always did with me what it wanted."

His paramour also worked at the Metropolitan Museum of Art, and Lumumba would visit often. As he recalls: "I began to spend a lot of time in the Egyptian area of that museum. You'd be surprised how much they stole from

Egypt." Egyptian history and imagery would play a large role in X-Clan, and Lumumba started studying African history voraciously.

While most parents would be thrilled to see their progeny succeeding in business enterprises and gaining respect in their chosen industry, Lumumba's weren't. Sonny Carson, a hugely important, highly visible activist in the Bed-Stuy neighborhood of Brooklyn, wanted Lumumba to use his intelligence and charisma to work in the community. Lumumba recounts: "As I became more immersed in hip-hop, all the while I had another life, the life I was born into. I was spoon-fed the politics of life since I was a child by my father. I was raised with pro-black nationalism. It was a confusing time for me, because I loved hip-hop and I also had commitments to my father.

"Seeing Run-DMC at the Beacon Theater for the first time, I knew that was the beginning of the rest of my life," Lumumba recalls. "I loved everything about it. The music, the image they had. I knew then and there that I should create a group." The final sign was Public Enemy's second-ever show at the Latin Quarter in 1987. "I was like: 'If they let *this* go on, then I am ready to go,'" Lumumba laughs.

Years before the first X-Clan album came out, producer and manager Claude "Paradise" Gray (aka the Grand Architect) was a behind-the-scenes veteran in the hip-hop world. He recalls: "My first involvement in hip-hop was growing up in the Bronxdale Projects (in the Bronx, obviously). Disco King Mario lived in my building, and he was (Afrika) Bambaataa's main rival. I was about eight years old. Then we moved to the west side of the Bronx, and I was linked up with this DJ named JC, who was Kool Herc's number-one DJ. I was JC's record boy, and I started DJing from there. I lived a block away from Pete's Lounge [owned by Pete "DJ" Jones], and the Fever was four blocks away. I've got flyers from 1979 with my name on them, when I was DJ Paradise, with my partner DJ Playboy." Paradise was even an MC for a short-lived group called The Brothers 3.

In the early eighties, Paradise was a self-admitted "computer geek," working a job in Manhattan in the same building where Russell Simmons had his first Rush Management offices. "Back then I was doing Telex service stuff, with a Radio Shack TRS-80 computer. It was like a fax before faxes and e-mail before e-mail. At the same time I used to go to a lot of spots to party, like the Funhouse, the Roxy, and I became a middleman for a lot of people. I used to help organize Russell's [recording] tape library, all the twenty-four-track reels he had." Paradise and Lumumba both knew Russell's right-hand woman, Heidi Smith, who introduced them. They hit it off immediately and a longtime partnership was formed.

Continuing to network and expand within the hip-hop community, Paradise ended up at the most important club in the hip-hop world at the time, the Latin Quarter (located on Forty-eighth Street, near Times Square). He says: "When I first went there, I was answering the request line for the Awesome 2's radio show [on WHBI], and they were presenting their night called Celebrity Tuesdays at the LQ. I went there every week after that, without fail." By 1986, Paradise was living in Crown Heights, Brooklyn, and had become the full-blown "host" of the club, booking acts and acting as liaison between the public and owner Mike Goldberg. Because of this, Paradise was on the speed dial of every important hip-hop act, high-power manager, and hip-hop record label of the eighties.

Lumumba was continuing to manage groups at the time, so the two men joined forces. Under the name Scratch Me Management, they booked and were involved with the careers of acts like Stetsasonic, Just Ice, King Sun, EPMD, and Positive K. Lumumba says: "It was a natural way to continue the next level of my career—as a manager. We started managing groups that we were already booking at the Latin Quarter, which was the epicenter of New York hip-hop at the time." Paradise explains: "The LQ became the incubator for hip-hop superstars, and we would showcase unsigned artists, people like Kid 'N Play, Queen Latifah, MC Lyte, Jungle Brothers."

As a result of the fly-by-night nature of the New York nightlife scene, the club closed its doors in 1988, and Paradise went on to manage another club called the World. "We had created Blackwatch by then," he says, "and from 1988 to 1989 we also developed X-Clan."

Grand Verbalizer Brother J (born Jason Hunter) was years younger than Lumumba and Paradise, and he came to be just the lyrical spark that the group needed to get their "funkin' lessons" to the masses. "Before it all, I was a DJ," J says from his current Cali homebase. "I was from Flatbush, Brooklyn, at a time where you had to earn the right to rock a block party. That was me, a little kid on a crate, cuttin' [Herman Kelly's] 'Dance to the Drummer's Beat.' I did family barbecues and learned how to move the crowd." He continues: "The microphone thing didn't start until I got into

Murry Bergtraum High. The Jungle Brothers and Q-Tip were there, before there was any kind of Native Tongues thing. Our high school was like ten-to-one ratio of female to male, so cats used to come to all our talent shows to check out the females. Our talent shows were like the Latin Quarter! Biz and Kane would come through, ODB was around back when he was calling himself A-Son. Shit was serious."

J was even in a very early incarnation of the Jungle Brothers, when they were called the Bugout Crew. He wasn't rhyming at the time, just beatboxing. After winning recognition at different Bergtraum talent shows, he caught the hip-hop bug for real—and also caught some of the ego that can come with the territory. He recalls: "After some success with those talent contests I was ready to drop out of high school right there. It souped my head up and I started failing my classes." He ended up leaving Bergtraum and attending Brooklyn College Academy, closer to his home.

"My lyrical content wasn't as positive until my father interjected himself into my life by showing me what was happening in the streets of the city," J remembers. "He'd say: 'Don't always just walk by a drunk guy and ignore him. Maybe buy him a meal and have a conversation with him, because you could learn something.' That's why I said, on [X-Clan's] 'Raise the Flag,' some of the strongest minds are in the Bowery. Walking the streets after my dad gave me permission to go into the city and move around started me writing the poetry that turned into the lyrics on *To the East, Blackwards.*"

Back in the mid-to-late eighties, J met the late Sugar Shaft the Rhythem Provider (Anthony Hardin, who passed away in 1995), who would become X-Clan's DJ. J recalls: "I went to school with one of his friends, DJ Spice. Those guys were best friends, and Shaft was just known as Sugar back then, so they'd cut together and it was Sugar & Spice. After I left the Bugout Crew, me, Shaft, Spice, and another guy called ourselves Quad Squad. One of the guys was biting his rhymes from someone uptown, so we cut him off, and then Spice dropped out, so it was just me and Shaft. We worked together all the time back in '86 and '87."

Shaft knew Paradise and through that connection, J was brought to the Latin Quarter. Since Paradise was managing the club, the two young hip-hoppers experienced greatness from backstage—a vantage point that few other up-and-comers had at the time. J says: "My dad gave me permission to go down there, and I got to witness so much history at the LQ through Architect [Paradise], by him opening those doors. I used to watch Red Alert DJ there and I would write rhymes to the beats he was throwing down."

Aside from being swayed by the greatest hip-hoppers of the mid-eighties during that time, by 1986 and 1987 J and countless others were influenced by a social and political organization that Professor X helped found called Blackwatch. Formed around the philosophies of the black nationalist movement that Sonny Carson put into action, Blackwatch wasn't a party crew. It was a meeting of the minds, and they gathered frequently at various locations in Brooklyn to discuss history and politics and, when needed, plan demonstrations in the community. Paradise says: "The meetings we had weren't regularly scheduled, but they were held frequently. Sonny Carson was always at the head of our meetings with the Council of Elders, and Lumumba was heavily involved too, of course." X-Clan became Blackwatch's ultimate "message group."

"The Blackwatch meetings took place at many different locations and featured teachings and conversations by many great elders from all over the globe," continues Paradise. "Some meetings were at Sonny Carson's Montague and Remsen Street offices in downtown Brooklyn, some were at Professor X's home, some were in the 'Clan Room' at the Klinic Hotel in Bedford-Stuyvesant, which was owned by one of our elders, Jim Cuffee. In fact, the 'Clan Room' was a major inspiration for the name X-Clan."

Although Paradise wasn't raised in the black nationalist movement, he deeply respected the African American self-reliance and empowerment that Blackwatch and Sonny Carson were all about. Paradise explains: "I'm a people person, I just love people. All the black nationalist stuff, including my and Brother J's involvement, came together under Professor X and Sonny Carson. And back in the eighties, the black nationalist meeting attendees were all older guys. We wanted to get the youth involved."

Paradise remembers meeting Sonny for the first time back in the mid-eighties: "I loved Sonny immediately. He looked me up and down and said: 'What kind of name is *Paradise* for a black man?' [*Laughs.*] I told him it was more of a goal than a name. And I told Sonny that we could use hip-hop for political uses, to draw people in with the music. He wasn't sold on the idea at first, but we made it happen with Blackwatch."

Brother J's father, who worked as a cab driver, wasn't a part of the black nationalist or Blackwatch movements. But he was part of another organization that was very influential on the still-young Brother J: the Freemasons. "The background in my family is Masonic," J explains. "I was being groomed to continue with the house. I grew up with order, and I studied the sciences. Blackwatch influenced me because they brought me around to hang out when I was only seventeen, and I saw Five Percent heads, Muslim heads. All of the sons of the elders were there. It was just such a universal spot. When I came there, I was like: 'Man, I can be free here. This is a lot looser than Junior Masons. I can learn black nationalism and everything that the Black Panthers were teaching.' That influenced me a lot."

J adds: "Blackwatch was the neutral ground for us to grow. I really salute Lumumba for creating that, bringing that black nationalist movement into a hip-hop frame of reference. Blackwatch was even more important than the X-Clan. But X-Clan became so popular and got so much hype that people just thought the movement *was* X-Clan. And I always tell Lumumba: 'You should be proud about what you did with Blackwatch.' "

Considering the father-to-son traditions handed down within Masonic structures, J's father was obviously concerned and curious about this new influence on his son's life. J remembers: "My father was concerned because I didn't want to go to the Junior Masons anymore, so he came down to a Blackwatch meeting and met Lumumba, like a parent is supposed to. He spoke with Sonny [Carson] and Sonny told Professor X to look out for me."

X-Clan actually became known on TV screens across the tri-state area in 1988 before they had even recorded a song. As Lumumba recalls: "Ralph McDaniels and *Video Music Box* (a music video channel in the New York area that was controlled by viewer requests instead of station programming; it debuted years before viewer-demand programs like MTV's *TRL*) was very important in our visuals. Just before we blew up, we were a curiosity on *Video Music Box*. That's actually how we started out. Between videos at that time, they'd have artist promos, and we did one too. I came on wearing a crown, with X-Clan in back of me. I'd say: 'Peace! Behind me is the group X-Clan, and when we're not reading the memoirs of Malcolm X or walking the pathways of Marcus Garvey, we watch *Video Music Box* with Ralph McDaniels.' The response was huge, and when I went into record labels after that, they knew who I was."

Of course the group would need a lyricist to achieve its lofty goals, but, as Paradise says, "Back then we hadn't ever even heard Brother J rap. His affiliation with us was just as one of the young brothers in the Blackwatch movement." J's spitfire MC skills, in fact, got pushed to the side for more than a year because X and Paradise were working with so many other top-level MCs at the time, like King Sun, Daddy-O and Stetsasonic, and Positive K. Also, Lumumba's and Paradise's Scratch Me Management was, at the time, most interested in working with the group Unique & Dashan, whose *Black to the Future* album (Warlock Records, 1989) was the first to come out of the Blackwatch organization. "They had crowns on the cover, before X-Clan was out," says Paradise, who co-produced the album with Lumumba.

But J's fight for attention changed dramatically later in 1987, when Paradise took J and Sugar Shaft to Ced-Gee's (producer of the Ultramagnetic MCs and a close friend of KRS-One and Scott La Rock) "Ultra Lab" home studio in the Bronx, where they cut a demo. The song was called "It's a Black Thing." J recalls: "Paradise brought us to Ced-Gee, but he didn't even know what I had until I opened my mouth and spit on that first track. I was talking about shit I was seeing in the streets and just trying to feel out how to fit into this Blackwatch organization. That's why the name of the song was so direct. I was proud to be part of a black movement. Lumumba had so much knowledge that he shared with us, and I tried to channel it. With that demo, it showed that I was living the order *and* spitting some different shit. When they heard that demo, that was the spark of what was to be X-Clan."

Paradise and Lumumba were very creative with how they financed their early projects. Paradise recalls: "X-Clan was actually signed to Warlock Records first. Al Tuga [aka Al "T" McLaran] was A&R for Warlock, and he gave X-Clan a single deal to do 'Raise the Flag,' which we had played him in demo form. He gave us a lot of money up front but we hadn't even signed a contract. He was so blown away by the song that he just gave us the money! So we took the money he gave us and produced the Unique & Dashan album, then took them to Warlock and said, 'You have to sign these guys too.' Because in reality we needed more money! So he signed them and Isis, too. Then we had the extra money we needed and we started actually working on X-Clan's album.

"Once we did the first six or seven songs for X-Clan, we knew it was going to be big," Paradise continues. "And we didn't think that Warlock could do enough with it. So we started shopping X-Clan, since we hadn't signed anything with Warlock. We knew Kookie Gonzalez at 4th & Bway, but someone higher in A&R turned the project down. Me and X wouldn't take no for an answer, so Kookie helped us get another meeting and we went directly to Chris Blackwell [the president and founder of Island, 4th & Bway's parent company]. He had signed Bob Marley and took a risk with him, so we knew that he would understand X-Clan. Halfway through the first song we played for Chris he stopped the tape and signed us for a single deal. We walked out the next day with a check, went to the studio, paid what we owed them for the X-Clan recording, took the rest of the money, and paid Al at Warlock back for the initial advance he gave us for X-Clan. After all that, we basically got a three-album deal out of it, and even though Warlock didn't have X-Clan, they still had Isis and Unique & Dashan. [*Author's note: Isis's debut,* Rebel Soul, *came out on 4th & Bway, not Warlock.*] Everybody got paid."

According to Brother J, X-Clan was initially called Rated X, although, he says, "Paradise knew that the name wasn't very marketable. So we decided to think about the name and I meditated on it. The name X-Clan just hit me. Because Blackwatch had me thinking with numbers, and numbers were strength." Considering that neither Paradise nor Professor X was a top-level MC and neither was a high-caliber DJ, their role at first, according to J, was more on the production and management side. He says: "If you look at the first group pictures, it was just me and Shaft in front of a gate, and there's a fence in front of it. It says, 'Who's on what side of the fence?' And Lumumba's face is faded into it."

J continues: "Lumumba was the manager, and he was like: 'Anything coming from Blackwatch will have my name attached, since I'm the founder. He was still calling himself Lumumba back then. Shaft named him Professor X. I was originally going to be Professor X, actually, because I was so mentally focused all the time. But I liked Grand Verbalizer better, so Lumumba used Professor X. And I named Sugar 'Shaft' because he knew the city so well. He knew the streets of New York like Shaft did in the movie." Lumumba says of the group's name, "It came from X-Men comics—we all read them. We were just a Technicolor version of what they were. And the nationalist movement knew what the 'battle of the mutant' was!"

"I was the chef, but everybody did the cooking," says Paradise. "They called me the Architect because I was laying the foundation for all the sounds. Everybody produced, but the final responsibility of how shit sounded was up to me. Professor X was the final word, but I was the one who got it ready for his approval." J recalls: "Paradise was great with his hands and with gadgets, so the Architect was perfect. He added 'Tracktitioner' because he was always on some producer shit. His style was still growing back then—he was with the Uptown [Records] sound, Teddy Riley and Heavy D. and all that."

J maintains that many things about X-Clan were a direct result of his ideas and work, but even back then his youthful confidence had to bow to Professor X's and Paradise's wisdom and experience. "If I would have had my way, we would have been the first Wu-Tang Clan," he says. "I was going to bring up my whole block, Twenty-fifth Street, Flatbush, all young cats spitting fire. But I knew that, considering the history of Lumumba and Architect, it would be so much more of a mature group to have them involved in our shit. We were young heads and didn't know anyone in the game, but whenever we went out with those dudes, everybody knew them. So having us all together was a great thing, because it was a balance."

With the beginning of Blackwatch's musical arm, put in motion by overseeing and producing Unique & Dashan's album, Lumumba's and Paradise's plan to start X-Clan was about to hatch. As noted by Paradise, X-Clan was signed for a single deal and released the powerful double A-sided single "Raise the Flag" b/w "Heed the Word of the Brother" in the first part of 1989. The group became known because of its involvement in the "Day of Outrage and Mourning" to protest the killing of Yusuf Hawkins in Brooklyn's Bensonhurst neighborhood in August. 4th & Bway knew they had a firebrand group on their hands, in certain ways akin to the controversial and popular Public Enemy, and they signed X-Clan for a full album.

Production on the album was a group effort, and most members have their own take on who did the most work. The easiest description is just how it was listed on the album: as a group. Lumumba explains: "We all agreed to have it as a group production, because on any given day it would be one of us that could be the main mover of any particular song. My production strength was that I was the oldest guy in the group, so I had an instinct about the older music [samples of funk groups like P-Funk and Zapp were used on several album tracks]. Sugar Shaft had musical knowledge and DJ mixing ability. Paradise, being the next oldest, had a knack for classic jams as well. J is a DJ at heart, so in reality we had several DJs in the group."

J gives his own impression: "In reality we'd start with a basic track, then go home and fill in the gaps with samples we wanted, then we'd tell [the album's engineer] Mike French where we wanted things to go. Mike put structure to our shit. We had ideas coming from the turntables, but he made it make sense. Bar counts, timing, editing, making sure that shit was punched correctly."

Lumumba agrees about Mike French's importance to the group's sound: "He was our engineer, and he had to be the first one in hip-hop to give us the understanding to stop hiding the voice behind the music, to bring it out front. If you had good voices in the group—and we did—you had to do that. Mike was the guy at INS [Recording Studios] who all the R&B cats wanted to use, so we had to fight with Keith Sweat for his time."

"Everybody contributed their part," J says. "Everything with us was always a partnership with everything, whether they wrote and produced on it or not. I very much wanted us to be credited as a team." Lumumba says: "It had to be a unanimous decision in the studio. If three of us was feeling a track more than the fourth one, then we had to get it to a place where the fourth one felt it in order for us to finish it."

To the East, Blackwards was recorded in one month's time, according to Professor X, and put on a full-steam-ahead promo track by the label. Perfectly described by the opening track's title, "Funkin' Lesson," the album mixed bouncing old-school funk samples with pro-black words of wisdom, perfectly and powerfully expressed by the muscular vocals of Brother J.

"I was raw on that album, like I was rocking at a block party," says J. "I don't put it on me, like I'm the most creative dude in the universe, but the light was shining through me on that album, and those brothers made sure that I had a conduit to shine through. Without them I would have been the rapper who never made it out of Flatbush. It was just a great dynamic that we had. We influenced so many people with our music and my team meant everything to me, as a family.

"We were the first real *movement* with a hip-hop budget behind us," continues Brother J. "We would take twenty members of Blackwatch around the country and show up at a venue looking thick. It was very impressive."

Brother J has one provocative beef with one of the group's most recognizable calling cards: Professor X's "sign off" monologues, which always ended with the word *sissy,* elongated and over-enunciated. He says: "I was very much against all the 'sissy' shit, because it made people ignore the message we were trying to get across. It had nothing to do with the music or our message. It was like some Flavor Flav shit, and Professor X wasn't Flavor Flav. Flavor Flav never founded a movement."

Professor X explains the catchphrase from his own point of view: "That was a way for me to say, 'If the shoe fits, then go ahead and have a problem [*laughs loudly*]!' It was a challenge. It was me responding to everyone using the word *sucka* all the time back then. If the shoe fits, then wear that motherfucka! I didn't ever mean it to be funny, but some people thought it was."

For the many fans who put X-Clan and Public Enemy in the same boat, there were several important differences. Professor X offers this distinction between the two different sides of the same struggle: "Public Enemy should always be protected, so don't misunderstand me. But their message—what it was and how it was delivered—just seemed so *complicated*. We felt that blackness was easier than that. If you were a brother or sister in Brownsville, it was right up under your nose. You only needed to talk to your grandmother to know how proud you were supposed to be and who you were."

"We offered a different type of expression," beams Brother J, looking back. "We allowed people to wear earrings and not be a punk rocker. We allowed people to live out that African cultural side of themselves that they used to be scared to show in public. They wore beads, carved their own sticks. We made people do research."

And the late, great Professor gets the last word: "Each person in that group was a piece of madness that you'd never believe could get along with the other three [*laughs very loudly*]. You'd never think we could be in a room together. And that's why it was magic together, because we made it work."

TRACKS

FUNKIN' LESSON

Paradise: We definitely combined our message with some funky music. But that's a pretty obvious thing, since people don't respond to shit if it ain't hot, whether there's a message or not. We were all about walking the walk, not just talkin'. We just really wanted to be funky and put the lesson in the funk. That's what the song was about. We were trying to redefine something, and have more culture in the music.

Professor X: I was a funkhead from back in the day. That was my contribution to our earliest music. The George Clinton vibe. I mean, who would have thought that the funk explosion in hip-hop started from a group in New York!

Brother J: Shaft was instrumental in how that song was composed like it was. I wanted to use "Dancefloor" by Zapp, but he brought [Funkadelic's] "Knee Deep" to the table. That was his favorite record. When we put both versions side by side, "Knee Deep" won because it was just more energetic. Lyrically, that's a great example of something I like to call "Funk Code." Sending a whole lot of information in a three-minute time frame. What made X-Clan different was that regardless of the complexity of the lyrics, you could dance all night and party and sweat your ass off!

GRAND VERBALIZER, WHAT TIME IS IT?

Brother J: I started using the name Grand Verbalizer way back, after I was out of Brooklyn College Academy and got my [Blackwatch] crown. Grand

Verbalizer defined MC differently for me. I didn't want to be MC Brother J—I needed a title that would describe me to the fullest. Grand Verbalizer was like a royal MC. Professor X didn't like that song because it looked like I was rubbing my ego. But that song never had anything to do with ego. It was about people asking the Verbalist what was going down. There's a line in there about polar bears swinging on the vines of a gorilla. A while back I saw that Eminem was bothered by that, in *Rolling Stone* or somewhere. He loved X-Clan but was intimidated, and thought I was trying to make all white kids into outcasts. I wasn't trying to do that at all. I was saying: "Be yourself." If I'm a gorilla and I go to the North Pole, I'm gonna be cold as fuck, I'm not going swimming! Play your position, that's all I've ever said to white artists. My biggest beef with 3rd Bass was that their label was pushing them as a black group. We were shocked when we saw the video and saw these white boys rhymin' on that dope-ass shit. We didn't want people to clone us by sounding like us. *Play . . . your . . . position* [*says very slowly*]. Be who you are. I could admire the Beastie Boys because they sounded like who the fuck they were: white boys getting drunk and fighting for their right to party. I could respect that.

Professor X: I'm sure everyone else in the group will say that that's their favorite track. The "crossroads" I mention in that song, and in other places on the album, was very important to us. We wanted to give recognition to all those who didn't know where they were at in life. It was the point in their lives where they were trying to get clear. We were drawing a picture where you were at so you could make decisions. And decisions start at the crossroads, and you're protected there.

Brother J: When I said "you must learn" in that song, people thought that there was a beef between us and KRS-One [because of the Boogie Down Productions 1989 song titled "You Must Learn"]. My thing to him was that I was a pit bull for black nationalism, and when I saw that he was trying to be a humanist and have everyone hold hands and build, I wasn't with it. It was like: "I can be friends with you all day, but before we're going to build organizations together, let me get my people together first, so we can come as a focused weapon." The beef with KRS got so high that it never became an intelligent conversation back then. It took sixteen years for me to sit down with him and explain. When I said that in the song, I *was* talking about Kris. If you're flip-flopping you can't teach people.

TRIBAL JAM

Paradise: A lot of people take Brother J for granted as a rapper. A lot of the things that he said were things that we or our elders lived personally. Everything we wrote came from the cultural experience of black people. It was all real. And we used the music to build a strong movement.

Brother J: It wasn't hard for our fans to embrace Africa. Everybody who listened to our shit had an elder who was like: "I told you!" Parents told their kids about Africa all the time and got ignored. But we presented it differently and redefined it. I didn't obey song-structure laws of sixteen bars, chorus, sixteen bars, chorus. I just *wrote,* and I spoke about everything from Hannibal to Legba to Yeshua. I was talking about our history and asking what happened to our power.

A DAY OF OUTRAGE, OPERATION SNATCHBACK

Professor X: The Day of Outrage was the day when the Brooklyn Bridge was taken by twenty or thirty thousand people, with Reverend Al Sharpton [in late August 1989, as a reaction to the murder of Yusuf Hawkins in Bensonhurst]. Those battles are what created songs like "A Day of Outrage." It's about how we were there, fighting for the right of recognition in that community [Bensonhurst]. I don't know about other hip-hop groups that were in the midst of it like we were. The day after we took the bridge, there was a picture of us in the paper being part of it, and the head of 4th & Bway saw it and signed us for the album right there, because of the picture. They were on the verge of getting rid of us up until then because of low sales on the single ["Heed the Word of the Brother"].

Brother J: I was fresh off the Brooklyn Bridge and went right into the studio and wrote that song. I wrote it on the way to the studio, and laid it out as emotionally as I possibly could. It was strict emotion.

Professor X: Ah yes, the pink Cadillac! I mention that on that track, don't I? We wanted to tell people to celebrate themselves. When I think of a pink Cadillac I think of my uncles, who were from South Carolina. Those guys had a Caddy every year. It meant something to them. We were talking about a 1959 pink Caddy because it represented a point in time. Once the elders saw that we were talking about that, they knew that we recognized the transition between a certain kind of Negro into a certain kind of black man. We wanted to celebrate the Caddy, too, because we had a little pimp in our crown. We got style from that. It was a metaphor. We wanted to celebrate things that some black people wanted to hide. Cornbread, grits. In every video of ours, Sugar Shaft is eating something. Chicken or watermelon. We love that food, and there's no reason to be ashamed of it. In fact, totally the opposite!

EARTH BOUND

Brother J: I wrote that whole song—Professor X didn't write anything on that one, although he performed on it. That was recorded right in the middle of the sessions for the album. I wanted to try a different style, a deep, scientific, raw approach. The title of the song meant that God is on Earth, and we have a mission that we must carry out. It was like *E.T.,* we're here on a mission but we're stuck.

SHAFT'S BIG SCORE

Paradise: Shaft was my best friend. He was quiet and funny and an incredible DJ. Very quiet and peaceful. A couple times when I was down he even bought Pampers for my kids. Food, whatever. He was amazingly generous and we all really miss him.

Professor X: Sugar Shaft had such an energy! We had to buy him new Technics turntables every two weeks because he destroyed them just doing his cuts. They would literally be no good to anybody after he was through. He would sweat so much when he cut, too. He just had so much inward energy. He also cut with his left hand, so he'd have to cross one arm over the other. I think that Shaft's influence is where the bounce in our music came from. We miss him. That particular track, which features Shaft's DJ skills, was a very hard track to do, because back then there was no automation. We had to do it over many times to get the punches in there correctly. We heard Terminator X's tracks [from Public Enemy] and we wanted to counter them on that level. Because we respected him so much. We all motivated each other in that way.

Brother J: We did that track so Shaft could just get his shit off, all that restlessness that was in him. Shaft wrecked a lot of turntables, but it was more out of negligence. He would use the 45 [adapter] holder as an ashtray [*laughs*]. We'd raid clubs for their turntables all the time, 'cause when an arm of the turntable would break off, they'd have a turntable graveyard in the back of the club. We'd take them and fix them up.

RAISE THE FLAG

Paradise: That was the first studio song that we did as X-Clan. I got that sample from a neighbor of mine in Crown Heights. She heard Run-DMC blaring through my walls and instead of yelling, she wanted to hear more about them and borrowed the album from me. Then one I day I heard that Roy Ayers "Red, Black and Green" song [which is sampled on the track] blaring through *her* walls. She had a crazy loud system that put mine to shame. She was a jazz lover more than hip-hop. So I banged on her door and asked her what the hell that music was.

Brother J: That was a record that Architect found and we sampled it and I wrote the lyrics in one day. I was working quickly like that back then. That track was definitely done quickly. That song was for the elders—it was Sonny's [Carson's] favorite.

Brother J: I had that song [the lyrics] written way back, before we were even called X-Clan. I wrote it with the "More Bounce to the Ounce" beat. That one was the club favorite. On that one, 45 King [who produced] replaced the sample. I wanted to rock the sample like EPMD did—I didn't want 45 King involved. But the record was a hit and the youth in me had to take the bench and let that motherfucker be a hit.

Paradise: That was the only song that anybody outside of X-Clan ever collaborated on with us, as an outside producer or artist. Mark the 45 King made the beat, and I produced the song. I put in the hook, and the "Flashlight" stuff in the intro.

IN THE WAYS OF THE SCALES

Professor X: That is definitely one of my favorite tracks on the album, if not my number-one favorite.

Brother J: In Egyptian science, when you leave your body you go to the scales, and they put your heart on balance with a feather in front of the gods. The song was the balance of all things. It was the boogie, the lyrics, and I think I did a small attack on 3rd Bass on there. I was saying: "We are balancing the game, don't challenge us." That song has sentimental value to me because I stayed in New York to record it when I was supposed to be down south with my father, who passed when we were recording that song. "Verbs of Power" and "In the Ways of the Scales" were the last two songs that we recorded, so I'll always remember that. My father believed in my group and he loved what I was doing. He adjusted to it and accepted it.

ACKNOWLEDGMENTS

All writers know that they would be nothing without the patience of their (usually very forgiving) families. My first and biggest thanks must go to my amazing and beautiful wife, Margot, who inspires me, is always there for me, and who was thankfully spared a lot of blindness-inducing proofreading this time around. My immediate family has always been unfailingly supportive, and I give them infinite love and respect: Mom, Dad, Darcie, Chris, Hope, Sadie, Pete, Pat, Kristi, Justin, George, Bev, Paul, Wade, Laurie, Charlene, Andrew, Sienna, Ryan, Jayce, and Julie. My in-laws are fresh, too; so thanks to Paula, Janet, Alex, Nate, and Jim.

As for this crazy book itself, I have to give the highest props and praises to everyone who lent me their time and input. The MCs, DJs, producers, managers, and record-label honchos whose words are all over this made *Check the Technique* happen.

When it comes to my friends, the trio of Michelle Mercer, Mitch Myers, and Ed Nawotka—all of whom are inspiring, top-shelf writers in their own right—offered sage advice and, against their better judgment, never blocked my e-mails, deleted me from their MySpace Top 8, or kept their restraining orders active for too long. Also much love and respect to Rani, Jenny Nawotka, Rich Benton, Jeff "Mr. Lif" Haynes, Linda and Tom, Jason and Kim, Seana and Nick, Garrou and Fitz, Gina and Tony, Frenchie and David, Kathleen and Tim, Matt and Susan, Zack and Anita, Mary Galli, Nyal and Becky, and many more of my pals who might not be listed but who know who they are.

I also have to give huge thanks to the following hip-hop journo peers for inspiration and encouragement: Dave Tompkins, Jeff Chang, Adam Mansbach, Adisa Banjoko, Bill Adler, and Dan Leroy helped at various junctures along the way, and I will always be indebted to them. On the biz side, many thanks to Paula Breen and Vince Kamin, who helped make my quest to sell out an easier one. Props also to my diggity-dope and hard-working editors

Adam Korn and Porscha Burke, who both helped in all aspects of this book. Also thanks to Bruce Tracy and everyone else at Villard and Random House who made *Check the Technique* a reality.

Artists, friends, and industry types who deserve mention for help and/or inspiration: Matt Conaway, Richard Nichols, Peter Agoston, Z-Trip, Peanut Butter Wolf and Egon at Stones Throw, Riggs Morales, the almighty DJ Red Alert, Matt Nicholas for design greatness on "Rakim Told Me," Andy Hurwitz at Ropeadope, Cut Chemist, 7L & Esoteric, Dante Ross, Evil Dee & Mr. Walt, Paradise Gray, Todd 1, Freddy Fresh, Jesse Ferguson, Ced-Gee, Kool Keith, Moe Luv, Chuck D, the legendary Greg Mack, Phat Gary, Qiana Wallace, Mike "Floss" Ross, DJ Premier, Bobbito Garcia, Nick Taylor, Kutmasta Kurt, Aimee Morris, Erik Blam, Wes Jackson & Alma Geddy-Romero at Room Service, Edo G, Violet Brown, Shauna Garr, Domino, Zach Katz, Rob Swift, Matt Life aka Matty C, Nomadik (Boston) and Nomadic (NYC), Dave Paul at BOMB, Jen Hall, Ice-T, Jennifer Ramsay aka Mrs. Schoolly D, Nat Robinson, Mr. Mixx, Roberta Magrini, James Ellis, Tony D, Monique Baines and Steve Rifkind at SRC, Noz, Edan, Prince Paul, Lord Finesse, Muggs, Jessica Weber, Papa D, Trevor Seamon, Cee Knowledge, Tim Linberg and O'Neal Rowe, Kym Norsworthy, Born Free, Jazzbo, Chris Craft, Teddy Tedd & Special K, Tom Silverman, Michelle & Gavin at Audible Treats, Tresa Sanders, Laz-E-Laz, Hitman Howie Tee, Mark Dienger, Jorge Hinojosa, Jeff Waye at Ninja Tune, Wood from Team Inspectah Deck, Corey Smyth, DJ T-Rock, Bonz Malone, Tony Ferguson, Nicole Balin, Mike Rivard, Simone Fader, Jamie Roberts and Joan Bolvin at Roadrunner, Pacey Foster, Wayne Marshall, Jayquan at The Foundation, Greg Miller, Faith Newman, Chris Van O at Boogiedownbeats.com, the anonymous hard workers at discogs.com, the guys in Tanya Morgan, Solomon Comissiong, Bill Banfield, Rob Hayes, and Allen Bush at Berklee, Sean Westergaard, Ann Braithwaite, Murray Forman, and DJ Spinna.

Writers who have inspired me are part of this, too: David Toop, Nelson George, Steven Hager, Ishmael Reed, Upski Wimsatt, Ronin Ro, Del Jones, Scoop Jackson, and Greg Tate.

Writers, editors, and radio peeps who helped along the way: Jerry Barrow, Alvin Blanco, Lizz Carroll, Jesus Trivino and all my peeps at *Scratch*, Andre Torres and Brian DiGenti at *Wax Poetics*, Josh Glazer and Kathryn

McGuire at *URB,* Chris Faraone, Hua Hsu, Larry Katz, Noah Uman at WFMU, Oliver Wang, Carly Carioli, Zaid and *Spine Magazine* UK, Michaelangelo Matos, Sarah Rodman, my dear friend Neil Bennun, Dru Ryan, Buddabong and everyone at SOL of Hip-Hop Radio, JToThaI at ThaFormula.com, Jeff Copetas, Julie Cohen, Mazi Mutafa at *Words Beats and Life* and his WPFW "Holla Back" crew in D.C., Phat Matt at *Elemental,* Theo Haumesser holdin' it down in France, Eric Arnold, Roy Christopher, Mary Nichols, Mike Endelman and Nina Willdorf, Davide Bortot and *Juice* in Germany, Sam Chennault, Paine at Allhiphop.com, Tony Wright at Rap News UK, Craig Smith, Dave Hofer at *Punk Planet,* Mike Wolf at *Time Out New York,* William Hernandez and *Urban America* in Miami, Camille Dodero, Jennifer Vineyard at MTV, Toph One from XLR8R, Chris Estey, Chris Force at *Alarm,* Ron Wynn in Nashville, Colin Helms, Soren Baker, Chris Porter, Elliott Wilson, Chairman Mao, Bonsu Thompson, Leah Rose, and Elisabeth Baco.

I can't forget retail, which helped *Rakim Told Me* make its way in the world: Christian, Mike, Trev, Matt, Will C, Big Dan, and everyone at Traffic Entertainment, Mike Lewis holdin' down the UK, Jasper Goggins and everyone at Turntable Lab, Joe Quixx and the Amoeba crew, Sound Library NYC, Fat Beats worldwide, Doug and the Dusty Groove Chi-town massive, Cool Chris at Groove Merchant, Giant Peach, Jesse Haley at Haley Booksellers, Sandbox, Newbury Comics, Dave Harris at Baghat Vinyl, and all the robot monkeys at Amazon who link me to books better than my own.

Publishing peeps whom I thank for their advice and encouragement over the years: David Dunton, David Barker, Beth Haymaker, Andrea Rotondo, Ben Schafer, Sarah Lazin, Sara Rosen, Lauren McKenna, Richard Nash, Brett Valley, and Meg La Borde.

I want to say that Philly's proud son, Ahmir "?uestlove" Thompson, is a great guy, a ridiculously funky drummer, and a true hip-hop fan and scholar. I'm honored to have his words in the book's Roots chapter as well as his kick-ass intro. Artists like Ahmir make a book like this an absolute pleasure to put together.

Finally, I am also indebted to photographer/writer/documentarian Brian "B+" Cross for providing *Check the Technique* with so many amazing photos, which truly bring their respective chapters alive. I have had the highest respect for him since I first peeped his 1993 book *It's Not About a*

Salary: Rap, Race + Resistance in Los Angeles (Verso), and he has gotten even iller since then. Props to his Mochilla partner Eric Coleman for his killer Wu-Tang photo, too.

Oh, and thanks to you, too, for purchasing, stealing, or otherwise acquiring this book.

I'm out,

Brian Coleman

INDEX

Page numbers in italics refer to illustrations.

ABOUT THE AUTHOR

BRIAN COLEMAN's acclaimed book *Rakim Told Me: Hip-Hop Wax Facts, Straight from the Original Artists: The '80s* was released on Wax Facts Press in 2005. Over the past decade, he has written hundreds of features and reviews for publications such as: *Scratch, URB, Wax Poetics, Complex, CMJ Weekly, CMJ Monthly, Boston Herald, Boston Metro, Boston Phoenix, XXL,* and *NY Press.* He resides in Everett, Massachusetts, with his wife and ten thousand pieces of vinyl. His website is www.waxfacts.com.

ABOUT THE PHOTOGRAPHER

BRIAN CROSS, aka B+, director of the acclaimed documentary *Brasilintime,* is the contributing photo editor at *Wax Poetics* and has photographed for *Rappages, Vibe,* and *The Fader.* His website is www.mochilla.com.